Traditions, Values,
and Humanitarian Action

Traditions, Values, and Humanitarian Action

edited by
KEVIN M. CAHILL, M.D.

A Joint Publication of
FORDHAM UNIVERSITY PRESS
and
THE CENTER FOR INTERNATIONAL
HEALTH AND COOPERATION
New York • 2003

International Humanitarian Affairs, No. 3
ISSN 1541-7409

The cover photograph was taken in a Somali refugee camp by Kathryn
Cahill.

Library of Congress Cataloging-in-Publication Data

    Traditions, values, and humanitarian action / edited by Kevin M.
Cahill.— 1st ed.
      p. cm. — (International humanitarian affairs, ISSN
1541-7409 ; no. 3)
    Includes bibliographical references.
    ISBN 0-8232-2287-X (hard cover : alk. paper) —
    ISBN 0-8232-2288-8 (pbk. : alk. paper)
    1. Disaster relief. 2. Humanitarian assistance. I. Cahill,
Kevin M. II. Series.
HV553.T73   2003
361.2'6—dc21   2003007550

Printed in the United States of America
07 06 05 04 03   5 4 3 2 1
First Edition

For Joseph A. O'Hare, S.J.

Who, during his long and
distinguished tenure as President of
Fordham University, established its
Institute of International
Humanitarian Affairs.

CONTENTS

ACKNOWLEDGMENTS

THIS BOOK is made possible by the generous contributions of many individuals and organizations. All the chapters were written by colleagues who accepted the challenge on short notice and for no honorarium because they shared my belief in the need to record their vast experience and knowledge for future humanitarian workers.

This book was supported, in part, by a generous grant from the William H. Donner Foundation. Special thanks are due to Ms. Phaedra Annan, Father Joseph A. O'Hare, S.J., Mr. Loomis Mayer, Ms. Felicity Edge, and the staff of the Fordham University Press. The Executive Secretary of the CIHC, Renee Cahill, helped with editing and made a complex and difficult task a pleasure.

A MESSAGE FROM THE UN SECRETARY-GENERAL

H. E. Kofi Annan

ONCE AGAIN, Kevin Cahill has brought together a remarkable group of people to consider a topic that is of great importance to us all.

Traditions are what distinguish each human society from all the others. They are what each society brings to the great banquet of human diversity. Indeed, they are the essence of that diversity itself, which is what makes the human species such a rich and splendid one to belong to.

The tragedy of human history is that so often people have allowed diversity to drive them apart instead of bringing them together, have interpreted their traditions exclusively, and taken refuge within them. Too often, in the name of tradition, anathemas have been pronounced and wars have been fought.

Values are what enable us to overcome those divisions—to approach one another with confidence and curiosity rather than fear and suspicion, to learn from each other, to respect each other's traditions, to cherish our diversity.

In short, if traditions can and should be kept distinct, values need to be shared. And first among our shared human values must be the humanitarian instinct, the instinct that drives us to help our fellow human beings in their hour of need, no matter how different from us they may be.

Kevin Cahill has devoted his life to humanitarian action, and to bringing people together so that they can learn from each other. It is entirely typical of him to have conceived and brought together this symposium and book.

INTRODUCTION

Kevin M. Cahill, M.D.

OUR MOST PROFOUND thoughts evolve, often very slowly, and co-alesce, sometimes, into workable concepts only after prolonged gestation. Someone asked me at the conference that led to this book, "How long did it take you to plan and organize this sympo-sium?" I thought for a moment and answered, "About forty years."

In the early 1960s, I worked for many months as a physician in the Southern Sudan. It was a time of great social unrest and revolution in an area long isolated from the impact of modernity. The missionaries, who provided the only health and educational services available, were ejected shortly after my arrival. I found myself the only doctor within hundreds of miles of roadless, swampy land, the Nilotic Sudd, home of the Dinka, Nuer, and Shilluk tribes.

Offering basic emergency medical services exposed me to cus-toms and practices of which, to that time, I was utterly ignorant. They were not based on our Western traditions and values and, initially, seemed to me the relics of a primitive culture. Over months, however, I came to respect the strength and beauty of their ways and beliefs. I gradually learned to see long-horned cat-tle not merely as a symbol of wealth but as a measure of a man's pride; I saw polygamy and family love in a new light.

I worked with an indigenous "healer" as my therapeutic part-ner. Together we saved some lives and helped alleviate much suf-fering, but part of the "therapy" offered was chicken bones and burnt cow dung. I quickly and humbly came to understand that the local population, my patients, believed more in those modal-ities than in the incomprehensible antibiotic pills I provided.

Shortly thereafter I began a series of studies in Somalia and spent part of every year for the next thirty-three years traveling with nomads across the Horn of Africa. The Somalis had no written language at that time and I spent many nights, around campfires under brilliant stars and the Southern Cross, listening to their songs and gabays, the poetry of a proud people, in which they recorded, for future generations, how they survived epidemics and famines. They told, in rhyme, of drought and warfare, and also, despite the incredibly harsh landscape, of love and flowers, of the joy of rain and of camels giving birth. This immersion in Somali culture utterly changed my perceptions of human dignity and strength. I learned how traditions and values allowed clans to handle severe deprivations without complaint. The Somalis faced death with courage, with loyalty, and with protection and care for their most vulnerable. Even in the midst of conflict, or in the face of starvation, I was always safe, for I was their guest.

I was in Somalia when the nation was born, and I was there when it collapsed in the early 1990s. The soul of the people had been destroyed by corruption, oppression, the introduction of alien, selfish ways, and the gradual abandonment of their own ancient ethos. Sadly, but inexorably, traditional customs that had bound the people together were shattered. There was no longer respect for the aged, for women, for religious leaders. The gun ruled the countryside. The fault lines got ever wider and Somali society, and the new nation, came crashing down.

Even earlier, in the late 1950s, I had worked in Calcutta and there I learned that cows could be sacred and insects so precious that one wore face masks to prevent accidentally inhaling them. I spent my mornings at the School of Tropical Medicine; and for the rest of the hot, sweaty day, I worked with Mother Theresa and her dying brood. She did not question the beliefs of those she cared for—they were human beings and that was enough. That was my introductory lesson in how the traditions and values of a people can influence the very process of death. Vast numbers of poor people were dying and palliative care, any care, seemed to be a much appreciated gift from God. Providing medical care became a far more complex undertaking when one tried to serve a living population and a vibrant community in foreign lands.

Here one learned to tread softly, to offer change with great care. One quickly found that existing customs and practices in any community, even in the chaos of a refugee camp, must not be altered without consultation and deliberation. The ways of a people, sometimes quite incomprehensible to one trained in a Western scientific system, are ultimately that group's own precious heritage and protection. Attempts to introduce new methods and replace time worn approaches can be devastating to a society, especially in times of crises, when the community is very vulnerable and dependent on strangers for the essentials for life.

These personal tales are the genesis of this book. For decades I have been privileged to work in remote areas among people far removed from the effects—good and bad—of modernity. The more I traveled, and read, and participated in the daily lives of isolated tribes, the more convinced I was that the richness of humanity lay in its incredible diversity. I do not share the belief that there is only one right way—whether that is how to rule, or how to worship, or court a mate, or establish a family, or express love, or even how to die. Any diminution in that diversity diminishes all of us. Attempts to homogenize the world, to impose uniform standards of behavior, to stifle differences of opinion and style, to impose restrictions on customs and practices because they are different from our own are regressive, usually destructive, acts. The biologic world thrives in its complexity, and artistic creativity flourishes best when there are multiple varying stimuli.

It was in this search for, and growing admiration of, other cultures that I saw that, everywhere, people prefer to help more than harm their fellow man. What are the universal bases of these different traditions and value systems, and how do they affect humanitarian action? What are the foundations on which we build caring societies? What are the acts we do—as individuals or as states—that can crack those foundations? And can anything be then done to put our humpty-dumpty world together again? This book reflects that triad of questions.

At the beginning of the book are chapters from representatives of some of the great religions of the world. I asked these contributors to reflect on those fundamental texts in their teachings that promote humanitarian action. I chose Christianity, Judaism, and Islam as examples of the great faiths, fully recognizing that space did not allow detailed consideration of Hinduism, Buddhism, and other religions. In international medicine, one quickly learns that there is no single approach to therapy, that peoples' backgrounds, their cultural heritage as well as their aspirations, may be very different. Where one culture sees an action that demands an immediate response, another might see alternatives as mere illusions that too will pass away. One group may find in their religion the basis for action while another finds that spiritual detachment is the best way to survive. Dialogue and a search for the universal common bases of humanity between people will, therefore, demand an understanding and acceptance of these differences. I also include a chapter on animist beliefs and practices of the Dinka of the Southern Sudan, and place that among the religious chapters since it demonstrates how similar are the world's different values systems.

In the second part, I have asked distinguished colleagues from four different disciplines to reflect on the unique codes of conduct, the often elaborate but unwritten rules and regulations that guide their professional lives. One could have selected many other occupations but I trust that the military, medicine, media, and academia offer adequate examples of some of the essential influences on our approach to humanitarian action.

Finally, in the Foundations section, I include a chapter emphasizing the positive aspects of migration. Throughout the centuries, mass movements of people have enriched societies, and the very diversity of cultures, the cross-fertilization of traditions and values, became the pride of modern nations. The United States of America, at one time, had an open door policy, "give me your tired, your poor, your huddled masses yearning to breathe free, the wretched refuse of your teeming shore." That unbridled welcome, for reasons to be discussed later, no longer exists. Around the world, but especially in Europe, the open approach is being questioned, and the benefits of immigration, the essential ferment for growth, is now threatened by ignorance and fear.

Life is never secure, and the strongest foundations, so carefully constructed, can crack under the pressure of fear or folly or evil. Fault lines in quake-prone areas cover moving earth plates that can collide and cause great damage. Individual—or governmental—acts that are in opposition to the foundations of a society can also cause devastation and destruction. This process can begin subtly. For example, it is almost easy to justify harsh interrogation methods of a suspected terrorist but such an approach can lead, inexorably, to accepting dehumanizing torture as a legitimate tool of government. The world is now engaged in a "war on terrorism," a war without borders and, possibly, without end. Here the fault lines are potentially catastrophic. In this part are two chapters on terrorism, one from a university-based center and one from terror-filled conflict zones of the world. Accepting gender exploitation, and trafficking in vulnerable women and children, may seem an obvious evil but it is, shamefully, accepted today as a way of life in too many parts of the world.

There are other fault lines that presage disaster to our global community. Especially in times of crises one can be tempted to abandon, for short-term advantage, those precious civil liberties for—and on—which a nation was founded. Sometimes even easier, one can forsake international conventions that bind civilized states together, even in times of war.

The overwhelming power of the Western media can be, as discussed in the Foundations section of this book, a positive force if it remains a free press. But there is another aspect to be considered in our complex world of so many different cultures. Can reporters, even fair and unbiased reporters, adequately understand the nuances of alien cultures and, if not, do their news articles and analyses merely reinforce existing prejudices? Migration, as noted in the Foundations section, has been an essential element in the growth of nations, but the sheer scope of human movement across sovereign borders as the twentieth century came to an end has pushed immigration policy in many lands to the boiling point.

There are other fault lines that are considered, even implicitly, in many of the chapters of this book on traditions, values, and humanitarian action. For example, even humanitarian assistance itself can be a tragic contribution to the destruction of a society. Good intentions and apparently generous deeds are simply not enough to avoid causing serious problems, ones that can perpetuate evil. Following the Rwanda genocide, humanitarian assistance helped killers survive in secure refugee camps where they re-established their murderous regimes. There are many dangers in the chaos that follows armed conflicts and one must be very aware of the almost predictable pitfalls that accompany external aid.

Supplying food to refugees may, to the innocent, seem like an unmitigated good action. But such donations can alter traditional farming practices, increase dependency, and radically change the fundamental relationship between children and their parents, because the children can now obtain sustenance from a stranger and need no longer rely on, or respect, their parents. If donated food becomes the vehicle for perpetuating deeply flawed systems of order, even inflaming rather than reducing tensions, then aid itself will become a fault line breaking the foundations of long-established societies. The more one is involved with international humanitarian assistance, the more one is aware how easily aid can be manipulated in ways that donors never considered. Being aware, however, must not become an excuse for inaction. Rather, the professional in humanitarian assistance must humbly but decisively plan, and constantly modify, programs to avoid fault lines and, hopefully, reinforce foundations.

Trying to correct the fault lines that we consider in this text—and the many others that challenge our civilization—is the job of governments, international bodies such as the United Nations, nongovernmental organizations, and even individuals. National borders are no longer sacrosanct, and sovereignty is now considered an inadequate protection in the face of widespread abuse of human rights and life. A decade ago, the former Yugoslavia disintegrated into civil war, the Soviet Union collapsed, Somalia imploded, and the world became aware of genocide in Rwanda. Out of all this, new concepts in statecraft emerged. Humanitarian need was used as a justification for armed interventions in many parts of the world.

Fundamental questions began to be asked regarding the primacy of inalienable individuals' rights over the rights of a state when the state failed to offer basic protections to their own citizenry. Is there a basic human right to humanitarian assistance in times of need? Some such rights for civilians have been codified into law in settings of armed conflict, whether internationally declared wars or in internal civil strife, but they unfortunately cover only essential provisions at this time.

International law defines both the rights of civilians in armed conflicts and the corresponding duty of combatants to alleviate suffering. But in today's complex emergencies, situations and combatants are rarely clear or easily amenable to the power of law. Nevertheless there is a growing movement to consider serious breaches or obstacles to providing humanitarian assistance to afflicted civilians as war crimes. In reality, most UN resolutions urging humanitarian assistance in conflicts are mere rhetoric, but the Security Council can employ a Chapter VII resolution that is binding on all members of the United Nations. Chapter VII resolutions can lead to the imposition of sanctions or even be the basis for "humanitarian interventions."

As these changes in law and diplomacy developed in the early 1990s, a group of diplomats and physicians established the Center for International Health and Cooperation. The Center was founded to explore *basic* problems in humanitarian action and to propose *practical* solutions. It has done so in education by developing a standard training program acceptable to academia while meeting the needs of field workers; it has devised and demonstrated practical prosthetic programs for land mine victims; it has imaginatively and effectively linked the disciplines of public health and diplomacy.

Now, through its sister Institute of International Humanitarian Affairs at Fordham University, we probe deeper, attempting to elucidate those basic forces that both help and destroy mankind's noblest urges. This book will, hopefully, stimulate the reader to appreciate the diverse strands that bind us together as a human family; to recognize those brutal acts that diminish the dignity of all mankind and endanger world stability and civilized intercourse; and, finally, in helping in the search for ways out of the current morass, it might encourage the reader to join the many thoughtful and good men and women, such as those who contributed to this volume, in the endless quest for peace, justice, and health around the world.

FOUNDATIONS

Part 1

The Foundations section begins, appropriately, with a consideration of the teachings of God on humanitarian action. These supernatural directions came, according to different faiths, by revelation or divine inspiration and were delivered through various holy men and prophets. The teachings have been refined, over the centuries, by careful theological study and interpretation of the Bible, the Koran, the Talmud, as well as other sacred scriptures in other formal religions. In societies without written texts there often are equally rich verbal references to the teachings of an almighty power encouraging peace and compassion for mankind.

In this part, four renowned scholars explain the origins of our most important moral and ethical bases. Avery Cardinal Dulles, S.J., is a Jesuit theologian whose profound influence has been recognized within his church by Papal elevation from priest to Cardinal reminiscent of the similar respect, and influence, of John Cardinal Newman in the nineteenth century. Dr. Harlan Wechsler is a highly respected Professor of Jewish Philosophy who also brings to his deliberations the insights of a practicing rabbi responsible for the pastoral care of a large synagogue community. Throughout his writings, Rabbi Wechsler finds textual support for his argument that mankind is not meant to be alone but, rather, to share in relationships with all their promises as well as their risks. His Royal Highness Prince El Hassan bin Talal is the senior member of the Hashemite family and, therefore, a direct descendant of the Prophet Mohamed. He has, for many years, tried to foster dialogue between opposing and even hostile neighbors in the Middle East, grounding his struggles for peace in relevant sura of the Koran that promote respect and understanding. Finally, I include in this part a

chapter on an animist culture by Ambassador Frances Deng, a remarkable diplomat-scholar who moved from a childhood herding cattle in
the almost unmapped Nilotic swamps to become Foreign Minister of
the Sudan, a senior member of the UN staff, and a revered teacher.

1

Christianity and Humanitarian Action

Avery Cardinal Dulles, S.J.

THE PROBLEM

WE COULD EASILY be tempted to imagine that Christianity would deter its followers from commitment to humanitarian action. Christian revelation teaches that life in this world is but a preparation for the life to come, which is immeasurably more important. Riches and comforts in this life are dangers, if not obstacles, to achieving the state of soul that brings eternal life. Poverty and suffering, patiently accepted, can be means of salvation. Anyone who believes all this would be content, one might think, to leave the destitute in their wretchedness rather than seek to relieve them.

But the fact is that the Christian Church since its beginnings has been a dynamo of humanitarian activity. Countless saints have given their possessions, their time, their talents, and their very selves to serve the poor and the needy. Historians tell us that the loving care that the Christian communities extended to the outcast was a major factor in the conversion of the Roman Empire. According to the distinguished sociologist Rodney Stark:

> Christianity served as a revitalization movement that arose in response to the misery, chaos, fear, and brutality of life in the urban Greco-Roman world. . . . To cities filled with the homeless and impoverished, Christianity offered an immediate basis for attachments. To cities filled with orphans and widows, Christianity provided a new and expanded sense of family. To cities torn by violent

ethnic strife, Christianity offered a new basis for social solidarity
. . . And to cities faced with epidemics, fires, and earthquakes,
Christianity offered effective nursing services.[1]

Throughout the centuries, Christian movements and religious
orders have dedicated themselves to caring for the sick, feeding
the poor, ransoming captives, comforting prisoners, freeing
slaves, and educating the unlettered. The church is always on
hand in situations of disaster.

CHRISTIAN ANTHROPOLOGY

How, then, do we explain the paradox that a faith that directs
its members to happiness in another world should be so heavily
engaged in ministering to the needy in this world? The question
can, I think, be answered on several levels.

Fundamental to any answer is the Christian vision of the
human person in society. Christians are convinced that human
beings stand at the very summit of God's creative work. On the
sixth day, Genesis tells us, after creating the inanimate world, the
plants, and the animals, God said, "Let us make man in our own
image, after our likeness" (Gen. 1:26). The Psalmist asks: "What
is man that thou are mindful of him, or the son of man that thou
dost care for him? Yet thou hast made him little less than God,
and dost crown him with glory and honor; thou hast given him
dominion over all the works of thy hands; thou hast put all things
under his feet" (Ps. 8:5–6). The whole visible world is related to
man as its center and crown.

The dignity that belongs to human persons by virtue of creation is further enhanced by the work of redemption. The Son
of God, Christians believe, became man and gave his life on the
Cross in order to cancel out the debt of human sin and reconcile
the human race with God. We have been purchased at a great
price and called to a destiny far beyond all that we could merit.

The Second Vatican Council, in its Pastoral Constitution on
the Church in the Modern World, teaches that human beings are

the only creatures on earth that God has willed for themselves.[2] Minerals, plants, and animals exist for the sake of man. The human person, by contrast, has intrinsic worth and inviolable dignity. Pope John Paul II, like many other contemporary Christians, agrees with Immanuel Kant that it is never permissible for us to treat other human persons as mere means to be exploited for our own pleasure or for their utility to serve our own ends.[3] Although persons can and should help one another, they have to be respected for what they are.

From the dignity of each person follows the concept of human rights. Because we have a duty to respect the dignity of others, they have a corresponding right to be treated with respect and reverence. Philosophers have tried to specify different levels of human rights. Christians would agree with the Declaration of Independence of the United States of America when it speaks of the rights to life, liberty, and the pursuit of happiness as basic and inalienable. Some less fundamental rights, such as gainful employment, education, health care, leisure, and retirement benefits, cannot always be implemented but they are, in any case, desirable social goals.

During the Second World War, Pope Pius XII, looking forward to a new world order, called for recognition of the rights that flow from the dignity of the person. In his Christmas address of 1942, he proposed a list of personal rights, including those to life, to religious freedom, to family life, to work, to choose a vocation, and to own private property while making use of it in a socially responsible way.

Christians of various denominational affiliations enthusiastically cooperated in the writing of the Universal Declaration of Human Rights approved by the General Assembly of the United Nations in 1948. In his encyclical *Pacem in Terris* of 1962, Pope John XXIII spoke appreciatively of the Universal Declaration and submitted his own list of human rights, in some ways more extensive than the charter's. Pope John Paul II has been a tireless advocate of human rights, which he grounds in the very nature of the human person and in the sacred relationship of human beings with God.

Our concept of the human person would be deficient unless we were aware that persons are by their very nature oriented to live in society. They cannot fulfill themselves except in giving themselves to one another. As stated by Vatican II, the human person "cannot fully find himself except through a sincere gift of himself."[4] To be locked up in one's private self-interest is to condemn oneself to a stunted existence. Since the friend is, as Aristotle said, another self, we enlarge ourselves through friendship with others.

Any well-ordered society aspires to be a network of human beings all working in concert for the authentic self-realization of each through interaction with others. From this mutuality there results what political philosophers call the common good—a condition of society in which all the members benefit because of their collaboration. If the common good were fully achieved on a universal scale, a state of general peace and prosperity would emerge, in which the good of the whole society redounded to the advantage of the individual members and private associations. Recognizing that this result cannot be achieved without mutual good will, Pope Paul VI called for the building of a civilization of love. In such a society, particular efforts will have to be made to assure that the benefits are distributed to all the members. Individuals and groups that are marginalized or excluded must receive special attention, as must those experiencing distress and deprivation due to calamities such as earthquakes and wars.

BIBLICAL BASIS: TEACHING OF JESUS

The social vision that I have been proposing has its roots not only in Greek philosophy but also, to an even larger extent, in biblical revelation. Many centuries before Christ, the priests and prophets of Israel were insisting on the two great commandments of love of God and love of neighbor. Love, they insisted, must be manifested in practical service. They pronounced woes on the rich who oppressed the poor, on moneylenders who charged usurious interest rates, on merchants who falsified the scales, and on judges who discriminated against orphans and widows. Reminding the Israelites that they were once strangers in the land of Egypt, the Law required them to love strangers and foreigners dwelling in their land as they loved one another (Lev. 19:34; Deut. 10:19).

The humanitarian dimension of the mission of Jesus is expressed in his inaugural sermon at Nazareth, in which he referred to himself as fulfilling the words of Isaiah: "The Spirit of the Lord is upon me, because he has anointed me to proclaim release to the captives and recovering of sight to the blind, to set at liberty those who are oppressed, to proclaim the acceptable year of the Lord" (Luke 4:18–19). While reaffirming the social morality of the Old Testament, Jesus extended it in directions that had already been intimated in the Mosaic Law and the prophets. For our purposes, three themes may be singled out for emphasis: universalism, mercy, and love of enemies.

Jesus gives unlimited extension to the command to love one's neighbor as oneself. In answer to the scribe's question "Who is my neighbor?" Jesus—himself a Jew—told the parable of the Good Samaritan, who bound up the wounds of the injured wayfarer, while the priest and the Levite did nothing to help. In directing the scribe to "go and do likewise," Jesus challenges all his disciples to show kindness to those of different races, nationalities, and religious affiliations.

Jesus noted that Elijah and Elisha had worked miracles for the widow in Sidon and Naaman the Syrian (Luke 4:25–28); he praised the Ninevites who did penance in response to the preaching of Jonah (Matt. 12:41). Though his own mission was only to the lost sheep of the house of Israel (Matt. 15:24), Jesus by exception worked miracles in response to the ardent pleas of the Roman centurion (Matt. 8:10) and the Canaanite woman (Matt. 15:28), and congratulated them on their faith. Encounters such

as these pointed forward to the universality of the coming Kingdom (Matt. 8:11–12).

A second distinguishing feature of the teaching of Jesus is his
emphasis on mercy. "Blessed are the merciful," he says (Matt.
5:7). He tells a warning tale about a rich man who feasted sump-
tuously in his lifetime but failed to respond to the pleas of the
starving beggar who wanted to be fed with the scraps that fell
from the rich man's table (Luke 16:19–31). In another parable,
Jesus describes the fate of a steward who had been forgiven an
immense debt by his master and then refused to defer repayment
of a relatively small debt owed to him (Matt. 18:23–35). The lesson is always the same: that we must be generous and forgiving
toward others as we want God to be toward us.

The third feature to which I wish to call attention is that Jesus
calls for a beneficence that extends not only to friends but also
to enemies. It is not enough to love one's neighbor and hate
one's enemies, as some Pharisees were apparently teaching. We
must love our enemies and pray for those who persecute us, as
Jesus did in his own Passion (Matt. 5:44; cf. Luke 23:34). This love
of enemies involves doing good to them, as the Lukan version of
the Sermon on the Mount explicitly declares (Luke 6:27).

It might be thought that Jesus, in calling for love and mercy, is
thinking only of spiritual favors, such as prayer for the needy or
preaching the gospel to sinners. But Jesus gives primary emphasis
to concrete and tangible acts. In the great parable of the Last
Judgment, he mentions six types of action that qualify people as
righteous: to feed the hungry, to give drink to the thirsty, to welcome the stranger, to clothe the naked, to care for the sick, and
to visit the imprisoned.

All this teaching of Jesus on beneficence toward the stranger,
the undeserving, and the enemy is difficult to put in practice. We
instinctively prefer to help family members, friends, and persons
who are in a position to help us in return. We are naturally disin-
clined to reach out to aliens and enemies. In order to follow the
gospel in its fullness, we stand in need of conversion. Jesus, aware

of this, proposes motives that could bring about a radical change of heart.

THEOLOGICAL MOTIVATION

If we had eyes to see the intrinsic worth of each human person, that would, I suppose, be motivation enough. Some of us might spontaneously achieve, with the help of the Holy Spirit, a truly Christ-like love for people to whom we are not naturally attracted. But moral intuition and spiritual enlightenment usually need to be reinforced by intelligible reasons. The Gospels themselves provide a number of theological motives.

To overcome our ethnocentric tendencies, Jesus points to the example of God, who makes his sun shine and his rain fall upon the just and unjust, upon friend and foe, upon Jew and Gentile (cf. Matt. 5:45). Since God is perfect, and since we are called to be perfect, we should seek to make God's attitudes our own. Then again, as I have mentioned, Jesus challenges his fellow Jews by recalling the example of prophets such as Elijah and Elisha, who worked miracles for Gentiles (Luke 4:23–27).

To induce us to reach out even to enemies, Jesus reminds us that God shows love and mercy toward us, even when we sin and are alienated from him. Since God gives us far more than we deserve, we ought to be generous toward others who depend on our mercy. If we are merciful toward others, we will be disposed to receive God's mercy, but if we are cold and pitiless, we forfeit God's mercy to us. In the Lord's Prayer, Christians are bidden to pray that God will forgive them as they forgive their debtors.

Still another motive is the way in which Jesus identifies himself with the needy. In the famous parable of the Last Judgment, as recounted in the twenty-fifth chapter of Matthew, Jesus makes the point that the merciful deeds done to the poor and marginalized are in effect done to him. What is done to the least of his brethren, he counts as done to himself (Matt. 25:40, 45).

A further motive, closely connected with the preceding, is

human accountability. We are not our own masters, but we have a divine Master to whom we must one day render an account of all that we have done in this life. When we die, we will be judged. If we have obeyed the commandments of God, we will enter into the joy of everlasting life, but if we have been disobedient and have failed to obtain forgiveness, we will be cast into the outer darkness to pay the full price for our misdeeds.

The final judgment, according to Jesus, is universal. It is not only Christians, but also men and women of every race, nationality, and religion who will have to encounter the Son of Man as their divine judge. All the nations of the earth will be gathered before his throne (Matt. 25:32; cf. Rom 2:15–16).

Hope of reward and fear of punishment are not the highest motives for doing good and avoiding evil. It is far better to act out of pure love for God and for our fellow men and women. But if our love is not yet strong enough, it is better to rely on somewhat selfish motives than to commit injustices. To do good for an imperfect motive is better than not to do good at all.

SUMMARY ANSWER

At this point I have sufficiently answered, I hope, the objection I raised at the beginning of this chapter. The realization that this life is but a preparation for eternity does not make us neglect the importance of our deeds here and now. On the contrary, it increases our sense of responsibility because we are conscious of acting in the presence of God who will judge us according to what we have done or failed to do in this life. We do not save ourselves by being rich and comfortable, but by making use of this world's goods in order to do the will of God. The rich are not condemned for being rich, but are admonished not to allow the pursuit of wealth, honors, and comfort to distract them from their duty to love and help others who are in need. The fact that the poor can save their souls without becoming rich does not excuse the rich and powerful for failing to help them in their distress.

The Christian teaching on humanitarian action is not just theory. It takes practical effect in the way faithful Christians live. I frequently hear of students, alumni, engineers, carpenters, social workers, physicians, and dentists who take time to travel to poor and even dangerous parts of the world where their services are most desperately needed. Every year the Jesuit Volunteer Corps, for example, sends young college graduates for a year or several years of their lives to help the impoverished to help themselves.

INSTITUTIONAL INVOLVEMENT

Thus far I have been speaking especially of humanitarian action on the part of individual persons. This aspect is sufficient for establishing the principles and the motives. But Christian experience through the centuries has shown the indispensability of organized efforts. In the complex world of our day, the major social problems cannot be effectively met without collaboration on a large scale. When there are disasters such as floods, earthquakes, volcanic eruptions, plagues, or terrorist acts such as the destruction of the World Trade Center, those who wish to help must band together. Christians of various denominations gladly contribute to secular nonprofit organizations such as the Red Cross, the United Way, and Bread for the World. The Second Vatican Council urged lay Christians to reach out to every person in need and to cooperate with all people of good will.[5]

The possibility of engagement in nondenominational charities does not eliminate the attraction of charitable organizations that are explicitly religious and bear a Christian or Catholic label. Many of the faithful want to bring the full weight of Christian motivation and the full guidance of Christian doctrine to bear on their efforts. They feel that in this way, they can better serve God, for whose sake they are making sacrifices.

In Christian antiquity, the monasteries were outstanding for offering care and hospitality toward the sick, travelers, and the poor. In the second millennium, many religious orders established orphanages, homes for the sick and elderly, and apostolates to prisoners and captives. Early in the nineteenth century, under the harsh conditions of the Industrial Revolution, a number of new social movements took their rise. In 1833, the French layman Frederic Ozanam launched the Society of St. Vincent de Paul. Shortly afterwards Adolf Kolping in Germany started the associations for Catholic workers, which are still known in his honor as the Kolping movement. Lay-founded organizations such as these have spread to other parts of the world and have endured. In the United States, saints such as Elizabeth Ann Seton, Frances Xavier Cabrini, and Katherine Drexel have recently been canonized for their heroic works of love in the fields of education, hospital care, orphanages, service toward immigrants, and charity toward neglected minorities such as African Americans and American Indians. The Missionary Sisters of Charity, founded by Mother Teresa to minister to the terminally ill in Calcutta, have become active all over the globe.

I cannot speak with competence about non-Catholic Christian organizations. I will, however, make my own the assertion of Vatican II that Protestant Christianity has "produced many organizations for the relief of spiritual and bodily distress, the education of youth, the advancement of human conditions, and the promotion of peace throughout the world."[6]

History seems to testify that church-administered charities have generally developed from below, through the initiative of lay persons and members of religious congregations who have been inspired to go out and help the needy. The National Conference of Catholic Charities, in the United States, was founded at the suggestion of leaders in the St. Vincent de Paul Society, who saw the desirability of a coordinating agency on the national level. In a similar way, the Catholic Hospital Association was founded to assist the many Catholic hospitals that had been founded by private associations, including religious orders. Catholic Relief Services, by contrast, was established by the United

States bishops in 1943 to continue the overseas relief work that had been initiated on the eve of World War II for the sake of resettling refugees and supplying food, clothing, and human services to ravaged areas. Since that time Catholic Relief Services has continued to take up collections and assist victims of disasters in all parts of the world.

On November 20, 2002, the day of the symposium that was the basis for this book, *The New York Times* carried a four-column story about the labors of half a dozen orders of Catholic religious sisters who have sent members of their communities to the Mississippi Delta to help out in destitute towns. They do not evangelize, but they serve as teachers, nurses, doctors, counselors, and community organizers among the poor and almost entirely black and Protestant population. The story concentrates on the town of Jonestown, Mississippi, where the Sisters of the Holy Name are credited with bringing hope to people on the verge of desperation.[7]

DUAL FINALITY

Institutions that are specifically Catholic have a dual finality. On the one hand, they seek to further the purposes of the church, which are necessarily related to supernatural salvation. Privately founded Catholic schools, hospitals, and welfare institutions operating under the aegis of the church make significant contributions to the work of the church in preparing for the full realization of God's Kingdom. Christ came announcing the arrival of the Kingdom of God in his own person. In his healings, his exorcisms, his feeding miracles, and his raising of the dead, he made signs indicating the inbreaking of that kingdom. The church is called to follow in this healing and serving ministry, making herself a sign and sacrament of the coming kingdom, and thereby realizing her inmost essence. Thanks to her manifest fruitfulness in good works, the church becomes, so to speak, transparent. People looking upon her and her members become aware of the dynamic presence of God's Kingdom within her.

On the other hand, church-sponsored activities are intended to achieve the particular social goals correlated with their specific nature as institutions of education, health care, or welfare, as the case may be. Schools exist to produce educated students; hospitals and medical organizations, to produce healthy people; social service institutions, to promote human well-being. Those who staff such institutions must have the requisite training and aptitudes in pedagogy, therapy, social service, or whatever their field may be.

Seeing themselves not only as instruments of the church but also as part of the community's educational, health, and social service resources, these institutions have one foot planted in the Catholic Church and the other in our pluralistic society. In a speech of the dual identity of such institutions, Cardinal Bernardin stated:

> The clients they serve, the contributors they approach, the staff and governing bodies they rely on include both Catholics and, increasingly, those who are not Catholic. They depend on federal, state, and local governments for such things as charters of incorporation, regulatory statutes, licensing, tax exemption status, and funding. They are also held accountable by government and the public, not only by the church.[8]

Standing as they do at the intersection between the church and secular society, these institutions cherish their Catholic identity as giving an added dimension to their work. Their personnel are likely to be motivated by religious convictions, and thereby inspired to work more eagerly, more altruistically, and more fully in accord with God's design. But, generally speaking, these organizations do not engage in direct evangelization, since this would interfere with their specific purposes, as already described. They would seem to meet the specifications laid down for government programs of public support for faith-based charitable initiatives.

John Paul II, in an address to the Pontifical Council "Cor

Unum" on April 18, 1997, confirmed this point. He stated that, "Actions of aid, relief, and assistance should be conducted in a spirit of service and free giving for the benefit of all persons without the ulterior motive of eventual tutelage or proselytism."[9] In an address to Catholic Charities U.S.A. in San Antonio a decade earlier, the Pope had declared that such organizations exist essentially to spread Christian love. He encouraged his hearers by his concluding words:

> For your long and persevering service—creative and courageous, and blind to distinctions of race and religion—you will certainly hear Jesus's words of gratitude: "You did it for me" (Matt. 25:40). Gather, transform, and serve! When done in the name of Jesus Christ, this is the spirit of Catholic Charities and of all who work in this cause, because it is the faithful following of the one who did "not come to be served but to serve" (Mark 10:45). By working for a society that fosters the dignity of every human person, not only are you serving the poor, but you are renewing the founding vision of this nation under God! And may God reward you abundantly![10]

While keenly interested in the charitable organizations that operate under her auspices, the Catholic Church keeps herself formally distinct from them. As stated in Vatican II's Constitution on the Church in the Modern World, the church must always keep in view her strictly religious, supernatural goal, which is to lead men and women to eternal salvation.[11] But to be faithful to her Lord, who attached salvation to loving service, she encourages her members to practice works of charity, both individually and in groups. She directs charitable organizations that claim to be Catholic, and oversees them so that they do, in fact, operate according to authentic Catholic principles. These organizations, if they are truly Catholic, willingly accept the teaching and direction of the Church.

ECUMENICAL IMPLICATIONS

The church's humanitarian initiatives have ecumenical and interreligious dimensions, which are especially pertinent to the goals of the present book. At the dawn of the ecumenical movement in the early twentieth century, leaders in the Life and Work Movement coined the slogan, "Service unites, doctrine divides." I have never liked that slogan, perhaps because it overlooks the unitive capacity of doctrine and the inseparability between doctrine and authentically Christian conduct. Yet, without minimizing the importance of doctrine, we may acknowledge that humanitarian action is, and could increasingly become, a unitive force among Christians and indeed among all human beings.

Catholic charitable activity is one of the areas mentioned by the Second Vatican Council as having great potential for ecumenical rapprochement with other churches. The words of the Decree on Ecumenism deserve to be repeated:

> Since in our times cooperation in social matters is very widely practiced, all men without exception are summoned to united effort. Those who believe in God have a stronger summons, since they have been sealed with the name of Christ. Cooperation among all Christians vividly expresses the bond that already unites them, and it sets in clearer relief the features of Christ the Servant. Such cooperation, already begun in many countries, should be ever increasingly developed, particularly in regions where a social and technical evolution is taking place. . . . Christians should also work together in the use of every possible means to relieve the afflictions of our times, such as famine and natural disasters, illiteracy and poverty, lack of housing, and the unequal distribution of wealth.[12]

Since its birth in the early decades of the twentieth century, the ecumenical movement has had two principal expressions: Faith and Order, concerned with matters of doctrine and ecclesiastical polity, and Life and Work, concerned with the promotion of peace and justice. These two expressions continue to supplement and stimulate each other. In times of social crisis, practical cooperation for humanitarian goals becomes especially important. In recent years, Catholics and Protestants have worked together in North Ireland to overcome the deep-seated hostilities and dispose people to accept peaceful solutions. In Catholic-

Orthodox relations, dialogues about doctrine and polity have predominated, but not to the exclusion of social teaching. It is significant that Pope John Paul II and Patriarch Bartholomew I of Constantinople, at a difficult juncture in the Catholic-Orthodox theological dialogue, saw fit to issue, on June 10, 2002, a major joint pronouncement on the need for a code of environmental ethics.[13]

INTERRELIGIOUS DIMENSIONS

The experience of the fifty years since the Council not only confirms the validity of its teaching on ecumenical humanitarian initiatives, but suggests the growing importance of involving the various religions. Interreligious cooperation has been promoted by organizations such as the World Conference on Religion and Peace, which held its first world assembly in Kyoto in 1970. From the Catholic side, organizations such as the Community of San Egidio in Rome and the Focolare Movement, which has its headquarters in Rocca di Papa near Rome, have promoted fruitful collaboration among different religions for objectives such as peace and social development.

Practical cooperation to meet moral and social challenges should be possible among the great religions. Cardinal Francis Arinze has memorably written: "After all, there is no separate Catholic drought, or Jewish epidemic, or Muslim urbanization, or Buddhist inflation, or Sikh poverty, or Hindu embezzlement of public funds."[14]

All too often in the past, and even now in some places, religions have proved to be divisive. The history of humankind is plagued by chronicles of religious wars. The very memory of such conflicts provokes present antagonisms, thus feeding the seemingly endless cycle of violence. This record should make us ashamed. For the good name of religion and for the very survival of civilization, it is urgent that religious faith becomes a force for peace and universal friendship. As Pope John Paul II said in Astana, the capital city of Kazakstan, shortly after the events of September 11, 2001:

> From this city, from Kazakstan, a country that is an example of harmony between men and women of different origins and beliefs, I wish to make an earnest call to everyone, Christians and followers of other religions, to work together to build a world without violence, a world that loves life, and grows in justice and solidarity. We must not let what has happened lead to a deepening of divisions. Religion must never be used as a reason for conflict.[15]

I would hope that all of us might be able to agree with these lofty principles. Each of the major religions, I believe, embodies valuable elements for a program of universal reconciliation.

Even without benefit of revelation, normal people sense that they ought to love and do good to one another. They spontaneously judge that there is something inviolable about the human person—a mystery of subjectivity that cannot be reduced to any definition or objective concept. I have tried to show that Christian doctrine reinforces this spontaneous sense, giving added motives for serving the universal good and helping persons in situations of need and distress. From my own perspective as a Catholic I am convinced that the Christian doctrines of creation, incarnation, grace, and eternal life clarify the dignity of the human person and provide singularly powerful reasons for humanitarian action. I believe, in fact, that the world will achieve peace and justice to the extent that it follows the teaching and example of Jesus Christ, the Prince of Peace and the King of Justice, and enjoys the assistance of his Spirit.

Subsequent chapters will offer the views of representatives of other faiths and beliefs. It will be exciting to learn whether they, from their several points of view, come to practical conclusions similar to my own, as I suspect they will. If this proves to be the case, humanitarian action could be recognized as a particularly stable platform on which to erect programs, dialogue, and cooperation among the major faith traditions.

2

For the Sake of My Kin and Friends: Traditions, Values, and Humanitarian Action in Judaism

Rabbi Harlan J. Wechsler

> For the sake of my kin and friends,
> Please, I pray for your peace.
>
> Psalms 122:8

JUDAISM is an old religion, and its traditions and values construct a framework of life and a form of living that encourages people to help one another. I shall look at the humanitarian perspective of Judaism based on three of the theological ideas that are part of the bedrock of the faith.

First, I shall examine the nature of *creation* in classical Jewish theology. What is Judaism's view of human nature? What is its view of human destiny and man's existential reality? And how do we learn about man from what we learn in Scripture about his Creator?

Second, classical Judaism is a religion that deals with God's will, or, as it is referred to in religious parlance, *revelation*. Here, I will suggest some ways that revelation can serve the purpose of bringing the human community together rather than splitting it apart. As well, I would like to look at a few examples of Jewish law to see what they say about the social relations between human beings.

The third category derived from classical Jewish thought is *redemption*. Judaism is the religion of the exodus from Egypt and is also a faith that hopes in a future redemption. Redemption thrusts the nature of man (creation) and the will of God (revelation) onto the stage of history, and since human beings operate on that stage we will need to see how Judaism views history and how history can ennoble the hopes we invest in humanity.

CREATION

In contrast to the creation stories that were widely taught in the ancient world, the Biblical story of creation tells us nothing about God before He begins to create. And, in contrast also to the view of Aristotle, who describes the activity of God as one of self-contemplation, the Biblical story of creation tells us of a God who decides to reach beyond Himself.

Imagine this: If there is a perfect being, and that perfect being is God, then Aristotle offers the compelling suggestion that such a perfect being would wish to spend His time in the contemplation of perfection. Since there is no perfection like divine perfection, then God, in Aristotelian terms, contemplates Himself.

Not Contemplation but Self-Giving

In contrast, the first thing we learn about the God of the Bible is that He takes an extraordinary step *outside of Himself!*[1] Abraham Joshua Heschel, the twentieth century Jewish philosopher, calls this the Divine Pathos.[2] He creates a world. The very act of creation, even before we examine its nature, is an act of going beyond the self. And it is certainly an act that shows a God who is willing to take an enormous risk: the risk of creating a world that is imperfect, the risk that there will be a world that is profoundly separate from divinity and, alas, the risk that the world will be a place for sin.[3]

The metaphor of creation is the metaphor of the artisan. In contrast to other religions where creation comes into being by virtue of the god giving birth to the new world, the Bible pictures

God not as a begetter but as an artisan. In paganism, for example, the begetter and the begat are, as in any birth situation, remarkably alike. There is a sameness of their substance. But in Judaism, God is utterly different from the world. We only know that God's creativity and something of his spirit is manifest in the world—just as we know that every artisan manifests his creativity and his substance in the creation he makes.[4]

Created in the Image of God

The Bible says, nonetheless, that "God created man in His image."[5] To Judaism, that means that there is something about man that connects him to God. Various Jewish thinkers throughout the ages have speculated on what that something is. Maimonides, for example, understood it to be man's intellectual faculties.[6] The tenth century Babylonian thinker, Rabbi Saadiah Gaon, understood the image to mean rulership. Just as God rules the world, so is man given dominion over all that is.[7]

Going beyond Saadiah and Maimonides, Heschel suggests that the image of God testifies to the essential dignity and nobility of man. "The basic dignity of man is not made up of his achievements, virtues, or special talents. It is inherent in his very being."[8] Whether we attribute that dignity to intellectual capacities, as did Maimonides, or to his nobility as controller and shaper of the world, we are supremely conscious of the unique nature of the human creation.

We have seen, so far, that the act of creation is an act of divine reaching out, an act of love and a great risk. The human creature is in the image of God as a statement of the extraordinary value of human life.

Nobility and Humility

The Bible portrays the creation of man at the end of a whole series of created things, progressing from the first day to the sixth. Implicit in this description is a hint of progress. Beginning with the inanimate objects and moving from there to the plant world, the simple animals, and the more complicated beasts, the Bible constructs a description where the end of it all is a human being, the pinnacle of the process.

But there is another way to read the story. As the Talmud points out, human beings are created on the sixth day in order to guard against arrogance. For, "if a man's mind becomes proud, let him be reminded that the gnats preceded him in the order of creation."[9] The story of creation both emphasizes human nobility and grandeur and, at the same time, the finite, broken, and lowly nature of the creatures—for even the gnat came first.

Moreover, chapter two of Genesis describes the human being as created from the dust of the earth. Of course, God blows into him the breath of life, and that emphasizes the paradoxical dynamic of human creation: on the one hand, the spirit of God is in him. On the other hand, he is of the dirt of the earth.[10] When God decides to create man, the text says, He said: "Let us make man in our image." To whom did God address His statement: "Let *us*"? The medieval commentator Nahmanides says that He was speaking to the only other parts of creation that were there, namely: nature. For the human being is a combination of the Godly and the natural, both mixed together.[11]

Not Alone but in Community

But there is one more piece to this existential reality: it is the pain of loneliness, which is apparent as soon as the creation is completed. Adam is alone.

Now it is possible for a person to be alone and to be happy. But the Bible tells us that the natural state of human existence is unhappy in its aloneness: "It is not good for a human being to be alone."[12] And so Adam looks to the animals of the garden as the way in which he will, perhaps, overcome his aloneness. Adam gives them names, and even though he does that, even though, as a superior creature he is able to classify them as he likes, it does not help him to be less alone.

Only another divine creation is able to overcome Adam's aloneness. God makes another creature who is like Adam in some ways—they share the same bone—and the other human being is absolutely different from Adam in other ways. As the Bible says, God puts Adam to sleep and then fashions the second creation. Therefore, the second one is filled with God's mystery, filled with all the enigmas of being a separate creature, and yet Adam says that this is finally good: Bone of my bones and flesh of my flesh. And he is satisfied.[13]

The story of God and the story of man, as we learn about them in the Bible, thus parallel one another. Each is unhappy to be alone. Each enters into a relation filled with promises and risks.

Social Ethics

"Give me friendship or give me death," the Talmud says.[14] Human existence finds its meaning in a world with others.[15]

The Talmud reminds us that when God created the world, He created one human being. Why? "For the sake of [the different] families, that they might not quarrel with each other."[16] Similarly, so that no one can say, My father is greater than your father.[17] There is a commonality to all human beings. We are all related. None of us has more distinguished forbears than the other. For, though we may have gone our separate ways a long time ago, we all go back to the same root. Rabbi Meir used to add his own angle to this by pointing out that in the rabbinic tradition, Adam was formed from dirt gathered together from various places throughout the world. Therefore, no place can claim it has richer soil and produces a better human being. Rather, there is a unity to all of humanity.[18] And, as well, man was created as a single creature in order to show that each human being is unique. For "if a man strikes many coins from one mold, they resemble one another, but the supreme King of Kings, the Holy One Blessed be He, fashioned every man in the same stamp of the first man, and yet not one of them resembles his fellow."[19]

Human Freedom

The human being, bearing upon himself the divine likeness, subject to nature and living in community with others, is conscious of the will of God and yet remains free and able to decide how it is that he will forge his destiny. As the story is told in Genesis, the human beings are given one commandment: "Of every tree of the garden you are free to eat, but as for the tree of knowledge of good and evil, you must not eat of it."[20] And, of course, they eat of it.

Crucial to the Jewish understanding of the nature of man is that man is free. He controls much of his own destiny. Man has the knowledge and the wisdom to be aware of the divine calling that is addressed to him. Man can surely blaze his own path, choose his own way, and either do right or wrong. For better or for worse, that is how God created the world.

God created man as a free human being. While of course he does not choose to be born, nor to have the inheritance, both physical and cultural, that he receives, man has both the intellectual and personal qualities to perceive God's will and to create his life in response to it. Therefore, while God has created the world, He has also created latitude for human beings to be able to exercise their free will.

In the Bible, no sooner is there a world than there is murder. Cain kills Abel; and by the time we arrive at the story of Noah, God has repented of all that He has made and decides to undo the creation and to try again.

Realize what Scripture is saying: there appears to be an unknown and ever-unfolding reality once the creation is made. God, too, learns about it as it unfolds. And God is filled with disappointment about what He has made.[21]

Theological Anthropology, Not Predeterminism

I have summarized this story of creation and underlined its main points because the beginning of the Bible possesses what to Jews is a theological anthropology. This reading of Scripture would be misinterpreted if it were to be understood to say, for example, that all future human beings suffer for the sin of Adam and Eve. To Jews, the Biblical story is important not because it describes the punishments and future limitations of humanity as a result of our ancestors' choices. It is, rather, a snapshot picture of what we consider human nature and human significance to be.

To describe that snapshot: Man is of absolute value. Every human being is unique. All human beings are of equal value. Man is self-conscious, aware, and incomplete as he comes to recognize his existential loneliness. Man is a creature endowed with will and the freedom to exercise it as he sees fit.

But as a human being searches for the meaning of his destiny, he is engaged in a quest that will be satisfied only as he lives not alone, but with others—other people and God.

REVELATION

Man lives a twofold existence: both as a creature alone, separated from God and even separated from other people. And man also lives an existence in relationship, in relationship to God and to other creatures. In each case, man must listen beyond himself to be able to be aware that the call of the other is there. In each case, as well, the other, in dialogue, in conversation, and, ultimately, in revelation, becomes the necessary desideratum to man's fulfillment; the other gives meaning to his lonely existence.

God and Man Both Live in Relation

Martin Buber spoke of I-and-Thou and I-and-It. The basic words, he said, are paired words for they define the quality of different relationships. When we experience the other as an "it," then the other is distant from us. At best, we know him objectively— though we do not bridge the gap that leads to intimacy. When we do, that relationship is I-Thou, a relationship that does not allow us distance or objectivity. It is marked by intimacy, empathy, and by meaning. And in every I-Thou between human beings, there is the Eternal Thou, the Thou of our relationship with God, who can only be understood as Thou, never as It.[22]

Meaning in existence is achieved in relationship, and nowhere is that more true than the meaning achieved in life with God. God has a relationship with human beings that manifests itself in many ways. For Jews, there is one aspect of that relationship that exceeds all others. As a result of God's love, God decides that He will create a people that has a covenant with Him. Abraham is the first Jew, but it is not until the later epoch of Moses and the redemption of the Jewish people from Egypt that, on Mt. Sinai, the covenant between God and the Jews is given clear and specific content.

The Covenant

It is important to know what the covenant is and what it is not. The covenant is a way of describing the unique relationship between God and the people of Israel, and it places upon the Jews the obligation of living according to the Law that was revealed as its content. As with all covenants, it involves obligations and benefits. God gives a Law to the people of Israel and, if they abide by His Law, which is His will, then it will be good for the people of Israel.

The covenant is an expression of Love. The Torah is the love letter of God to Israel. The Torah is the content of that relationship; it provides the way for Jews to come close to their Father in Heaven. "You shall love the Lord your God with all your heart, with all your soul, and with all your might,"[23] we say twice a day, quoting Scripture in our daily prayers; those words are immediately followed by another Scriptural passage, which says: "If you will abide by my commandments . . ."[24] The theological idea is: First accept the fact that there is a kingdom of heaven. Then, accept the yoke of the commandments.

It is inaccurate to interpret the Law as being somehow inimical to love. The Law *is* the expression of God's love.[25] And it is through the Law that a Jew draws near to God. Secondly, the love of God, known through the revelation of the Torah, does not preclude a unique relation that God will have with every human being and, potentially, with all cultures on the face of the earth. The covenant with the Jews does not put any limitations on the rest of humanity to develop a relationship of love and of content with the God of the world.

In addition, classical Judaism maintains that, just as there is one God of all the universe, He makes certain demands on all human beings. Judaism assumes that all people are obligated to observe a universal law. That law, spoken of as the Seven Noahide Commandments, is applicable to everyone. These laws are: (1) the establishment of courts of justice so that law will rule in society, and the prohibitions of (2) blasphemy, (3) idolatry, (4) incest, (5) bloodshed, (6) robbery, and (7) eating the flesh of a living animal.[26]

It is important to realize the implications of believing in a universal covenant as well as the particular covenant between God and Israel. It means that Jews do not believe it is necessary for others to convert to their faith. Maimonides and subsequent decisors all make it clear that "the pious of all the nations of the world have a place in the world to come."[27] A basic tolerance that is the result of the brotherhood of mankind is therefore expanded, rather than limited, by such an idea of covenant. There are many paths that may lead to heaven. But there are some shared ideals on all of those paths.

Transcendent Truths

It is important to realize that such a view of God's will provides for a universally appreciated transcendent truth. It means that people of all faiths can and must share certain understandings with each other. It means that underlying a sense of the possibility of the human community to create a just world is a community in which there is a universal appreciation for the divine gifts that are universally at the source of the meaning of all of our existences.

Let me spell that out more directly. I think that it is widely thought today that religion is a major impediment to the working of a universal mankind. Many, particularly in our Western society, assume that if religion withered away, there would be universal bliss. No doubt, there is much reason to point to the strife so often the result of religious expressions. At the same time, though, I think that it is crucial for us to appreciate the need for a universal recognition of certain transcendent truths in order for there to be any universal law or any universal community.[28]

Let us take the popular idea that all the nations, to know what is right and just, would simply vote on it. The result of that would, while enticing, be an opportunity for every idea, be it bad or good, to be the source of a universal brotherhood. It could easily justify the murder of some while protecting others. It could justify economic systems, for example, that try to equalize wealth at the expense of the sacred rights of the individual. This was the basis of communism and its mass killings throughout the twentieth century, a system of murder justified for economic reasons. The murder of millions was in the service of a secular, not a religious, ideology, I note. While monotheism presupposes that there is a possibility of human community, it also requires the community to reach a consensus on a transcendent, universally acceptable truth that will reinforce the essential dignity of God's creation of humanity.[29]

I would therefore like to make a plea to all faiths, a plea that we engage in dialogue with one another so that we can, in each other's presence, communicate the power of the revelations we have received from God. Not so that we can become adherents of each other's faiths but so that, by bearing witness to the God of the world, we will hone, slowly but surely, a deeper respect for the universal truths that must be at the basis of a universal community.

The Law in Action

Fundamentally, the Law embodies the values of the tradition. Let us look at some examples, therefore, to probe their meaning and to see how traditions and values are constructed out of the building blocks of ancient words.

Leviticus 19, verse 32, contains a very simple admonition that a person is supposed to "rise up before the aged and give respect to those who have white hair." The rabbis studied this and, placing it together with the Biblical verse that requires "honoring one's father and mother,"[30] they elaborated a rather detailed series of laws that tell us how we are to treat the old.[31]

The treatment of the old is divided into two types of old: namely, one's parents and those who are not one's parents. Perhaps surprisingly, the commandment to honor parents is not seen in our tradition as principally directed toward young children, but rather toward adult children who have elderly parents. Honoring a parent means giving them food and drink, dressing them and covering them, bringing them in and taking them out. We are obviously talking here about parents who can't do these things for themselves.

When the Torah mentions standing up before the old, the Talmud discusses whether there are any limitations on who is old. If, for example, an old person is not a learned person, are we still required to treat them with such deference? The answer is, of course, yes. As the Talmud says: All the old have learned from the troubles that life has meted out.[32]

Now one might, therefore, think that Judaism is a religion that thinks, without any hesitation, that it is good to get old. And while that is generally true, the trials and tribulations of aging are carefully noted, both in the Bible and in the Talmud. The pain of arthritis, hair loss, vision, hearing, and digestive problems are all carefully documented in the texts.[33] So what one might have thought—that perhaps the ancient rabbis never really knew old people but rather imagined that old age was good since no one ever got to the ages we know—this is just not true.

According to the Talmud, the average life span of someone who made it past childhood was seventy years of age. Of course, a very large number of people never made it past childhood. But those who did were assumed to live to a reasonably old age. Though, as described, it was far from golden.[34]

But here is the crucial insight: The human being is created in such a way that, inevitably, the finite processes that make us work cease to function well and, finally, to function at all. A disjunction is created between a theological idea and the experience of everyday life. The theological idea is that the created person is noble and of enormous, infinite worth. But what does experience teach? That age brings with it pain and suffering. Therefore, a person's own experience belies the religious value that is at the basis of the tradition.

What happens? When his own body doesn't work, *other people begin to stand up in his presence.* You see, just as one's self-image begins to plummet on the physical scale, Scripture requires the society to take over and to reinforce the lofty nature of human creation.

When you need help, it is the job of other people to help you. Creation is noble and creation is also fragile. The community of people, working together, removes the rust that accumulates on the creature's wheels. *Only other people can do that.*

The Evil Tongue

A second example, Leviticus 19:16, states: "Do not go about as a talebearer among your people." This is one of the most difficult laws of the Torah to observe for it is the prohibition against gossip. In the Jewish religious tradition, gossip does not mean the telling of false tales about someone else. The law against defamation prohibits false tales. Tale bearing is the sharing of information that is true, not false. So what could be wrong with sharing *true* information? Simply that it is nobody else's business.

There is a high value placed on privacy in Judaism and there are many ways that people can cheapen each other's lives. Talking about others is one of the ways we take away their importance and lower the esteem in which they are held.

In Judaism this simple verse leads to laws concerning "lashon hara," the evil tongue, for the tongue is seen as an instrument that can do more damage than the most potent poison arrows. Words are the vehicles of our interpersonal lives, and the way in which we either respect or cheapen each other's value is frequently the result of the words we use.[35]

Just think of the current status of words. What are our words causing us to do to each other? In our modern world, much of our culture is media generated. It knows few inherent rights of privacy. It uses words and advertising to create needs that, frequently, we should not have; it molds us into opinions that frequently encourage us to hate each other, rather than to cultivate mutual respect. Words are cast out onto the airwaves; pictures may accompany them. Arrows shoot around the world in ways that would impress a Nazi propagandist.

It is the function of religion to sensitize human beings to the destructive power of their tongues, just as it is the job of religion to encourage us to use our tongues for the betterment of the world.

The Value of Life

The Law embodies the value of human life as one of the supreme values in Judaism. Since man is in the divine image, few things could be worth more. One may suspend nearly all the laws of the Torah to save a human life. The Sabbath and even the Day of Atonement may be transgressed.[36]

But there are situations where life may be forfeited. If a person were to be forced to commit idolatry, a sexual act forbidden by the Torah, or to commit murder, then, in very limited circumstances, it would be obligatory to give up one's life.[37]

War is permissible, but it must be conducted according to certain rules that, among other concerns, protect non-combatants and offer the option of peace to an enemy. Judaism abhors the phenomenon of terrorism. It is opposed to suicide for any reason. The use of suicide to commit murder is doubly abhorrent.[38]

Ritual and Ethics Are Totally Intertwined

The Torah of Israel, and by the Torah I mean the tradition that begins with Scripture and continues even to our own day, that Torah is concerned with the welfare of human beings just as it is concerned with people's relation to God. The Ten Commandments were written on two tablets. The first tablet tells us to believe in God and not to make or worship idols, not to bear the name of the Lord in vain, to observe the Sabbath, and, finally, to honor parents. Tablet one symbolizes the Law's concern with the relation of man to God. The fifth commandment provides a point of transition: honoring parents brings us from the realm of relating to God to the realm of relating to human beings. The second tablet concerns entirely ethical mandates: not to murder, commit adultery, or steal, neither to bear false witness nor to covet.

The section of the Torah from which I drew the examples of respect for the aged and the prohibitions of the evil tongue is a perfect example of the total intertwining of ritual and ethics in Judaism. The nineteenth chapter of Leviticus says that a Jew should strive to be holy because the Lord, God, is holy. Judaism is a religion of commandments between man and God and commandments between man and man. But they are all God's will, meaning that our relations with each other are not only *our* concern, they are *God's* concern as well.

This holiness spans the two paradigmatic relationships, man and God as well as man and his fellow man. Thus in Leviticus 19, the Torah commands reverence for parents and the Sabbath and then condemns the worship of idols or the making of molten gods. That is followed by laws of sacrifices and immediately thereafter by the law to leave the edges of a harvested field for the benefit of the poor and the stranger. No stealing, no defrauding, no favoritism in judgment. Hate not your kinsfolk in your heart.

Take not vengeance or bear a grudge. Love your neighbor as yourself.[39]

The challenge to be holy because God is holy is a challenge met by acts of devotion toward God and practical responses that embody the sanctity of every human being. Thus the image of God—a human being—is, while not worshipped, made clear and certain as the holiest of all creations. Loving devotion to our fellow human beings is the clear and abiding will of God. The love of God in the covenant demands a corresponding love for human beings.

Imitation of God

The greatest devotion involves *imitating* God. Imitating God results in service to human beings. Thus Rabbi Simlai in the Talmud points out the value of lovingkindness, for the Torah begins with lovingkindness and ends with lovingkindness. At the beginning it is written: "And the Lord God made garments of skins for the man and the woman and He clothed them."[40] And at the end it is written: "And He (God) buried him (Moses)."[41] What God does is what man is supposed to do, and both engage in loving acts of devotion to others.[42]

Similarly, Rabbi Hama, son of R. Hanina, said:

How does one explain the text: "Ye shall walk after the Lord your God"?[43] Is it, then, possible for a human being to walk after the Divine presence; for has it not been said: "For the Lord thy God is a devouring fire"?[44] But the meaning is to walk after the attributes of the Holy One, blessed be He. As He clothes the naked, for it is written: "And the Lord God made for Adam and for his wife garments of skins, and He clothed them,"[45] so do thou also clothe the naked. The Holy One, blessed be He, visited the sick, for it is written: "And the Lord appeared unto him by the oaks of Mamre,"[46] so do thou also visit the sick. The Holy One, blessed be He, comforted mourners, for it is written: "And it came to pass after the death of Abraham, that God blessed Isaac his son,"[47] so do thou also comfort mourners. The Holy one, blessed be He, buried the dead, for it is written: "And He buried him in the valley,"[48] so do thou also bury the dead.[49]

Maimonides, in his monumental *Guide for the Perplexed,* concludes the volume with a discussion of imitating God's ways. Here, in a philosophical exposition of the tradition, the same conclusion is drawn: love of God is realized by acts of kindness to human beings.

Maimonides recalls the verses in Jeremiah: "Thus saith the Lord, Let not the wise man glory in his wisdom, neither let the mighty man glory in his might, let not the rich man glory in his riches; but let him that glorieth glory in this, that he understandeth and knoweth me."[50] In a verse that we might have read as a directive to only know God, both intellectually and experientially, Maimonides explains it with a surprising twist.

> The Divine acts which ought to be known, and ought to serve as a guide for our actions, are lovingkindness, justice, and righteousness. . . . The object of the passage [of Jeremiah] is, therefore, to declare, that the perfection in which man can truly glory, is attained by him when he has acquired—as far as this is possible for man—the knowledge of God, the knowledge of His Providence, and of the manner in which it influences His creatures in their production and continued existence. Having acquired this knowledge he will then be determined always to seek lovingkindness, justice, and righteousness, and thus to imitate the ways of God.

Imitation of God is, therefore, the highest level of religious experience, and imitation of God consists of devotion to our fellow human beings.

REDEMPTION

Human beings need to work together for the common good, finally, because Judaism has a notion of history that is grounded in the experience of redemption.

Because God is an active participant in history, history itself has meaning and is moving in a direction that, as it unfolds, bears witness to God's wish for the world to be redeemed. There are some views of history that see it as a wheel that continues to turn around. In that way, there is no beginning and no end, nor any real progress at any point. What was yesterday will be again tomorrow.

Judaism is a religion that locates the relation of God and man on a continuum of time that has both a beginning and an end. The beginning is creation. The end is the Coming of the Messiah, the End of Days, when all strivings for a better world will finally be welcomed in the era of perfection. And hope is pointed in that direction, "to perfect the world into the Kingdom of the Almighty."[51]

Judaism believes that the world, as we know it, is an unredeemed place. It is a place where perfection, righteousness, and peaceful living can be worked for; they can be partially, but not completely, achieved. All of life as we know it is inevitably tinged with pain and disappointment, with the certainty that, as good as it might become, it will never achieve perfection. The unredeemed world is a world in which one must accept less than the best. It is a world in which utopian hopes inevitably lead to disastrous consequences, for their expectations will not be fulfilled. Unfortunately, because these hopes become the center of people's faith, they often lead, instead, to great devastation and destruction.

The belief in the ideal future, in the end of days that is characterized by an era of peace is, however, the guiding light. Without a beacon, there is no vision in a world of fog and sometimes darkness. Without hope, there is no striving. All of humanity needs to grow toward the sun that gives it energy and strength.

Creation Is a Partnership Between God and Man

Judaism views history as a field of deeds in time where the possibilities of human beings, possessed with free will, can change the course of events. Free will thus allows man to be an active agent in history. Ours is not a view of history where all is decreed from above. God's will becomes evident in history. It is a will that leads toward a messianic future. But it doesn't remove man's responsibility from playing a crucial role.

Human activity, therefore, has value, and there is an ongoing creation that is a partnership between man and God. The rabbinic midrash makes the point in this way. Tyranus Rufus, a pagan Roman general, asks Rabbi Akiba whose deeds are more becoming, those of God or those of human beings. Rabbi Akiba replies that man's deeds surpass those of God. Surprised, Tyranus Rufus says: Behold the heavens and the earth, can any human being make something that compares to them?

Rabbi Akiba then brings together sheaves of wheat and loaves of bread. The sheaves are God's creation, the loaves, man's. Akiba does the same with flax and the beautiful clothing made from it.[52]

Rabbi Akiba was teaching the Roman that God and man both work to continue the creation of the world. Man is God's partner in that task. History is the context in which this partnership is played out, day after day, eon after eon.

As Rabbi Norman Lamm notes in his study of Jewish social ethics, "When R. Shelomoh Eger, a distinguished Talmudist, became a hasid, he was asked what he learned from R. Menahem Mendel of Kotzk after his first visit. He answered that the first thing he learned in Kotzk was, 'In the beginning God created.' But did a renowned scholar have to travel to a Hasidic Rebbe to learn the first verse in the Bible? He answered: 'I learned that God created only the beginning; everything else is up to man.'"[53]

Human beings have a role in the creation and, although they should not expect perfection, they should always labor to bring it about. As Rabbi Tarfon teaches in the Talmud: You do not have to finish the work, but neither are you free to desist from it.[54]

Historical Memory of the Exodus

Since history is a place where communal meaning is found, the exodus from Egypt becomes a historical event in the life of the

Jews that not only evokes memories, but requires an ongoing response. The response is one of requiring acts of love and fellowship toward other human beings.

Jews, for example, are required to be kind to the stranger. Why? "You shall love him as yourself, for you were strangers in the land of Egypt."[55] On the Sabbath, not only a Jew must rest, but also his servants and the strangers living in his midst. Why? "Remember that you were a servant in the land of Egypt, and that the Lord your God brought you out from there with a mighty hand and with a stretched-out arm."[56] Similarly, when an indentured servant goes free, "You shall furnish him liberally out of your flock, and out of your threshing floor, and out of your winepress; of that with which the Lord your God has blessed you, you shall give to him. And you shall remember that you were a slave in the land of Egypt, and the Lord your God redeemed you; therefore I command you this thing today."[57] The widow and the orphan are protected, together with the stranger, for precisely the same reason: because you were slaves in Egypt.[58] Likewise, the poor shall be left their gleanings. Again: "You shall remember that you were a slave in the land of Egypt; therefore I command you to do this thing."[59]

Historical memory is therefore a basis for humanitarian action.

The End of Days

It should also be noted that in classical Judaism, the final end of days is not only spiritual in nature. It will witness a resurrection of the dead. Therefore, the perfection of the end of days involves not only the perfect soul, but it involves the embodiment of a soul in the world of matter. Matter that heretofore had been inimical to perfection is now the realm of perfection.

No circumstances of human experience can possibly offer evidence to deny the hope in the future that is grounded in faith. Therefore, when Jews were sent to the gas chambers by the Nazis during World War II, it was common for them to repeat Maimonides's statement of belief in the Coming of the Messiah: I believe with perfect faith in the Coming of the Messiah. And though he tarry, still I believe.

The experience of history, though filled with many disappointments, provides the ground on which to realize the doing of the commandments and the continual redemption of the world.

This redemption is universal. The Messianic age is to be enjoyed by all of humanity and all will gather in Jerusalem to proclaim that the Lord is King over all the earth, that He is one and that His name is one.[60]

Its blessing is peace. The Biblical blessing that the priests are commanded to utter before the people ends with a prayer for peace: "May the Lord lift His face to you and grant you peace."[61] The prayer that is central to Jewish liturgy and is repeated three times daily ends with a prayer for peace. Great is peace, for the prophets have taught us to care for nothing as much as peace. Great is peace, for it is given to the meek; as Scripture says, "But the humble shall inherit the land, and delight themselves in the abundance of peace."[62] Great is peace, for it outweighs everything else. The morning prayers say, "He creates peace and creates everything." Therefore, if there is no peace, there is, so to speak, nothing left in creation.[63]

For the Sake of My Kin and Friends

Lonely and disappointed is the God of the world unless there is hope for humanity. And the very fact of creation, the very involvement of God in it, is an intimation that God was willing to take the risks because it was worth it in the long run. This is God's promise, even to his people who are exiled: "Keep your voice from weeping, and your eyes from tears, for your work shall be rewarded, says the Lord. Your children will come back from the land of the enemy. And there is hope for your future, says the Lord."[64]

For God's presence and concern, God's relation to the world and His hope for it, devolves upon the noble but flawed humanity that is in His image. It is for the sake of the other, for the sake of my kin and friends, that God creates the hope for peace, the hope that sustains the world.

3

Strategies for Disagreement

His Royal Highness Prince El Hassan bin Talal[1]

THE RELIGIOUS DIMENSION of cultural misunderstanding is central to all discussions of the issue at this time. In speaking of interfaith conversations, it is the process that concerns me—conversations between the adherents of the faiths, not between the faiths. Such conversations do not touch on creeds and metaphysics. It is necessary that one side respect what is sacred to the other; and, in the words of Imam al Shatibi, *nu'adhem al-juwaame' wa nahtarem al-furooq* (we enhance what is universal and we respect what is different).

Where respect does not exist, the problem arises of how to engender it; where creeds and metaphysics *are* discussed, the problem arises of how to accommodate contradictions. The theory espoused by numerous well-intentioned peace activists and promoters of interfaith and intercultural dialogue revolves around—in spirit, at least—the familiar notion that "to know is to love"; that mutual awareness and knowledge, the often-heralded fruits of education, help to *humanize* the other, creating a better understanding of his or her fears and trials, and eventually lead to empathy among former adversaries. Of course, while this may be true as far as it goes, we must bear in mind that some of the bloodiest and most brutal conflicts have occurred between people who know each other only too well and have little mutual empathy as a result, including—alarmingly—co-religionists.

Let us look at some examples of confrontation among co-religionists and co-nationalists. In the Caucasus, for instance, Christian Russia backed Muslim Abkhazia against Christian Georgia, while Muslim Iran played off Christian Armenia against Muslim

Azerbaijan. The list continues: Ossetians against Georgians (both Christians); Lezgins against Azeris; Circassians against Karachai (both Muslim). Elsewhere, in Lebanon, savage battles raged between Muslims, Christians, and Druze, all of whom knew each other sufficiently well; but the most savage of all battles often took place *within* each sect. In the Balkans, too, where for each conflict pitting Muslims against Christians, there was another conflict involving co-religionists; for instance, Moldovans versus Russians; Hungarians versus Romanians; Macedonians versus Greeks; Serbs versus Croats.

Familiarity, therefore, does not always eradicate enmity. It is perfectly possible for us—for people—both to know *and* hate each other. And my call is for a civilized framework for disagreement.

I believe that only by accepting responsibility for words and actions at all levels will this ever be possible. Whether or not history has come to an end or whether or not we are heading for a clash of civilizations is not really the point. If we want to clash we will clash. What is needed is to create programs and ideas that bring certain unacceptables to an end—war, terror (with or without its "isms"), violence, and disregard for the inherent dignity of man.

The notion of international implementation of a code of human responsibilities to balance the code of human rights most widely accepted in the form of the United Nations Declaration of Human Rights (UNDHR) has received a considerable amount of attention lately. The work of Hans Küng has been especially noteworthy in this regard. The Declaration toward a Global Ethic that he coordinated, approved by the Parliament of the World Religions, promoted much discussion on the issue and is published alongside a "Universal Declaration of Human Responsibilities."[2] As the preamble of the Declaration of Responsibilities states:

> The initiative . . . is not only a way of balancing freedom with responsibility, but also a means of reconciling ideologies, beliefs, and political views that were deemed antagonistic in the past. The

proposed declaration points out that the exclusive insistence on rights can lead to endless dispute and conflict, that religious groups in pressing for their own freedom have a duty to respect the freedom of others.

Part of any implementation of the Declaration of Responsibilities to reconcile antagonistic views must be the re-explication of the specific values in each tradition and culture that support and confirm the principle of living in freedom while respecting the freedom of others to be different *without* necessarily reconciling differences. The difficulty of observing the principle of reciprocity in freedoms and rights—the polar opposite of vengefulness, as it were—was well expressed by the Christian historian, Arnold Toynbee, when he wrote just before his death in 1973:

> In the biosphere, life has found for itself a habitable but inhospitable setting, and life's reaction has been grasping and greediness. The Buddha held that grasping *(tanha)* is the root cause of suffering. All the higher religions call, with one voice, for renunciation. But renunciation is a still greater *tour de force* than the self-assertion that has been life's original response to the inhospitability of the biosphere.[3]

The promotion of the "value of peaceful disagreement" thus requires not only the establishment of institutions such as conflict avoidance centers and citizens' conferences, and sustained educational and media support at each step, but also the backing of religious leadership with reference to their faith and cultural traditions. Religions have always emphasized the responsibilities of man toward self, other, society, and environment; have attempted to teach values (such as humility, moderation, altruism) and institute mechanisms (such as fasting, alms-giving, and *zakat*) that will minimize selfishness and graspingness; and in some cases have provided for the fact that disagreements inevitably do arise.

The media and educational programs must, simultaneously, address the role of *perceptional revisionism*. As an essential component of education—especially in the troubled Western Asian region—we must examine reciprocal perceptions among Jews, Christians, Muslims, and other faiths—including secularism. As yet we do not have access to an analytical concordance of values in the three holy books, let alone a document aiming at coordination of traditions worldwide. Meanwhile, the role of responsible scriptwriters for the media and for the world of informatics, in distance-education, in literature, in mass communication, in textbooks, in religious and scholarly works, in the performing arts, in the visual arts, in ethnographic materials, and others, is hugely important in minimizing artificial differences or differences that arise from misunderstanding or blind assertions.[4]

Part of this program is the dissemination of a philosophy of positive difference, of progress and refinement through difference. As President Muhammad Khatami of Iran has written:

> . . . it is possible to eliminate differences, except for those which are natural, for people are by nature different; we do not all think alike, and we do not have identical interpretations. Therefore, in light of agreements and numerous common elements, we can minimize differences and render them a means to perfection and progress. Similar thoughts never confront each other. To have two ways of thinking set against each other is not only problem-free, but they ought to confront each other, for this causes the evolution and perfection of the thought. What is important is that the dichotomy of thoughts not turn into disagreements, contradiction, aggression, and war.[5]

President Khatami goes on to call for wisdom and rationality in dialogue to avoid the scenario threatened in the last sentence. In the absence of wisdom and rationality in many human encounters, it is necessary to devise and to put into practice institutional and legislative means to address the globalization of communications and power, the threat of a "clash of cultures"—if not Huntington's infamous "clash of civilizations"—and the fact that, with the proliferation of every kind of weapon, violent disagreement is becoming easier than ever before. *Realpolitik* and petro-politics must at all costs give heed to an overarching ethic with human welfare as its center and goal.

The education of these values in society begins with the individual and his or her relationship with the institution. Religious schools have a particular responsibility to foster pluralist and international thinking. The famous Jesuit education provides a well known, if controversial, example. Father Peter-Hans Kolvenbach, Superior-General of the Society of Jesus, spoke at Santa Clara University in the year 2000 on the topic of this Christian educational tradition and today's changes:

> For 450 years, Jesuit education has sought to educate "the whole person" intellectually and professionally, psychologically, morally, and spiritually. But in the emerging global reality, with its great possibilities and deep contradictions, the whole person is different from the whole person of the Counter-Reformation, the Industrial Revolution, or the twentieth century. Tomorrow's "whole person" cannot be whole without an educated awareness of society and culture with which to contribute socially, generously, in the real world. Tomorrow's whole person must have, in brief, a well-educated solidarity.

The argument for an educated solidarity is one that I have made myself many times.[6] Without a global ethic of human solidarity, cultural misunderstandings and political expediencies will continue to tear us apart, both between and within communities. Yet to educate only the idea of solidarity is not enough when, in so many encounters, basic disagreements cannot be negotiated without degenerating into attempts to dominate, by force or violence. It is necessary, therefore, to educate further, ideally through personal experience, the possibility of civilized disagreement within a wider structure of agreed values.

What means to promote non-violent disagreement already exist? Moreover, to what extent may previously workable mechanisms have become invalid or ineffective in the larger, globally connected, and widely informed societies in which we live? In all discussions, we now have to take account of the fact that the previously dependable relationship between the human being and natural geography—the "size of the world"—has been removed from or altered in every equation that had previously served mankind's interests in promoting and negotiating traditions, values, and humanitarian action.[7] We lack the exact experience with which to deal with this fact, but we do have numerous records of intercultural and intracultural advice with which to work to expand the sphere within which we may safely disagree and still work toward common goals.

It should be emphasized that the promotion of mechanisms enabling peaceful disagreement goes hand in hand with both educating our capacity also to agree (through universal values, varied debate, responsible media activity, formally placing value upon diversity in society, etc.) and, very importantly, enforcing international norms and standards of humanitarian law as they already exist. Indeed, if all Abrahamic believers really believed in and implemented Moses's Ten Commandments, I suppose no need would have arisen for the symposium that led to this book.

A complete catalogue of traditional injunctions to find civilized means to disagree would be an extremely useful resource and will surely form part of any global matrix of religious and philosophic values. It may be useful, as a starting point, to note some possible Islamic beginnings from which to develop a global "framework for disagreements."

I open with the Qur'an and a late surah which is rendered in English as follows:

> Say, "O you unbelievers!
> I do not worship what you do,
> Nor do you worship what I do.
> Neither shall I ever worship what you do,
> Nor indeed shall you worship what I do.
> You have your own religion, and I have my own!"

This is explained as an instruction to Muhammad to turn down an offer by non-Muslims that he should worship their gods and that they worship Allah in return. It constitutes a refusal to compromise or syncretize Islam, and also an acknowledgment of fundamental division between religious beliefs. The surah does not, however, demand that the unbelievers shall worship Allah—even though, in its context, Islam is the true religion. It is not a missionizing exhortation; it is a statement of the *status quo* constituting a recognition that some differences are not to be papered over, ignored, nor resolved.

This is a step that may not be omitted from any attempt to engage in dialogue toward solidarity—the formal recognition and agreement that there are areas of utter difference. Here, I do not refer to situations such as political negotiations over land disputes, water use, or the right of return of refugees, in which a compromise acceptable to both sides is sought. Non-negotiable difference in the cultural and religious sphere does not necessarily result in mutually incompatible demands or stalemate.

To accompany the surah cited above, and supporting the ideas of seeking peaceful agreement throughout diversity and implementing extant laws and norms, the Qur'an again states:

(2:256) There shall be no compulsion in religion.

(6:106) Follow that which has been revealed to you from your Lord, other than Whom there is no God, and turn away from the polytheists.

(107) Had Allah willed, they would not have joined partners to Him. We have not appointed you as their controller, nor are you a guardian over them.

(108) Do not revile those [deities] which they invoke besides Allah, lest they revile Allah aggressively and unknowingly. Thus We have caused every group to see their deeds pleasant in their eyes. Then they will return to their Lord, who will tell them what they used to do.

(10:99) Had your Lord willed, all those who are on earth would have believed. Can you force people to be believers?

(16:125) Call [people] to your Lord's path with wise and tactful preaching, and debate with them using a gracious way of speech.

(17:53) Tell My servants to use good speech in their parlance, because Satan arouses animosity between them. Truly, Satan is an avowed enemy to man.

(25:56) We only sent you [Muhammad] as a boder of good tidings and as a warner.

(57) Say, "I am not asking you a reward for [my message], except that you walk in the way to your Lord, if you so wish."

(25:63) The servants of the Merciful One are those who walk gently on the earth, who, if the ignorant speak [badly] to them, they say "Peace" [in reply].

Other Muslim thinkers have developed upon these themes. The mystic Sufi Muslim tradition's long history of "connectivity" with other religions is exemplified in the following lines of Jalal ad-Din ur-Rumi—one of the great poets of the Islamic world, born in a happier Afghanistan in the thirteenth century—who said:

> Come now whoever you are!
> Come without any fear of being disliked.
> Come whether you are a Muslim, a Christian, or a Jew.
> Come whoever you are!
> Whether you believe or do not believe in God.
> Come also if you believe in the sun as God.
> This door is not a door of fear.
> This is a door of good wishes.

A Muslim tradition of Jesus (who is highly revered as God's prophet before Muhammad) reports as follows:

Jesus said, "Leave people alone. Be at ease with people and ill at ease with yourself. Do not seek to earn their praises or merit their rebuke. Perform what you have been commanded to do."[8]

"Leaving people alone"—accepting the existence of radically opposed views to one's own without feeling threatened—requires trust that the other will, in turn, permit one's own views to continue to exist. I speak here not only of the fear of the other that follows our mistrust of difference and—for those who dare to engage in dialogue or inclusionist discourse—the fear of the folks back home and what they will say or do, but also the paradoxical fear of peace itself. It is ironic, but all of us, in our close exclusionist circles, share a certain agoraphobia, a fear of open spaces, which amounts to a fear of peace with the other.

Too often, as a consequence, we find defensiveness, self-arming, and the threat of force. The Qur'an is well known to take up issues of punishment and use of force, including military force, in the defence of one's Muslim beliefs against attackers. The reader should also note that this religious scripture uniquely asserts the rights of prisoners, especially women and children, in any such scenario. Implicit in the idea of minimal mutual trust is a notion of a shared governing value: that profound disagreement is acceptable and that peaceful disagreement without threat is the acceptable norm. Hence the importance of instituting a global ethic of human solidarity so that forceful self-defense becomes absolutely the last resort.

Problems arise when expressions of the value of "non-negotiable difference" run into the value of "universal human rights" (and when both values are rejected in favor of a claim to superior authority or force). We see such situations in the Muslim world today in debates over—for example—freedom of conscience, the implementation of strictly literal Shar'ia criminal law and, more generally, women's rights. Further problems arise when the "right to be different" that is argued to preclude certain accusations of human rights infringements defends the idea of an innate, non-negotiable superiority—that "Islam" rather than "human rights" (in one form or another) is the only correct and acceptable code. Conversely, any suggestion that "human rights" are the only acceptable code and must supersede "Islam" is unlikely to meet with approval.

The idea of unity as an essential attribute of God, to be reflected by mankind who was created from a single soul and its mate, is very important in Islamic thinking. Disunity, by contrast, is of the devil. What is needed is an awareness that unity does not mean identity and that differences need not disappear within a variegated whole. The Qur'an emphasizes the variety of creation, the alternation between day and night, the striped and changing colors of rocks and animals and the different tastes of fruits irrigated by the same water. B. A. Dar has commented beautifully on the Qur'anic treatment of this topic, and for ease of reference, it seems worthwhile to quote him at some length:

The Qur'an aims at establishing a peaceful social atmosphere where people belonging to other faiths can enjoy freedom of conscience and worship (2:256) . . . It is as a consequence of this attitude of tolerance that, according to the Qur'an, all those who believe in God and the Last Day and practice righteousness, whether they are Muslims, Jews, Christians, or Sabaeans, shall get their reward from their Lord (2:62; 5:72).[9]

The disvalues of discord and disunity are the result of the denial of the unity of God (59:14). The unbelievers and those who associate partners with God are always subject to fear and lack a sense of unity and harmony (2:151; 8:65). It is the devil that incites people to discord (7:200; 41:36) and, therefore, the Qur'an very forcefully forbids people to be divided among themselves (3:103), and looks upon disunity as the result of lack of wisdom (59:14). It denounces divisions and splits in religion (6:159; 30:32; 42:13) and disagreements among different sects and schisms through insolent envy (42:65; 45:17). Similarly, all those acts which tend to spread mischief and tumult after there have been peace and order are condemned because they tend to create disorder, disunity, and disharmony in life (2:191–92, 205; 7:85; 11:85).[10]

Dar was writing in the early 1960s, a more hopeful time perhaps than today; but the "opposition" so often dwelt upon in the images and soundbites fed us by our various more-or-less propagandistic media is still by no means an opposition of monoliths. There is a great variety of opinion within the "Muslim world" concerning human rights and their implementation, and the idea of cultural relativism itself derives from the same Western intellectual milieu that brought forth the UNDHR. Indeed, the interpretation of the UNDHR in the context of issues of national sovereignty, religious majority, or social integration is problematic for the Western nations who first approved the document.[11] However, criticisms of today's "universal" human rights have from the beginning focused on the idea that their definitions and statement were characteristically Western, not universal.[12]

With regard to the idea of Muslim variety, dialogue within the Muslim communities and between different branches and sects of Islam is seriously lacking today. The four schools of Sunni Islam and two schools of Shi'a Islam are not engaged in conversations to clarify similarities and acknowledge differences and, consequently, there was no unified Muslim stance on the terrible attacks of September 11, 2001. Part of the solution lies in acknowledging that internal differences also exist and emphasizing that these differences are not a threat to the existence of Islam and that the traditional process of *ijtihad,* or careful analysis and reform of Islamic thinking, is by no means incompatible with orthodoxy. The cultural differences that have inevitably grown up in far-flung communities of a global religion need not preclude unity of faith but should be recognized by all when discussing cultural clashes. Muslims too were killed in the bombing of New York's World Trade Center.

Muslims themselves need an education that will convey some grasp of the analyses, commentaries, and reforms that have characterized the history of Muslim philosophy and political thinking. With reference to the proliferation of extremist Islamist groups today, and the supposed opposition between "Muslim" and "Western" values it would be helpful to recognize that, to the Mu'tazilites, the Sufis, and indeed to some of the modernizing thinkers who lay behind the nationalist movements in the Arab world, there was not necessarily any incompatibility to begin with.[13] During the second half of the twentieth century, disagreements between "Western" and "Muslim" culture were framed in terms of purpose and rationale rather than rational scientific methodology, which was promoted as an approach shared by both. Indeed, in one of the most beautiful allegories of the Qur'an, the light of God is compared with the luminous rays cast by a lamp whose oil itself verges upon the luminous and comes from an olive-tree "neither of the east nor or the west."[14] This is fuel for centrist thinking.

I hope that we can take a rational approach in developing the four basic principles of *A Global Ethic,* as the Declaration of the World's Parliament of Religion underlined, to forming a minimum common ethical understanding between current religions and the cultures adopting them. It is interesting to note that both the "Dialogue of Civilizations" and *A Global Ethic* have, if not their origins in modern Islamic thinking, at least an integrated and inherent Islamic component.

Controlling anger and "opening the gates of *ijtihad*" means teaching people to allow for the possibility of fundamental disagreement and to realize that agreements continue to be possible as many bridges across few divides. Rigid adherence to the notion of a monopoly upon the truth is the basis of exclusionism whether propagated by a Muslim or a Western secularist. Thus *ijtihad* is an activity to be cultivated not only by Muslim thinkers in the course of intra-Islamic and interfaith debate but also by proponents of Western values, whose roots in the Renaissance and Enlightenment surely demand the continuation of a rigorous and vigorous self-questioning. At these times of simultaneous globalization and polarized thinking, open markets and blind faith, it may be that the formal process of *ijtihad* and the idea of providing cross-faith and cross-cultural rules and guidelines for how to disagree will be very useful contributions from Muslim thinking to the world.

4

The World of the Dinka: A Portrait of a Threatened Culture

Ambassador Francis Mading Deng

Introduction

Culture is an embodiment of values that have evolved over a long period of time and have become crystallized into institutionalized patterns of behavior. Cultures and the values they engender are what give human beings their innate dignity and social cohesion. While cultures are dynamic and change with the imperatives of experience, they also provide predictable standards for prescriptive behavior. The result is a normative system that reinforces perspectives, expectations, and conformity. Change then takes the nature of discrete reforms, with occasional revolutionary zeal, prompted primarily by prophets, inspired leaders, or crises of grave magnitude. Otherwise, life is evolutionary and predictable.

Applying these concepts to the African scene, it is obvious that the continent has suffered a trauma that has severely damaged its structures, perspectives, behavior patterns, and expectations. Politically, economically, culturally, and spiritually, the peoples of Africa were assumed to be in a void that had to be filled by imported concepts, values, and aspirations for self-enhancement through the emulation of the supposedly superior outsiders. Rather than see development as an evolution or a process of self-improvement from within, Africans began to see it as a commodity alien to them that had to be imported, with indispensable assistance from outsiders.

Of course, judged by objective modern criteria of the gross national product or per capita income, or by the social indices of life expectancy, literacy, and the benefits of science and technology, indigenous Africans can appropriately be described as poor. But from a subjective standpoint, a people whose aspirations, expectations, and patterns of life were adapted to their environment, and who, to give the example of herding societies, may possess large herds of cattle and sheep and fertile soil endowed with sufficient rainfall for subsistence farming, far from seeing themselves as poor, may, indeed, view themselves as blessed and perhaps even envied by others. Linkage to the outside world and opportunities previously outside their purview can begin to damage these self-gratifying assumptions. But it is, in fact, the destructive intervention of the outside world, often manifested in devastating violence, that begins to impoverish the communities that, in their splendid isolation, had thought themselves in a worldly paradise.

The Nilotics of the Sudan—Dinka, Nuer, Shilluk, among others—have been well documented by anthropologists as an exceedingly proud people, who glorified in their livestock, their land, and their culture, resisted any foreign influences, much of which they deemed inferior to their culture, and, as a result, lagged behind the process of modernization.[1] Once they realized that education and socio-economic development had become essential to their status and welfare in the modern context, the same values that had inhibited their adaptation to change suddenly provided them with the incentive to adapt and modernize. But then an even worse source of destruction than the invasion of foreign ideas came in the form of a devastating civil war, whose core is the competition for the soul of the nation. Indeed, the Dinka and the indigenous peoples of the Southern Sudan are more known today for the humiliating humanitarian tragedy that the devastating civil war that has raged intermittently since 1955 has imposed on them than for the pride and dignity for which they had been known.

While they are now set on a course of radical change from

which there is no return, tradition remains a force in the life of most Dinkas. Tradition emanates from experience, and that experience is not ancient history; it is a significant part of the present. And although it is now threatened by various forces, it is a system that is still observable, definable, and useable to reinforce the people's sense of worth and a self-motivated development from within. This is why it is described in the present tense in this chapter, despite the radical changes traditional society is undergoing. Exceptions will be made only in those cases where the past tense is clearly called for.

Building on the case of the Dinka, this chapter presents their indigenous value system, the way it has interacted with the adventitious Arab and European influences, and the challenge it poses for building a pluralistic nation that should be enriched by its diverse legacies, instead of continuing to be torn apart by conflicting visions for the nation. But the challenge is more than political and touches on a contextualization of the principles of democracy, human rights, and equitable development from within. Although the focus is on the Dinka, the evidence and the arguments provided are arguably applicable to other indigenous groups in the Sudan and elsewhere in Africa.

The Dinka and Their Values

Overview of the Dinka World

The Dinka are the largest ethnic group in the Sudan, numbering about four million in a country of around thirty million people and several hundred tribes. Though they engage in agriculture and grow a wide variety of crops (sorghum, millet, maize, sesame, beans, groundnuts, pumpkins, okra, and tobacco), their culture is dominated by cattle (and to a lesser extent by sheep and goats), to which they attach a social and a moral significance far beyond their economic value. Their land, a flat configuration of thick forests and open plains, lacks stone, iron, or any material resource of significant durability. This is perhaps why their culture is poor in visual arts but strikingly rich in verbal skills. Poetic abilities and the powers of articulation and persuasiveness are inculcated and encouraged in a child from the earliest years, and continue to be highly prized as determinants of intelligence, character, influence, and social stature. And yet, the Dinka are excellent builders, constructing huts and cattle-byres that have circular mud walls reinforced with wattles and conical roofs with rafters of remarkably smooth thatching. Their houses, indeed, have been described as among the best native dwellings on the African continent.[2]

The world of the Dinka is a combination of environmental attractions and hardships. During the dry season, which lasts for six months from November to April, the blazing tropical sun bakes the land, killing virtually all vegetation and turning the area into a thirsty arid zone, with shimmering mirages of pools and lakes separated by a cracking pavement of dark clay soil. With the coming of the rainy season, which lasts for the remaining six months from May to October, the land is miraculously transformed: first, with the early rains, deep green grass carpets the plains; lush natural vegetation follows, and the world suddenly becomes alive with the hustle and bustle of birds[3] and insects of all shapes and colors, the flashing of plentiful fish in the rivers, the concerted tunes of frogs and crickets, combined with the characteristic bellowing of cows and the bleating of goats and sheep. Despite the hardships of the extreme climatic conditions, the Dinka have a burning love for their land, and, until the late 1950s when the allurements of modernity began to pull them toward urban centers, to leave Dinkaland was considered a depraved action that was almost certain to provoke a slanderous song.

The Dinka are spread out over a vast territory covering over one-tenth of the nearly one million square miles that make the Sudan the largest country in Africa. Territorially, the Dinka are organized into tribes, sub-tribes, sections, clans, and lineages (which are factions of clans) determined by descent from a common ancestor. Dinka residential patterns are also widespread.

There are usually several miles between clusters of huts and cattle-byres in settlements or villages, each accommodating only a few families whose homesteads are also well separated. Large in numbers, widespread in settlement, and segmented by the topography of their land, the Dinka are a conglomerate of some twenty-five independent groups that are also divided into autonomous subgroups, all of which share a striking pride in their race and culture.[4]

The Age-Set System as an Institution of Identity and Dignity

A vital institution that reinforces territorial identification among the Dinka is the age-set that every Dinka joins on coming of age, usually in his mid-teens, after undergoing an initiation ceremony. This is a painful ordeal that, in most tribes, involves scarring deep lines across the forehead varying in number from seven upward, according to the height of the forehead and the bragging courage of the young man. Some tribes exempt women from this ordeal, although they are organized into age-sets that correspond to those of their male counterparts.

Painful as initiation is, the aesthetic and social dignity associated with it is a source of great joy and gratification for every Dinka. It allows a young man to graduate from the status of a boy, *dhol* (or *dhok*, depending on the dialect), to that of *adheng*, a word with the positive connotation of "gentleman." To see a young Dinka man before and after initiation is to witness the remarkable power of symbolism and ritual, as the dignity of bearing, the responsible conduct, and the overall poise of a gentleman take over the carefree, servile status of boyhood.

Age-setting is essentially a system of military regimentation aimed at developing courage and fighting abilities in young warriors. That is why age-sets are functional institutions of the territorially determined sub-tribes as the warring units. Within the sub-tribe, fights may break out between the sections or the lineages, but only clubs, not spears, are used. In the more serious fights between the sub-tribes and the tribes, spears and shields are used.

Age-setting is correlatively also an institution of intergenera-
tional competition and succession. On graduation from initiation, members of the preceding age-set compose and perform
mock insult songs against the newly initiated set, provoking them
into an institutionalized fight called *biok,* which is in part a game
but can result in serious injuries.

Biok is not only training for warfare, it is also a manifestation
of rivalry between age-sets both for the position of military dominance and for the attention of the girls. As a rising generation of
young, robust, and eligible men, the newly initiated warriors are
seen by their seniors as a threatening group that must be hum-
bled, if only playfully, to keep them in their place.[5]

While the functions of the generations change with age and
status, the age-set system confers a lifelong corporate identity,
comradeship, and mutual dependency on its members. They
grow from warriors to family men and gradually age to be tribal
elders with an authoritative voice in public affairs.

The Family and Its Spiritual and Moral Dimensions

Although territorial organization and the age-set system are the
pillars of Dinka political order, the central unit that injects the
blood of life into all the organs of Dinka social structure, whether
based on territory, descent, or age, is the family. To the Dinka,
the family is the backbone of society and the foundation of its
social, moral, and spiritual or religious values. The overriding
goal of every Dinka is to marry and produce children, especially
sons, "to keep the head upright," *koc nom* (or *nhom*), after death.
Dinka religion does not promise a heaven to come, and although
the Dinka believe in some form of existence that conceptually
projects this worldly life into a hereafter, death for them is an
end from which the only salvation is continuity through posterity.

The British anthropologist who specialized on the Dinka, Godfrey Lienhardt, noted, "Dinka fear to die without male issue, in
whom the survival of their names—the only kind of immortality
they know—will be assured."[6] When a man dies without issue

to carry on his name, members of his family are under a moral obligation to marry a woman for him, to live with a relative and beget children to his name. Equally, a man who dies leaving behind a widow of childbearing age devolves a moral obligation on his kinsmen to have one of them cohabit with her to continue bearing children to his name.

This worldly orientation of religion has the effect of making the Dinka intensely religious, with high standards of moral values. The consequences of good and evil for the Dinka are not deferred; they are here and now. And every illness or misfortune is believed to have some moral cause in the actions of the victim, a close relative, or an evildoer. Charles and Brenda Seligman observed, "The Dinka, and their kindred the Nuer, are intensely religious, in our experience by far the most religious peoples in the Sudan."[7] Major Titherington, whose encounter with the Dinka went back to the early days of colonial rule, wrote of the "higher moral sense of the Dinka."[8] In the words of Godfrey Lienhardt:

> God is held ultimately to reveal the truth and falsehood, and in doing so, to provide a sanction for justice between men. Cruelty, lying, cheating, and all other forms of injustice are hated by God, and the Dinka suppose that, in some way, if concealed by men, they will be revealed by him. . . . God is made the final judge of right and wrong, when men feel sure that they are in the right. God is, then, the guardian of faith—and sometimes signifies to man what really is the case, behind or beyond their errors of falsehood.[9]

The hierarchy of spiritual authority in this world is headed by the father as the representative of God and the ancestors. God is believed to create every person in the mother's womb, using man's "urine of birth," and although this means that both parents are partners in creation, the values of ancestral continuity give the father seniority over the mother. But dominant as men are in Dinka society, women occupy a paradoxically pivotal role, not only because they are the main source of wealth through marriage, but especially because society depends on them to rear the children and inculcate in them the values on which the lineage system is founded. Because the relationship between the mother and child is so intimate during the formative years of infancy and childhood, her influence is critical. A Dinka mother will nurse for two to three years, during which period she must devote her full attention to the child and avoid any sexual relationship with her husband. To violate this taboo is believed to cause a spiritual contamination that may bring illness and perhaps death, not only to the child, but also to other babies in the neighborhood.

On reaching the age of weaning, a child, whether male or female, especially a first-born, is sent to the mother's relatives, where the maternal connection is reinforced. The relationship between a child and the maternal relatives, especially the grandfather and the uncle, is regarded as very special. Maternal relatives are generally believed to spoil their daughter's children. This is why the maternal grandfather and uncle are believed to be uniquely effective in their power to bless or curse, for they give a great deal that must affect the child's conscience, in which is rooted the efficacy of the curse.

And yet, while they develop in the child a special regard for his maternal side, the influence is not directed toward turning him against his paternal kin. On the contrary, the maternal relatives realize that his position in society is dependent on his role in his father's family and how well he manages to promote the interest of his clan. It is by succeeding among his parental kin that a child can best project the image of his maternal relatives.

Of course, the Dinka, including the women, recognize as a fundamental premise the continuity of the male line and the way it subordinates women to men, but mothers, both directly and through their male relatives, exert such a dominating influence on their children that society must guard against their potential threat to the male-oriented ancestral values.[10] The Dinka resolve this paradox by recognizing two modes of filial love and affection and ways of expressing them. Love for the mother is understood to be a function of the heart, which everyone knows a child feels but which society dictates should not be too conspicuously expressed or displayed. On the contrary, a child is expected to be very discreet about showing love and affection toward the mother, avoid calling her "Mother," and address her by her name. From an early age, a child is required to resist his mother's influence, especially if it detracts from the ancestral ideals of family unity and solidarity.

On the other hand, since love for the father is considered a function of the mind, it is expected to be cultivated and developed in a child and should be more visibly displayed, to make up for any deficiency in the natural sentiments of love. One must always refer to him as "Father," never by his name, must obey and revere him, and should take him as the model of what to be and do in the service of ancestral ideals. As the symbol of unity and solidarity around which family sentiments revolve, it is with and toward him that all should identify and demonstrate unreserved loyalty, even if that should entail an open disavowal of the sentiments for the mother and maternal connection. By and large, the mother and her kin-group will understand that this in no way detracts from their closer bond with the child.

The delicate balance between the collective interest of the family and the exclusive interest of the individual member is obvious in the manner in which marriages are celebrated.[11] Generally, the Dinka recognize two parallel procedures in the performance of marriage. Legal, social, and material formalities are left to be arranged or negotiated by the elders, while courtship aimed at winning the love, or at least the consent, of the girl is left to the man and his friends or members of his age-set. Theoretically, these two sets of roles should complement one another, but, in fact, they do not always go together; indeed, they often come into conflict. When they do, the position of the elders ideally should prevail; but disregarding the wishes of young men or women is not without risk. Quite often, to counter the position of their elders or otherwise to assert themselves, young people will resort to such alternatives as pregnancy, elopement, abduction, and, rarely, especially for women, suicide, more often than not as a threat. Since Dinka social attitudes allow a considerable measure of freedom for young men and women to meet and socialize, there is always the opportunity for a couple to plan and do whatever they wish. It is therefore both pragmatic and prudent to cater to their wishes.

The Social, Moral, and Spiritual Value of Cattle

The most important aspect of marriage among the Dinka is the exchange of cattle. Conversely, one of the most significant values of cattle is that they are directly responsible for the continuation of the lineage and the race, since it is with cattle that men procure wives to beget children and perpetuate the ancestral line. When a man is killed, whether intentionally or accidentally, his relatives are compensated with cattle, which must be used to find a wife who will live with one of them to beget children on behalf of the dead man. Because they are so important to the attainment of their overriding social and spiritual goals, the Dinka regard cattle as sacred, approximating human beings in value. They are indeed regarded as God's special gift to the Dinka, and therefore the most noble form of wealth.

Dinka mythology has it that at the beginning of things, God gave the Black Man, by which they mean the Dinka, a choice between the cow and a secret thing called "What." When the man reached for the cow, God warned him to consider carefully, for there were great things in the secret of "What," but the Dinka kept eyeing the cow. God then said, "If you insist on having the cow, then I advise you to taste her milk before you decide." The Dinka tasted the milk and declared, "Let us have the cow and never see the secret of 'What.'" That secret was later given to the other races and became a source of their inquisitive minds, which eventually led them to scientific and technological inventiveness. The Dinka, on the other hand, has continued in his obsession with cattle.

And yet, except for the sacred bulls, which are consecrated to the ancestral spirits and are kept in the possession of the family head as studs, the most important animals from the viewpoint of aesthetic cultural preoccupation are oxen, which have the least economic value, but with which young men identify themselves and are identified by the society. This is why they are known as "personality oxen." Ownership of personality oxen is determined by their colors. The Dinka distribute all conceivable color patterns to the male members of the family according to their mother's seniority of marriage and their own order of birth. Any bull born into the herd or accruing through marriage automatically goes to the person whose color pattern it is. Once initiated, a man is then formally recognized as the owner of the ox or oxen with his color pattern, or is otherwise presented with one; and from then on, the ox becomes a symbol of the young man's personality, individuality, and social status. Both in terms of courtesy and intimacy, he becomes known by a metaphoric name derived from the color pattern of his ox and otherwise fully assimilates himself into a world of poetic imagery and fantasy associated with his ox in any way, color, or shape.

While young men view personality oxen as symbols of virility, power, and defiance, a personality ox is a bull castrated from early calf-hood and, therefore, also symbolizes docility and submissiveness to the will of the "father," a term the Dinka apply to the relationship between the owner and the personality ox. The castrated bull-calf is raised by an owner who may ultimately not be the one to derive aesthetic pleasure from the full-grown bull. Once the ox has reached maturity, it may be kept by a member of the family or bartered for a cow. Usually, the prime mover is not the owner of the ox but a man interested in acquiring a personality ox, for which he is willing to give the more materially valuable cow-calf. Bartering for a bull is itself an important event celebrated by song, dance, and—ironically—a festive slaughtering of other animals for feasting.

The Ideals of the Dinka Social and Moral Order

Despite the warlike profile of the Dinka, their moral values emphasize the ideals of peace, unity, harmony, persuasiveness, and mutual cooperation. These values are highly institutionalized and expressed in a concept known as *cieng* (pronounced "cheng"), which is fundamental to Dinka moral and civic order. Godfrey Lienhardt wrote of *cieng:* "The Dinka . . . have notions . . . of what their society ought, ideally, to be like. They have a word, *cieng baai* [*baai* meaning home, village, community, or country], which used as a verb has the sense of 'to look after' or 'to order,' and in its noun form means 'the custom' or 'the rule.'"[12] Father Nebel, who lived among the Dinka and became a leading expert on their culture and way of life, translated *morals* as "good *cieng*" and *benefactor* as a man who knows and acts in accordance with *cieng*. He also translates *cieng* to mean "behavior," "habit," "nature of," or "custom."[13]

At the core of *cieng* are such "human" values as dignity and integrity, honor and respect, loyalty and piety, and the power of persuasiveness. *Cieng* does not merely advocate unity and harmony through attuning individual interests to the interests of others; it requires assisting one's fellowmen. Good *cieng* is opposed to coercion and violence, for solidarity, harmony, and mutual cooperation are more fittingly achieved voluntarily and by persuasion.

Cieng has the sanctity of a moral order not only inherited from the ancestors, who had in turn received it from God, but also fortified and policed by them. Failure to adhere to its principles is not only disapproved of as an antisocial act warranting punishment, but, more importantly, as a violation of the moral code that may invite a spiritual curse—illness or death, according to the gravity of the violation. Conversely, a distinguished adherence to the ideals of *cieng* receives temporal and spiritual rewards. Although *cieng* is a concept with roots in the heritage of the ancestors who still sanction adherence to its principles, it is largely an aspiration that is only partially adhered to and, indeed, often negated. Hence, it can be improved upon even through innovation.

The contradiction between the requirements of *cieng* and the violent reputation of the Dinka can be explained in terms of the gap between the ideal and the real, institutionally manifest in the differences between generational roles. While elders strive to live by the ideals, the young warriors find self-fulfillment, social recognition, and dignity in their valor, fighting ability, and defensive solidarity. Consequently, they tend to overindulge in militancy, often provoking wars that must then be fought by all. Nevertheless, frequent and pervasive as it is, warfare reflects a negation of the ideals, an alternative that should only be resorted to when peaceful methods have failed.

By the same token, chiefs, even when young, must be men of peace. One chief, reacting to the assertion that, traditionally, force was the deterrent behind Dinka social order, articulated the delicate balance between the violence of youth and the peacemaking role of chiefs: "It is true, there was force. People killed one another and those who could defeat people in battle were avoided with respect. But people lived by the way God had given them. There were the Chiefs of the Sacred Spear. If anything went wrong, they would come to stop the . . . fighting and settle the matter without blood . . . Men [chiefs] of the [sacred] spear were against bloodshed."[14] And in the words of another chief, "There was the power of words. It was a way of life with its great leaders . . . not a way of life of the power of the arm."[15]

While it was not always easy for the elders to control the overzealous warriors, it was a clearly established principle that the warriors should adhere to the will of their chiefs and elders. When they had to confront aggression and justifiably go to war, they were blessed by their spiritual leaders, chiefs, instructed on the ethics of warfare, and, trusting in the justice of their cause, counted on their ancestral spirits and deities to ensure their victory against the forces of evil. Among the ethical principles of warfare were that the enemy must not be ambushed or killed outside the battlefield and that a fallen warrior covered by a woman for protection [women accompany men in battle primarily to help the wounded] must be spared, as harming women and children in war was strictly forbidden.

It is particularly noteworthy that despite the lack of police or military forces, civil order was maintained with a very low level of crime, other than those incidents associated with honorable fighting or pursuit of self-help forms of justice. Major Court Treatt, who traveled in Dinkaland in the late 1920s, described the Dinka as "a gentleman" who "possesses a high sense of honor, rarely telling a lie," and with "a rare dignity of bearing and outlook."[16] And Major Titherington, who served as a colonial administrator among the Dinka also in the late 1920s, wrote of "the higher moral sense which is so striking in the [Dinka]. Deliberate murder—as distinct from killing in fair fight—is extremely rare; pure theft—as opposed to the lifting of cattle by force or stealth after a dispute about rightful ownership—is unknown; a man's word is his bond, and on rare occasions when a man is asked to swear, his oath is accepted as a matter of course."[17] Sir Gawain Bell, who served as District Commissioner among the Ngok Dinka in the 1950s, observed, "I can't remember that we ever had a serious crime in that part of the District. Among the Baggara [Arabs] . . . there was a good deal of serious crime: murders and so forth; and the same applied to the Hamar in the North . . . The Ngok Dinka were a particularly law-abiding people."[18]

One of the ways in which Dinka culture sustains a level of conformity and continuity is by providing alternative access to dignity that accommodates and institutionalizes even elements of what would otherwise be a violation of the norms. As already mentioned, an initiated man is *adheng*, a "gentleman"; his virtue is *dheeng* (pronounced "thëng"). But initiation is only a key or a point of entry to the complex values of *dheeng* and their varied avenues to individual and social dignity. *Dheeng* is a word of multiple meanings—all positive. As a noun, it means nobility, beauty, handsomeness, elegance, charm, grace, gentleness, hospitality, generosity, good manners, discretion, and kindness. Except in prayer or on certain religious occasions, singing and dancing are *dheeng*. Personal decoration, initiation ceremonies, celebrations of marriages, the display of "personality oxen"—indeed, any demonstrations of aesthetic value are considered *dheeng*. The social background of a man, his physical appearance and bearing, the way he carries himself, walks, talks, eats, or dresses, and the way he behaves toward his fellowmen are all factors in determining his *dheeng*.

From its various meanings, one can discern at least three kinds of *dheeng* or dignity. The first derives from birth or marriage into a family with already-established status. The second is the status people acquire through material resources and social responsiveness, which is measured not only in terms of generosity and hospitality, but also by personal integrity and responsible conduct. The third is more sensual in nature and stems from physical attractiveness and various forms of aesthetic display.

To the Dinka, power and wealth must serve moral and social ends, or else they do not confer *dheeng* on the holder. The word for chief, *beny*, also means "rich," or "wealthy," but a man of wealth who is stingy or frugal is *ayur*, the opposite of *adheng*, and his indignity is *yuur*. Conversely, a man of modest means who is generous and hospitable is praised as *adheng*, and even as *beny*. On the other hand, a man who is exaggeratedly generous or hospitable far beyond his means is considered vain and a show-off, *alueth* (a word which also means "liar"); although he is not despised in the way a stingy person with means would be, his performance falls short of *dheeng*. The ideal behavior is for a person to have the means and to display a social consciousness commensurate with them. That is *adheng* in the ideal sense.

Divine Leadership and Intergenerational Dynamics

A final set of concepts crucial to the values of leadership are *dom*, establishing control over a group, *muk*, maintaining and sustaining the group, and *guier*, improving the lot of the group. Each of these concepts connotes the observance of the principles of *cieng* and *dheeng*. A chief establishes control and "holds" the land for the people, not only by the mere fact of wielding legitimate power and authority, but also by using his position wisely to ensure peace, security, and prosperity. The continuity and stability of that state of affairs is maintained through *muk*, which literally means "keeping," a word also applied to child-rearing, including handling, feeding, looking after, protecting, and raising. *Guier* goes a little further to imply improvement of the existing situation, whether through reconstruction or reform within the framework of existing societal norms. These values are mutually reinforcing and cyclic in nature. When a chief has taken over the reins of power *(dom)*, has stabilized his benevolent control over the situation *(muk)*, and has introduced reforms to ensure a constructive and stable leadership *(guier)*, he is described as having held *(dom)* the land.

Traditionally, a Dinka chief is not a ruler in the Western sense but a spiritual leader whose power rests on divine enlightenment and wisdom. In his installation ceremonies, people raise his right hand toward the sky, symbolizing the will of his people and acceptance by the divine powers above. In order to reconcile his people, the chief should be a model of virtue, righteousness, and, in Dinka terms, "a man with a cool heart," who must depend on persuasion and consensus rather than coercion and dictation. The word for "court" or "trial," *luk,* also means "to persuade." Godfrey Lienhardt wrote on this aspect of the Dinka:

> I suppose anyone would agree that one of the most decisive marks of a society we should call in a spiritualized sense "civilized" is a highly developed sense and practice of justice, and here, the Nilotics, with their intense respect for the personal independence and dignity of themselves and others, may be superior to societies more civilized in the material sense. . . . The Dinka and the Nuer are a warlike people, and have never been slow to assert their rights as they see them by physical force. Yet, if one sees Dinka trying to resolve a dispute according to their own customary law, there is often a reasonableness and a gentleness in their demeanor, a courtesy and a quietness in the speech of those elder men superior in status and wisdom, and attempt to get at the whole truth of the situation before them.[19]

Paul Howell, who served as District Commissioner among the Dinka in the 1950s, observed that the chief "represents the 'voice of the people' and articulates . . . moral values inherent in the social system. He has the power to curse but is not expected to use his powers to his own ends and certainly does not impose his authority by threat or curse, unless, in so doing, he is in fact representing the opinion of the more level-headed elements."[20]

Despite the ideals of Dinka concepts of power, a conspicuous factor in their law was the minimum effectiveness of the chief prior to the advent of colonial government and the reinforcement of the spiritual authority by the secular power of the state. But it would seem consistent with the ideals of the system to view violence as a negative aspect of an otherwise positive system of values, or as the outcome of the upheavals of the nineteenth century when, in local perception, the world, as they knew it, was "spoiled" and the fundamental role of the warrior became an exaggerated necessity. As Major Titherington expressed it, "That the system worked at all speaks well for the higher moral sense which is so striking in the [Dinka]."[21]

Tradition and the Cyclical Stability of Society

A good illustration of the self-contained viability, stability, and continuity of the system is that there are hardly any words in the vernacular language that approximate the concept of "development" in modern usage. The notion of endeavoring to elevate society or individuals to a yet unrealized higher (and better) level of existence through a process called "development" was traditionally foreign to the Dinka. Individual and societal goals, even to the optimum degree, were considered part of experience, which was achievable, and, indeed, at one time or another, actually achieved. *Cieng* and related values are seen as part of a heritage that has proved its worth over generations and has become sanctified and elevated, even though it may have negative aspects. Such negative aspects are hardly ever visible to the Dinka. When a Dinka was asked what he thought was negative in his people's ways, he responded with an expressive silence, a puzzled look, a smile, and then said, "How can there be anything bad in the Dinka way? If there were, would it not have been abandoned long ago?"

DINKA SELF-PERCEPTION OF WEALTH

While certain objective factors are globally accepted as indicators of affluence or poverty, whether individuals or groups perceive themselves as rich or poor may not always be a matter of objective determination. Subjective factors attributable to culture may play a vital role in the way people view themselves in terms of wealth or poverty. Global perspectives on poverty imply both integration into the comparative framework and marginalization or exclusion within that framework, which then closely corresponds to a state of poverty or relative deprivation. From a policy standpoint, there are both positive and negative implications to the way people are classified or perceive themselves. To be labeled poor is to establish a case for corrective measures toward poverty alleviation, which is positive; but it could also breed apathy, self-pity, and dependency. A positive self-perception might breed complacency, which would be negative; but it could also enhance the sense of worth as a resource for self-reliance.

Self-Exaltation in Reverence to the Ancestral Legacy

Dinka self-perceptions of wealth reflect their cultural values, which are intrinsically geared toward a positive self-image as a legacy of reverence for the ancestors. The goal of immortalizing a person in an ancestral chain through remembrance depends largely on continued social esteem and veneration. To the Dinka, poverty implies a demeaning status that is inimical to the exalted image required for honoring the dead through living memory. A corollary of this is the social, moral, and spiritual value the Dinka place on cattle as the resource for ensuring the continuity of the lineage through bridewealth. And indeed, while there are no reliable statistics, the Dinka are probably among the wealthiest in cattle on the African continent. The average bridewealth (i.e., what a man pays in marriage) is around fifty cows, while the bridewealth for daughters of prominent families can go as high as two hundred cows. Bloodwealth (i.e., compensation paid for homicide) is normally estimated to be the equivalent of the average bridewealth as it is intended to be used in obtaining a wife to beget children to the name of the deceased, or, in the case of a female, to compensate for the loss of potential bridewealth or reproductivity. The distribution system itself fosters a degree of social equity through the exchange of cattle in marriage and other reciprocal kinship obligations.

The Dinka always exalt their forebears as the ideal model of their cultural values—material, social, moral, and spiritual. No Dinka ever claims to have done better than his forebears. Traditionally, no Dinka would even entertain such a thought. What one does, and however successful one is, tends to be seen as an effort to live up to the standards set by the forebears. These lines indicate the extent to which the Dinka brag about their forebears as the epitome of prosperity:

My father, Ring, was called by his father
He seated him down by his side
Affectionately rubbed his head
And left him these words,
"Son, Ring, *there* are the cattle.
Cattle are the prosperity of man."
My great father had a cattle-camp
His house became rich with herds
The cattle-byres were full.[22]

****

Our clan has never been in need
The clan of Ajong de Monydhang has never been in need of cattle
From our ancestor, Jok,
To Achai, our girl with the River Spirits
Prosperity has remained forever with us.[23]

****

When my father left me
I was only a small child,
But I grew up and matured
To revive the legacy of my father.

While the dependent members of the family are subordinated in the control over cattle, wives and dependent sons compensationally preoccupy themselves with cattle symbolized by personality oxen. For male youth, status is enhanced not only by the man's identification with his personality ox, but by the exaltation of his ancestry and the lineage through which he acquires the ox.

> When I rise to sing [over my ox], gossipers disperse
> I am like my forefathers
> I rise to be seen by my ancient fathers
> I rise to be seen walking with pride
> As it was in the distant past
> Where our clan was born.[24]

The payment of cattle as bridewealth accounts for the stability of marriage and the rarity of divorce. Bridewealth is contributed by a wide circle of a man's relatives and distributed among a correspondingly large circle of relatives on the bride's side. If a divorce should occur, unless the marriage has been stabilized through children (in which case divorce is even less conceivable), bridewealth cattle must be returned; traditionally, the original cows and their offspring were traced and returned. Since some of them would have been passed on for the bridewealths of other relatives, one divorce could threaten other marriages. Divorce is therefore viewed as a tragedy to be avoided, except in the most compelling cases of extreme incompatibility.[25]

As important as cattle are to the Dinka, land has an even greater intrinsic value to them, not only because they depend on it in a wide variety of ways, including farming, gathering, and grazing, but also because it is associated with the ancestors. A Dinka will swear on the land to establish his truthfulness, symbolizing his submission to the judgment of the ancestors. Before drinking or eating, especially in a new setting, one must offer to the ancestors portions on the ground. And before adults can share in the consumption of new crops, festive offerings must first be made to the ancestors. These rituals, which are associated with the value of ancestral land, have a bearing on the rules favoring perpetuity in traditional land tenure.

The Conservative Implication of Self-Perception of Wealth

The outcome of these values and processes is that the Dinka traditionally saw themselves as members of a society whose reciprocal relationships were mutually beneficial; a people endowed with a land of plenty and blessed with the ideal wealth—cattle. As one Dinka elder proudly expressed it, "You are the Dinka inhabiting this vast territory of rich grassland and the keeper of cattle."[26] Another elder went further: "It is for cattle that we are admired, we, the Dinka . . . All over the world, people look to us because of cattle. And when they say, Sudan, it is not just because of our color, it is also because of our great wealth; and our wealth is cattle. . . . It is because of cattle that people of other tribes look to us with envy."[27] Yet another elder saw Dinkaland as the source of wealth and sustainability for the country: "One day, should tragedy befall this country, the survival of the black people will start here . . . Should we abandon this land with all its blessings, our descendants will blame us."[28] And that was before oil was discovered in their land.

Dinka pride in their culture, cattle wealth, and land has been heavily documented and given to explain their conservative attitude. A Christian missionary observed in 1949: "One of the determinants of the rapid or slow spread of Christianity in the South [Sudan] has been provided by the contrast between semi-nomadic, cattle-breeding Nilotic tribes (Shilluk, Nuer, and Dinka) and the settled agriculturists. The life of the former is bound up with a cow economy, this animal being a veritable god. They are intensely conservative and very proud of their civilization."[29] The anthropologist, Audrey Butt, also wrote of the Nilotics: "They consider their country the best in the world and everyone inferior to themselves. For this reason they . . . scorn European and Arab culture . . . They are self-reliant and extremely conservative in their aversion to innovation and interference."[30]

But Nilotic conservatism has been grossly exaggerated. It has now become apparent that throughout earlier historical phases, they rejected what they considered not worth adopting and selected what they considered desirable, assimilating it into their own culture to the point where it eventually lost its foreign character. Their so-called resistance to change was indeed augmented by the colonial policies, which kept the tribes isolated and tried to preserve traditional cultures. As a result of intensive cross-cultural interaction and of modern education, the process of adopting foreign ways has been accelerated and revolutionized so much that the Nilotics are demonstrating more adaptability to change than could have been predicted only two decades ago. One can hypothesize that the same values of pride and dignity that had made them resist change may well provide them with the motivation to enhance their status and self-image through modernization.

MODERNITY AND DIMINISHING SELF-IMAGE

Colonialism brought the various groups in the Sudan together within the modern state, but kept them apart and introduced modernization selectively and discriminatingly, especially as between the North and the South. In the South, limited social services in the fields of education and health care were provided through the Christian missionaries, whose primary objective was proselytization. There was also some exposure to the market economy and labor migration into towns.

The Impact of Labor Migration

Labor migration elicited a mixed response. It provided young men with the opportunity to acquire independent wealth, but paid labor was seen as servility, an indignity that was inappropriate for a "gentleman." They mitigated this indignity by migrating for labor far away from the Dinka context and in a country where one was unknown. The Dinka saying goes, "*Dheeng,* Dignity, remain; *yuur,* indignity, let us travel," which means pocketing one's pride in a foreign land. Another saying states that, "*Adheng,* a nobleman of one's tribe is not known to a nobleman of another tribe." Despite the mitigating factor in labor migration, the conditions experienced in the urban setting were considered inimical to Dinka values, especially the solidarity of kinship ties:

> I have become a slave,
> Laboring in a foreign land,
> Cracking my back-bones like a captured bird,
> I worked in the cotton field until my hair turned grey,
> It was not the grey of age;
> It was the bitter pain of the words in our heads,
> As we wasted away in foreign lands.
> O Marial, what I have found, I will not say. . . .[31]
> The riches that I hear of in towns;
> People live to old age buying and selling . . .
> The family has lost its value;
> Blood ties have been severed in the pockets,
> Even a son of your maternal aunt
> When you ask him for help
> Will first invoke the name of God,
> "May I die, Brother, see my pocket
> If you find a millieme (a penny), you are lucky."
> In towns, people dance to the drums in their pockets
> If one has nothing, one goes with nothing.[32]

The Devastations of the Civil War

The civil war that has raged intermittently for nearly five decades between the Arab-Muslim North and the more indigenously African South has been perhaps the most radicalizing and destabilizing factor in Dinka life. And by creating conditions of extreme deprivation and degradation, it has ironically been a source of motivation in the quest for a modernizing change.

It is now estimated that the war has cost the South over two million lives, displaced over four million Southerners inside the country, and forced half a million into the neighboring countries as refugees. Quite apart from its death toll, the war has inflicted on the people of the South unprecedented conditions of deprivation and degradation. Even the life of a refugee, which ensures a reasonable level of protection and assistance from the international community, is a source of great indignity for a people who had grown up thinking of themselves and their country as second to none. These lines from a song of lamentation during the first phase of the war are illustrative:

> Gentlemen grind grain in the land of the Congo;
> The Arab has remained at home
> He has remained in our land.
> We left our herds in the cattle-camps
> And followed Deng Nhial.
> Gentlemen beg in the land of the Congo;
> A Congolese said, "Dinkas are *matata*."
> I asked Ngor Maker,
> "What does *matata* mean?"
> Ngor Maker replied,
> "He says we are bad."
> My heart was destroyed
> And I thought of Anger, the daughter of Wol Ayalbyor,
> I wish I could see her again.[33]

The current war is revealing another side of the people of the South. Unlike the 1955–72 movement, which called for secession, the Sudan Peoples Liberation Movement/Army (SPLM/A), which has championed the Southern cause since 1983, has postulated the goal of creating a New Sudan that would be free from any discrimination based on race, ethnicity, religion, or culture. This is perceived as tantamount to the reversal of Arab-Islamic hegemony in favor of a more African identity for the country. Although Southerners would overwhelmingly choose secession and the call for a new united Sudan is perceived by many as a euphemistic disguise of separatist aspirations, radical Arab-Islamic elements in the North took the threat from the South seriously and began to counter it by organizing and mobilizing

Islamic revivalism, which eventually seized power in 1989 through a military coup. Their success in radicalizing Islam politically has only led to the polarization of the nation in a militaristic contest for the soul of the country. The competing vision from the South rejects any scheme of power sharing that would give Southerners only local control: "What about the Sudan, to whom shall we leave it?"[34] The Arab is now seen as an intruder who must give way to the true owners of the country:

> It is Omdurman which we shall contest
> It is Khartoum which we shall contest
> It is Sudan which we shall contest
> O people, the land is our land.[35]

This positive self-assertiveness by the freedom fighters tells only an aspect of the story, one that is perhaps spotlighted by its military fervor and the nationalist aspirations that it represents. In the broader social context, a more tragic process of self-doubt and diminishing self-image appears to be the consequence of change and its dehumanizing integration of the indigenous population of the South into the state framework, dominated by the Arab-Muslim North. As a consequence of their relegation to an inferior status in the modern Sudanese and global contexts, the Dinka now appear to have accepted that their traditional culture and way of life are indeed wanting. Since their religious thought dictates that everything has an intrinsic meaning, ultimately related to the origin of things and the manifestation of God's will, they have begun to internalize this new awareness into their belief system to give it a convincing explanation. A body of oral literature has begun to emerge in which the Dinka are beginning to rationalize their relegated position. Even the myth of their original acquisition of cattle as the most noble symbol of wealth is being seen more as an explanation of their scientific and technological backwardness, attributed to their original choice of the cow in preference to the thing called "What," which is now being perceived to have been later given to the Europeans and the Arabs and became the source of their material superiority and power. In the following lines, the singer attributes the hardships of urban labor to the inequitable distribution of resources among the races at the time of creation.

> God hates us for the things of the past.
> The ancient things he created with us,
> When he gave the black man the cow
> Leaving behind the Book of his father,
> Our curse goes to the elders of the original land;
> The man who threw the Book away,
> Is it he who gave us into slavery?[36]

Another myth explains that the black man was relegated to a status inferior to his white and brown brothers because his mother favored him, forcing their father to plead with God to take care of the disadvantaged children. As one elder commented, "That has remained a curse on us. Our father did not show us the ways of our ancestors fully. . . . Otherwise, we would have known more things than we know."[37]

Godfrey Lienhardt analyzed the process by which the Dinka, who had taken their superiority for granted, came to accept a significant degree of inferiority. "The Dinka view of age-sets, based on a cyclical notion of local history, begins to be displaced by a dynamic view of history, accompanied by a philosophy of progress, and with teleological overtones."[38] The new notion of "getting ahead" begins to be directed toward some distant, more universal end, defined in foreign terms and for a society based on foreign models, rather than one conceived of by the Dinka.

THE NEW CHALLENGE FOR THE DINKA

As the impact of the outside world on the Dinka intensified, traditional pride began to wane, occasionally resurfacing defensively, but otherwise submerging in the quest for self-improvement through development. In a series of interviews conducted in the 1970s with chiefs and elders from different parts of Dinkaland, this ambivalent merger was most striking. The seventeen-year civil war (1955–72) had just ended with the Addis Ababa Agreement that granted the South regional autonomy. Development was projected as a national ideology that would replace the war psychology. The ruling socialist revolution had abolished native administration in the North and, although it was allowed to continue in the South, chiefs had reason to be apprehensive that they, too, might be affected. That presumably added to their determination to prove themselves capable of meeting the demands of development.[39]

As a result of this new challenge, the principle of continued identity and influence, essentially geared toward a backward-looking veneration of the ancestors and the forefathers, with age as the source of knowledge and wisdom, began to be reconceptualized in a forward-looking emphasis on educated youths and their contribution to building the future. Chief Arol Kachwol articulated this in terms that delicately balanced tradition and change:

> It is God who changes the world by giving successive generations their turns. For instance, our ancestors, who have now disappeared, by the way their world began and the way they lived, they held the horns of their life. Then God changed things; things changed until they reached us; and they will continue to change. When God comes to change your world, it will be through you and your wife. You will sleep together and bear a child. When that happens, you should know that God has passed to your children borne by your wife the things with which you lived your life.[40]

Arol Kachwol was even more empathetic about the generational change:

> Our stories are gone. New stories will now begin with you. The ancient stories you were asking us about have had their turn. The time has now come for your own stories to begin. So, instead of us being the story-tellers, it is now for you to be the story-tellers. It is also for you to bear your children for the stories you are now about to tell.[41]

In response to the question of how he saw the future relations between the North and the South, Chief Arol Kachwol re-

sponded: "It is not really for you people to ask us that question
. . . It is you people who know the good things that will come out
of this. And it is you people who know what may go wrong in it
. . . It is also for you to tell us, 'Our people, this is the way we can
make our country go ahead.' "[42]

Chief Ayeny Aleu addressed himself to the prevention and
cure of human and animal diseases, the procurement of tractors
for cultivating the fields, the provision of potable water, and the
promotion of education. Chief Thon Wai also spoke on education, agriculture, marketing, and health services:

> Let all the chiefs speak about opening schools. Let them speak
> about cultivating crops. Crops provide food as well as products for
> sale . . . to provide cash which can be used for developing the
> country . . . Diseases are on the increase. There is a disease called
> kalazaar, which is killing people, and a disease which causes head-
> aches . . . Diseases which did not exist at the time of our grand-
> fathers. And what brought them? It is because those foreigners
> came and other foreigners came and people intermingled. All the
> disease which were absent are now amidst us. For these we need
> hospitals.[43]

And yet, some of the old self-perceptions of the Dinka as
wealthy linger on, as evidenced by the fact that the chiefs consider their people capable of financing their own development.
Chief Thon Wai posed a question and provided the answer: "And
with what money will [schools and hospitals] be built? They will
be built with the money of [our] people. The chief must collect
the money, . . . ask his people to build houses and then say to the
government, 'We want a doctor to be brought.' "[44] So radical
have the Dinka become in their commitment to development
that, according to the chiefs' accounts, there is now a striking
willingness to change the traditional Dinka ways, including their
attitude toward cattle. According to Chief Makuei Bilkuei: "I told
all my people, 'The North burned down our villages during the
war. Everything is now gone . . . You people are going to remain
behind. When I come back from Juba, I want the cattle to be
made use of. We have to make use of our cattle.' "[45]

Development, the chiefs contend, requires considerable self-sacrifice as an investment in a better future. In line with their procreational values, the present generation is called upon to sacrifice for the benefit of generations to come: "We have to leave them in a cleared field [where] no scrubs will pierce their feet and no thorns will hurt their faces and nothing . . . will happen to them . . . nothing like the things we are now experiencing."[46]

Whether it is a manifestation of characteristics hitherto hidden by their isolationism, the result of the impact of the civil war, or simply adaptability to their present circumstances, the Dinka are demonstrating a degree of commitment to development that would surprise the observers of the 1950s. Development appears to be both an objective pursuit and a subjective resort—a material and moral defense against current insecurities. At the initial stage, focus appears to be on the provision of social services, such as education and health, but the long-term objective is the transformation of society in modern terms, sadly impossible under the prevailing war conditions.

From the Cow to the Pursuit of "What"

The civil war that has ravaged the Southern Sudan since 1955 has inflicted upon the people one of the worst humanitarian tragedies and indignities of modern times. To the world, the Dinka are now known not for their cattle wealth, cultural pride, and general self-esteem, but rather for their destitution, starvation, and even the indignity of slavery.

In response, the Dinka not only yearn for peace and security, but have become keenly aware of the need to improve their lot and try to catch up with development, previously alien to their culture, but now voiced with an almost obsessive sense of purpose. And yet, not once did any of the chiefs and elders interviewed describe their condition as one of poverty. Quite the contrary, what comes through is a paradoxically positive determination to overcome their predicament, with considerable self-confidence that they possess the human and material resources to do so. It is that self-confidence in both the conversion of cattle to the cash economy and the mobilization of human resources that makes Dinka positive self-perception a significant asset for development. The Dinka now demonstrate willingness to give up the cow in pursuit of the thing called "What," given a conducive environment of peace, security, and the power to determine their own destiny.

Will a downward slide in self-perception lead the Dinka to recognize that they are poor, or will they sustain a degree of positive self-image, even as they recognize their underdevelopment and the need to improve their lot by modern standards? The answer to this question will probably depend on the outcome of the civil war and the post-war strategy for reconstruction and development. If the South succeeds in achieving self-determination, whether within the framework of a united Sudan or through separation, and if their program of reconstruction and development is culturally oriented as a process of self-enhancement from within, then it is possible that Dinka tradition could not only sustain a positive self-image in the process, but could indeed be a vital resource in a self-reliant development. Appreciating these options is essential to the conceptualization, formulation, and implementation of appropriate development policies and strategies.[47]

Although all that is now being shattered by the civil war, the premise of this chapter is that notions of wealth and poverty are only meaningful within a given cultural context. Attitudes similar to those of the Dinka have been observed among pastoral peoples throughout Africa, and, while the poverty of the continent is taken for granted, there are voices throughout Africa that resist this blanket classification, invoking the wealth of the continent in untapped natural resources, vibrant indigenous cultures, and dynamic human potential. For policy purposes, a positive self-image is, in itself, a vital resource for self-reliant development. To be constructive, development policies and strategies must be appropriately contextualized to make effective use of people's traditional values and institutions behind a positive self-image.

Part 2

The traditions and customs of different occupations and professions have evolved over thousands of years and greatly influence both individual and societal reactions to humanitarian crises. For example, a physician might respond to the exact same challenge in a manner quite at odds from that of a policeman, and yet there are universal values that can be found in almost any occupation. Honesty, dependability, loyalty, respect for others and for the land are common traits in every field. In this part, I asked highly respected representatives of four different disciplines to view humanitarian action, and its needs, from their own unique professional viewpoint.

Major General Timothy Cross has had a distinguished military career with involvement in most of the major wars in the last three decades. As a good soldier must, he has been formed by the practices and customs that sustain armies as cohesive fighting forces. He also has had the opportunity to work with humanitarian agencies in relieving civilian hardships in the midst of armed conflict. He contributed a chapter on the interaction of military and NGOs in crises to a sister volume *(Emergency Relief Operations)* in this series.

Joseph A. O'Hare, S.J., to whom this book is dedicated, was a missionary teacher and editor before assuming the presidency of a large urban university. He knows the constraints as well as the potential of academia and reminds us that in intellectual debate and the search for truth, the goals of institutions of higher learning, the old virtues of respect and civility, must prevail.

Tom Brokaw, the leading television network news anchor in the United States, documents the price his profession must be prepared to pay in order to maintain the basic freedom that we expect from our press and communication system. He brings to society a perspective grounded partially in the skills of reporting the daily news, and partially in the proud traditions that bind journalists into a global family.

Finally, I include in this part a chapter on my own profession, medicine. In Western medicine, we trace our clinical approach back to ancient Greek physicians. But the foundations of healing, the emphasis on respect for the patient, on confidentiality, on the need for a scientific assessment, and continued efforts to maintain competency by continuous study are common in almost all other cultures. I have asked a colleague, Eoin O'Brien, M.D., to not only present the traditions and values of medicine but to reflect on how our noble profession might improve its capacity to contribute to humanitarian actions.

5

Military Values and Traditions

Major General Timothy Cross, CBE, FCIT, FILT

> Every man thinks meanly of himself for not having been a soldier.
>
> Dr. Johnson

> The safety and honour of Britain depend not on her wealth and administration, but on the character of her people. This in turn depends on the institutions, which form character. In war, it depends, in particular, on the military institutions which create the martial habits of discipline, courage, loyalty, pride and endurance.
>
> The Lord Bishop of Durham
> Walker Trust Lecture on Leadership, 1934,
> before the University of St. Andrews

INTRODUCTION

I HAVE BEEN ASKED to write on the values and traditions that the military bring to the world of complex emergencies and humanitarian operations. But before setting out my stall, I must first lay some foundations.

I write as a professional soldier of over thirty years, and as a British Commander who has taken part in a number of deployments around the world; Northern Ireland on bomb disposal work in the 1970s; Cyprus with the United Nations in 1980; the 1990–91 Gulf Campaign as the Commander Supply of the U.K.'s 1st Armoured Division; and the Balkans with NATO Implementation Force (IFOR), Stabilization Force (SFOR), and Kosovo

Force (KFOR), the latter bringing me in particularly close contact with the international aid agencies and nongovernmental organizations in Northern Macedonia, Albania, and Kosovo. As I write this chapter, I am also heavily involved in the planning for potential operations in the Gulf again.

While this all gives me some experience in the world of complex emergencies, I do recognize, as H. G. Wells once said, that:

> The professional military mind is by necessity an inferior and unimaginative mind. No man of high intellectual ability would willingly imprison his gifts in such a calling.

I am such a man! And my thoughts set out below must be set in that context!

That said, I must first stress that there is no such thing as "the military"—no more than there is "the NGO." We are not dealing here with a single, generic, and impersonal organization, but a mix of professional and amateur, effective and non-effective, efficient and inefficient. All organizations are made up of unique, individual people, and that applies to the military as well as any other. And around the world there are many types of military organizations. Some are conscript; some are full-time professionals. Some are a part of the state's governing machine, be that a dictatorship or military regime; some are servants of a democratically elected government. Some military are in well-paid careers; others forced into poorly paid, short-term "contracts." In some continents the military are the cause of the problem; in others, they are but a part of the solution. And there are many different values and traditions.

I can only write about the values and traditions of the British Forces, primarily the British Army, which I happen to believe is a pretty professional, effective, and efficient organization. It is an organization with wide operational experience across the globe stretching back many centuries, from fighting wars to assisting with disaster relief, and one with credibility and reputation. But we—like every other army—have good and bad attributes. Within our ranks, at all levels, are officers and soldiers who range from the brilliant, lateral thinking, and open-minded, to the less brilliant, orthodox, and somewhat less open-minded—men and women whom H. G. Wells would instantly recognize! There is, therefore, a danger that the picture I will now paint is an over-rosy one. The reader must be the judge of that. My aim, nonetheless, is to establish a reference point against which the right military values and traditions can be judged—recognizing that all too often, the reality is different. Throughout, I will refer mostly to the army and soldiers, noting that it is largely they who engage in land operations—but the arguments apply across all three services.

THE MILITARY COMMUNITY

To assess the professionalism of any military organization, U.K. defense policy says we must consider three components of fighting power. The first of these is the physical component—their equipment, training, and logistic sustainability. The second is the conceptual component—their understanding of warfare; how they think, how they develop their concepts and strategies, and how they have put them into practice historically. And the third is the moral component—their leadership, values, ethics, and culture. In one sense, this chapter is about all three, because values and traditions are nothing without the right equipment and training, and the ability to use that equipment wisely and to good effect; to bring relief to bear—to make a difference. But my real focus here is on the moral component of fighting power. For it is the strength of the moral component that, first, separates out the "good" military from the "bad" and, secondly, separates out the military from the non-military players involved in complex emergencies and operations. Napoleon once said, "the moral is to the physical as three is to one." My own experience confirms that the ability to get things done, to achieve success in any operation or in any task, is as much, if not more, a state of mind as a piece of equipment or an intellectual understanding of how to use that equipment. War, as Van Crefeld has said, is, before anything else, a question of psychology; we must bear that in mind if we are to understand military traditions and values.

The British Army is very committed to the concept of the moral component, taking it very seriously indeed. One of the most recent concrete examples of that is the publication in March 2000 of the *Values and Standards of the British Army* booklet. This booklet, which comes in two parts (one for Commanders and one for every soldier), was issued by the then Chief of the General Staff to reinforce that commitment, and to formally codify the standards of conduct essential to sustain the moral component of fighting power.[1]

THE MILITARY VERSUS THE NON-MILITARY

I will take my two earlier premises in reverse order. First, what separates out the military from the non-military players?

Let me stress at the outset that the soldier is not chiefly a military figure; he/she is primarily a social figure, influenced by home, upbringing, and historical traditions. A soldier is a soldier (or sailor or airman) only because military training has imposed a certain fixed pattern of behavior; above and beyond that the soldier is a citizen of the nation. The army is inevitably (and rightly) woven into the social fabric of a nation and it is, or should be, an integral part of that nation. The true and ultimate strength of a nation lies in its people, in their capacity to work, in their vitality; in their national character. This national character helps produce the fighting soldier—and gives the soldier many of the attributes he/she brings to an operation. The national character is therefore of immense importance, for anything that weakens the national character weakens the army.

Notwithstanding the impact of national character, and no matter what may be instilled, the soldier will nonetheless retain much of his/her individuality. In part, this individuality is derived from what I call the "hardware" of life—genetics, the raw building blocks that make up human inheritance. But genes do not dictate, control, or direct life; they simply permit and limit—they are, in effect, the cards that make up the hand we have been dealt by the Almighty. How we play those cards is another story. That is the interplay with the environment in which we are nurtured—the "software" of life. A soldier's individual character, like that of everyone else, is thus a blend of the "hardware" and "software" of life; it includes the environment of their upbringing, their national character, and their uniqueness—their own particular gifts and abilities.

Now the world of nation-states is largely focused on the two sectors that, on the face of it, are all that is needed to run a successful society. The state and the economy, the government and the market, politics and economics. The state/government/politics is about society as a collective body; collectively the citizens agree to abide by certain laws, recognizing that it is their collective but also (largely) individual interest to do so—we may survive running a red light occasionally but most of us recognize that our luck will run out if everyone were to do so on a regular basis! The economy/market is about society made up of private individuals who are free to choose to do what they like within the framework of the law; to buy and sell as long as there is someone willing to sell to them or buy from them. That's the essence of it. Power mediated through government, laws, politics, and the courts; exchange mediated by money and the markets. Nations/societies of any shade or color around the world have approached the execution of these two over the centuries in different ways, but most would still argue that any problem can be solved by one or other, the state or the individual.

The military is, of course, bound into these two as well, getting its legality and resources from both in turn. But the British military, like all military organizations within democratic societies, is apolitical in its allegiance—my commission is from my Sovereign, Her Majesty the Queen, not the British Government of the day—and, to some degree, at least, the military lies outside the normal economic cycle; it does not (not yet, anyway) run a profit or loss balance sheet! But it stands aside in a much more important way.

The military is usually a distinct community within society. The individuals who together make it up are separated from the rest of society by, on the one hand, military law—distinct and separate from civilian law[2]—and, on the other hand, by a strong sense of identity. Unlike politics and economics—which are essentially zero sum games—the strength of the military comes from words that lie within the moral component of fighting power; words like integrity, honor, duty, commitment, trust, friendships, loyalty, and love. Jonathan Sachs, the British Chief Rabbi, calls such things spiritual goods—as opposed to other goods, which we label economic wealth or political power. Such spiritual goods can't be accounted for in terms of politics or economics, but they are enormously powerful drivers in their own right. Sachs cites friendship as an example. Suppose someone were to help me because there were a law that says that in certain circumstances they have to; then they are not helping me as a friend. Or suppose someone were to help me because I pay them; then again they are not helping me as a friend. You cannot analyze friendship in terms of the law or the market; it is more than that. Nor can you analyze integrity or duty in such a way. Yet on such goods rests much of the values and traditions of the military community—labeled, under the umbrella of the moral component, as ethos and culture as well as values and traditions.

Now the military is not the only institution that deals with spiritual goods—clearly religious institutions like the church do so, too, as do other communities in their many different ways. But society as a whole is less focused on such goods; there is less deference to authority and a greater awareness of individual rights. It is also a less cohesive society, one in which traditional, shared values are less effectively transmitted and concepts such as honor and loyalty are, if still present, less well understood. Yet these values are not abstract concepts to the military. Together they must be nurtured in peace to ensure that they survive the testing ground of battle. And this is why the military is different. Being made up of communities within a single community, regiments and battalions, ships and air force squadrons with rich, individual and collective histories, come together within a wider community whose principal endeavor is unique.

Before looking at that principal endeavor, consider first the regimental histories and traditions.

REGIMENTAL TRADITION/SPIRIT AND COMRADESHIP

> The men did not expect every officer to be a brilliant leader, and they strongly hoped he would not be a "pusher," but they expected him to put more than the next man into the general reservoir of courage. They did not look to him for ringing words of inspiration, but they liked to be reminded that they were the best mob in the line. No subaltern on the Western Front had read, or heard of, Wolseley's Pocket Book, but all grew to recognize the truth which Wolseley set out: "The soldier is a peculiar being that can alone be brought to the highest efficiency by inducing him to believe that he belongs to a regiment that is infinitely superior to the others round him." That was the Old Army's source of strength; and that faith in the regiment could be agreed through twenty battalions with very little dilution.
>
> E. S. Turner, *Gallant Gentlemen*

A Polish Jew was once asked how he gained the courage and strength to survive the horrors of a concentration camp. He replied that while character is the sum of many things, much of it stems from all we do and learn in our early years. He explained that Jewish history is full of examples of tragedy but also of individual and collective courage, from the Exile in the Old Testament to the purges/pogroms throughout the centuries. As a child and a young student, he had learned all about that history, and he had resolved that if a testing time should ever come to him he would do his utmost to stand firm. He learned the lessons of the past and he carried them with him through his life; and when the testing time came he did, indeed, stand firm, in conditions that most of us can never, if we are honest, really comprehend.

The traditions and regimental histories of the British Armed Forces have always tried to provide this same kind of resolve. Military traditions around the world are built around historical successes (and, sometimes, failures). All young officers and soldiers quickly become rooted in their regiment/battalion's past in order to help them maintain and uphold their honor in the future. Embedded in their lives today, men and women within army regiments, naval ships/submarines, or air force squadrons have a sense of the history that precedes them; through it they find pride, both in the unit's particular history and in the collective history of the Army, Navy, and Air Force in which they serve. Regimental spirit is the soldier's pride in the values and traditions of his/her regiment and the determination to be worthy of those values and traditions; and it can be a powerful driver. Remembering, with thanksgiving, the lessons of the past, bringing the lessons of the past into the present, and then carrying them with us into the future.

But there is a difference between comradeship and regimental spirit. Comradeship develops between a small group of men and women who live and work and fight together. It is the spiritual good of "friendship" that Sachs speaks of and, if regimental traditions are a powerful driver, comradeship is even more powerful. In the crisis of battle, the majority of soldiers will not derive encouragement just from the glories of the past, but will seek aid primarily from their leaders and comrades of the present. In other words, most soldiers do not fight hard simply because their ancestors fought well at the Battle of Minden two centuries ago, but because their particular platoon or battalion has good leaders, is well disciplined, and has developed the feeling of comradeship and self-respect among all ranks on all levels. It is not devotion to some ancient regimental story that steels men and women in crisis; it is devotion to the comrades who are with them and the leaders who are in front of them. Soldiers learn to have faith in each other. Comradeship is a great antidote to fear—of which more later—because it gives a person friends; true friends forged in adversity from whom a soldier will derive strength from their presence and be anxious not to let down in battle. Everyone has within them a streak of generosity and unselfishness—a touch of nobility—and these qualities will be brought out in their attitude to their friends. Friendship causes soldiers to give of their best. It surrounds them with an atmosphere of warmth and strength at the very moment when they are feeling cold and weak. It encourages their finest instincts, and the demands of friendship serve to strengthen them in battle.

THE SOLDIER'S PURPOSE—THE PRINCIPAL ENDEAVOR/THE OPERATIONAL IMPERATIVE

Regimental spirit and comradeship are important because the armed services exist to conduct operations on behalf of the nation, if necessary by engaging in battle—to fight the nation's wars. The aim of any army is to achieve success, usually in battle against the enemies of the nation, sometimes in other ways. Everything is directed toward this end, and it must never be forgotten. An army's professional competence is measured in adversarial times; we win or we lose. There is no competition; to be second is to lose. Those books listing and comparing nations' navies, armies, and air forces, or describing all their equipment, or those parades—or the modern equivalents, like exercises, when we show ourselves off—do not in themselves foretell the future or the outcome of employing those forces. The test is war and battle. The measure: triumph or defeat; life or death. If the outcome were measurable in terms of the quantity and quality of means (the physical or conceptual components), then probably we would not have wars. But we do have them.

Operations are, by their very nature, physically and mentally demanding, extremely unpredictable and potentially dangerous—characterized by uncertainty, fear, fatigue, and discomfort, all of which have to be faced and overcome. "War," said General Rupert Smith in his 2002 lecture to the Kuwait Staff College, "is the province of uncertainty." Such operations are a group activity, whether the task is a full-scale war or a peace support operation or support to the civil authorities in a time of crisis (like a fire strike or a natural disaster). Everyone is a part of the team, and the effectiveness of the whole depends on each individual, seen or unseen, playing his or her full part. The military is a fighting organization, molded by discipline and controlled by leaders. And this is *the* key point. It is by discipline that a military unit is welded into a fighting weapon, and it is by leadership that it is led to victory; leadership that is decisive when in action and calm in a crisis. And leadership that recognizes and seeks out what timely decisions need to be made, is comfortable about making them, and disciplined about implementing them. This is what separates us from the other, non-military players.[3]

Let me expand on this, considering each in turn. First, leadership.

LEADERSHIP

War is pre-eminently the art of the man who dares to take the risk; of the man who thinks deeply and clearly; of the man who, when accident intervenes, is not thereby cast down, but changes his plans and disposition with the readiness of a resolute and reflective mind, which so far as is possible has foreseen and provided against difficulties.

Brigadier Maunsell
Extract from the Royal Military Academy
Sandhurst study, "Morale, Leadership, Discipline"

There are many forms of leadership. Political parties have their leaders, so does every organization in industry or commerce and, at the other end of the scale, so do dance bands and youth clubs, and so do gangs of thieves and smugglers. There are many qualities that apply equally to every type of leader, but we are concerned here with one particular type of leadership—and that is leadership on the battlefield; where it has to be exercised under conditions of great difficulty and considerable danger, in conditions of fatigue and fear, uncertainty and ignorance, and often in isolation. That is what makes it extremely difficult, and that is why leadership in the military calls for the very highest qualities.

We constantly look for and reward good leaders, and we search for those few who are commanders. Remember, we lead and command in adversity. We succeed by changing the situation. We are not looking for the comfortable man; we are looking for the man who does it differently with the confidence of his subordinates; leaders who can practice the art of war within the science of war.

The difficulties, dangers, and discomforts inseparable from the battlefield make soldiers cry out for leadership they can do without in times of peace. At such moments they are too weak to stand alone; they find the burdens too great to bear and their own selves unequal to the task. Everyone is afraid at one time or another, to a greater or lesser extent. In moments of fear we band together and look for guidance; we seek a person to give decisions; we look for a leader.

The leader himself accepts the burdens of others and by doing so, earns their gratitude and the right to lead them. The soldiers recognize in their leader some quality that they themselves do not possess; that quality is "decision." Fear makes men sluggish and indecisive, unable to decide or act for themselves. The leader's power is based on the ability to cut through this "fear paralysis," and in so doing, enable others to escape from it. The rightness of the decision taken by the leader is irrelevant. What matters is that the decision should be taken and that the leader should shoulder the responsibility for that decision. The leader must convince his soldiers of its rightness, even though he himself may be uncertain of his own judgement. If the leader will decide, others will follow and will fight. If there is indecision, they will hesitate and flee. In short, "fight and survive" or "fear and be slain;" the leader decides.

Leadership in such circumstances is a lonely business. Field Marshal The Viscount William (Bill) Slim, perhaps the greatest British field commander of World War II, tells of a moment late in the retreat from Burma in the face of the Japanese in 1942 when he faced his staff, and a number of Chinese staff officers:

> They stood there silent and looked at me. All Commanders know that look. They see it in the eyes of their staff and their men when things are really bad, when the toughest soldiers want holding up and they turn where they should turn for support—to their Commander. And sometimes he does not know what to say. He feels very much alone.

I, too, in much smaller ways, have found myself in such positions. From the 1970s on the streets of Northern Ireland as a bomb-disposal officer amid the rubble of a bombed-out restaurant or on a lonely, cordoned-off road with suspect cars to be dealt with; through to the 1990s in Kuwait/Iraq and in the hills of Bosnia around Kupres and Sipovo with IFOR/SFOR; and later with KFOR in the north of Macedonia, faced with the tens of thousands of Kosovar Albanian refugees flooding across the border.

The leader's power of decision results from his ability to remain imperturbable in the crisis. His greatest asset is the ability to act normally in abnormal conditions, to continue to think rationally when those under him have ceased to think; to be decisive in action when they are paralyzed by fear. The object of military training is thus, first, to select those who possess within them these qualities of leadership and, secondly, to give them responsibilities that enable them to develop their leadership qualities. To learn to guard against becoming unduly elated by success or depressed by failure; to never take counsel of their own fears. To learn that there are no hopeless situations; when things look bad and difficulties loom large, leaders must be cheerful, reasoned optimists; and when success has been achieved not to pause, but to exploit it to the full. And when that success has been exploited, to focus their first thought and action on the welfare of their troops; the leaders' own comfort and rest must come last. This is not an easy business. The key is to develop leaders who, before they learn to lead others, must learn to lead themselves—to understand the blend of "hardware" and "software" within themselves. Sun Tzu, in *The Art of War*, written around 350–500 B.C., said: "If you know the enemy and know yourself you need not fear the result of a hundred battles."[4] and General Franks, the Commander of 7 U.S. Corps in the 1990–91 Gulf War, commented in a lecture to a recent British Higher Command and Staff Course that "Commanders must observe themselves, learn from themselves, and gain valuable insights into themselves, for an understanding of who you are and what you are made of is essential."[5] Once leaders and commanders can learn to understand themselves, acknowledging their own strengths and, more importantly, their weaknesses, then they gain the confidence to lead and command well, and to be loyal to themselves and others.

Loyalty is an essential quality in a military leader; it extends to subordinates as well as to superiors. Never sheltering behind the shortcomings or mistakes of subordinates, when plans for which they are responsible go wrong they must take the blame, correcting the mistakes of the subordinates themselves. Every military leader has the right to express his or her views to superiors on any question under consideration, but once a decision has been reached, it must be supported loyally with every means in his or her power, and an immediate stop must be put to any criticisms.

If it can be got right, military leadership is a finely tempered sword and shield, a dynamic, confident, assertive, and "up-front" style—but not arrogance!—with an understanding heart for those being led. As Yen Tzu (493 B.C.) said of Ssu-ma Jing Chu: "His civil virtues endeared him to the people, his martial prowess kept his enemies in awe. The ideal commander unites culture with a warlike temper; the profession of arms requires a combination of hardness and tenderness."[6] The hardness, and indeed the tenderness, stems from discipline, which we must consider next.

DISCIPLINE

> To obey God's orders as delivered by conscience—that is duty; to obey man's orders as issued by rightful authority—that is discipline. The foundation of both alike is denial of self for a higher good. Unless the lesson of duty be first well learned, the lesson of discipline can be but imperfectly understood.
>
> Sir John Fortescue, *A Gallant Company*

The word "discipline" has a somewhat nasty smell to some people, perhaps more so today than ever before. Many simply do not understand what is meant by it, which is unfortunate because the idea of discipline, properly understood, underlies civilian life in the same way as it is the basis of military life. In other words, discipline is both a civilian and a military necessity, even if more so for the latter.

Too often those outside the military community see discipline as a mindless activity—harsh punishment or courts martial. It is true that punitive measures are part of ensuring discipline, but there is much more to it than that.

Discipline is the glue that holds men and women together in the face of adversity. People of high morale and discipline triumph in adversity, and, remember, the military are trained to operate in adversity. Discipline ensures the achievement of the objective, whether expressed as an order or not, in the worst conditions. Put another way, it ensures that a soldier does what's right when it is easier to do what's wrong. The military do not consist of unthinking automatons, but men and women who achieve their objectives with initiative, imagination, and resource.

The object of discipline in the military environment is the conquest of fear. The basis of fear is the awareness of danger. Soldiers become aware of danger when they feel themselves up against something more powerful than they are. It is here that discipline shows its value, for it can help soldiers to lose their own identity and become part of a larger and stronger unit; to lose their individual feelings and become an integral part of the battalion, division, and army to which they belong. In this way, discipline will conquer fear. Fear acting through soldiers' thoughts can so reduce their hard core of courage that they will become nervous and fearful. Discipline strengthens the mind so that it becomes impervious to the corroding influence of fear. It teaches soldiers to confine their thoughts within certain definite limits. It instils the habit of self-control. This corporate sense that discipline creates helps soldiers to face the unknown, and the method by which the conquest of fear is achieved is through the obedience to orders. To get soldiers to give of their best, discipline seeks to instil into all ranks a sense of unity by compelling them to obey orders as one man. This obedience to orders is the indispensable condition of good discipline, and it is the basis of all military effort. Soldiers learn to gain confidence and encouragement from doing the same thing as their fellows; they derive strength and satisfaction from their company; their own identities become merged into the larger and stronger identity of their unit. Soldiers learn to obey orders when all their own instincts cry out for them not to be obeyed. They learn to obey orders in times of stress so that they will do so in times of danger, and they learn to carry out their tasks under any conditions and despite all difficulties. In this way the mass of loose individuals, with their fears and weaknesses, are welded into a united whole, ready to act on the word of a leader.

Rather than being imposed from above, the basis of all discipline is self-discipline, which must come from within. Whatever its source, it involves the idea of self-control and self-restraint. This concept of self-restraint underlies the whole of Christian (and most other religious) teaching on personal conduct, and it is impressed on most, if not every, child from nursery days onward. Obedience to, for example, the Ten Commandments, means that we submit ourselves to the necessary self-discipline to enable ourselves to carry them out. Discipline thus has a moral foundation, and most in the military are not afraid to admit it.

Such discipline implies a concept of duty. Nothing will be accomplished in the crisis by the soldier without a sense of duty. The sentry in an outpost holds ground in the face of an attack because he has a sense of duty to those behind him. This sense is instilled by discipline because it teaches soldiers to obey orders as a matter of course, to know that it is wrong not to obey them, and right—that is, their duty—to do so. For the soldier, this conception of duty does not embrace abstractions such as freedom or empire or democracy. In battle, a soldier's sense of duty largely extends only to the friends who are around him.[7]

In brief, discipline seeks to conquer fear by welding soldiers into a cohesive whole, united by obedience to orders. It aims to create a body strong enough to carry each of its members through dangers and difficulties that they themselves would be unable to face alone, and in this way it promotes comradeship, which although present in many parts of society is uniquely powerful in the military community. Soldiers, sailors, and airmen thus agree to subordinate their own interests to those of the unit. This is the immune system, the antibody to rampant, selfish individualism on the one hand (reflected in the wider economic life of society) and the overbearing state on the other (reflected in political power play).

> Any military organisation today without such discipline is no more than a mob, alternating between frightened sheep and beasts of prey. Discipline, as the British soldier amongst others has demonstrated it in peace and war, is the old Christian spiritual virtue of unselfishness; of standing by your neighbour, your comrade. It is the sacrifice of a man's comfort, inclination, safety, even life, for others, for something greater than yourself. It is the refusal to be the weak link in the chain that snaps under strain.[8]

The best traditions of the British military are rich in such leadership and in what I would call enlightened discipline. Take, for example, the Royal Navy at Trafalgar in 1805. Consciously or unconsciously, Nelson, in those last weeks off Cadiz, was fashioning a tradition and a legend that was to be of a priceless service to England. He reminded the Navy that, whatever the bonds of authority, leadership was not a mere matter of transmitting orders but of evoking the will to serve. Building on all that was the best in the great naval tradition in which he had been nurtured, and discarding all that was bad, he established an ideal of discipline that was as revolutionary as it was practical. It was founded not on a corporate abstraction, but on the individual who alone, as he saw, embodied the principle of life. Its ideal was liberty in a framework of discipline—a liberty that worked and was grafted, in the English mode, on nature. Captain Fremantle testified how pleasant it was, after Lord Nelson's arrival, to be given constant change of scene and occupation, freedom of choice and method, yet to know precisely how far one might go.

It was this that, as an officer said, double-manned every ship in the line. Nelson was essentially a humanitarian who, wooing men to duty, trusted them and had the imagination to see into their hearts. By his reckoning, the best disciplinarian was he who most loved and understood men, who remembered that they were human beings and treated them accordingly. One of his first acts was to order that the names and families of all killed and wounded should be reported to him for transmission to the Chairman of the Patriotic Fund, and that an account of every man's case should accompany him to hospital. In this spirit, he allowed Sir Robert Calder to return in his own flag-ship to England to face a court martial, thus depriving the fleet of one of its precious three-deckers at the very moment that he was fretting for every gun to annihilate the enemy. "I much fear I shall incur the censure of the Board," he wrote to the Admiralty, "but I trust that I shall be considered to have done right as a man to a brother officer in affliction—my heart could not stand it." It would have been idle for authority to complain; such tenderness and consideration were an essential part of Nelson's success. He could not discard them without ceasing to be Nelson.[9]

There are many other examples. Nelson is of course the hero of the Royal Navy. The British Army has many of its own:

From its earliest days, the efficiency and the success of the standing army of Great Britain have been largely derived form the high qualifications of many of its officers. Practically every important campaign has produced at least one great leader, and many good ones; and almost all of them have been well educated. The training of some, such as Cromwell, Marlborough, and Clive, has been altogether practical; their wits sharpened and their intellect strengthened, as was also the case with Nelson and St. Vincent, by long and varied experience. These, however, are the exceptions, and it is not to be overlooked that their natural genius for war was of the highest order. The majority, including Wolfe and Wellington, have been deep students of the military art, relying not merely on the knowledge derived from their own personal practice and conclusions, but assimilating the practice and conclusions of the great captains. The era of Napoleon, when war first became a science, was peculiarly prolific, so far as the British army was concerned, in characters so trained. Wellington's lieutenants in the Peninsula and his colleagues in India were as earnest and as industrious as himself, and the tradition of hard work they handed down, though at times obscured, was never completely lost to sight. At no time was the importance of study more generally accepted as a guiding principle than at the end of the nineteenth century. The brilliant successes of Moltke and his Prussians, due almost entirely to a thorough knowledge of war and its practical application, had rekindled the torch. Competitive examination both for first commissions and the staff gave an impulse to intellectual activity; while the influence and example of Field-Marshal Lord Wolseley, the best-read soldier of his time, who from 1882 onwards was the moving spirit in the path of progress, had a marked effect upon the younger generation. Apathy became unfashionable, hard work the rule; study was no longer considered useless; and the professional acquirements of the officers reached a far higher standard than they had attained since Waterloo.

The standard, however, might easily have been higher still. Zeal was never lacking in the army. The troops had always been well disciplined and well drilled. The internal economy of the different units was everywhere admirable. The health and comfort of the men were most carefully looked to; and the rivalry between regiments, and even between squadrons and companies, though confined to the exercises of the parade ground, to soldierly bearings, and to good conduct, was a token not only of a strong *esprit de corps* but of a strong sense of duty and professional pride among the regimental officers. They were supported, it is true, by an excellent body of non-commissioned officers; but although these men, who have been rightly styled the backbone of the army, furnished an invaluable link between the private soldier and the higher grades, their powers were strictly limited; they were merely assistants to their superiors; and it was impossible, under the system of regimental administration, that they could become their substitutes. Thus between the company officer and the rank and file no obstruction whatever existed, and in no army were their personal relations, especially on foreign service, closer, or more constant.[10]

The Good Military Versus the Bad

This is what separates out the military from the non-military players. What then separates out the good military from the bad?

A good military community is a community prepared for the controlled use of force, but is also one tuned to show restraint even when doing so involves personal danger, and to witness injury or death to friends and foe alike but still continue with the task in hand. This requires courage—both physical and moral, the latter being the more crucial. Courage to do what is right even when it may be unpopular and to insist on the highest standards of decency and behavior at all times and under all circumstances. To maintain a sense of justice under fire is not easy, which is why all forms of deceit or dishonesty, or breaches of trust or confidence, are treated severely in the British military and in some others. Such breaches constitute a lack of integrity, and call into question whether an individual can be relied upon to be loyal to himself, his friends/comrades, and the wider military community when the going gets tough. So the core values of a good military organization include selfless commitment; courage; integrity; loyalty; respect for others (see note 1). A military without these things is like a society without love or friendship, trust or honor. It is like a city without homes, only hotels; a place of strangers, not friends. I will develop just two; courage and integrity.

COURAGE

> A man of character in peace is a man of courage in war.
>
> Lord Moran, *The Anatomy of Courage*

It has been well said that there is no man alive (or dead, come to that) who, in his heart of hearts, wouldn't rather be called brave than have any other virtue attributed to him. And this elemental, if somewhat unreasoning (and largely male), attitude is a sound one. Field Marshal Bill Slim argues that courage is not merely a virtue; it is *the* virtue. Without it there are no other virtues: "Faith, hope, charity, all the rest don't become virtues until it takes courage to exercise them. Courage is not only the basis of all virtue; it is its expression. True, you may be bad and brave, but you can't be good without being brave."

Courage is self-evidently a mental state, an affair of the spirit, and it gets its strength from spiritual and intellectual sources, blended to produce essentially two types of courage. The first is an emotional state that urges soldiers to risk injury or death—physical courage. The second is a more reasoning attitude that enables them to coolly stake career, happiness, perhaps their whole future on their judgement of what they think is either right or worthwhile—moral courage.

These two types of courage, physical and moral, are very distinct. Many men have marked physical courage, but lack moral courage; some in high positions fail to be great in themselves because they lack it. On the other hand, some men undoubtedly possess moral courage but are very cautious about physical risks;

that said, few, if any, with moral courage would not, when it is really necessary, face bodily danger. Moral courage is a higher and rarer virtue than physical courage. Slim argues that to be really great, a person—or a nation—must possess both forms of courage. And the good military certainly must.

Everyone has some degree of physical courage—it is often surprising how much. Lord Moran, Winston Churchill's doctor, says that courage is like having money in the bank. We start with a certain "capital" of courage, some large, some small, and proceed to draw on our balance; courage is thus an expendable quality. It can be used up. If there are heavy and, what is more serious, continuous calls on our courage, we begin to overdraw. If we go on overdrawing, we go bankrupt—we break down. This overdraft can be seen clearly in servicemen and women who endure the most prolonged strains in war: the submariners, the infantry platoon, the bomber crew. A growing impatience and irritability; a hint of recklessness; a sort of "Oh, to hell with it—attack!" spirit; next, real foolhardiness, what is sometimes called "asking for it"; and last, sudden changes of mood from false hilarity to black moroseness. The crucial point is that if, before that stage is reached, the soldier's commander has spotted what is happening and has pulled him/her out for a rest, then the soldier will recover and in a few months be back again as brave and as balanced as ever. The capital in the bank of courage will have been built back up, and he/she can start spending again.

Can courage be taught? In one sense physical courage can be, by training soldiers not to draw too heavily on their stock of courage. Teaching them what to expect, not to be frightened by the unknown. Bill Slim again:

> If you send an untrained British soldier on patrol in the jungle, every time a branch creaks, every time there is a rustle in the undergrowth when an animal slinks across the track, when a bush moves in the wind, he will draw heavily and unnecessarily on his stock of courage. And he will come back a shaken man, with a report of no value. But if you train that man beforehand, let him live in the jungle, teach him its craft, then send him on patrol, he

will come back with his balance of courage unimpaired and probably a couple of enemy helmets into the bargain.

To teach moral courage is another matter—and it has to be taught because so few, if any, have it naturally. The young can learn it from their parents, in their homes, from school and university, from religion, from other early influences, but to inculcate it in a grown-up who lacks it requires not so much teaching as some striking emotional experience—something that suddenly bursts upon him; something in the nature of a vision. That happens rarely, and that is why most men and women with moral courage learned it by precept and example in their youth. It is thus very much a part of the soldier's national character, and it is certainly one of the important distinctions between the good military and the bad.

After the death of Moses in the Old Testament, Joshua, his deputy, found himself in command. As he prepared to lead the people of Israel in the campaign to conquer the Promised Land, God spoke to him:

> No man will be able to stand up against you all the days of your life; as I was with Moses, so I will be with you; I will never leave you or forsake you. Be strong and of good courage; for you will lead these people to inherit the land I swore to their forefathers to give them. Be strong and *very* courageous, being careful to obey all the law which Moses my servant gave you; do not turn from it to the right or to the left, that you may be successful wherever you go.[11]

Be strong and of good courage, Joshua, because you will lead your army through over forty physical battles in the coming campaign. You will need to be physically courageous to ensure victory. But be strong and *very* courageous, Joshua, because you will lead your people in a continuous spiritual battle—moral battles when you and the people you lead will be tempted to abandon righteousness, and succumb to worldly temptation—and it is these moral battles in life that are the most difficult, and often require the greatest courage. As Clausewitz commented in his treatise "On War":

As the moral focus in one individual after another becomes prostrated, the whole inertia of the mass gradually rests its weight on the will of the Commander; by the spark in his breast, by the light of his spirit, the spark of purpose, the light of hope must be kindled afresh in others.

Which leads us to integrity.

INTEGRITY

> I contend that fortitude in war has its roots in morality; that selection is a search for character, and that war itself is but one more test—the supreme and final test if you will—of character. Character, as Aristotle taught, is a habit, the daily choice of right instead of wrong; it is a moral quality which grows to maturity in peace and is not suddenly developed on the outbreak of war. . . . Man's fate in battle is worked out before the war begins.
>
> Lord Moran, *The Anatomy of Courage*

The next value that separates the good military from the bad is integrity; integrity within the leadership and with the men and women they lead and with whom they work. Integrity—like honesty—cannot be compromised, cannot be altered. From such honesty and integrity flows the ability to deal with the conflicting realities of complex emergencies in a fair and balanced way. Lecturing recently in Lithuania, I was asked by an officer from Azerbaijan how, when the British Army was deployed to places like the Balkans, we knew what side we were on. It took some time to convince him that the whole idea was not to be on one side or the other, but to be determined to be neutral and fair-minded to all sides. Such an attitude is not new, for the British Army at least. Bill Slim, in one of his lectures recalls the story of how, on one sweltering afternoon in the Red Fort at Delhi, a company of British infantry was hurriedly falling in. There was a riot in the city, Hindu against Muslim. Heads were being broken, men stabbed, shops looted and burned. As the troops struggled into their equipment, an officer said:

> "Now remember, in this quarrel you are neutral." A young soldier turned to his Sergeant, "Wot did 'e mean by nootral, Sergeant?" he asked. "Nootral my lad," replied the N.C.O., "Nootral means that when you go down that adjectival bazaar, you're just as likely to be 'it by a Mo'amedan brick as by a 'Indue brick."

Unruffled by brickbats or bouquets, the good soldier has marched in such a way across history. Success that might turn another's head he greets with studied understatement; disaster that would appal most he meets with a jest; at its best with courage always laced with humor, a natural humor that is quick and topical and good-natured through the centuries.[12]

But this is not just historical. A young civil servant working in the recently created Defence Logistic Organisation in the U.K. met its first boss, General Sir Sam Cowan, the Chief of Defence Logistics, in the corridor of the headquarters. Explaining that she and a number of others were beginning to meet for prayer once a week, she wanted to know what to pray for him personally: "Pray for strength, that I can preserve my integrity," he replied. And they did.

Integrity, like moral courage, cannot easily be taught; but it must be a part of the framework of the military community, built into the architecture as it were. Thus, within the good military organizations, issues like the Geneva Convention, the Laws of Armed Conflict, Rules of Engagement, and the concept of the Just War are both taught and debated.[13] Civilized behavior requires self-control and self-discipline at the personal, group, and corporate level. In the context of this chapter, it marks out the civilized soldier/military from the brute. This does not mean that there must be a superabundance of integrity in every soldier in every unit—that is an impossibly tall order; but it does mean that there is, within the organization, a desire and an intent that there should be. It is too late to turn to such intent when the campaign/conflict is about to start. When the moment comes, the responses must be instinctive.

There are many examples of instinctive integrity that I could quote. This one, told of the Regimental Medical Officer (RMO) of the Gloucester Regiment during the Korean War, sums things up rather well:

> Nearby, I met Bob (the RMO) returning to the Regimental Aid Post from a talk with the Colonel. The signallers had already destroyed their sets, and Harry was stamping on the ashes of the codebook he had just burnt. We were all ready to move. In small groups, the Headquarters split up and ran over the ridge. When they had gone, I, too, came up on to the ridge crest and prepared to descend the other side. Bob was standing alone by the path that led to the steep slopes below us.
>
> "Come on, Bob," I said. "We're about the last to go; you ought to have gone before this. The Colonel will be off in a minute and that will be the lot." He looked at me for a moment before saying:
>
> "I can't go. I must stay with the wounded."
>
> For a few seconds I did not comprehend his meaning: we were all making our way out—there seemed a very fair chance that some of us would make it: to stay here was to stay certainly for capture, possibly for death, when the Chinese launched their final assault on the position. And then I realised that he had weighed all this—weighed it all and made a deliberate choice: he would place his own life in the utmost jeopardy in order to remain with the wounded at the time when they would need him most. Somewhere, the words appear, "Greater love hath no man than this . . ." I knew now exactly what those words meant. Too moved to speak again, I clapped my hand upon his shoulder and went on.[14]

So What?

What does all this mean in practical reality? It means that the good military demand clear leadership; calm in a crisis, decisive when all around is chaos. They demand, too, leaders whose principal virtue is to serve those they have the privilege to command. It is not by chance that the cap-badge of the Royal Military Academy, Sandhurst, is "Serve to Lead" and the prayer is this:

Almighty God, whose son Jesus Christ, the Lord of all life, came not to be served but to serve, help us to be master of ourselves that we may be servants of others and teach us to Serve to Lead.

Good military organizations seek leaders who build up self-belief in others and encourage the gifts that are present in everyone to grow and to contribute to the needs of the team. Leaders who confront wrong; recognize it and deal with it—not condoning it or walking away from it. Leaders who have a sense of "spiritual" truth,[15] and can recognize when it is right to lay force aside and work to establish peace. To fight when necessary, for example in the Falklands or the Gulf, but then to stop the shelling of the retreating enemy, or ensure vehicles, food, and water are made available to the captured POWs, or ensure equality of treatment to all sides of an internal conflict, be that in Cyprus or the Balkans, in East Timor or Sierra Leone. Such soldiers stand aside and are separate from those who slaughtered women and children in the Far East and Europe in WWII, or who ethnically cleansed villages and towns throughout Bosnia, Croatia, and Kosovo, or in Cambodia or numerous other countries around the world.

One of the most potent ways of recognizing the reality of this in an organization is that when things pass beyond their own authority or initiative, everyone knows to whom to turn for further direction, and doesn't hesitate in doing so. If it is the right kind of organization, soldiers will turn to their leaders in the confidence that they will get sensible and effective direction. And they are not just efficient; they look efficient. If you enter the lines of a regiment where the guard is smart and alert, and the soldiers you meet are well turned out and salute briskly, you cannot fail to get an impression of efficiency. You are right; ten to one that unit is efficient and well disciplined. If you go into a headquarters and find the clerks scruffy, the floor unswept, and dirty teamugs staining flyblown papers on office tables, the unit may be efficient, but I doubt it.[16]

These, then, are some of the values and traditions that the military brings to the world of complex emergencies. Leadership and discipline, courage and integrity. They are not virtues that all military organizations possess. Those that do possess them are rightly proud of them. I stress, as I did at the opening, that this chapter is about principles; the practice is all too often different, even in the best of military organizations. But the best strive to meet the principles, recognizing that they are the stuff of military hyperbole and ideology. But take them away and you are left with pure militarism. These virtues are not absolutes, but variables, more often than not diminished between intent and actions—varying between and within military units, the presence of danger, stress, physical deprivation and cognitive confusion and the course of the battle or operation. But taken as a whole, the good military organizations will recognize their need for them and display their intent to embed them in their men and women. And when they are embedded, then history can recall the effect.

Two closing examples:

WATERLOO

No incident is more familiar in our military history than the stubborn resistance of the British line at Waterloo. Through the long hours of the midsummer day, silent and immovable the squares and squadrons stood in the trampled corn, harassed by an almost incessant fire of cannon and of musketry, to which they were forbidden to make reply. Not a moment but heard some cry of agony; not a moment but some comrade fell headlong in the furrows. Yet as the bullets of the skirmishers hailed around them, and the great round shot tore through the tight-packed ranks, the word was passed quietly. "Close in on the centre, men"; and as the sun neared his setting, the regiments, still shoulder to shoulder, stood fast upon the ground they had held at noon. The spectacle is characteristic. In good fortune and in ill, it is rare indeed that a British regiment does not hold together, and this indestructible cohesion, best of all the qualities that an armed body can possess, is based not merely on hereditary resolution, but on mutual confidence and mutual respect. The man in the ranks has implicit faith in his officer, the officer an almost unbounded belief in the valour and discipline of his men; . . .

Colonel Henderson, *The Science of War*

THE SOLDIER WRITES HOME

Woolwich, February 26, 1793
Dear Mother, Brother, Sister, and acquaintances,

This is the last from us in Ingland. I have just received orders for Germany under the command of the Duke of York, with 2,200-foot guards. We expect to embark tomorrow with 1 Captain, 4 Subalterns, 8 non-comishened Officers and 52 gunners to go with His Royal Highness as a Bodyguard of British Heroes. We are to lead the Dutch Prushen and Hanover Troops into the field, as there is none equal to the British Army. We are chosen troops sent by His Majesty to show an example to the other Troops, to go in front, & lead the combined army against the French which consists of 150,000 able fighten men. You may judge if we shall have anything to dow. I had the pleasure to conquer the French last war; but God knows how it will be this war. I cannot expect to escape the Bullets of my enemies much longer, as non has ever entered my flesh as yet. To be plain with you and not dishearten you, I don't expect to come off so cleare as I did last war. But it is death or honour. I exspeck to be a Gentleman or a Cripel. But you never shall see me to destress you. If I cannot help you, I never shall destress you.

Dear Mother, I take my family with me. Where I go, they most go. If I leave them, I should have no luck. My wife and 2 children is in good health, & I in good spirits. Fear not for us. I hope God will be on our side.

Your Loven Son & Daughter,
GEO. & MARY ROBERTSON

(Sir John Fortescue, *Following the Drum*)

6

The Academy and Humanitarian Action

Joseph A. O'Hare, S.J.

HUMANITARIAN ACTION is ordinarily understood to involve a response to the needs of individuals and communities afflicted by different kinds of calamities, both those that are natural, like earthquakes and typhoons, and those that are the result of human intervention, like wars and political repression. Some calamities, of course, represent a convergence of natural disasters and human mischief; famine, for example, can be the result both of climactic changes in a particular region and a flawed distribution system created by a world market dominated by a profit motive.

Humanitarian action can also be understood in a broader sense, namely the continuing attempt to achieve a more human world, one where wealth and opportunity are more evenly distributed among nations and among classes within nations. In this sense, humanitarian action is the enduring effort to create a world where a respect for human dignity and the inalienable rights of the individual are the cornerstone of society.

At first glance, the world of the academy is more directly engaged in the second, broader meaning of humanitarian action. The expansion and communication of knowledge, which is the life of the academy, is more directly related to the continuing search for wisdom and a vision of the human than to the more episodic responses to the needs of victims of wars and famines. At the present moment, however, the possibilities of direct humanitarian action in support of the afflicted in different parts of the world are limited and threatened by a new kind of world conflict that is rooted in a clash of the fundamental values and traditions that have always engaged the energies of scholars and teachers. The possibilities of humanitarian action, in the conventional sense of a response to a crisis but also in the broader sense of a continuing search for a more human world, are today linked together in an unusual and more immediate relationship.

As an attempt to bring the perspective of the academy to bear on the theme of this symposium, "Traditions, Values, and Humanitarian Action: Foundations, Fault Lines, and Corrections," I propose to first describe the special character of the present world conflict that threatens the possibility of humanitarian action and the threat this conflict poses for the integrity of the academy or, more specifically, the freedom of the university. I will then argue that the dangers of the present moment underline the urgency of recognizing that the contemporary university must be an international institution, one that fosters authentic intercultural understanding and maintains an environment where interreligious dialogue can take place and religious traditions can be renewed. One important dimension of this conflict involves the inexorable process of globalization, which demands that contemporary education must be international in character, on every level in appropriate fashion.

THE UNIVERSITY AND INTERNATIONAL TERRORISM

The university, only the most typical institution of academia, encourages differences, believing that the free competition of ideas is a necessary condition for the expansion of knowledge that can lead to a glimpse of the truth and the best available wisdom to guide our lives and our world. Given this inherent diversity, does the contemporary university offer a distinctive perspective on the possibilities of humanitarian action in a world where traditions and values can be locked in conflicts that can seem insoluble?

The dangers of the present moment arise from a network of international terrorists and terrorist organizations whose motivation and objectives are far more obscure than the causes that have, in the past, led nation-states into armed conflicts. International terrorism transcends national borders and political ideology. Its objectives appear vague and shifting, its passion rooted in popular resentment rather than any patriotic cause, its vision of the future vague and inarticulate. The amorphous character of international terrorism—the absence of any proposal for an alternative future coupled with its willingness to attack the innocent at random—only adds to the unsettling, because undefined, character of its threat to international society.

In such a climate of fear and uncertainty, legitimate concerns about national security can escalate into unnecessary restrictions on civil liberties and the repression of legitimate differences on how to meet the dangers of international terrorism. In the wake of the terrorist attack of September 11, the desire to retaliate overwhelmed the need to better understand the passions behind this murderous assault. Debate on university campuses over the Middle East crisis quickly became politicized, and the legitimacy of conflicting views on the Israeli-Palestinian conflict was challenged. In the rush of patriotic feeling, many were impatient with any call for an examination of the international posture of the United States as the sole remaining superpower in the world.

Yet any attempt to contain and eventually eliminate the dangers of international terrorism must include a better understanding of its dark and tangled roots. This search for understanding is the mission of the university. To fulfill this mission, however, the university must protect its autonomy and encourage the kind of academic freedom that is a condition of authentic discovery. Such freedom, which encourages the competition of ideas, is not a luxury that can be surrendered in a time of national danger, but a necessity if we are to understand the nature of the danger that surrounds us.

The Internationalization of Education

One source of the energy of international terrorism is resentment of the current division of wealth and power in the international community. Such resentment can create coalitions of protest among groups with different agenda and ideologies. The demonstrations against the present economic order that have marred international meetings around the world have brought together a wide variety of groups and organizations; religious activists calling for the cancellation of the debts of poorer nations and anarchists seeking to undermine civil order, united only in a resistance to the inexorable but bewildering process of globalization, driven by the dynamics of world markets and information technology. In this new world economy that transcends national boundaries, new wealth is created and whole societies can be transformed, but the distribution of this wealth is uneven and individuals and communities can be left behind and left out.

The very process of globalization seems to strip individuals and communities of their autonomy and self-determination, and provokes the fury of those who consider its costs, both economic and cultural, dehumanizing. These critics of globalization insist that it has created a wider gulf between the rich and the poor, between nations and regions, and between classes within nations. Meanwhile, distinctive cultural traditions are being undermined by a homogeneous popular culture that comes with mass consumerism.

Resentment of the economic and cultural consequences of globalization is a common passion that connects a broad array of critics with different causes and agendas. The violent protests that have exploded in recent years at several international meetings, e.g., Seattle and Genoa, have bewildered many, while legitimate questions concerning globalization have been obscured by the destructive behavior of radical groups. But the process of globalization, driven by the appeal of world markets and the revolution in information technology, cannot be reversed, nor should it be.

If the university is to contribute to a better understanding of both the challenges and the opportunities that globalization presents, then the university must be transformed into an international institution, recognizing that in our contemporary world, all education must be international in nature.

This does not mean that individual institutions must compromise their distinctive identities and missions. In the twenty-first century we live in one world, whether we like it or not, but it is a world of differences, and our challenge is not to diminish those differences or paper them over in the interests of some superficial unity. On the contrary, the challenge for the university as an institution is the same challenge that confronts all nations and institutions in this new millennium: How to make our differences a source of enrichment rather than division? How to better appreciate our own traditions and values by recognizing and respecting the traditions and values of others? How to redeem the promise of cultural and religious traditions by a creative renewal of their deepest meanings? How to find in the renewal of such traditions a more human response to the opportunities made possible by the technological revolution? How to make it clear that modernization does not, in the end, mean Westernization?

The Development of Intercultural Understanding

The most obvious sign of the increasingly international character of higher education is the growth in exchange programs that bring students and scholars from other nations and cultures to our campuses here in the United States and encourage faculty and students from the United States to spend time at other institutions in other nations and cultures. But while the exchange of faculty and students is necessary, it is not enough. The university must encourage and support the development of authentic intercultural understanding.

The promotion of multiculturalism on American campuses can be an easy target for those critics who see it as a surrender of the defining values of Western civilization. It was with some chagrin that I learned some years ago of a campus debate here at Fordham that posed the question: Multiculturalism versus the Jesuit educational tradition. We need only think of historic Jesuit experiments at inculturation, like those that led to the Chinese Rites controversy and the Paraguay Reductions, to realize that

Jesuit education over the past four and a half centuries has always been multicultural.

It is unfortunate that the debate about multiculturalism in American education has too often been mired in arguments about what texts should be included in college curricula in order to include underrepresented groups. It is a debate that has often degenerated into academic politics in its least appealing posture. To achieve the goals of an authentic intercultural sensibility, a program of immersion in another language and culture should be part of the required curriculum in any program of liberal studies. At the present time, for example, the Beijing Center for Language and Culture offers a program for undergraduates at Jesuit colleges and universities in the United States that is far more demanding and far more rewarding in terms of an intercultural experience than prescribed readings, in translation, of a faculty member's favorite neglected author.

An understanding and appreciation of non-Western cultures should enrich our understanding of Western civilization and not diminish it. To achieve this end, however, the enduring goals of a liberal education have to be continually affirmed and realized. The study of other cultures should not lead to a collapse of community into separate national and ethnic enclaves but rather should lead to a deeper and richer appreciation of the common human values we share.

This process is assuredly not automatic. To be successful we cannot shy away from cultural critiques and ethical judgments. Accepting a bland moral relativism as the necessary corollary of multicultural appreciation will not guide the development of a more human world. At the same time, moral judgments that have no appreciation of different cultural sensibilities will remain irrelevant abstractions.

THE CHALLENGE OF INTERRELIGIOUS DIALOGUE

The university has always been an institution where tradition is not only recovered and remembered but also renewed and transformed. In its classrooms, libraries, and laboratories, the wisdom of the past should confront each day the questions of tomorrow. In the life of the ideal university community, new questions are not feared and suppressed but welcomed and debated. In actual life, of course, university communities do not always resist the narrow politicization of activists and advocates that declare what is and is not acceptable thinking.

In the wake of the September 11 terrorist attack and the continuing violence in the Middle East, debate over the fundamental causes of these conflicts has often become polarized and the legitimacy of dissident scholars challenged because of their political views. If the university is to fulfill its historic role as a forum for competing views, we must insist on the conditions for civil debate: mutual respect and honest recognition of differences. Civility does not compromise moral commitment, although this is not obvious to campus activists who find demonstrations more satisfying than debates.

The need to balance passion and civility is particularly acute in the continuing conversation that should be interreligious dialogue. Perhaps the secular university is not the most congenial environment for such dialogue, since the recognition of the importance of religious experience and the legitimacy of intellectual inquiry into such experience can be absent from the prevailing ethos of the secular academy, the legacy of the children of the Enlightenment.

For the secularist, religion itself, with its absolutist claims, can appear to be the source of inevitable conflict, and certainly human history has demonstrated in many different ages that violence to the human spirit can be done in the name of religion. The terrorist attack on September 11 was not the only instance in history of the destructive purposes to which religious passion can lead. To protect the purity of the faith, heretics were tortured and beheaded in the name of Christendom. Closer to our own day, we have seen false messiahs inspire mass suicides by their followers.

Religious passion is a powerful flame that can inspire the radi-

ant example of St. Therese of Lisieux and the heroic service to
the poor by generations of missionaries. But religious passion, we
recognize, can be turned to darker and more destructive purposes, as it surely was on September 11 when the terrorists committed the ultimate blasphemy of destroying the innocent in the
name of the Almighty.

All religious traditions, if they are to be continually renewed,
must be engaged in a dialogue with history. In the Catholic tradition, we speak of the development of doctrine, where the test
of continuity is applied to new understandings of the received
tradition. Every religious tradition, if the tradition is to be a living
tradition, must deal with the tension between fundamentalism
and modernity. There is no easy resolution of this tension; instead, it involves a continuing conversation, and the university
offers a privileged forum for such a conversation. This has been
the experience of Catholicism from the first development of the
university as an institution born from "the heart of the church"
(Ex corde ecclesiae) in the medieval universities of Europe.

This challenge of renewal confronts the powerful tradition of
Islam. The dangers of Islamic fundamentalism can, in the end,
only be resolved within Islam itself. The renewal of Islam, as a
living religious tradition, must take place in that dialogue with
history and modernity that must engage all religious traditions.
The world of the university remains a privileged forum for this
indispensable conversation and renewal. Those universities that
are themselves animated by a living religious tradition would
seem to be a particularly congenial home for such dialogue.

In our observance of the first anniversary of the September 11
terrorist attack at Fordham University, interreligious memorial
services were held at each of our campuses. The readings for
these services were drawn from the New Testament, Buddhist
texts, and the Koran. Though obviously different in tone and
accent, all of these readings converged on the primacy of human
dignity as the test of any religious passion. Respect for those who
differ from us in national identity or religious belief does not
imply an indifference toward the truth. A healthy religious plu-

ralism fosters the renewal of distinctive religious traditions and respect for the truth claims they make, even when one chooses to disagree with those claims. But the critical test of such claims is their relevance to the dignity of the human person. Does this religious vision recognize and enhance the human person or diminish and violate human dignity? While different cultures may manifest different expressions of what it means to be human, the assumption of liberal education is that there is a common humanity we all share. To destroy the innocent on behalf of a religious cause is the ultimate blasphemy. Religious passion, then, becomes a vicious abstraction, demonic in origin rather than divine. Part of the legacy of September 11 is the painful reminder that religious faith can be betrayed by those who use it to justify violence. The search for understanding among differences, the mission of the university, is an essential guardian of religious integrity.

The fundamentalist instinct in all religious traditions, of course, can slide into a kind of anti-intellectualism that resists the kind of questioning of tradition that is part of the life of the university. The university, as an institution of inquiry rather than indoctrination, is suspect to the fundamentalist. The irony here is that without such inquiry religious tradition can become distorted, frozen into harmless irrelevancy or distorted into the more dangerous sense of absolute righteousness that can become absolute ruthlessness. Dare one suggest that the blasphemous attack of September 11 was an extreme instance of a religious tradition that had refused the essential dialogue with modernity that is the mission of the Catholic university and remains the best hope of a creative renewal of the deepest truths of the Islamic tradition?

CONCLUSION

The contemporary university should provide a context for humanitarian action in the broad sense of creating a more human world and enable individuals to respond to the needs of the afflicted in the more narrow sense of humanitarian action by fostering an authentic intercultural understanding and encouraging the renewal of religious traditions, and particularly the Islamic tradition, through interreligious dialogue. In a world threatened by international terrorism, the university must resist restrictions on academic freedom that would inhibit the task of understanding the sources of the deep-seated, if inarticulate, resentment at the heart of such terrorist campaigns.

7

Is Any News Good News?

Tom Brokaw

IN THIS NEW WORLD in which we're sailing across unknown seas, navigating by the stars because so many of the familiar navigational guides are of little use, the role and the responsibility of the press, both print and electronic, are critical to a successful journey.

However, the very conditions that brought us to this perilous and anxiety-inducing state are constantly in danger of blowing up into a perfect storm in which the press is buffeted by primal forces colliding with a ferocity that shatters the old landscape of perceptions and expectations. It is a fierce wind made all the more powerful by the accelerant of the ceaseless demand to constantly replenish the air waves, Web sites, print outlets. Judgments, declarations, interpretations, descriptions blow through the greatly expanded universe of the traditional and new media twenty-four hours a day, seven days a week, in a dizzying fashion. For those of us at the helm, navigating through these conditions is challenge enough. To our viewers and readers, it can be overwhelming and disorienting.

In the West, the press is swept into an ancient culture anchored in another region, struggling to understand the new imperatives of a popular faith that, nonetheless, remains mysterious in origin and practice to most of its viewers and readers. That there is a struggle within that faith for its soul and future makes the assignment all the more vexing to an outsider.

There are certain objective truths that provide a framework for determining the direction and the mission of the media in this bewildering new environment.

First, the faith from which the violent acts emanated is not monolithic, but it is indisputably popular. For most of the twentieth century, Christianity represented 30 percent of the world's population and Islam 20 percent. Given current birth rates, those numbers will flip by the year 2025. The mass of Islam, however it is interpreted, is a reality that demands more attention from those outside the faith.

Next, the global war on terrorism has many layers, but a common theme: it is much more a war of cultures than a war between sovereign nations. All of the conventional definitions of what it takes to be successful in war—choosing the battlefield, standing armies, great power in the air and sea as well as on the ground— now compete with fanatical guerrillas who are nationally rootless acolytes of shadowy figures who send them happily to their suicidal deaths with no remorse about the loss of innocent life, all in the name of Allah.

So a primary function of the press in this new world is to not just demonize a great faith but also not to ignore the cruel realities of too many of its interpreters. It is testimony to the power of faith, spirituality, and fundamental human values that they retain their place on the agenda of constant examination and explanation, more than holding their own in the presence of breathtaking advances in the expanding universe of physical sciences and economics.

Simultaneously, the press, in all of its forms, must address the issue of its own prisms. There has been at once a great expansion and a great consolidation of media power in this new world. Even a casual traveler to any remote corner of the globe quickly realizes that there are two realities: the one in the villages and fields, in the temples and mosques of the region, and the other on the small screen attached to a satellite dish taking in reports, commentary, discussion, and images from distant studios, almost all of them centered in the West. Those images are at once welcomed, envied, and resented.

One of the most dramatic developments in this new era is the rise of competing media outlets on the other side of the divide, so to speak. Al-Jazeerah, the satellite news service originating in Qatar, is not a propaganda megaphone, but it does have a distinctly Arab point of view, just as outlets in Tel Aviv reflect the Israeli culture or MSNBC, CNBC, CNN, and Fox News reflect layers of the American culture.

It is all part of what I call The Big Bang of media expansion. When I was a young man in Yankton, South Dakota, in the late 1950s, I was thrilled by the choices I had every evening: a fifteen-minute newscast from Huntley and Brinkley, one local newspaper, and two local radio stations.

Now, were I teenager in Yankton, I'd have a greatly expanded menu on NBC and CBS, but also ABC, Fox, CNN, MSNBC, Fox News, and the BBC on cable or satellite. I'd still have the local newspaper, but with a few clicks on my personal computer, I'd also have access to the great newspapers on a real-time basis in all the world capitals.

However, there is a striking difference between what's available to a teenager in South Dakota and to a young Muslim in Africa, the Middle East, the Subcontinent, or Southeast Asia. Ninety-six percent of the Internet use in the world is confined to 15 percent of the world's population. But even if we were able to wave the twenty-first century version of the magic wand and assure Internet access everywhere, it would not be enough, for it does us little good if we wire the world and short-circuit our secular souls. There is no delete button for hate and intolerance, no cut and paste to shift the values and ethos of one culture to another.

Just as we are outraged, puzzled, bewildered by the failure of other cultures to understand ours, we must also remember that there has been pitiful little appreciation for other cultures when they are viewed through a prism looking from West to East. It is here that the press has its most critical role. Just as there is globalization in economics and consumer markets, it is equally important to have globalization of the mass media marketplace. That requires publishers and broadcasters, editors and producers, reporters and anchormen to rise above parochial origins and examine a world of many colors, faiths, and economic and ideological interests in an enlightened and engaging fashion. Examine and analyze, not merely reflect and regurgitate.

In the current environment, there is far too much of the latter and too little of the former.

In this new universe created by The Big Bang of media expansion, there is always the danger of inciting rather than informing, and it happens at warp speed. Once the chain reaction of misinformation and deliberate deceit begins, it is difficult to stop, and the consequences can be disastrous.

Most of all, it is imperative that the primary media outlets remain fiercely independent, especially of government control, manipulation, and pressure. Those pressures come in many ways, even in the so-called "free press" societies. One of the most pernicious is the pressure to conform to a single perspective or face the lash of organized special interest groups, commentators, and cultural conformity.

In societies where the news and information media in all of its forms is directly controlled from the top down, the suppression of the people's right to know is a critical component in any evaluation of the human rights of the people involved. The ancient call, "Let my people go!" is now as much about intellectual freedom as it is about physical freedom.

As we begin this new millennium with the world of human rights and fundamental freedoms in such turmoil, we'll do well to remember that no superpower can administer just punishment or force societies to change their ways with military power alone, however great that military application may be.

The old lessons endure. The battle for hearts and minds remains as critical as the battles for streets and ports, skies and high ground. Enlightened, courageous, and independent journalists must be the honest brokers of this complex and dangerous new world.

It is not an assignment for the timid.

As a founding member of the Committee to Protect Journalists, I long have been interested in improving the legal, political, and cultural climate in which journalists operate around the world. It has been a constant struggle, and the following announcement from CPJ at the end of 2002 is a chilling reminder of the price too many journalists pay for their courageous and critical work.

ANNOUNCEMENT FROM THE COMMITTEE TO PROTECT
JOURNALISTS
NINETEEN JOURNALISTS KILLED FOR THEIR WORK IN 2002

Lowest Number on Record; Russia, Colombia, and the
West Bank Top List

New York, January 2, 2003—A total of nineteen journalists were killed worldwide for their work in 2002, according to the Committee to Protect Journalists (CPJ). This number marks a sharp decrease from 2001 when thirty-seven journalists were killed, eight of them while covering the war in Afghanistan. Of the nineteen journalists killed in 2002, most were targeted in direct reprisal for their work, and their killers had not been brought to justice at year's end.

This is the lowest number of journalists killed in the line of duty that CPJ has recorded since it began tracking the deaths in 1985. The dramatic drop is partially attributed to a decline in the number of world conflicts. According to CPJ research, a direct correlation exists between the number of journalists killed on the job and the incidence of violent conflict, which can give those who target journalists the ability to do so with impunity because of the instability that war fosters. In 1994, for example, sixty-six journalists were targeted for their work while civil wars raged in Algeria, Bosnia, and Rwanda.

Another factor in the decreasing number of journalists' deaths may be the result of the international attention that *The Wall Street Journal* reporter Daniel Pearl's kidnapping and murder early last year garnered. In the wake of Pearl's death, journalist safety became a priority for news organizations; many sent their staff to hostile-environment training, and reporters were better prepared in the field. At least two journalists survived being shot in the West Bank last spring because they were wearing flak jackets, while in Venezuela, bulletproof vests saved the lives of two more journalists.

Still, in 2002, journalists remained at great risk. In countries such as Russia, Colombia, Pakistan, India, Bangladesh, and the Philippines, local journalists were murdered in direct reprisal for their reporting on crime and corruption, most of them with impunity. Cameramen and photographers were especially vulnerable to cross fire and targeting by military forces—five were killed in 2002, including two who were covering conflict in the West Bank.

"While we are encouraged to see the number of deaths decrease this year, journalists are still being targeted and assassinated for doing their jobs," said CPJ executive director Ann Cooper. "Drug traffickers in Brazil, paramilitary groups in Colombia, and corrupt politicians in the Philippines are trying to silence journalists through intimidation and murder, and it has to stop."

In addition to the nineteen cases described in this report, CPJ continues to investigate four journalists who are missing and thirteen others whose killings may have been related to their professional work.

Russia and Colombia: Perennial Offenders

Some statistics fluctuate from year to year, but others remain constant in such countries as Russia and Colombia, where journalists die virtually every year because of their work. Three journalists were killed for their work in Russia in 2002: An editor of a newspaper known for its coverage of organized crime was shot eight times at point-blank range; a cameraman died in cross fire covering the fighting near the Chechen border; and a business reporter was bludgeoned to death on her way home.

In Colombia, three journalists also died in the line of duty:

The owner of a radio station and host of programs that criticized all sides of Colombia's civil war was pulled from his car, shot, and killed; a newspaper columnist who wrote about human rights abuses was shot in the head while walking to work; and a cameraman was killed in cross fire while covering fighting between the army and a paramilitary group.

The following list is a brief summary of the circumstances surrounding the deaths of each of the nineteen journalists killed for their work in 2002. For a more comprehensive list, go to: http://www.cpj.org./killed/killed02.html.

BANGLADESH: 1
Harunur Rashid, *Dainik Purbanchal,* March 2, Khulna
Rashid, a crime reporter for the Bengali-language newspaper *Dainik Purbanchal,* was ambushed by gunmen while riding his motorcycle to work. He was later brought to a hospital, where he died from a bullet wound to his chest, according to one account. Rashid, known as Rashid Khukon, wrote several stories exposing official corruption and linking criminal syndicates with outlawed Maoist guerrilla groups. He had received anonymous death threats throughout his career.

BRAZIL: 1
Tim Lopes, TV Globo, June 3, Rio de Janeiro
Lopes, 50, an award-winning investigative reporter with TV Globo, was kidnapped, tortured, and brutally murdered by drug traffickers while on assignment in an impoverished community on the outskirts of Rio de Janeiro. Working undercover with a hidden camera, Lopes was investigating a story about drug traffickers abusing drugs and minors. According to two suspects, Lopes was kidnapped, beaten, shot in the feet to keep him from escaping, and sentenced to death at a mock trial. A known drug trafficker then stabbed him with a sword and killed him, said the suspects.

COLOMBIA: 3

Orlando Sierra Hernández, *La Patria,* February 1, Manizales

Sierra, 42, a deputy editor and columnist for the newspaper *La Patria,* was shot in the head on his way to work and died two days later. Sierra wrote a popular Sunday column that criticized corrupt local party bosses and highlighted human rights abuses committed by leftist guerrillas, right-wing paramilitaries, and state security forces.

Héctor Sandoval, RCN Televisión, April 12, outside of Cali

Sandoval, a cameraman with RCN Televisión, died of gunshot wounds sustained while covering a firefight between the Colombian army and leftist rebels. He and his crew came under fire while traveling in a mountainous area where the army was pursuing rebel fighters who had just kidnapped a group of lawmakers. The crew had decided to turn back when an army helicopter opened fire on their vehicle, killing Sandoval and the vehicle's driver.

Efraín Varela Noriega, Radio Meridiano-70, June 28, Arauca

Varela, a radio host and station owner of Radio Meridiano-70, was killed while driving home after gunmen yanked him from his car and shot him in the face and chest. Varela hosted news and opinion programs that criticized all sides of Colombia's long-running civil war. Most recently, he had told listeners that right-wing paramilitary fighters had arrived in the area and were patrolling the streets.

INDIA: 1

Ram Chander Chaterpatti, *Poora Sach,* November 21, Sirsa

Chaterpatti, editor of the Hindu-language newspaper *Poora Sach,* died from injuries sustained one month earlier, when gunmen fired several shots at him. According to officials, members of a religious sect ordered Chaterpatti's murder after he wrote several articles about sexual abuse and other crimes allegedly committed in the sect's compound. Police have arrested three suspects.

NEPAL: 1

Nava Raj Sharma, *Kadam,* June 1, Kalikot

Sharma, editor of the Nepali-language weekly *Kadam,* was kidnapped and later killed by Maoist rebels who are fighting a guerrilla war to overthrow Nepal's constitutional monarchy. Sharma's badly mutilated body was found in mid-August; his eyes had been gouged out, his hands and legs cut, and he had been shot in the chest. One local journalist said Sharma had resisted pressure from rebels to turn *Kadam* into a Maoist propaganda organ.

PAKISTAN: 2
Daniel Pearl, *The Wall Street Journal,* date unknown, Karachi
Pearl, 38, South Asia bureau chief for *The Wall Street Journal,* was abducted while on his way to an interview at a restaurant in downtown Karachi on January 23. A group claiming responsibility for his kidnapping sent several e-mails to news organizations containing photographs of Pearl, calling him a spy, and threatening to kill him if a list of demands were not met. In late February, a graphic video received by U.S. government officials confirmed that Pearl had been brutally murdered by his captors. Four suspects were tried and found guilty of his murder in July.

Shahid Soomro, *Kawish,* October 20, Kandhkot
Soomro, a well-respected correspondent for the Sindhi-language newspaper *Kawish,* was assassinated in reprisal for his reporting on abuses committed during general elections held two weeks earlier. Three men came to Soomro's house at night and tried to abduct him. When he resisted, they shot the journalist at least nine times, killing him almost instantly. Members of an influential local family have been detained for questioning.

PALESTINIAN AUTHORITY TERRITORIES: 3
Raffaele Ciriello, freelance, March 13, Ramallah
Ciriello, an Italian freelance photographer on assignment for the Italian daily *Corriere Della Sera,* was killed by a burst of machine gun fire from the direction of an Israeli tank during the Israeli military offensive in the West Bank and Gaza. According to a journalist accompanying Ciriello, the photographer was trailing a group of Palestinian gunmen at the time of the incident. An Israel Defense Forces spokesman had no information about the shooting.

Imad Abu Zahra, freelance, July 12, Jenin
Zahra, a Palestinian freelance photographer, died after being hit
by Israel Defense Forces gunfire in the West Bank town of Jenin.
Together with a colleague, he had gone to photograph an Israeli
armored personnel carrier (APC) that had slammed into an electricity pole. They were facing two Israeli tanks when they started
taking pictures of the APC. Moments later, gunfire erupted from
the tanks, according to his colleague. Zahra was hit in the leg,
and died the next day.

Issam Tillawi, Voice of Palestine, September 22, Ramallah
Tillawi, a journalist and program host for the official Palestinian
National Authority radio station, Voice of Palestine (VOP), was
killed after being shot in the head by Israeli gunfire during protests in the West Bank city of Ramallah. According to Palestinian
sources, Tillawi was both covering and participating in demonstrations against the Israeli army's siege of Palestinian leader Yas-
ser Arafat's compound. VOP officials said he was wearing a jacket
marked "press."

PHILIPPINES: 2
Edgar Damalerio, *Zamboanga Scribe* and DXKP Radio, May 13, Pa-
gadian City
Damalerio, 32, managing editor of the weekly *Zamboanga Scribe,*
and a commentator on DXKP Radio, was shot and killed while
driving home from a press conference. Two witnesses in the car
identified the gunman as a local police officer, but he was only
briefly detained and was never charged. Damalerio was known
for his critiques of corruption among local politicians and the
police.

Sonny Alcantara, "Quo Vadis San Pablo" and *Kokus,* August
22, San Pablo
Alcantara, 51, a newspaper publisher and cable TV commentator,
was shot in the forehead and killed by a lone gunman near his
home. Investigators believe at least one accomplice informed the
gunman by cell phone of Alcantara's departure. He had recently
broken a story on his cable TV program about a local politician

in a corrupt land deal, while his newspaper covers politics and community affairs. No one has been charged with the murder.

RUSSIA: 3

Natalya Skryl, *Nashe Vremya*, March 9, Rostov-on-Don

Skryl, 29, a business reporter for the newspaper *Nashe Vremya*, died after being attacked from behind while walking home at night. She was struck in the head about a dozen times with a heavy, blunt object and died in the hospital the next day. Skryl reported on local business issues and was investigating an ongoing struggle for the control of a local metallurgical plant. Although none of her money or jewelry was taken, local officials initially announced robbery as the motive of the murder before closing the case in September.

Valery Ivanov, *Tolyatinskoye Obozreniye*, April 29, Togliatti

Ivanov, 32, editor of the newspaper *Tolyatinskoye Obozreniye*, was shot dead at point-blank range while entering his car outside his home. The gunman used a pistol with a silencer to shoot Ivanov eight times in the head and fled the scene on foot. Colleagues believe the killing is connected to the newspaper's reports on local organized crime, drug trafficking, and official corruption. No one has been charged in the case.

Roddy Scott, Frontline, September 26, Galashki Region, Ingushetia

Scott, 31, a British freelance cameraman working for Britain's Frontline television news agency, was killed following clashes between Russian forces and Chechen fighters near the border with Chechnya in Ingushetia's Galashki Region.

UGANDA: 1

Jimmy Higenyi, United Media Consultants and Trainers, January 12, Kampala

Higenyi, a student at United Media Consultants and Trainers, was covering an opposition rally as part of his journalism course work when he was killed. All political activity is banned in the country, and soon after the large group gathered, police fired into the crowd, killing Higenyi. Police acknowledge responsibility for the shooting, but no disciplinary action had been taken against the responsible officers at year's end.

VENEZUELA: 1

Jorge Ibraín Tortoza Cruz, *2001*, April 11, Caracas

Tortoza, 48, a photographer for the Caracas daily *2001*, was shot while covering violent clashes between opposition demonstrators and government supporters. He died later that same evening. The journalist was carrying his camera and a vest identifying him as a member of the press when he was shot in the head. Eyewitness accounts and videos of the scene implicate both the Venezuelan National Guard and the Caracas Metropolitan Police in the shooting.

Documenting the deaths, CPJ researchers apply stringent guidelines and journalistic standards to determine whether journalists were killed on assignment or as a direct result of their professional work. By publicizing and protesting these killings, CPJ helps change the conditions that foster violence against journalists. The death toll that CPJ compiles each year is one of the most widely cited measures of press freedom worldwide.

For more information about journalists killed in 2002, visit CPJ's Web site at http://www.cpj.org or call CPJ communications coordinator, Abi Wright, at (212) 465-9344, ext. 105.

The journalistic profession paid a very high price for covering the war in Iraq. For an updated list of those killed, consult the CPJ website.

CONCLUSION

If ignorance is enforced at the point of a gun or the threat of long imprisonment, all of us are diminished, for that ignorance is a cancer on the fundamental right of everyone everywhere to freely decide what they need and want to know about the world they occupy.

It is not just the freedom to make informed political judgments, but also the freedom and the necessity to make informed personal judgments without fear of reprisal from the state, the culture, or the community.

Only a vigorous and independent free press in all of its forms—from broadcast to print and the Internet—can provide that antidote to intellectual oppression.

As Thomas Paine wrote in *The Rights of Man,* ". . . though man may be kept ignorant, he cannot be made ignorant."

8

Human Rights and the Making of a Good Doctor

Eoin O'Brien, M.D.

> Public health professionals are among the most edu-
> cated and, occasionally, the most respected members of
> the community. Yet, except when an issue impinges on
> their particular interest, their impact on government
> policy is miniscule. . . . By mutual sharing, the good
> physician becomes part of the body and soul of the per-
> son he serves. If that trust and confidence are not
> abused, and if, with warmth and humility and compe-
> tency, the doctor proves his worth over time, the bond
> becomes as durable as love. When people and nations
> can agree on little else, those common bonds may be-
> come the bridge to understanding and peace. There is
> certainly no reason not to utilize this bridge, especially
> in the light of the dismal record of standard diplomacy.
>
> Kevin M. Cahill, M.D., *A Bridge to Peace*[1]

THE CENTER for International Health and Cooperation was
founded to promote the ethos that the physician in society can,
as the above quotation illustrates, be a bridge between politicians
and peace, or as an earlier publication put it, if every politician
has a doctor, is this not a great "untapped resource," a resource
with the potential to influence for the good? That is assuming, of
course, that the doctor in society is prepared for such a role.[2] In
The Untapped Resource (edited and introduced by Kevin Cahill),
Hugh Carey, then a member of the United States Congress, said:

"In fact, a review of our own history will show that when we had less we did more proportionately. When we were not so strong, we were more generous to the weak. When we were less well fed, we helped others fend off famine." He went on prophetically (this was 1971): "If our country is not to act as a policeman of the world and wield the bomb as a club, then perhaps it is in our own interest and in the interest of humanity we might consider ourselves as corpsman to mankind, bearing the balm of healing and helping. Exporting our know-how in health care at relatively little cost to ourselves should be an attractive alternative to some high-cost, low-yield programs of foreign aid that we now support under the name of mutual security."[3]

The Traditional "Good Doctor"

This book has within its shell three strata of discussion— "foundations, fault lines, and corrections." The doctor must be seen as indispensable to the "foundations" of any tradition in humanitarian rights, but more importantly, I hope to show that "corrections" are needed, and needed urgently, if the doctor is to fulfill his/her potential in contributing to humanitarian action. In short, the good doctor in today's world must be versed in human rights, and if this is to happen, the undergraduate student has to be taught the subject.

The doctor in society has been a figure of immense influence since the beginning of time. The physician has been portrayed in literature, music, film, and caricature, not always with kindness, but the status of the physician in society has greatly exceeded that of other professions, probably even exceeding that of the cleric. Many assumptions are made in the portrayal of the doctor, and many commentators fail to acknowledge that a doctor is as susceptible to the failings of humankind as anyone else. Or, as Shaw would have put it: "Doctors, if no better than other men, are certainly no worse."[4]

The good doctor has to be all things to all men. He has to

fulfill the requirements of a taxing undergraduate curriculum; he then has to undergo a postgraduate period of betterment, which, depending on his chosen specialty, can be very arduous; he must then be trusted by his patients; accepted by his peers; fulfill the dictates of the jurisdiction in which he practices; acquiesce with the dictates of his professional bodies so as to gain admission to them; and perhaps, depending on the role he casts for himself, also be a scientist and researcher prepared to write and present on his chosen avocation; be a teacher; head a large department; be an administrator; be capable of communicating with his patients, his colleagues, and scientific peers; be prepared not only to keep himself abreast of advances in an ever-changing discipline, but to have his knowledge and skills assessed regularly; be able to cooperate with colleagues in the delivery of health care and with colleagues abroad in the furtherance of science; be willing to work antisocial hours and to adjust his private life accordingly; he must not contract an illness that might endanger his patients' health; he must be prepared to face the medico-legal consequences for incompetence, real or imaginary; and above all, and most difficultly, he must acknowledge the Socratic dictum, "Know thyself."

Not many, one would think, could be attracted by such a job description, yet, thankfully for society, many are. My advice will add to the burden of the good doctor by calling for a further quality that carries an inevitable demand. In a world faced with humanitarian strife and with large populations in turmoil seeking refuge in stable and more prosperous nations, today's good doctor must be alert to the complex discipline of human rights, which brings the inevitable moral imperative of being aware of the prejudices that doctors, as others in society, inherit through the cultural, religious, and ethnic influences of their formative environment.

I suspect more has been written on the making of a good doctor than what makes, for example, a good solicitor, fireman, or accountant. Apart from numerous books, there are university courses devoted to the topic; for example, the Northeastern Ohio Universities College of Medicine offers a course over two months entitled, "In search of the Good Doctor."[5] The *British Medical Journal* saw the subject as one of such importance as to merit an issue devoted to "What's a good doctor and how do you make one?"[6] The editor accepted at the outset that his journal faced an impossible task, but one that nonetheless was worth undertaking. This in-depth analysis, running to some 50,000 words, discusses, among other relevant issues, the making of a good doctor as seen from the perspective of the patients, nurses, medical students, women, and doctors; it assesses the expectations of society, governing bodies, and the health services; and considers the necessity for the good doctor to be able to communicate, to remain knowledgeable and skilled, and to be subject to assessment of competency. However, only in the correspondence columns (a letter from Khartoum Hospital) can any reference be found to the need for a good doctor to be aware of human rights issues: "In the developing world with its deficient facilities and patients who need to eat before they need medical care, the medical profession needs input from a belief in humanity and the ethics of the job more than scientific professionalism."[7]

The journalist, Polly Toynbee, reviewing the qualities that the General Medical Council sees as necessary in the making of a good doctor, had this to say:

> What makes the perfect modern doctor? The General Medical Council has drawn up new guidance for medical schools as a framework on which to base their curriculums and assessments. *Tomorrow's Doctors* is an idealistic compendium of the best qualities every new doctor should acquire. If medical schools could, indeed, turn out doctors molded to this template, then we should expect a new generation of scholar saints and gentle scientists— wise, knowledgeable, sensitive, collegiate, humble, and good beyond imagining.[8]

In short, the traditional good doctor as epitomized by Luke Fildes in his famous Victorian painting, *The Doctor*.[9]

THE HUMANITIES IN THE MAKING OF A GOOD DOCTOR

If human rights and humanitarian affairs seem to be neglected in the making of a good doctor, it does not seem to be the case with the teaching of the humanities, which has seen a remarkable resurgence in the last few decades, especially in the U.S. The Internet provides a truly remarkable compilation of curricula, such as the New York University on-line syllabi of courses in medical humanities,[10] or the U.K. equivalent "Medical Humanities Resource Database," compiled by the Centre for Health Informatics in Multiprofessional Education, University College London.[11] The importance of this is not so much the relevance of the humanities to human rights, but rather that an awareness of the former serves as a means of bringing students close to the moral dilemmas of medicine. An acquaintance with the humanities, especially literature, imparts an appreciation of the profundity of human existence and a deeper realization of the human condition. Literature is not only enjoyable, but when it enables us to discover how great writers view illness, suffering, and death, it becomes an enriching formative experience.

Take, as an example, Samuel Beckett writing on the humanitarian tragedy of Saint Lô, the small town in Normandy that was devastated in one night by an allied bombing blitz that left hardly a house standing,[12] and the efforts of a bewildered group of Irish physicians grappling with all that was so foreign to them:

> And yet the whole enterprise turned from the beginning on the establishing of a relation in the light of which the therapeutic relation faded to the merest of pretexts. What was important was not our having penicillin when they had none, nor the unregarding munificence of the French Ministry of Reconstruction, . . . but the occasional glimpse obtained, by us in them and, who knows, by them in us (for they are an imaginative people), of that smile at the human condition as little to be extinguished by bombs as to be broadened by the elixirs of Burroughes and Welcome, the smile deriding, among other things, the having and not having, the giving and the taking, sickness and health. . . . I suspect that

our pains were those inherent in the simple and necessary and yet so unattainable proposition that their way of being we, was not our way and that our way of being they, was not their way. It is only fair to say that many of us had never been abroad before.[13]

Or if one moves forward to read of a unique tribute paid by maestro Leonard Bernstein to his physician:

It is hard not to love Kevin; it is equally hard to know which Kevin you are loving. He is that complicated creature once called a "Medicine Man," a term that presents us with a host of dualities: pillar of society/leprechaun; medieval alchemist/medical master; shaman/clinician; witchdoctor/psychologist; juggler/saint. I have observed him in all three phases, I think; I have appeared at his office in despair, begging for some magic pill, only to leave like Fred Astaire, lighter than air, with not even a placebo to con me on my way. How does this happen? What went on in there during that hour or more, aside from a cardiogram, some palpation, and what I think of as the *Stethoscopic Follies,* the shortest show in New York. Oh, yes, the prerequisite blood sample; but all that surely didn't take an hour plus. Of course not; we *talked.*[14]

These quotations from a rich literary archive are chosen merely to suggest that the humanities can at least prepare the intellectual soul of the doctor-in-the-making for the tougher stuff of human rights. The artist can hone the sensitivities, kindle a desire to participate, even contribute toward the betterment of the panorama of living and dying in which the doctor is always center-stage. The arts cannot teach us to be good human beings but they can kindle in us a desire to try to be more humane, to banish prejudice, to be kinder and more considerate of the foibles and irritations that constitute the non-medical presentation of all clinical dilemmas. Put another way, medicine demands compassion and feeling, or such, at least, would be the public's perception of the good doctor. Paradoxically, the practice of medicine makes the exclusion of sentiment a prerequisite for the survival of self, and the process, begun in early studentship, soon becomes so integral a part of the scientific persona that the dissipated gems of idealism, among which, of course, may be found compassion, become unrecognizable. The years of training so carefully constructed by our institutions initially blunt and, finally, pervert the purity of avocation and the sensibility of youth, essences to be found in most medical students but so few doctors. It is chastening but not necessarily a balm to existence, to have this protective wall around one annihilated. At least being aware of the contradictory influences that will confront the doctor in society places the medical student at an advantage in choosing the correct moral stance.

HUMAN RIGHTS AND THE UNDERGRADUATE CURRICULUM

The need for the teaching of human rights in medical schools has been long recognized. For example, in 1992, the British Medical Association (BMA) declared: "We recommend that all medical schools incorporate medical ethics into the core curriculum and that all medical graduates make a commitment, by means of an affirmation, to observe an ethical code such as the WMA's (World Medical Association) International Code of Medical Ethics."[15] In 1993, the General Medical Council in the U.K. stated that a core-objective of the undergraduate degree in medicine included a "knowledge and understanding of . . . ethical and legal issues relevant to the practice of medicine," as well as an "awareness of the moral and ethical responsibilities involved in individual patient care."[16] In 1999, the World Medical Association resolved that in so far as medical ethics and human rights form an integral part of the work and culture of the medical profession, and of the history, structure, and objectives of the World Medical Association, "it is hereby resolved that the WMA strongly recommends to Medical Schools worldwide that the teaching of Medical Ethics and Human Rights be included as an obligatory course in their curricula."[17] Moreover, the United Nations has published, among other documents relating to the topic, *Guidelines for National Plans of Action for Human Rights Education,* in which it envisages human rights education as being part of the education of "pre-school and primary, secondary, university, and other institutions of higher learning levels of education."[18] The many international declarations and standards on medical ethics and human rights are available in a number of compilations.[19,20] However, these recommendations have fallen largely on deaf ears. Despite these prestigious and authoritative mandates for the teaching of human rights to medical undergraduates, there appears to be no systematic human rights education within the curricula of the U.K.'s twenty-seven medical schools.[21]

DOCTORS AND PREJUDICE

Why should doctors, particularly those living in affluent, stable societies, have to concern themselves with humanitarian issues? The *New Dictionary of Medical Ethics* has postulated four reasons:

> First, as citizens of the modern world, they should know about the most dynamic, complex, and challenging modern movement; after all, their own rights and dignity as well as those of their patients are at issue. Second, health policies, programs and practices, and clinical research may inadvertently violate human rights. Thirdly, violations of each of the rights have important adverse health effects on individuals and groups. Finally, promoting human rights is now understood as an essential part of the efforts to promote and protect public health.[22]

No one can disagree with these recommendations, but do they go far enough?

To me, there would seem to be at least three other reasons why aspiring doctors should be taught human rights. The first is that young doctors (and some old ones) are fundamentally good and even better than good, they are idealists who are often anxious to give back some of what society (or parental affluence) has given to them. Or as Shaw (who said so much so well nearly a century ago) put it: "Unless a man is led to medicine or surgery through a very exceptional technical aptitude, or because doctoring is a family tradition, or because he regards it unintelligently as a lucrative and gentlemanly profession, his motives in choosing the career of a healer are clearly generous. However, actual practice may disillusion and corrupt him, his selection in the first instance is not a selection of a base character."[23] If the idealism of the young doctor is not exposed, at least in theory, to the calamities of humanitarian crises in the world and the means of alleviating them, the fire of youthful idealism is denied.

A second more practical reason is that the movement of populations is such today that the doctor practicing even in the most settled and affluent of societies is likely to be called upon to care for displaced people. Or as a group of bodies involved in human rights expressed it:

> Throughout history, society has charged healers with the duty of understanding and alleviating causes of human suffering. In the past century, the world has witnessed ongoing epidemics of armed conflicts and violations of international human rights, epidemics that have devastated and continue to devastate the health and well being of humanity. As we enter the twenty-first century, the nature and extent of human suffering have compelled health providers to redefine their understanding of health and the scope of their professional interests and responsibilities.[24]

Finally, and most importantly, the teaching of human rights should serve as a means of dispelling, or at least of bringing into focus, the prejudices that are present in us all, and which can lead to discrimination at many levels of health care. A report to the UN Committee on Economic, Social, and Cultural Rights presented alarming evidence that decisions about access to investigations and treatment in the U.K. are sometimes motivated by who the patients are rather than by their health care needs. The report highlights serious shortcomings in protecting the international right to the highest attainable standard of health as a consequence of which some doctors discriminate against vulnerable groups, such as the elderly, prisoners, patients with HIV/AIDS, people with learning disabilities, and, surprisingly, women with coronary heart disease are denied the treatment facilities afforded to men.[25]

At an international level, the former High Commissioner for Human Rights, Mary Robinson, has identified discrimination and stigmatization as important impediments in the global battle against HIV and AIDS. "HIV/AIDS is one of the greatest human rights and health challenges facing the world today. HIV/AIDS-related stigma and discrimination—including discrimination in health care settings—continue to be the primary driving forces behind the epidemic by undermining prevention, treatment, care, and support . . . Health care professionals have a crucial role to play in ensuring respect for human rights, and the right to health and to nondiscrimination in particular."[26] Indeed the issue of discrimination in medicine is one of considerable concern globally, and is evident not only in the U.K. but also in the U.S.,[27] in India,[28] and no doubt in any country that cares to examine the issue.

What many doctors will not know, simply because they have never been told, is that discrimination contravenes a number of ethical codes. First, it violates the Hippocratic Oath, which anticipated the Universal Declaration of Human Rights by nearly 2.5 millennia, and which is just as relevant to contemporary international law today as it was in 400 B.C.[29] Second, it violates one of the six nonderogable obligations within Article 12 of the International Covenant on Economic, Social, and Cultural Rights, which asserts the human right of each individual to the highest attainable standard of health.[30]

However, there are some promising happenings that augur well for dealing with the problem of stigmatization in medicine. The appointment of Paul Hunt from the Human Rights Centre of the University of Essex as Special Rapporteur on The Right to Health to the UN Commission on Human Rights, whose overall brief is to "promote and protect the international right to health," suggests that after a long period of neglect, "the human rights system, WHO, and other members of the UN family are beginning to treat seriously the international right to health . . .

Nobody can be sure of the implications of the renewed international interest in the right to health. But I suspect the implications are long-term and, at least for some countries, far-reaching."[31] The impressive Publications Program of the Office of the United Nations High Commissioner for Human Rights (OHCHR), which addresses training and education in human rights for "indigenous peoples, minorities, professional groups, and educational institutions," is another welcome move.[32] The launch of a global campaign to integrate health and human rights in undergraduate and postgraduate medical training in an effort to "expunge stigmatization from medical practice" can be seen as another step in the right direction.[33] All the more reason, therefore, for the medical schools of the world to join in and play their crucial role in the international move to establish a right to health for all.

WHAT SHOULD MEDICAL STUDENTS BE TAUGHT ON HUMAN RIGHTS?

Human rights is a complex discipline in its own stead, but not one that has yet developed into a specialty in the traditional manner in medicine, whereby an expert becomes a head of a department attracting others with a kindred interest to devise a suitable curriculum for undergraduate teaching. So, at least for the immediate future, even if the deans of medical schools were prepared to introduce the subject into the undergraduate curricula, most universities would simply not have the staff with the necessary interest or expertise in the subject to prepare and teach its many complexities. The British Medical Association (BMA) has examined the issue in detail by concentrating on: (1) the composition and scope of ethics and human rights training; (2) what doctors need to know; (3) how they can obtain that knowledge, and (4) how they can use that knowledge effectively.[34]

As all medical schools have a course on medical ethics, the BMA begins logically by examining the mutually complimentary roles of ethics and human rights. Ethics helps students to understand *why* abuse should be resisted, and human rights should help them discover *what* should be done and *how* to resist abuse. Though there is considerable overlap between ethics and human rights, "ethics teaching needs to be supplemented by human rights guidance."[35] Medical ethics has been taught in medical schools for many years in most countries of the world, but the quality of the courses available varies greatly and herein lies a further caveat for the teaching of human rights; the content and standard of the courses are related to the availability of teachers with the knowledge and enthusiasm to inspire their students, and various bodies have responded by producing case-based teaching packs, evaluated through workshops.[36]

Three conclusions that may be drawn from the comprehensive BMA review relating to medical ethics are: (1) many of the current courses on medical ethics are in need of revision; (2) the teaching of medical ethics and human rights should go hand-in-hand, but be designed in unison so as to avoid the repetition that seems inevitable if they are designed in isolation; and (3) the achievement of the later objective would serve as an ideal opportunity for effecting the former.

At first glance there appears to be a wealth of teaching material available for the teaching of human rights to medical students, but more careful assessment shows that the material is fragmented and lacking the collaborative cohesion that should be possible with contemporary distance learning techniques, which is likely to be the key to success. Moreover, it must be borne in mind that the teaching of medical ethics and human rights on an international scale must be sufficiently flexible to take account of the political, religious, and social mores that will to some extent govern the national attitude to human rights issues, though this should not be taken as implying that international principles governing human rights can be compromised, but rather be seen as a means of influencing doctors within the sensitivities of the environment in which they will later practice and face abuses to human rights.

The range of material available for human rights education extends from that which medical organizations produce for doctors practicing in societies in which particular human rights abuses occur, for example, the International Rehabilitation Council for Torture Victims (IRCTV) based in Denmark has established training programs dealing with the rehabilitation and care of torture survivors in Asia, Africa, the Balkans, and Latin America. Likewise the Asia-Pacific Forum runs teaching programs and rehabilitation services in Australia, Bangladesh, India, Indonesia, Nepal, New Guinea, New Zealand, Pakistan, Papua, the Philippines, and Sri Lanka. Specific programs in ethics and human rights for prison officers have been established in the former Soviet Union and Southeast Asia by the International Committee of the Red Cross. The organization International Physicians for the Prevention of Nuclear War (IPPNW) works closely with the International Federation of Medical Students concentrating on human rights issues from the perspective of conflict prevention. Another medical student initiative, Human Rights Union for Medical Action (HURUMA), grew out of the work undertaken in Africa by the International Federation of Medical Students and African student groups.[37,38] The Commonwealth Medical Association (CMA) has developed an ethics training manual for developing countries,[39] which integrates ethical principles and extracts from human rights conventions with the aim of making it necessary for all health professionals to attend one training module annually as part of the requirements for renewal of the license to practice.[40] Moreover, the CMA has taken the innovative step of linking each statement of ethics to the provisions of the various UN human rights conventions and declarations, thereby allowing that while doctors in developing countries would not necessarily share the same cultural standards or views about medical ethics, they should nevertheless be aware of an obligation to respect the health-related human rights specified in international instruments that their governments have legally ratified.[41]

After the fall of the Marcos regime in the Philippines in 1986, the new government made a strong commitment to promote human rights through education, and this resulted in a framework for human rights education that "has been seen by some commentators as a useful model of who should be involved and what can be achieved."[42] The Consortium for Health and Human Rights, with a mandate to carry out education, research, and advocacy work, consists of the François-Xavier Bagnoud Center for Health and Human Rights, Global Lawyers and Physicians, Physicians for Human Rights, and International Physicians for the Prevention of Nuclear War. Each of the constituent bodies of the Consortium has produced training courses in various aspects of health care and human rights.[43] In the Netherlands, the Johannes Wier Foundation has produced a teaching module designed for doctors, nurses, and paramedics, which, using a case study approach, places students in "real life" situations with victims of violent crime, torture and death in custody, rape in wartime, forensic anthropology, and the administration of justice.[44]

Most of the material I refer to is designed for specific groups, or for doctors working in areas where human rights abuse is likely to occur. What is happening in the medical schools? A survey of medical schools in the U.K. and U.S. showed a willingness to consider human rights in the curriculum, but there was considerable confusion between what constituted medical ethics and human rights, and overall these surveys revealed that, in reality, little was being taught on human rights.[45] Indeed, there is some evidence that in countries in which human rights abuses occur, the medical schools and medical organizations are active in teaching awareness of human rights, examples being Turkey, India, the Philippines, Indonesia, Malaysia, and Nepal.[46] Increasingly, the pressure and impetus for the teaching of human rights has come from medical students' organizations even though they, like their deans, are very conscious of the demands being made for more subjects to be compressed into an already overloaded curriculum.[47] In many medical schools, the students organize work experience in areas of need and deprivation, which may impart more about human rights than didactic teaching.

In the U.K., Physicians for Human Rights,[48] in conjunction with Rachel Maxwell and Derrick Pounder, has developed a cross-disciplinary course entitled, "Medicine and Human Rights," which is available free on the Internet and has been adopted by the University of Dundee as part of the undergraduate curriculum, and has now been taken up by other medical schools in the U.K.[49] This module on the Internet is designed "for those with no prior knowledge about human rights as they impact on the practice of medicine." It deals with issues that include medical involvement in torture, the diagnosis and rehabilitation of torture victims, doctors' involvement in the death penalty, human rights and public health, women's rights and rape in war, mechanisms of redress for human rights abuses in member states of the European Community, and seeking asylum.[50] The module had been used in Russia, India, and Israel to teach human rights to lawyers and scientists, as well as to medical students. It has also been incorporated by the Centre for Enquiry into Health and Allied Themes (CEHAT) into a one-year diploma in the Civics and Politics Department of Bombay University,[51] and into an intercalated BSc in International Health at the University College London.[52]

Another initiative that differs from other available options is one that cuts across the boundaries of academe and makes no distinction between undergraduate and postgraduate status, the younger or older participant, but seeks rather to educate those working, or contemplating work, in the field of humanitarian crisis relief. The International Diploma in Humanitarian Assistance, which is conferred by the Center for International Health and Cooperation at Fordham University, the Royal College of Surgeons in Ireland, and the University of Geneva, has been conferred on more than 400 graduates from over eighty nations. The one-month intensive residential course has a distinguished faculty that comprehensively covers the ethical and human rights aspects of humanitarian assistance including, among many topics, the historical background to humanitarian assistance, coping with humanitarian crises and protecting human rights, international law and human rights, planning and management of humanitarian relief in strife-torn communities, preventive diplomacy, law and ethics, environmental health, torture, land mines and trauma, sexual violence and rape, the military aspects to humanitarian crisis, the role of the media, and the psychological and personal health of international relief workers.[53]

If the growing imperative for teaching human rights to medical students is to be achieved, rhetoric and the passing of international resolutions will not solve the problem. The biggest difficulty for the deans of medical schools will not be any lack of acknowledgement of the importance of human rights for the doctors graduating from their medical schools, or, indeed, of willingness to introduce the subject, but rather the impossibility of implementing a meaningful and well-structured course without having suitable teachers. In this regard, medical schools would do well to take heed of what has been achieved in the Open University with distance learning, and the international experts in human rights would do well to pool their expertise in producing electronic learning modules in medical ethics and human rights for incorporation into the undergraduate curricula of medical schools across the world. In this regard, it is of relevance to note that European Biomed funding was obtained in 1996 to produce distance-learning workbooks on core themes in medical ethics for use across Europe. This project, known as the European Biomedical Ethics Practitioner Education (EBEPE) project, was co-coordinated by the Imperial College School of Medicine in London in partnership with the Instituut voor Gezondheidsethick in Maastricht, the Instituto Psicoanalitico per la Richerche Socali in Rome, the Zentrum fur Ethik in der Medizin in Freiburg, and the Department of Philosophy at the University of Turku in Finland. The training pack was published in 1999 with the objective of encouraging health professionals to assess differing approaches to resolving dilemmas by illustrating how the same ethical challenges are handled in different European countries.[54]

In concluding, it would not be unreasonable to ask skeptically if there is any evidence that the teaching of human rights to medical students makes them better doctors. Intuitively my response would be affirmative, but we live in a world where evidence is demanded for all statements, and to be fair, the incorporation of human rights in the medical school curricula, as I have stressed, is not one to be undertaken lightly. A few international surveys have indeed shown that the teaching of human rights to medical students does increase awareness by allowing doctors to detach themselves from the prejudicial influences of their social background, but where doctors are faced with human rights abuse education alone will not solve their dilemmas, and the need for collegiate support then becomes necessary.[55] More evidence on the value of teaching human rights is clearly needed but in fairness may be difficult to obtain, at least until the teaching of the subject is standardized to internationally accepted minimum standards.

If medicine, with its long-established tradition of caring, has been slow in acknowledging human rights, I hope I have not so much excused the profession for its shortcomings in this regard, but rather enunciated the real difficulties it faces in achieving what it recognizes as an urgent imperative. The symposium, "Traditions, Values, and Humanitarian Action," has served as a timely stimulus to assess the place of humanitarian action within the tradition of medicine, not merely as an audit of the current state of affairs within the undergraduate curriculum, but as the impetus to develop structures for the future implementation of human rights in the training of doctors. The teaching of human rights will not, of course, abolish the worldwide abuse of human rights, but it is an essential component in the fight to make the world a better place for all to live.

Part 3

Civilization cannot survive without the stimulation provided by the movement of goods, ideas, and people. There are problems associated with mass human migrations but, historically, the benefits have far outweighed the price of a policy of isolationism. I include, therefore, a chapter on immigration in the Foundations section of this book. There is another chapter in the Fault Lines section. In this section, Ambassador Jan Eliasson presents the positive, even necessary, aspects of immigration in an area, Europe, where misunderstanding, and even manipulation of economic statistics, have caused serious political tensions.

9

Immigration in Europe: Promise or Peril?

Ambassador Jan Eliasson[1]

> We should strive towards one single global set of princi-
> ples for all types of migration in the long run. In an
> ideal world, international migration would not be more
> difficult for the individual than migration within coun-
> tries.
>
> Swedish State Secretary for Migration Affairs,
> Gun-Britt Andersson[2]

THE EUROPEAN UNION (EU) is basically a project of common
values aimed at creating a life in dignity for all its inhabitants.
Granted, this is often overshadowed by economic and political
matters; by the enlargement process, the development of the
Euro zone, and other issues that make up the substance of the
construction of a union.

Even though the Union began as an economic association, its
founding partners always viewed it as an important tool to ensure
that Europe would never again be torn apart by war, or fall back
into totalitarianism. Economic and political integration, it was
thought, would make war between members unthinkable, and
improve living conditions for their populations.

As such, it has performed remarkably well. The EU has successfully worked to reduce differences between member countries
through a redistribution of resources from the wealthier members to the less affluent. And the Union is now in the process of

enlargement, attempting to bring the same positive effects to the Eastern and Mediterranean parts of Europe.

In a similar vein, the EU is one of the biggest donors of development and humanitarian aid in the world. The only five countries to live up to the goal promoted by the United Nations (UN) of giving 0.7 percent of GDP as foreign aid are all European—Norway and EU members Denmark, Luxembourg, the Netherlands, and Sweden.[3]

Over the years, the EU has been a major supporter of international humanitarian assistance and action, mainly through the UN. All EU members have joined the Universal Declaration of Human Rights and the 1951 Refugee Convention. Europe has made a collective effort of enforcing human rights through the European Convention on Human Rights, and the European Court of Human Rights. The EU as a group has been a strong supporter of most major international treaties on humanitarian issues such as the rights of children, migrants, and women, and is today a driving force behind the International Criminal Court.

The European Union's traditional support for humanitarian values may now be challenged, as an effect of reactions to recent developments in the area of immigration. Attitudes toward immigrants appear to be increasingly negative. According to human rights organizations, EU support for the absolute right of asylum is wavering.

The direction the EU chooses to go on the issue of immigration will have strong ramifications not only on life in Europe, but also on the whole international climate in a day and age when religion and ethnic origin increasingly become dividing rather than uniting factors. There is an urgent need internationally to define common values across religious and ethnic divides.

THE IMMIGRATION CRISIS

Throughout history, individuals, groups, and peoples have moved to Europe and within Europe. The continent has also been a huge area of origin for migrants. Millions of Europeans left for America during the nineteenth and twentieth centuries. Migration has always been a major feature of European life.

When different cultures come into contact with each other, none of them are left unchanged. Thus, migration has helped form our countries as they are today. But this is a simple fact of life and history that seems all too easily forgotten. It certainly appears to be held in little regard in the current period.

In recent years, a wave of xenophobia has again affected the European continent. Country after country has seen populist anti-immigration parties spring to prominence, calling for restrictions on immigration, tougher guidelines for immigrants, and sometimes for their forcible expulsion.

These messages have hit a raw nerve and received favorable responses from parts of the electorate. Fear appears to have set in among the political strategists. Fear of losing power and control. Fear that this apparent right-wing surge would turn into something ugly. Europe has seen it all before, and the memories are frightening.

Certainly, some have also seen it as an opportunity.

In order to fight these tendencies, or to exploit them, many political parties have moved to the right on immigration issues, embracing some of the ideas of their anti-immigration colleagues, while rejecting their ideologies. Several left-of-center administrations have been swept from power in what began to look like a major political shift to the right in Europe. It has become conventional knowledge that Europe is in the midst of an immigration crisis, facing masses of asylum seekers and illegal immigrants.

Time for a Different Argument

Anti-immigration parties claim that the crisis with immigration stems from the numbers, that there are too many immigrants in our societies.

We will argue that this image of immigration is false and that the opposite is true. Europe needs *more* immigrants.

Europeans are growing older and are having fewer children. Without immigration, the population of most EU countries would already be sinking. For Italy, this is already the case. Our economies are sluggish. Diversity is seen by many as threatening, at the same time that business schools are teaching diversity management and extolling its many benefits. Many thousands of immigrants go unemployed, yet there are large skill gaps in the labor market.

The effort to close the door to illegal immigrants and asylum seekers is creating a conflict of conscience for many humanitarian-minded Europeans. Our support for global solidarity, human rights, and equality makes it difficult to justify sending people back to unstable countries or abject poverty. Policies of restriction may also add to xenophobia, in fact legitimizing it.

Taking a tough stand on illegal immigration and border controls may pick up votes in the short run. However, it may hurt long-term goals such as securing European growth and welfare, fighting racism and xenophobia, and projecting generosity and humanity.

Recent actions and statements indicate that this is already clear to large segments of the political and business sectors. However, they have been ineffective in communicating these arguments in the public forum. The arguments for immigration need to be stated clearly and honestly, without avoiding a discussion of the problems and risks involved. Otherwise, the field will be left open for populist rabble-rousers to continue to ply their trade.

Nevertheless, increased immigration is not a solution to the fundamental causes of global migration, for example, the fact that many millions of people feel compelled to leave their home countries in search of freedom and better opportunities to live decent lives.

Therefore, it is also high time to strengthen the dialogue and the partnership with the immigrants' countries of origin. In an overarching sense, large-scale immigration can be seen as a symptom of deep-seated development problems that industrial and developing countries have to address in close cooperation. If we can successfully promote global economic and social development, migration does not have to be a desperate and risky activity, but a strong engine for flexible and growing economies.

THE RECENT HISTORICAL FRAMEWORK

We believe that Europe should absorb more immigrants than we currently allow, both for humanitarian reasons and for reasons of self-interest. At the moment, this is a matter of dispute in Europe. A brief review of the postwar era may shed some light on why.

The current political environment of immigration did not develop overnight. Some of the far-right parties now enjoying political successes have roots in the ideologies that tore Europe apart in the 1930s and 1940s.

In the aftermath of World War II, Europe did not have an inclination for racism and xenophobia. There was a continent to rebuild, and lost years to recuperate. During the following two decades of recovery and growth, local labor markets could not supply enough workers, especially in Northern Europe. Immigrants were actively recruited, mostly within Europe. Hundreds of thousands of Greeks and Italians—and, later, Turks—moved north, to countries like Germany and Sweden.

Most labor immigrants were expected to be temporary visitors, but many chose to stay permanently. In a climate of low unemployment and rapid standard-of-living increases, they were needed, and societies had relatively few problems absorbing large numbers of foreign workers.

END OF A GOLDEN ERA

Much of this changed with the oil crisis and the stagnation of the late 1970s and early 1980s. Unemployment rose as economies faltered. Labor immigration in Europe declined drastically.

The end of the 1980s and the early 1990s brought a new trend—large numbers of refugees fleeing from conflict zones inside and outside of Europe. The lifting of the Iron Curtain and the end of the cold war brought unforeseen consequences. Old rivalries and animosities, frozen by decades of ideological, superpower struggle, now heated up again.

Places like Yugoslavia, Afghanistan, and Somalia erupted in violent ethnic and religious conflict. Asylum seekers flocked to the EU in previously unprecedented numbers. At the peak in 1992, 675,460 people applied for asylum in the EU.[4] A decade later, in 2001, the number was only about 57 percent of that, or 384,530 applicants.[5]

In 1992, immigration to the EU reached top levels. Family reunification immigration soared, and Germany opened up a generous return program for ethnic Germans from the former Soviet bloc. All in all, three million people migrated to the EU in 1992,[6] compared to an average over the ten years since then of around 1.4 million per year.

States were not prepared for this sudden influx. They started amending asylum regulations that were deemed too generous, and increased efforts to curb illegal immigration. Anti-immigrant sentiments grew.

In a European-wide EU survey of racism and xenophobia, the Eurobarometer opinion poll of 1997, 65 percent of respondents agreed that there were already enough minority residents and that accepting more would cause problems. Twenty percent agreed that all immigrants, legal and illegal, and their children, even those born in the EU, should be sent back to their country of origin.[7]

It has become increasingly clear that drawing political capital on the fear of strangers has made a comeback with a vengeance.

Taking a Stand against Xenophobia . . . and Failing

The 1999 national elections in Austria created a crisis for the EU. Joerg Haider's far-right Freedom Party won massive support and was invited into a coalition government. Haider had expressed sympathies for aspects of the Nazi regime in Germany, and his party used and encouraged xenophobia to gain votes. Critics warned that this would legitimize and give a boost to xenophobia across Europe. It was seen as an intolerable development and an embarrassment to the Union.

The EU reacted strongly and imposed sanctions on Austria's participation in EU affairs in 2000. However, the move was controversial, with many predicting that it would be counter-productive. After seven months of divisive debate, the sanctions were lifted. The Freedom Party remained in power.

In Search of a Response

Less than a year later, when media mogul, Silvio Berlusconi, became Prime Minister of Italy with the help of the ex-fascist National Alliance and the xenophobic Lega Nord, the response from the EU was restrained. As Danish Foreign Minister Mogens Lykketoft observed: "I believe we learned a lesson from Austria."[8]

The United Nations High Commissioner on Refugees (UNHCR) has criticized Italy repeatedly for being the only EU country without adequate asylum legislation. In August 2002, a new asylum law was finally enacted. But the Bossi-Fini law (named after its sponsors, the leaders of coalition members Lega Nord and the National Alliance) is controversial. It has drawn strong criticism from the UNHCR, among other things, for not allowing appeals to halt expulsion.[9]

By current EU standards, however, Italian immigration policies now appear more mainstream in character. In a very short period of time, the focus on the immigration issue has shifted from the fight against racism to the fight against illegal immigrants and asylum abusers.

IF YOU CAN'T BEAT THEM, JOIN THEM?

In France, President Jacques Chirac, after facing off with surprise opponent, extreme right-winger Le Pen, has made it his top priority to fight crime, an issue closely connected to immigration in Europe these days. Meanwhile, Spanish Prime Minister José Maria Aznar says he will restrict immigration in order to prevent the rise of a Spanish Le Pen. Similar signals have come from British Prime Minister Tony Blair and German Chancellor Gerhard Schröder, among others.

At the European Council summit in Seville in June 2002, the fifteen member countries debated efforts to deal with the problem of illegal immigration and the large numbers of asylum seekers. Measures were adopted to make border controls more effective and improve cooperation with transit countries and countries of origin. Uncooperative countries may find that their relationship to the EU will suffer. On the whole, the emphasis lay clearly on reducing the total numbers of people reaching the Union.[10]

In other words, national leaders and the EU have chosen to respond to the recent rise of the populists on the right by trying to steal the wind from their sails.

TRYING TO CUT THE NUMBERS

The shift in attitude toward immigration has had concrete effects on policy in many countries. Denmark, previously known for its liberal immigration policies, has been strongly influenced by the populist momentum. The anti-immigrant Danish People's Party (DPP) received 12 percent of the vote in last year's national elections. The government, relying on DPP support in parliament, has openly declared a policy partly aimed at discouraging some groups of potential asylum seekers.[11]

During the first six months of this year, asylum applications in Denmark almost halved. The Danish authorities claim to save 200 million Euro per year as fewer people apply for asylum.[12] In the meantime, neighboring Sweden and Norway have seen substantial increases in applications during the same period.

In Austria, a law has been proposed that could mean that non-EU citizens could be expelled if they fail to pass a German language test within four years of their arrival.[13] Similar tests, and other proposals that would serve to "force" integration on immigrants, have been on the agenda in several EU countries, most of which have recently acted to curb immigration or make conditions for immigrants less generous.

Instances such as Le Pen's elevation to second-round presidential candidate, Fortuyn's provocative statements about Islam, and Berlusconi's similar ones have met with strong official protests. But the fact remains that the official position of most EU countries on immigration and asylum has moved toward rejection of the many in favor of selection of the few.

In connection with Seville, the weekly political magazine, *The Economist,* suggested, under the headline, "Huddled Masses, Please Stay Away," that the inscription on a European Statue of Liberty might read: "We have vacancies for a limited number of computer programmers and will reluctantly accept torture victims with convincing scars. Migrants looking for a better life can clear off."[14]

"FEAR IS NOT A GOOD BASIS FOR MAKING POLICY"[15]

While there has been much discussion about creating a uniform EU asylum policy, harmonizing legislation, and setting common standards, governments mostly have been unwilling to commit to this process. Rules vary within the Union, causing frictions between countries.

Human rights watchdogs like the European Council on Refugees and Exiles (ECRE) and Amnesty International have been highly critical of recent EU immigration policy. They have claimed that the lofty declarations and the specific proposals do not match, and have expressed concern that a sense of crisis has been created when in fact there is little cause for alarm.

The focus on border controls and the fight against illegal immigration may be creating a climate, they say, in which people's irrational fears are validated. "The term 'illegal immigrant' will too easily be seen to fit everyone, and create the risk of criminalization and discrimination," writes Amnesty.[16]

The Public Image of Immigration

The public image of immigration is a problem. All across Europe, election results show that anti-immigrant sentiments have grown stronger, as immigration has moved to the top of the political agenda, not least after the terrorist attacks in the U.S. on September 11, 2001.

Much of what has been brought forward by the main political parties, however, has not had an anti-immigrant bias in itself. Moreover, it is understandable that many sensitive political issues, including immigration, are now viewed through a security lens. But taken as a whole, the political discourse has built up a sense of impending crisis on the immigration front.

A similar phenomenon has been evident in the media. Whether reporting on immigrants dying on Europe's borders, the failure of integration policies, racist attacks on immigrants, or crimes perpetrated by immigrants or their children, an overall image of immigration and immigrants as a problem has been created.

According to a comparative study by the European Research Center on Migration and Ethnic Relations (ERCOMER), the news media tend to focus on "negativity, problems, crime, and conflict" when reporting about migrants and ethnic, cultural, and religious minorities. The study examined media practices in all of the fifteen EU states during 1995–2000. While practices vary from country to country, some common themes were found.[17]

When immigrants or ethnic minorities are involved in crimes, their origin is often linked, directly or indirectly, to their criminal behavior. Crimes are sometimes presented in more dramatic terms and are often related to a specific minority group (Russians in Finland, Albanians in Greece and Italy, etc.).

In several countries, the study found a tendency to report in terms of "us and them," where "we" are the victims and "they" are the problem. The arrival of asylum seekers was often described using metaphors like disasters and invasions—presenting immigration as a national threat.

Negative media reporting was not balanced by positive images. Only rarely did media focus on individual immigrants or minority members or offer perspectives on their everyday lives. Immigrants were presented as dishonest and ungrateful abusers of welfare and asylum systems. Reporting on illegal immigration tended to include references to police action and supposed criminality, reinforcing a negative image.

According to the study, stereotyping was common, especially in countries where large-scale immigration is a relatively new occurrence. Stereotypes were especially prevalent and negative for Roma and Muslims.

Open racism disappeared from the media in most countries during the 1990s, while subtle racism sometimes remained. The problem of reporting on immigration and minorities was discussed, and some measures were taken. Minorities and immigrants have had more opportunities recently to offer their perspective in the media. Unfortunately, this may add to the negative picture, as those stories, again, tend to focus on problems.

The main conclusion of the ERCOMER report is that the media tends to overemphasize negative aspects of immigration and minority cultures. The focus on problems risks reinforcing prejudice and negative opinions.

In a situation characterized by hardening economic conditions, the threat of foreign terrorism, and political leaders dramatizing immigration, there is fertile ground for misunderstanding. An often stated or implied message that immigration is a problem can easily be misconstrued as immigration being *the* problem.

Immigration is a highly emotional subject on which many people have strong feelings and opinions. Unfortunately, opinions are not always based on facts. They may reflect long-lived myths, sometimes conveyed through the media, that tap into our inherent skepticism of strangers. They provide scapegoats and suggest easy solutions to difficult problems. They are the staple ammunition of the populist. "It's the immigrants' fault. They are not like us. If we get rid of them, everything will get better."

A rational discussion of immigration and its consequences for Europe should be based on facts, not myths. So, let us look at some of the notions that are in sway and being spread.

"Immigrants Are Swamping the Continent"

Many seem to believe that we are currently experiencing record levels of immigration in the EU, and that the numbers of immigrants in our countries have reached critical mass.

As we have seen, immigration actually peaked over ten years ago, in 1992, and is down significantly compared to then. Asylum applications rose during the late 1990s from very low levels. But in 2000 and 2001, they decreased: in 2001 there were 384,530 applications.[18]

There have been some attempts to encourage labor immigration, but the numbers are small. In any case, skilled immigrants moving directly into the job market are unlikely to concern most people; illegal immigration does. Illegal immigration is naturally hard to measure with any amount of certainty. It is estimated that around 500,000 people enter the EU clandestinely each year. Despite all the drama, it has not been substantiated that illegal immigration is increasing.

In comparative terms, the EU is not receiving a uniquely large number of immigrants. Over the last ten years, total yearly immigration into the EU has averaged about 1.4 million people. In the same period, 2.3 million have immigrated to the U.S. every year.[19] With about 90 million less inhabitants (290 to 380 million), the U.S. is, on average, absorbing almost one million more immigrants per year than the EU.

Finally, the EU does not have an unusually large share of foreign-born residents. At 5.3 percent, it is quite low compared to some other countries. In the U.S., it is around 11 percent, and in Australia it is as high as 25 percent. If these countries can manage, then our smaller share of foreigners should not be an insurmountable threat, even if it increases.[20]

". . . Abusing the Asylum System"

There is a persistent argument that very few of the refugees or asylum seekers who come to our countries are really qualified for refugee status. First-review numbers are often quoted to show that only a small percentage of those seeking asylum are accepted, leaving room for speculation that as many as 90 to 95 percent lack sufficient grounds. So, the argument goes, a large majority of them are just abusing the system.

This is a misrepresentation of the reality of the asylum process. The first review is, by definition, not the end of the matter. There are further investigations and appeals, and the number of refugees finally allowed to stay is significantly higher.

For example, the U.K. decided almost 120,000 asylum cases in 2001. In about 9 percent of them, 11,180 cases, the applicants were granted asylum, while 19,845 people, or 17 percent, were allowed to stay for humanitarian and other reasons. The remaining 74 percent were rejected. But 75 percent of rejected cases were appealed and, of the appeals reviewed in 2001, another 19 percent were granted asylum.[21] Assuming that these numbers can be applied to refugees arriving in 2001, almost 40 percent of asylum seekers were finally allowed to stay.

Higher numbers can be seen in other countries. A Swedish study found that of all asylum seekers who arrived in 1997, as many as 65 percent had received some sort of residency status in

Sweden by 2000.[22] This is not to say that unfounded applications are not a problem. They, no doubt, undermine public support for the right to asylum and put strain on already burdened migration authorities. But the problem is highly exaggerated.

Also, a look at UNHCR statistics reveals that in the last decade, the top ten countries of origin for asylum seekers in the EU were, in descending order: the former Yugoslavia, Romania, Turkey, Iraq, Afghanistan, Bosnia and Herzegovina, Sri Lanka, Iran, Somalia, and the Democratic Republic of Congo.[23] All of these countries have been the stage for violent conflicts or repressive regimes in the last ten years, as have most of the major countries of origin.

Asylum seekers generally do not come from safe and secure countries. Granted, some are economic migrants looking for better opportunities rather than protection. But the lines between these two groups are blurred, and the distinction may not always be clear to asylum seekers.

". . . Undermining the Welfare System"

Another common complaint is that immigrants come to our countries to live off welfare and are not interested in working or contributing to society.

There is, indeed, a higher rate of welfare dependency among the foreign-born than in the native population. For example, a study of welfare in Germany found that in 1996, 23.5 percent of recipients were foreign-born, at a time when they made up 8.9 percent of the population.

However, the study also found that this over-representation was entirely due to demographics. Immigrants were generally less educated, younger, and had more dependent children, factors that made them more prone to rely on state assistance.[24]

Studies in the U.S. have seen results along similar lines. A Carnegie project reached the conclusions that working-age non-refugee immigrants have the same rates of participation in welfare use as working-age natives. Immigrants with incomes below the poverty line actually use less welfare than natives in the same situation.[25]

Welfare dependency is not a factor related to ethnicity, religion, or some innate quality that the diverse group of immigrants shares, but to integration in the job market. Immigrants are just as willing to work as natives, but they have a harder time finding a job.

Illegal immigrants are likely the most work-seeking group in society overall. As they are not covered by welfare systems, they have to earn their way from day one. They come to work hard, and often to send money home to relatives. Their lack of legal status steers them toward the "gray" economy, and they often end up working for low pay under substandard conditions.

However, there is one group of immigrants that stands out. Refugees have distinctly higher rates of welfare dependency than other immigrants, on both sides of the Atlantic. The reasons for this are obvious. Asylum seekers are usually forbidden to work for several months after their arrival. Moreover, refugees, unlike legal immigrants, are not admitted because of any special skills they hold and they usually do not have sponsors or relatives who can support them. They are offered protection because they are fleeing from persecution, frequently arriving in ill health, sometimes traumatized by their experiences, and often without financial resources. It is hardly surprising that this leaves them vulnerable and more dependent on state assistance.

". . . STEALING OUR JOBS"

Eventually, immigrants enter the job market and as they do, competition increases. An increase in labor supply has been shown to decrease wages. This will hurt some groups in the labor market, especially in sectors requiring less education.

Still, immigrant labor is not responsible for the high unemployment in much of the EU. Most experts would rather put the blame on the inflexible nature of the labor market. The U.S. admits almost one million more immigrants every year into a smaller population, and still has an unemployment rate that, at 5.7 percent, is well below the EU average of 7.7 percent.

Immigrants have also been found to compete asymmetrically in the labor market, filling high-end jobs where there is a skill gap, and low-end jobs that most natives would rather avoid. Providing labor is just one of many ways in which immigrants contribute to the economy of their host countries.

IMMIGRANTS AND THE ECONOMY

While attitudes toward immigration have much to do with emotions and social adaptation, it is also to a high degree an economic matter. As previous eras have shown, immigrants are more welcome when times are good and unemployment low.

Unfortunately, this is not the case at present in Europe, where non-growing economies cause concern and probably contribute to xenophobia. The European Commission reported in November 2002 that the average growth rate for the Euro area is estimated at only 0.8 percent in 2002. Growth for 2003 is forecasted at 1.8 percent, much lower than the 2.9 percent predicted in the last Commission report. The expected recovery is being pushed further into the future.[26]

In this environment of unsatisfactory growth and job creation, the burden of immigration on state finances becomes a recurrent argument for the populists. Immigration, it is said, siphons off money from the state that could be better used to provide for the citizens already living there.

Clearly, it is costly to receive, house, and investigate asylum seekers. They need somewhere to live and something to live off while their applications are reviewed. This usually means welfare, as asylum seekers are often not allowed to work for a period of time after their arrival. The Swedish Migration Board reports that in 2001 it spent roughly $220 million (SKr2 billion)[27] handling 23,520 asylum applications.[28]

However, considering only the immediate costs does not give us a fair idea of the overall economic effects of immigration. It fails to take into account factors that, in a longer perspective, are positive for the economy. In the long run, immigrants who are accepted into society will contribute in the same way as the rest of us, by living their lives, working, spending, paying taxes, raising families, and participating in society.

In spite of the multitude of stories about impoverished minority ghettos and welfare dependency, there are thousands of success stories as well. When *Time* magazine surveyed immigration in 2000, it found that 16 million immigrants in Europe earned more than $460 billion each year, opening businesses, creating jobs, and fueling the economy. They bring an entrepreneurial spirit, which is much needed in Europe.[29] In addition, their remittances to various home countries have a number of effects that are positive for the international economy.

Taxes versus Welfare Benefits

What is the effect of immigration on state finances? The findings are mixed. A study by the Institute for Economic Research in Dresden, Germany, stated that immigrants pay $150 billion in taxes every year in Germany, surpassing the $120 billion they receive in welfare benefits.[30]

Similar reports in the U.K. in 2001 and 2002 reached the conclusion that immigration is an economic plus. In 1999/2000, migrants in the U.K. paid £31 billion in taxes and consumed £29 billion in tax-supported public services, generating a fiscal surplus of £2 billion.[31]

In Sweden, Jan Ekberg has studied the effects of immigration on the Swedish economy. Up until the 1980s, predominantly labor-oriented immigration contributed to the economy. Growth was high, unemployment low, and the need for foreign labor great. More recently, immigration has had a somewhat negative influence on the overall Swedish economy. Recent immigrants have had a hard time entering the job market, making welfare costs outstrip tax income.[32]

Immigration does not have to be a drain on state finances. Evidence suggests that under the right conditions, it is a positive factor. But access to the job market is essential.

FILLING THE GAPS

Immigrants and state finances would not be the only beneficiaries of better integration into the job market. As many European firms have found out, labor shortages can be very costly. In 2001, the International Labor Office in Switzerland found that unfilled vacancies in the information technology (IT) sector alone had cost EU member states approximately $106 billion in lost GDP growth.[33]

This is already a problem in Europe. With the baby boom generations about to retire in large numbers, it is a problem destined to grow. Immigration can provide a partial solution. This is well known to European governments. Several of them have already tried various programs aimed at particular professional groups, such as computer programmers or health care workers.

Germany introduced the first European "green card" scheme in 2000, issuing 12,500 five-year work permits to non-EU computer specialists between August 2000 and July 2002.[34] The U.K. has set up special categories for high-priority migrants, such as managers, students, artists, investors, and academics. There is a fast-track work permit system in place to attract desirable workers, like nurses and midwives. France has had a similar system, especially geared toward IT workers. The Netherlands has given priority and special treatment to IT and telecommunication industries, and has recruited nurses from abroad.[35]

In Sweden, the newly re-elected Social Democratic government has rejected targeted labor immigration. Prime Minister

Göran Persson has declared that efforts should first be made to integrate those immigrants who are already in the country. A Swedish think tank argues that targeted labor immigration misses the goal. As the baby boomers retire, the effects will be felt across the entire economy. Countries will not need just the elites, but people of all kinds.[36]

In *Willing Workers,* a study on illegal Mexican migration to the U.S., Daniel Griswold reports that, according to the U.S. Department of Labor, demand for less skilled labor will continue to grow in the years ahead. Meanwhile, the supply of American workers suitable for such work will decrease through aging and increasing education levels.[37] Considering Europe's demographic situation, this effect should be felt even more strongly there.

The skill gap is not just something that affects high-tech industries or specialized professions. In the developed world, there are vacancies not only for doctors and programmers, but also for waiters and gardeners. Therefore, if we are to manage migration flows, the task is much more complex than just prioritizing specific categories of skilled labor.

LOWERING WAGES, STIMULATING GROWTH

Apart from alleviating skill gaps, an increase in the supply of labor can be expected to lower the costs of labor. This is controversial, as it hurts those who see their wages go down or rise less than they otherwise would. But for the economy in general, it is usually considered positive, stimulating industry and growth.

In *Heaven's Door,* a recent book by a leading researcher in the area, George Borjas, the author confirms that immigration increases the U.S. labor supply and that as an effect, wages and prices are lowered. This process increased U.S. GDP by about $8 billion in 1998. The cost of providing public services to immigrants exceeded the taxes they paid, according to Borjas, who concludes that the positive economic contribution of immigrants

is limited. He finds that the effect of immigration is largely distri-
butional, shifting $160 billion a year from workers whose wages
are depressed to employers who benefit from lower wages and
consumers who benefit from lower prices.[38]

As argued by Griswold, immigrant labor can also serve as a
flexible buffer for the economy, providing labor that can be mobilized quickly to serve fluctuating needs. It makes the economy
more efficient and stimulates growth. Under current rules on immigration in Europe as well as the U.S., this is especially true of
illegal immigrants, who are very demand-sensitive. He suggests
that encouraging temporary migration could achieve the same
effect in a legal way.[39]

Immigration actually could be a better economic proposition
for Europe than for the U.S. The skill shortages are higher, making larger gains possible. On average, immigrants to Europe also
tend to have higher educational levels than their U.S. counterparts. Realizing these advantages will, however, require an open
and well-functioning internal market. This is a critical area for
the EU. If the internal market is successful, coping with immigration will be considerably easier.[40]

The U.K. treasury has produced studies that suggest that immigration contributes to economic growth in the U.K., adding an
extra quarter-point of growth each year.[41] This may not appear
impressive, but 0.25 percent growth is not an insignificant number, especially not in Europe.

And even though costs to some native workers are real, the
benefits to the entire economy, and to immigrant workers who
achieve significant wage increases, far outweigh them.

ENTREPRENEURSHIP AND DIVERSITY

There are other possible positive effects. It is often argued that
immigrants, by virtue of having taken the leap and settled in a
new country, are a more entrepreneurial group than the general
population. The decision to migrate cannot be an easy one. As it

carries considerable costs, economic as well as social, it takes strength and confidence to leave one's native country. After all, those that take the chance are a select minority. They tend to be younger and have higher skills and education than the average population of their home countries.[42]

Diversity management is now a standard topic at many business schools. Its proponents argue that companies and organizations have a lot to gain from encouraging and welcoming diversity and different cultures in the workplace.

The same can be said for countries. Historically, the most vibrant and successful societies have not been the ones that closed their gates to the world, but those that became meeting places where different cultures and influences could interact. That is the sort of environment in which new ideas thrive and a society's long-term vitality is preserved.

In previous eras, nations like France and England became focal points of science, industry, and culture, giving birth to the enlightenment and the industrial revolution. Today, our eyes naturally turn to the U.S. While the great melting pot may have its blemishes, it continues to be an economic and cultural powerhouse.

As Tony Blair said recently, "In the modern world, an open and tolerant society that welcomes newcomers is a condition for growth and prosperity."[43]

THE SOCIO-CULTURAL DILEMMA

The first two years of the twenty-first century will not go down in history as a great time of tolerance and openness. The horrible terrorist attacks in the U.S. on September 11, 2001, the war on terrorism, and new terrorist attacks in 2002 have been detrimental to the relations between the Western and Islamic worlds.

Recent tragic events have added to old prejudices and suspicions and fueled xenophobia on all sides. The fear of international terrorism, closely associated with Muslim fundamentalists, is now the top perceived threat listed by both Americans and Europeans, according to a study by the German Marshall Fund and the Chicago Council on Foreign Relations.[44] And American flags are burning on Arab streets in the Middle East again.

What we see is not a clash of civilizations, but Muslims are currently the most visible immigrant group in Europe and have been the focus of many anti-immigration campaigns. In some of them, denunciation of Islamic culture and promises to curb Muslim immigration were cornerstones of anti-immigration party strategy.

Muslims and other non-European immigrants are targeted because they differ in many respects from natives, as well as from earlier groups of immigrants. One generation ago, most immigrants came from within Europe. Overall, the socio-cultural differences were not overwhelming.[45]

Modern immigration has brought with it new cultural challenges. Today, a large and increasing portion of immigrants come from outside of Europe, from Africa and Asia. They stand out more and the societies many of them come from are built on different foundations and history. They bring their own traditions, values, and ideas on culture, society, politics, and family. Integration has proven more difficult for a number of reasons, prejudice and fear not least among them.

Immigrants challenge our lifestyles, our traditions, and, to some degree, our values. But why should this be perceived as necessarily negative? Societies have always thrived on the exchange of ideas and influences, on diversity, not on uniformity. And if we never need to defend our own values, they may lose their relevance and content and turn into empty phrases.

Some people argue that immigrants threaten social cohesion by challenging and undermining traditions and values that are essential to native culture. According to proponents of this view, the purity of a culture is indicative of its relative worth and vitality. We would argue that the opposite is true, that interaction strengthens a culture and that it withers in isolation.

The notion that any culture can be preserved in some sort of pure condition is far-fetched and dangerously ethno-centric, especially in our time of global communications and interdependence. But even earlier in history, cultures have always been works in progress. What it means to be European or American today is not the same as it was one hundred years ago. Cultures evolve and respond to outside stimuli. The culture that a purist may want to preserve is itself a product of this process of evolution.

This is not to say that the mixing of cultures, religions, and ethnic groups cannot put strain on the social fabric. But strain does not have to be negative. The world is constantly changing, and we need to change with it.

Of course, minority groups cannot be allowed to place themselves outside of our legal systems or democratically accepted norms. For example, in the Western world there are laws against female circumcision and laws guaranteeing the equality of women. These and other aspects of human rights are essential to our systems and must be equally respected by all inhabitants of our countries.

On other matters, it would serve us well to show more flexibility. Why, for example, the desire to wear a turban or a veil should be considered a threat and sometimes lead to legal action is a mystery to us.

However, you can argue against immigration on socio-cultural grounds without being a cultural purist. On the practical side, critics point out the failures of integration—the segregation in housing, high immigrant unemployment, crime rates, and cultural collisions over women's rights and other issues—and claim that immigration must be curtailed.

Across the EU, immigrant or minority "ghettos" are familiar features of most large cities. Sometimes, the problems are severe. In some European suburbs to big cities, the unemployment rate can be as high as 50 percent, criminality out of control, and police afraid to respond.[46] People in such areas probably feel little positive connection to the rest of society. Subcultures may develop, where values are different than those of society at large, and language skills may suffer. Integration then becomes very difficult indeed.

Social marginalization can bring with it unemployment, drug abuse, and criminality, independent of ethnic, religious, or cultural background. Many of the problems afflicting such immigrant communities are not related to any specific cultural or religious background. This situation is not just a failure on the part of immigrants, but also a failure for European integration policies.

We should do our utmost to break social marginalization, which is undermining the positive contributions that these communities have to offer. It is important not only for their sake but also for ours. Romani Prodi, President of the European Commission, has called immigration, "a fountain of vitality and energy that is indispensable for a Europe that's aging."[47]

THE DEMOGRAPHIC CHALLENGE

In recent years, increasing attention has been paid to the serious demographic development in Europe. The UN population projections for 1995–2050[48] calculated that during the first half of the twenty-first century, the populations of most European countries are likely to become smaller and older as a result of low fertility rates and increased longevity. The European median age will increase from 37.7 to 52.7 years. The support ratio may decrease to two workers per retiree. These are dramatic developments, which will have considerable implications for both the economy and public policy.[49]

The U.S. situation is radically different. In the past decade, the U.S. has taken in over eleven million legal immigrants, up from six million in the 1970s and seven million in the 1980s. In addition, another eight million may have entered the country illegally, many of them staying permanently.

Most of these immigrants, both legal and illegal, come from Mexico and other Latin American countries. As the fertility rate for Latin-Americans in the U.S. is roughly 3.0, this infusion gives a tremendous boost to population. Compared to Europe, in 2050 the U.S. could be younger, more ethnically mixed, and more dynamic.[50]

Of course, a large and young population is not in itself a guarantee for economic well-being. But the opposite can be a real problem for societies who are accustomed to high levels of public assistance in times of ill health or old age. Basically, it means that there will be fewer people who pay for the welfare system, and more who expect to receive from it.

WHAT CAN THE EU DO TO DEAL WITH THIS SITUATION?

Specific reforms, for example creating more robust pension systems, would be an important contribution. In certain countries, measures designed to increase the female participation rate would also be helpful. Some governments are discussing ways to increase birth rates. Moreover, increased economic growth can offset rising costs for pensions and health care. But it seems unlikely that this increased growth will materialize.

On the contrary, growth can be expected to fall as the population ages, for a number of reasons. Retirees will leave gaps in the work force that will be hard to fill. Burdens on health care systems may force increases in taxes. National debts may increase if the tough choices of cutting benefits or raising taxes are not faced. An older population is also generally assumed to be less dynamic and inventive.

We will not be able to find the people we need inside the existing EU. All the EU countries are experiencing roughly the same trend of declining birth rates, event though some, like the United Kingdom and France, will be less affected than others, such as Italy and Spain.

The EU is about to embark on another round of enlargement, and will probably include ten new members within the next few years. Can this be a solution to the demographic dilemma?

According to the EU's own estimates, around 335,000 people will migrate each year from Eastern Europe to Western and Northern Europe once the borders are opened. Of these, 100,000 will be of working-age. This migration will close some labor gaps but will not have a significant effect on the overall situation.[51]

The population trends of the candidate countries are similar to EU trends, and they too are becoming receiving countries, rather than sending countries. Thus, new labor will have to come from outside of Europe, probably from Asia and Africa, where the youth bulge provides large numbers of people with somber prospects in their home countries.

THE MAKINGS OF A WIN-WIN SITUATION

In many developing countries, the challenge governments face is quite different. Instead of growing numbers of retirees, they face the advent of a youth explosion, that is, a disproportionately large part of the population being fifteen to twenty-nine years old. This creates its own problems.

The labor force of the developing world is expected to grow rapidly from 1.7 billion people in 1998 to 3.1 billion in 2025. It is highly unlikely that there will be sufficient job opportunities to meet demand.[52] Governments will find themselves in a difficult situation, with social upheavals as distinct possibilities.

Migration has traditionally worked as a safety valve in such situations, and continues to do so today. Emigration is a favored escape route for the disaffected. It can relieve social and political pressures that follow when you have an expanding and largely unemployed youth group.

What we have here is a win-win situation. Europe can alleviate its own demographic problems and at the same time assist parts of the developing world by receiving immigrants. Immigration is the reason why the EU population has not already begun to decline. But Italy, with the lowest EU birth rate of just 1.1 children per woman, provides an example of what is to come. Its population is already falling, despite an influx of 70,000 immigrants per year.[53]

According to UN calculations, the EU as a whole will be able to offset population decline with immigration maintained at about the level it has today. In order to prevent the number of people of working age from declining, the EU would have to receive significantly larger, but still feasible, numbers of immigrants.

However, in order to counter population aging and maintain support ratios at where they are today, very large numbers of immigrants would be needed. Germany alone would need three million immigrants per year in order to maintain its current ratio of workers to retirees in 2050, if the current trends hold. At twice the total yearly immigration to Europe over the last ten years, this is a level of immigration that is unlikely to be practicable, or acceptable to citizens.[54]

Immigration is no panacea. It cannot eradicate Europe's demographic problems. But it will help take the edge off the problem, and allow more time for reforms, such as increasing the age of retirement or creating a more flexible labor market.

THE NEED FOR A BALANCED, HUMANITARIAN APPROACH

Finally, when it comes to immigration, we are talking about more than numbers or statistics. We are talking about people. This brings a whole new range of arguments into play; moral arguments, that present us with an ethical dilemma. Perhaps part of the intensity of the current debate has less to do with actual numbers than the unease that many experience when confronting this issue.

When it comes to asylum seekers, it is clear what is expected of us. We have a moral as well as legal obligation to offer protection to those in need, stemming from our commitment to the 1951

Refugee Convention. We are expected to protect the right to asylum, avoiding measures that may undermine it.

Some critics say we are not doing that today. Commenting on the focus at the Laeken summit on border controls and curbing illegal immigration, ECRE writes: "Regrettably, this exemplifies a trend witnessed in the asylum work of the European Union during the last two years, whereby deterrence rather than protection seems to be the key priority of the majority of Member States."[55]

For example, the UNHCR has recommended that visa requirements not be used for countries where there are civil wars, generalized violence, or widespread human rights violations. Yet, the EU has visa requirements in place for most of the major refugee-generating countries, according to ECRE.[56] Usually, it is impossible to get a visa in order to apply for asylum, and it is often not possible to apply for asylum at embassies or consulates.

Further, asylum seekers may be sent back to countries they passed through before reaching the EU, according to the "safe third country" policy. This, says ECRE, penalizes countries for being close to conflict areas, it encourages destruction of travel documents and smuggling, and it is time-consuming and expensive. It also puts the burden of refugee protection on countries ill equipped for the situation. The poorest nations already care for the largest numbers of refugees.[57]

Amnesty goes further, warning that the EU may be in breach of international human rights and refugee law by refusing access to EU territory and fair asylum processes.[58]

ILLEGAL IMMIGRATION EQUALS SUFFERING

The lack of legal options and the efforts to restrict access to Europe opens up the door to illegal immigration. Both asylum seekers and economic migrants are willing to face the risks and costs involved in order to achieve entry, slipping across borders or traveling on temporary visas and then overstaying them.

This has created a market for human smuggling, which, like trafficking, has rapidly become a global concern. Hundreds of thousands of migrants are willing to pay smugglers considerable amounts of money for assistance in reaching affluent Western countries. And many people are trafficked against their will for purposes of sexual exploitation or forced labor.

In 1994, research by the International Center for Migration Policy Development showed that 15 to 30 percent of all illegal migrants to Europe paid a smuggler or trafficker to get into a European country. Three years later, the German Federal Refugee Office stated that about half of their asylum seekers were smuggled into the country. The Dutch Immigration Service put the number for the Netherlands in the 60 to 70 percent range in the late 1990s.

Illegal immigration leads to human suffering, even deaths. There have been numerous reports of illegal immigrants suffocating in the back of trucks, drowning in the Mediterranean, or freezing to death on the Bosnian border. The tragedy of the fifty-eight Chinese immigrants who were found suffocated in a truck in Dover in 2000 is perhaps the single, most well-known example. Members of the Chinese community in Rotterdam say that it was not the first time. Many have left for the U.K. and never been heard from again.[59]

The waters off Spain are said to have claimed even more victims. Four thousand people may have died in the Strait of Gibraltar and in the Atlantic waters between Africa and Spain's Canary Islands in the last five years alone.[60]

And the immigrants' troubles are not over once they arrive. Those illegal immigrants who do not apply for asylum often end up in the underground economy, pushed there by their illegal status. There, they work for low pay under bad conditions, with no legal protection. Exploitation is common.

As we have seen, the EU response has been to focus on border controls and cooperation against illegal immigrants. The argument that allowing for more legal immigration might lower incentives for illegal entry, however, has not found much support.

"We know from America's experience that allowing lots of legal immigration does not put a stop to illegal immigration," observed one EU diplomat, quoted by *The Economist*.[61]

The EU seems less inclined to draw another possible lesson from the U.S. experience; that intense and expensive border controls only yield limited results. The U.S., in spite of strict border controls, is estimated to receive about as many illegal immigrants as the EU per year, around 500,000.[62]

A policy solely focused on restricting access is costly, ineffective, and morally dubious. It encourages illegal activity and drives hundreds of thousands of people into a twilight existence of exploitation and lack of legal protection. With more legal options at hand, fewer people will probably be attracted to the dangerous and costly option of illegal immigration. And fewer people can be expected to abuse the asylum system.

But the most efficient way of combating illegal immigration is by improving conditions in transit and origin countries. This means building decent reception systems and efficient border control systems. It also means helping weak societies create environments where people can hope to improve their lives. For this to be successful, however, those countries need to be willing to change and reform. And they must be supported in their efforts.

Focusing on transit countries and countries of origin must not be used as a pretext for turning people away before they reach our borders. Rich countries must carry their part of the burden for global refugee problems. In this era of global and instant communications, we cannot claim ignorance of the difficult conditions in which most people of this world live out their lives.

CONCLUSION—TURNING THE CORNER

Immigration is less of a problem than it is currently made out to be. Immigrants are an integral part of European society, and an important social and economic phenomenon. They have been so for a long time. The recent public discussion has been overly focused on problems and negative aspects, neglecting the positive contributions immigration can bring to our societies.

To recapitulate, immigrants by many accounts constitute a positive factor for the economy. Tax revenues from immigrants roughly equal or surpass the costs of the welfare benefits they receive as a group. Their contribution to the economy increases GDP, not dramatically, but still significantly so. Diversity is in itself a positive factor. As long as the transfer to the labor market functions, immigration is a good economic proposition for all involved.

Demographically, Europe is facing a development that, in the medium to long-term range will seriously threaten growth and living standards and, at the very least, necessitate painful reforms. At present, immigration is the one factor that is keeping the population of many EU countries from declining. To prevent the working-age population from declining as Europe ages, we will need considerably higher levels of immigration than today. To preserve our welfare systems as we know them, we will also need to reform our pensions and welfare systems. Immigration is not the whole solution. But it can reduce the size of the problem, and help pay for reform.

On a humanitarian level, we must not jeopardize the absolute right to asylum by wavering in our commitment to the 1951 Refugee Convention. We believe that too many steps have already been taken in that direction, and that the EU should live up to its oft-stated promise to balance restrictive and preventive measures with guarantees for access and protection. Much could also be gained by opening additional legal avenues for immigration to Europe.

Socially, some can perceive immigration as a threat. We need to be receptive to the needs of those groups in society that pay the most direct cost of immigration through depressed wages and increased competition in the labor market. They are already vulnerable and may constitute a willing audience for populist messages promising easy solutions, blaming immigrants for the nation's problems.

The voters' rights to a voice in immigration policy must be respected. But politicians must also take their role as public educators seriously. Political leaders have two options before them when dealing with the growing resentment of immigration.

They can respond by making immigration the problem. We would argue that this populist tactic has exacerbated the situation and is leading us down a dangerous path. We are now confronted with a situation where xenophobic parties are making gains in several EU countries.

The other approach would be to reject simplistic arguments and easy solutions, and put the blame where it belongs. Most of the difficulties afflicting immigrant communities are effects of weak economies, social marginalization, and lack of access to the job market. Leaders of politics and business who already see the benefits of immigration need to communicate this insight. Surely we are not willing to give up the idea that people of different cultural, religious, or ethnic backgrounds can coexist peacefully and gain from this association?

What is needed in Europe and elsewhere is a comprehensive approach that deals with issues of asylum, immigration, integration, and development in an integrated manner. More efforts must be made to develop a generous, common policy on asylum and immigration. This should be combined with an active dialogue with the immigrants' countries of origin, focusing on stimulating growth, the rule of law, and human rights.

What is needed now is a common policy that sees immigration as a promise, not a peril. If this is to be successful, mutual respect for traditions and values must be the guiding norm.

FAULT LINES

Part 4

The Fault Lines section of this book examines some of the major acts that individuals and, more significantly, states commit that cause serious, and sometimes permanent, damage to the very foundations on which civilized society rests. Some fault lines are fundamental evils while others are in response to new challenges. In this part, four topics are presented as universal fault lines.

Professor Timothy Harding is a forensic pathologist who has had worldwide experience examining the maimed bodies and corpses of torture victims. His comprehensive chapter provides a frightening picture of the cruelty of man, of the role of doctors, lawyers, and government officials in perpetuating an evil that has been condemned in international conventions and humanitarian law.

We are living in the midst of a "war on terrorism," and no one can accurately predict the next phase or set a timetable for its end. To make matters worse there is often no agreement on the definitions of basic terms or concepts in this war. Even job titles change. My own duties as a Professor of Tropical Medicine and Director of an Institute of International Humanitarian Affairs now include an added jurisdiction; I serve as the Chief Medical Advisor for Counterterrorism in the New York Police Department, partially because I have had significant experience with diseases such as anthrax and smallpox, diseases that can be used as bioterrorist weapons.

In this part, Professor Paul Wilkinson, director of a famed academic center for the study of terrorism, provides a thoughtful and thorough chapter reviewing the history, typology, and effectiveness of both traditional and new forms of terror and political violence. Larry Hollingworth spent thirty years as an officer in the British Army before joining the United Nations High Commission for Refugees. He has worked, on the ground, for long periods, at the very center of many of the worst conflicts and disasters in modern history. His reflections on the reality of officially sanctioned terror, as seen by a field worker serving civilians under siege, provide an added insight into the tragic fault line of terrorism.

Finally, in this part, Ambassador Nancy Ely-Raphel cites a sordid fault line, gender exploitation, that is both a cause and consequence of trafficking in human beings. The most vulnerable, women and children, are still held in bondage and forced to work as prostitutes, as domestic servants without compensation, or under incredibly harsh conditions as slave laborers in fields around the world. The Ambassador then details the multi-pronged effort of one government, the United States of America, to right these intolerable wrongs.

10

Torture

Timothy W. Harding, M.D.

INTRODUCTION

TORTURE HAS BEEN and remains a constant in human society; its history is closely linked to the evolution of state powers and the exercise of authority.[1] In all circumstances, the notion of torture has two essential elements: the purposeful infliction of pain, usually described as excruciating, and an ulterior motive in the interests of the authority responsible for the torture.[2] The pain can be either physical or psychological in nature, and most authorities would accept that provoking intense fear through mock executions or threats to family members can be considered a form of acute psychological pain. Furthermore, the notion of humiliation is considered by many authorities as central to the process of torture, being antinomic to the principle of human dignity at the origin of modern concepts of human rights.

The most frequently cited motive for torture is the extraction of a confession or the obtainment of information during interrogation. The Japanese word for torture, *gōmon,* is made up of two *kanji,* the first, rather rarely used in Japanese language, meaning "to flog" or "to beat," and the second a commonly used *kanji* meaning "to question." However, torture is also used as a form of punishment, intimidation, and coercion outside the interrogation process. The use of torture on a large segment of the population, including rape and mutilations, is recognized as a means of intimidation against populations or minorities.[3]

The word for torture in most European languages is derived from the Latin "to twist" or "to distort," reflecting techniques of torture involving forcible extension of the body or twisting of limbs, provoking intense musculo-skeletal pain. The word can also be taken to reflect the fundamental distortion in the human relationship between the torturer and the tortured person. It should be recognized that, as well as the tortured person losing his or her fundamental human dignity and suffering long-term consequences, both psychological and physical, the torturer is also debased and humiliated by his activity. A key question, therefore, is why individuals are prepared to torture. At one time, it was thought that only particularly sadistic individuals were capable of committing torture. However, psychological experiments show clearly that most normal individuals are capable of inflicting even apparently intense pain under experimental conditions.[4] It is the perception of the victim and his or her difference and inferiority, as well as dangerousness, that allows individuals with a normal psychological make-up to commit acts of torture. A striking example is the systematic rape of civilian women by soldiers during armed conflict, for example when the Japanese Imperial Army entered Nanking in 1937,[5] or, more recently, by Serb forces during the war in Bosnia. In both instances, there was an open permissiveness and even encouragement by senior military officers, as well as a perception of Chinese or Muslim women as racially inferior.

BRIEF HISTORICAL REVIEW

Paradoxically, it is easier to provide a well-documented account of torture in early civilizations in ancient Greece and Rome, as well as in the Middle Ages in Europe up until the eighteenth century, than in the modern world.[6] This is because torture was openly practiced and was part of judicial procedure, both during investigation and as part of punishment. In both ancient Greece and Rome, slaves were systematically tortured if they were involved in a judicial procedure, whether as accused or simple witnesses, in order that their testimony could be heard in court. The earliest debates about torture come from Roman times, when both Seneca and Cicero criticized the torture of free men as being likely to lead to false confessions: "Even the innocent may lie when tortured." This is a utilitarian and legalistic argument against torture, rather than a moralistic or humanitarian opposition. Saint Augustine is often cited as the first to oppose torture on the grounds of its moral perversity. However, even his opposition is centered on the risk of punishing a person for a crime falsely confessed under torture. He did not take a clear position against the humiliation and infliction of pain during criminal procedures or as part of punishment.

The late Middle Ages and the period of the Reformation and Counter-Reformation saw an institutionalization and a reutilization of torture; many woodcuts of this period give explicit details of torture instruments and methods. The use of torture was common during times of religious divide (see the example from sixteenth-century Geneva at the end of this chapter). The use of torture during the period of the Inquisition in Spain has probably been exaggerated and its main victims were not religious dissenters but the Jewish and Moorish minorities.

In the eighteenth century, during the period of the Enlightenment, the first clearly enunciated oppositions to torture on moral and humanitarian grounds were published by Voltaire, Rousseau, and Hobbes. Their philosophical position was linked to the new concept of the relationship between the individual and the state enshrined in the American Constitution and the Declaration of Rights of the Citizen following the French Revolution.

Torture was first abolished in Sweden in 1734, and almost all European countries had abolished torture from the provisions of criminal procedure by the early nineteenth century.

There is surprisingly little written about the effects of this prohibition on interrogation procedures, and only fragmentary accounts of torture exist after its abolition in nineteenth-century Europe. Many political activists claimed to have been beaten or subject to prolonged solitary confinement, particularly in czarist Russia. In North America and Europe, the term "third degree" method came into use for police questioning of difficult suspects, and certainly involved methods that today would be considered as torture. It was the unprecedented and systematic abuses committed by the Third Reich and the Japanese Imperial Forces in the form of genocide, other forms of mass murder, human experimentation, and abuse of prisoners that led to the Universal Declaration of Human Rights and the outright prohibition of torture in any form.

It is therefore just over fifty years ago that torture was prohibited in a series of interlocking provisions of international law; nevertheless, all objective assessments about the prevalence of torture in the world today lead to the conclusion that systematic torture occurs in one form or another in the majority of states despite the fact that they have confirmed their adherence to the Universal Declaration of Human Rights and have ratified the United Nations' International Covenant on Civil and Political Rights. Article 7 of this covenant reads: "No one shall be subjected to torture or to cruel, inhuman, or degrading treatment or punishment."[7] Torture is also prohibited in times of armed conflicts by the Common Article 3 to the Geneva Conventions. It is outlawed by the 1994 United Nations's Convention Against Torture. In the statute of the International Criminal Court, torture is recognized as a crime against humanity when it is committed as part of a widespread or systematic attack directed against a civilian population.

Torture is, therefore, one of the few issues in which international human rights and humanitarian law is unambiguous and for which no exceptions are provided. For example, under the European Convention of Human Rights, any high contracting party may take measures derogating from its obligation under the convention in time of war or other public emergency threatening the life of the nation. However, no derogation is permitted for Article 3, prohibiting torture.[8]

The provisions of international law prohibiting torture did not give clear definitions of what would constitute torture. In most texts, the concept is linked to that of inhuman and degrading treatment, while the International Covenant on Civil and Political Rights (1966) indicates that being subjected to medical or scientific experimentation without free consent is a particular form of torture or cruel, inhuman, or degrading treatment.

The definitions were to come from several sources; first, through the work of the European Court of Human Rights (and later the subsidiary European Convention for the prevention of torture and inhuman or degrading treatment or punishment of 1989). In the decision concerning the case of Ireland versus the United Kingdom over techniques of "interrogation in depth" carried out by the British Army in Northern Ireland, the court ruling included a detailed account of wall standing, hooding, subjection to noise, deprivation of sleep, and deprivation of food and drink, which were considered as a violation of Article 3 of the European Convention. The reports emanating by the CPT (the committee set up by the 1989 Convention) also give some detailed consideration as to what constitutes torture.

Second, the reports of the special reporter of the UN Commission of Human Rights investigating torture on a global scale also provide descriptions of the wide variety of abuse and treatment that should be considered as torture.

In 1975, the United Nations General Assembly adopted a declaration on Protection from Torture, in which torture is defined as "an aggravated and deliberate form of cruel, inhuman, or degrading treatment or punishment." The essential elements in the definition are the intentional infliction of severe pain or suffering, whether physical or mental, at the instigation of a public official. Torture is thus defined as an intentional act under the authority of the state with the purpose of obtaining information or a confession, but also as a punishment or to intimidate. The 1984 United Nations' Convention Against Torture has a closely similar definition, although the role of a "public official or other person acting in an official capacity" is widened to include not only direct infliction, but also instigation, consent, or acquiescence. Both definitions from the United Nations exclude "pain

or suffering arising only from, inherent in, or incidental to lawful
sanctions."

CASE STUDY: THE ANGELOVA AFFAIR[9]

In 1996, a seventeen-year-old boy was seen by the police hanging
around parked cars in a small town in Bulgaria. He was chased
and apprehended by a policeman and was then seen by members
of the public handcuffed to a tree while the police carried out a
search of the area. He was taken to the local police station. No
written detention order was issued and the register did not have
an entry for him. The following morning, the boy was taken by
the police to a local hospital, where he was pronounced dead
shortly afterwards. An autopsy established that the cause of death
was internal bleeding in the brain as a result of a fractured skull
around the left eyebrow. The autopsy report established that the
trauma had occurred between four and six hours prior to his
death. There were also marks of recent trauma on several other
parts of the body. The medical legal conclusions were therefore
clear: the boy had died as a result of a blow received while in
police custody, furthermore, there had been a delay of several
hours before the boy was brought to hospital; when he arrived, it
was too late to provide any care.

Since the police were involved, the criminal investigation into
the boy's death was taken over by a military investigator, who appointed five medical experts from the police and military to re-
examine the conclusions. Without providing any fresh evidence
or arguments, the experts concluded that the trauma could have
been received more than ten hours before the death, and, therefore, prior to his arrest. On this basis, the investigation was termi-
nated. No administrative or discipline reaction of any kind was
taken.

So ends a typical case of death in custody, giving rise to serious
suspicions of ill treatment and possible torture by the police, in-
vestigated by another state authority, which concluded clearly

that no abuse had occurred. If we add that the victim belonged to the Roma ethnic group, a minority subject to discrimination and social exclusion in many Eastern European countries, we can understand easily why such a boy could be subject to abuse by the police and why the government's investigation was so half-hearted and inconclusive.

The story would normally end there, had Bulgaria not ratified the European Convention of Human Rights in 1992. With the support of an NGO and a human rights activist lawyer, the boy's mother made an application to the European Court of Human Rights on the basis of Article 2 of the European Convention, which guarantees the right to life. The mother complained simply of an unexplained death in police custody, the failure to provide adequate medical care, and the ineffectiveness of the subsequent investigation. The proceedings before the court established that the police had manipulated the detention records and that the government's explanation of the death was implausible. The police had delayed provision of medical assistance and this contributed in a decisive manner to the fatal outcome. Therefore, there had been a violation of the state's obligation to protect the life of persons in custody. Furthermore, the court considered that the investigation carried out by the military authority lacked the "requisite objectivity and thoroughness." In particular, the police officers were never asked to explain why detention records had been forged and why they had given false information on the boy's arrival at the hospital.

The court went further in its condemnation of the Bulgarian government by concluding that the injuries shown at the autopsy were clear signs of inhuman treatment. It was therefore concluded that a violation of Article 3, which prohibits torture and inhuman or degrading treatment, had also occurred.

Finally, the court considered the mother's complaint that the police's abusive treatment was based on their discriminatory perception of him as a gypsy was grounded on "serious arguments," but proof beyond the reason brought out had not been provided.

The mother received 19,000 Euros in nonpecuniary damages.

This case is recounted in some detail in order to demonstrate how easy it is for inhuman treatment amounting to torture and death to occur while in custody, particularly when the victim is from a minority group; and how difficult it is to investigate and bring to account the perpetrators.

ALLEGATIONS, DENIAL, AND IMPUNITY

Despite the clarity of legal prohibition of torture, the Angelova case illustrates the problem of investigation, which, in turn, leads to the widespread problem of impunity and denial. On each occasion, when reputable human rights organizations such as Amnesty International or Human Rights Watch provide well-documented reports of torture in a particular country, there is a ritual exchange of documented allegations followed by official denials.

One example of such an exchange: on Monday, February 12, 2001, the BBC World Service reports as a main news item:

> "The human rights group Amnesty International says torture and ill treatment of prisoners and detainees in China has become widespread and systematic;" the victims are members of the banned Falun Gong spiritual movement, Muslim separatists in Xenjiang, prisoners in Tibet, many of whom who were reported to have died in custody. Amnesty suggested that the Chinese government's commitment to curb torture was often undermined by its directives to use "every means" in anticorruption campaigns and political crackdowns. Furthermore, the torture and inhuman treatment were often carried out almost publicly in order to "instill fear and discipline."

The message is therefore clear: commitments to end torture do not survive government drives against political opponents or what are perceived as dangers to the fabric of society such as corruption or separatist or religious movements.

The following day, Tuesday, February 13, 2001, the BBC World Service News carried the rejection by China's Foreign Ministry of the report by Amnesty International. "The allegations are totally groundless," the Foreign Ministry's spokesman was quoted as saying. Later in the same week, the BBC News carried a further item in which a senior Chinese government official denied the allegations of torture and inhuman treatment of members of the Falun Gong spiritual movement. This spokesman accused Falun Gong of being politically motivated and "maiming and killing people." He gave the example of the recent immolation of five Falun Gong members in Tiananmen Square as a testimony to the group's inhumanity and deadliness. Furthermore, the official protested about the interference from outside in China's internal affairs, in particular the protests by the European Parliament at that time concerning violation of human rights in Tibet, the destruction of mosques, and the arrests of teachers of the Koran.

We can see therefore that the problem of torture is not limited to individual occurrences of ill treatment in police custody, prisons, or other state detention centers, however common they may be. Torture is intimately linked to the powers of the state, the belief by those in authority of the need to defend, at all costs, the state's authority and policies, and the perception of individuals and groups as dangerous to the state. The denial of torture by governments is always accompanied by reminders of threats against the state and the dangerousness of certain minorities. The unspoken message is, of course: if torture does occur, it is because it is necessary to defend the state.

The ritual waltz between human rights organizations and governments, with its well-defined, pre-arranged steps of allegation, denial, denial, occurs dozens of times every year. China, Egypt, Burma, Israel, Russia, Guantanamo, Turkey—the list goes on and on, and the dance always remains the same. And, to be honest, our own perception of these allegations is invariably related to our feelings about the regime concerned. The ritual exchange quoted here took place early in 2001. More recently, of course, the ritual has evolved further: every government response to allegations of torture mentions the threat of terrorism.

Is the Prohibition of Torture in International Human Rights Law Credible?

The issue of torture today therefore exposes not only the deep-seated fault line about the relationship between the state and vulnerable individuals or groups, but also the very credibility of International Human Rights Law. We have to ask the question whether we are not living an illusion. The unequivocal outlawing of torture in human rights instruments has become a cruel farce in relation to what actually happens in police commissariats, interrogation centers, and prisons in most countries of the world. By participating as lawyers, medical experts, international civil servants, or academics in the ongoing debates and processes at an international level, while ignoring what really happens in the shadows of states' power and structure, we are actively participating in this farce. Would it not be more honest to face up to the ineffectiveness, the impotence, of International Human Rights Law in the face of the power and prerogatives of individual states?

Such a position might seem heretical to most observers of the human rights scene and participants in international organizations and NGO militants. It would be seen as an acknowledgement of defeat, a surrender, or, in more subtle terms, an appeasement. However, such a position would be more in line with historical reality. Torture has existed under all civilizations. (We should perhaps pause a moment to note the paradoxical nature of this simple statement: can torture really be part of a civilization? Or does civilization necessarily imply some form of state authority that, in turn, opens the way to torture and inhuman treatment?) Well, according to historical perceptions of civilization, torture has almost always been an integral part of it; the question is whether it always will be. As indicated above, for most of recorded history, torture has been a formal part of judicial procedure, used for obtaining information, forcing confessions, and also for punishment and execution. In China and Japan, torture practices are reflected in specific language and terminology, which was found also in the detailed, almost obsessional, inventory of torture techniques and instruments developed in Europe in the late Middle Ages and during the Inquisition.

The persistence of torture in the so-called modern era of human rights since 1948 leads us to two kinds of analysis. First, whether torture is the inevitable response of the state under threat, for example in time of war, when faced with acts of terrorism or deep-seated social ills, and second, how it is that the complex and wide-ranging provisions of international law are so consensual in public discourse and so ineffectual in reality. Law can only be understood in a historical context, and International Human Rights Law is no exception. The preamble of the Universal Declaration describes the context clearly: "Whereas disregard and contempt for human rights have resulted in barbarous acts which have outraged the conscience of mankind. . . ." It is therefore a reaction to the horrors of the Third Reich and the Japanese Imperial occupying armies in the middle of the last century. The preamble also places the inherent dignity of all members of the human family as the foundation of freedom, justice, and peace in the world.

This was a period when the concept of the state was undergoing a fundamental change. Keynesian economics and the foundation of the Welfare State was changing the relationship between the individual citizen and the authorities. It was clearly seen that genocide, torture, mass rape, and abusive human experimentation undermined the dignity not only of victims, but also of perpetrators and the state itself. Eleanor Roosevelt described the "basic character" of the Universal Declaration in these terms: "It is not a treaty; it is not an international agreement; it is not . . . a statement of law or of legal obligation; it is a declaration of human rights and freedoms . . . to serve as a common standard of achievement for all peoples of all nations." It was a time, therefore, that the people and the nation could be placed on the same footing with an appeal to the dignity of both. The aim was clearly to eradicate the kind of relationship that had existed between the Nazi regime and Jews, gypsies, and the mentally ill, or the

Japanese military forces and the civilian population in Nanking or Manchuria.

The failure of International Human Rights Law to reduce substantially the practice of torture is part of wider failure of international public law. The proliferation of conventions covering women, children, minority groups, indigenous peoples, the disabled, the mentally ill, and many others, are all floored by the absence or the inadequacy of enforcement procedures. The special reporters of the United Nations Commission of Human Rights are often hampered in their work by governments, and there is more and more resistance to the idea of international investigative powers and jurisdiction. The idea that International Human Rights Law would progressively influence national law has had some success, but there has been little success in fields such as the investigation, exposure, and sanctions against torture. Many government leaders express satisfaction about the growing body of Human Rights Law, but are resistant to its direct application for vulnerable people. A substantial part of International Human Rights Law is therefore essentially cosmetic.

THE EUROPEAN EXCEPTION

The most fertile ground for the realization of the human rights approach has proved, without any doubt, to be Europe. The political and economic context, the recent traumatizing experiences of the Second World War, lent themselves to a proactive approach to human rights, going further than the hortatory tone of the United Nations' texts. Thus, the Convention for the Protection of Human Rights and Fundamental Freedoms signed in Rome in 1950 opens with the statement that the "Western European" governments were resolved "to take the first steps for the collective enforcement of certain of the rights stated in the Universal Declaration." However presumptuous this might seem to the rest of the world, it is undoubtedly true that investigation and enforcement are excessively weak, if not entirely absent, from almost all International Human Rights Law. It is, therefore, hardly surprising that the investigation and punishment of torture is so ineffective and weak at the national level. However, the European Convention did put into place procedures that allowed for the first time an independent supranational body to investigate allegations of human rights violations committed by state parties themselves. Furthermore, the complaints could be launched not only by other state parties, but also by individuals. Thus, in 1978, the court condemned the United Kingdom for systematic violations of Article 3 during the interrogation of Irish Republican Army (IRA) suspects arrested and interrogated by military investigators in Northern Ireland. The court has rendered a number of other decisions on the Article 3 of the Convention in recent years, involving a number of former communist countries, one case of which has already been cited.

It was rapidly recognized that the impact of the court was limited by its lack of investigative power, especially in situations of detention and interrogation. The revelations at the end of the 1980s and in the early 1990s of abusive interrogation techniques and falsification of evidence in cases against suspected terrorists in Britain, which had led to prolonged imprisonment of many innocent individuals, shocked many people.

It was at this time that the Council of Europe introduced a new convention with extraordinary powers of access to places of detention and with the explicit objective of preventing torture and inhuman or degrading treatment: the CPT. In the early years of the CPT's work, visits and investigations were carried out, which allowed, for the first time, a rather detailed picture of the anatomy, physiology, and pathology of systematic torture to be described. It is not surprising that the early reports of the CPT on visits to Turkey have remained, for many years, unpublished, or that the Spanish authorities were equally embarrassed by the findings of visits to interrogation centers of the civil guard in the Basque region. More recent visits, both in Turkey and in a number of decent European countries, reveal that interrogation rooms, corresponding in almost every detail to the torture chambers found in Ankara and Istanbul in the early 1990s, still exist.[10] Clearly, both the European Court and the CPT have much work to do, especially as their remit now extends from Lisbon to Vladivostok. The commitment of the forty-odd members of the Council of Europe to collectively prevent and banish torture has therefore achieved some impressive results. Furthermore, the CPT has widened the scope of its work progressively to cover not only police stations and prisons, but also psychiatric hospitals, detention centers for immigrants, and juvenile detention centers.

However, from the earliest years of the Council's existence, there was a deeply hypocritical vein to this commitment. France and Great Britain, the self-declared defenders of human rights and democratic values, were becoming embroiled in long and drawn-out colonial wars. We have now certain evidence of the systematic and extensive use of torture and illegal killings as the violent struggle for independence evolved in Africa and Southeast Asia. It is now clear that the most senior military commanders and government ministers were fully aware of these abuses and, indeed, provided additional resources and expertise. Thus, in both Malaya and Kenya, the British set up so-called re-education camps for terrorists, involving prolonged sensory deprivation, humiliation, mock executions, and unrelenting physical abuse. France is trying to come to terms with the admissions by most senior military officers of widespread torture and illegal killings during the Algerian war. The revelations and apologies or, in at least one case, unrepenting justification are at the same time moving and disturbing.

All these instances of documented and confessed torture help us to understand better the nature of torture and the fundamental distortion of human relationships that are implied. The Bulgarian policeman's perception of a Roma adolescent is of the same order as the Japanese soldier's perception of a young woman in Nanking when the Imperial Army entered in 1937, the same as British interrogation officers' toward Catholic terrorist suspects in Northern Ireland, or of the British and French army faced with military uprisings by people who, until then, had been colonial subjects.

THE MEDICAL PROFESSION AND TORTURE

It is widely believed that doctors can and should play an important role in the fight against torture.[11] First, they have the competence and expertise to detect and document torture. When they examine prisoners or ex-prisoners, they may observe physical lesions or the psychological consequences of abuse. Doctors who work regularly in prisons or visit police stations can use epidemiological models to follow the incidence of certain kinds of injuries and draw conclusions about the overall prevalence of physical abuse. They are also able to observe certain patterns of injury and correlate them with types of torture. The forensic pathologist has a special role for cases of death in custody, providing objective and irrefutable evidence of traumatic lesions, their pattern, and timing (see Table 10.1).

However, this role is limited by the fact that some doctors working for the state are not free to speak out and may be fearful of authoritarian regimes. Indeed, there are many well-documented cases of doctors who have spoken out about cases of torture who have been arrested, mistreated, and even tortured themselves. Doctors, who occupy a privileged position in all societies, should be able to criticize the authorities more freely than ordinary citizens, especially if they have the support of professional organizations. However, this is not always the case, despite the fact that most national medical associations are affiliated with the World Medical Association, which has codified the responsibilities of doctors in relation to torture in the 1975 Declaration of Tokyo. Another limitation is the fact that many doctors are not trained to carry out forensic examinations; few doctors can accurately detect the signs of asphyxia and interpret different kinds of bruising or abrasions. The British Medical Association has been particularly active in leading the campaign of "doctors against

Table 10.1

MEDICAL DOCUMENTATION OF TORTURE

1. Examination of acute lesions
- Skin—abrasions, contusions, lacerations, incised wounds, burns, electrical injuries, gunshot wounds
- Asphyxia—signs of strangulation, conjunctiva hemorrhages
- Bones and joints—X-ray signs of fractures, dislocations
- Psychological—acute stress syndrome
- Autopsy

2. Long-term effects
- Scars and deformities (difficult to assess)
- Special investigations—CT scan, bone scintigraphy
- Post-traumatic stress syndrome

3. Exhumation of victims
- Forensic anthropology
- DNA testing
- Ballistics

torture." The association published a substantial report on torture in 1986,[12] followed by a remarkable publication, *Medicine Betrayed: The Participation of Doctors in Human Rights Abuses,* published in 1992,[13] in which the active role of doctors in a process of torture and other human rights abuses is extensively documented. The conclusions about doctors' motives for participating in torture are probably applicable to other professional groups working for the state, particularly police officers, army interrogation experts, prison guards. The seminal study in this field is Lifton's account of the Nazi doctors, which puts emphasis on the way in which societal pressures progressively distorted medical ethical values.[14] This view has been elaborated by Staub, who also emphasizes the role of military training and obedience, the tendency to "blame the victim," and, above all, the discrimination against and labeling or devaluing of a victim group.[15] Nazi doctors were thus living in a society where fundamental human values had been denied; they, therefore, yielded to the psychological process of fear and threat of loss of their professional identity by adopting the credo of assigning a subhuman status to Jews, gypsies, and the mentally ill.

The report includes a summary of an account by a Chilean doctor who became involved in a more recent period of torture and abuses and spoke of "pressures and physical threats" leading to "the desperate sense of isolation experienced by doctors . . . in a closed society." Other factors leading to medical complicity in torture include "ideological sympathies with the objectives of the torturers" and "accepting exaggerated accounts of the danger of particular prisoners," combined with a social marginalization of a particular social or political group, which can lead to individuals being regarding as subhuman and stripped of all their rights. In other instances, doctors set out in their work with prisoners to help and protect them, only to become aware later of the extent to which "they have become compromised."

Much effort has, therefore, been made to introduce training in human rights into the undergraduate medical curriculum and to insure that the doctors working for state authorities, and particularly the police, the prison service, or the military, have the full support of their professional colleagues. Forensic skills have also been neglected in basic medical training, so that many doctors have found themselves on humanitarian missions confronted by apparent victims of torture or illegal executions and unable to carry out the most basic forensic assessment.

An important stimulus to medical involvement in the fight against torture has been the role of medical journals. Until 1985, there were very few articles or editorials in the field of prison medicine, human rights, or torture published in medical journals. Since then, the lead has been taken by certain editors, in particular in the *Lancet* and the *British Medical Journal*, to open their columns to accounts of torture by doctors working for humanitarian organizations, as well as to more scholarly accounts of torture victims. Overall, the number of papers on the subject of torture (to be found in citation lists) has grown from between ten and twenty in 1985 to well over a hundred articles published each year since 2000. This professional and editorial interest provides a degree of vigilance with constant questions about the participation of doctors in detention and interrogation procedures. (See, for example, recent exchanges concerning Turkey, Israel and the territories, China, and Guantanamo.)[16] The medical commitment to fighting against torture has also led to a more systematic repertory of torture techniques, which are summarized in Table 10.2.

Third, different types of medical documentation have been systematically described.

Much of the medical evidence of torture comes from centers for the rehabilitation of torture victims, for example, in Copenhagen or Toronto. Since the centers often see torture victims many months or years after the torture experience, much of their work concerns the long-term effects of torture, in particular chronic pain, persistent mental symptoms, but also neurological and motor handicaps and sensory loss. The post-traumatic stress syndrome, with criteria defined in the International Classification of Diseases,[17] has often been used to document and describe the chronic effects of torture. But many authorities now believe that this syndrome is difficult to apply, particularly to those victims who have experienced many traumatic events in life and who remain politically involved. The consensus is now that a multidisciplinary approach to treating victims of torture is needed, rather than a single therapeutic model (Table 10.3).

AMBIVALENCE

Torture and inhuman treatment are a fault line that runs deep and long in almost every human society. Its history is as long as the history of state power and its geographical distribution is planetary. Since the prohibition of torture in International

Table 10.2

METHODS OF TORTURE

1. Beating
Kicks, fists, truncheons, canes *(lathi),* whips *(sjambok),* electric cables, plastic bags, *falanga* (beating of soles of feet), *telefono* (beating of both ears with palms)

---

2. Postural

Prolonged standing	Extension
Suspension (Palestinian hanging)	Binding / fixed position
	Confined space

---

3. Burning

Cigarettes	Hot metallic objects
Acid	Hot water

---

4. Electric shocks
Electrodes (with hand-driven generation)
Shock baton (battery driven)
Metallic bed (attached to main electricity)

---

5. Piercing
Genitals, tongue, hands, fingernails

---

6. Asphyxia
Plastic bag
Gas mask *(elephant)*
Submersion *(submarine, la banera)*
Strangulation

---

7. Psychological

Pressure	Anticipation (in earshot of torture)
Threats	Humiliation, ridicule
Mock execution	

---

8. Extrajudicial killings
Faked suicide
"Attempted escape"

Table 10.3

PRINCIPLES OF TREATMENT OF TORTURE VICTIMS
1. Listening
2. Documentation
3. Avoid encounters reviving torture experience
4. Psychomotor approaches: relaxation / massage / exercises
5. Psychotherapy—cognitive, supportive
6. Psychopharmacology
7. Psychosocial rehabilitation

Human Rights Law, we can best describe the attitude of the state authorities toward torture as ambivalent. The risk factors, to employ a public health model, are clear: detention for interrogation, deep-seated perception of inferiority of the victim, and the conviction that the state is under threat (the so-called "war and terrorism" syndrome) certainly increase the risk of torture of those arrested as terrorist suspects.

Today, just as there are international networks of crime, money laundering, corruption, and terrorism, there is also an international network of repression and torture. There is no doubt that security forces, antiterrorist agencies, and secret police maintain contacts and share information, not only about investigations and suspects, but also about techniques of interrogation and torture. There is no doubt that the police officers and military investigators concerned believe sincerely that their corporation and the resort to interrogation amounting to torture is justified, whether in Chetchen, Israel, China, or Turkey. In every case, this belief, this justification, is underpinned by a distortion in the perception of the human relationship concerned.

The pessimistic but realistic conclusion of this analysis is that existing human rights law and procedures are powerful enough to counteract this network. Despite this, it is fundamentally important to face up to the historical realities of torture, whatever political, religious, or national affinities may be. Thus, the case brought against General Pinochet and the details of torture carried out under his regime informed public opinion both about the reality of torture and also its underlying purpose as an instrument of state terror. Another case, which has had the same effect of forcing a reluctant public's attention, is that of Teniet El-Hhd, who was born to a sixteen-year-old Algerian girl who had been tortured and repeatedly and brutally raped by more than thirty French officers in an Algerian internment camp. In 2001, a French court awarded damages to the son, thus breaking the pre-existing taboo about official recognition of torture and rape by the French army in Algeria.

The final example of belated recognition of torture and illegal killing is drawn from Geneva, Switzerland, home of many international and human rights organizations. Many visitors include in their itinerary the impressive and monumental Wall of the Reformers, at the foot of the old town of Geneva, commemorating Jean Calvin and his fellow Protestants. The visitor can have little doubt of the pride that underlies such a memorial. Few visit another memorial, just next to Geneva's medical school, which is in memory of Michel Servet de Villeneuve d'Aragon, who was tortured and burned at the stake in 1553, one of the many Catholic victims of the theocratic regime of Jean Calvin. The inscription reveals the deep-seated ambivalence that exists when condemning torture: *"Fils respectueux et reconnaissants de Calvin notre grand réformateur mais condamnant une erreur qui fut celle de son siècle et fermement attachés à la liberté de conscience selon les vrais principes de la Réformation et de l'Evangile nous avons élevé ce monument expiatoire."* ("Respectful and grateful sons of Calvin our great reformer but condemning an error which was that of his century and strongly attached to the liberty of conscience according to the true principles of the Reformation and the Evangile we have erected this expiatory monument.") It is a clear illustration of the ambivalence toward the perpetrators of torture and the failure to recognize the fundamental flaw in the relationship between the state and the individual, which underlies such abuses.

11

Terrorism: The Concept

Professor Paul Wilkinson

THE CONCEPT OF TERRORISM is often totally misused, as when employed as a synonym for political violence in general or when it is used as a pejorative for any insurgency campaign of which we disapprove. It is also frequently used loosely and inconsistently. In this respect it shares the same problem of other key strategic concepts, such as "revolution," "imperialism," and "democracy." None of these concepts lends itself to universally agreed one-sentence definition, yet all of them are indispensable for political discourse, and there is a sufficiently widely shared acceptance of the core meaning of such concepts for them to play a central role in international political and social scientific debate.

Alex Schmid and Albert Jongman have produced impressive evidence of the extent to which a minimum consensus definition of terrorism has become accepted among the international community of social scientists who study conflict.[1] Equally significant is the development of a whole body of international resolutions, conventions, and agreements dealing with aspects of prevention, suppression, and punishment of acts of terrorism[2] in which there is a near universal acceptance of the terminology used to describe the form of behavior to be condemned or prohibited. Contemporary international academic, diplomatic, and juridical debates no longer become bogged down in days of definitional debate. The major disputes that arise concern culpability for specific attacks or for sponsoring or directing them, and over the kind of international measures that should be taken in response.

Terrorism is neither a political philosophy nor a movement, nor is it a synonym for political violence in general. It is a special means or method of conflict that has been employed by a wide variety of factions and regimes. It is premeditated and systematic, and aims to create a climate of extreme fear or terror. The modern words *terror* and *terrorism* are derived from the Latin verb *terrere*, to cause to tremble, and *deterre*, to frighten from. *Terrorism* and *terrorist* did not come into use until the period of the French Revolution in the 1790s. The term was used by Edmund Burke in his polemic against the French Revolution, and came to be used to denote those revolutionaries who sought to use terror systemically either to further their views or to govern, whether in France or elsewhere.

A key feature of terrorism is that it is directed at a wider audience or target than the immediate victims. It is one of the earliest forms of psychological warfare. The ancient Chinese strategist, Sun Tzu, conveyed the essence of the method when he wrote, "kill one, frighten ten thousand." An inevitable corollary is that terrorism entails attacks on random and symbolic targets, including civilians, in order to create a climate of extreme fear among a wider group. Terrorists often claim to be carefully selective and discriminating in their choice of targets, but to the communities that experience the terrorist campaign the attacks are bound to seem arbitrary and indiscriminate. In order to create the widespread sense of fear he or she seeks, the terrorist deliberately uses the weapon of surprise and disproportionate violence in order to create a sense of outrage and insecurity. As Raymond Aron observes: "an action of violence is labeled 'terrorist' when its psychological effects are out of all proportion to its purely physical result. . . . The lack of discrimination helps to spread fear, for if no one in particular is a target then no one can be safe."[3] It is the characteristic that differentiates terrorism from tyrannicide and individual political assassination.

As Hannah Arendt has observed, the belief that one could change a whole political system by assassinating the major figure has clearly been rendered obsolete by the transition from the age of absolutist rulers to an age of governmental bureaucracy.[4] In all but a handful of regimes today, real power is wielded by the bureaucratic elite of anonymous or faceless officials. Arendt provides a powerful explanation for the fact that the age of bureaucracy has coincided with burgeoning of political terrorism. Terrorism has become, for its perpetrators, supporters, and sponsors, the most attractive low-cost, low-risk, but potentially high-yield method of attacking a regime or a rival faction. The bomb plot against Hitler, had it succeeded, would have been an act of tyrannicide not terrorism. Who could deny that Hitler was the linchpin of the Nazi system? Is it possible to find an analogous case today where the removal of an all-powerful dictator would dramatically change the system? Some have argued that Saddam Hussein is one such case, but others have suggested that if he were assassinated, he would be succeeded by a powerful Ba'thist general of comparable brutality.

The concept of terrorism used in the contemporary academic literature is essentially political. What about the use of terrorism in the name of religious causes? Or of the purist of criminal gains? It is true that militant religious fundamentalists have often throughout history waged holy terror as part of a holy war, and there is much concern about the rise of contemporary fanatical Islamic fundamentalists groups such as Hezbollah, Hamas, and al-Gama'a Al Islamiyya and al Qaeda. But the major reason why moderate Muslim leaders and secular movements see these particular fundamentalists groups as such a threat is precisely because their revolutionary Islamic agenda aims not merely at the purifying of religious practice, but at the overthrow of existing governments and their replacement by fundamental theocracies. Hence these movements are inherently religious and political. The worrying trend whereby powerful criminal gangs, such as the Italian Mafia[5] and the Latin American narco-barons[6] have adopted some of the tactics and weapons of terrorist groups, does pose grave problems for the relevant law-enforcement authorities. But it does not detract from the value of the core concept of political terrorism. In reality, the overwhelming majority of perpetrators of contemporary terrorism use the weapon to influence political behavior.

Typology

It is important to note the above defining criteria of political terrorism are broad enough to encompass states' use of terror as well as that performed by group. Typologically it is useful to distinguish *state* from *factional* terror. Normally, in the literature, a state's use of terror is referred to as terror, while substate terror is referred to as terrorism. This distinction is employed throughout this chapter. Historically, states have conducted terror on a far more massive and lethal scale than groups. They have employed terror as a weapon of tyranny and repression and as an instrument of war. Another important distinction can be made between *international* and *domestic* terrorism: the former is terrorist violence involving the citizens of more than one country, while the latter is confined within the border of one country, sometimes within a particular locality in the country. This distinction is useful for analytical and statistical purposes. However, in reality, it is hard to find an example of any significant terrorist campaign that remains purely domestic; any serious terrorist campaign actively seeks political support, weapons, financial assistance, and safe haven beyond its own borers.

Once we move beyond these very broad categories, it is useful to employ a basic typology of contemporary perpetrators of terrorism based on their underlying cause or political motivation.

Nationalist Terrorists

There are groups seeking political self-determination. They may wage their struggle entirely in the territory they seek to liberate, or they may be active both in their area and abroad. In some cases, they may be forced by police or military action or by threat of capture, imprisonment, or execution to operate entirely from their place of exile. Nationalist groups tend to be more capable of sustaining protracted campaigns and mobilizing substantial support than ideological groups. Even those nationalist groups that can only claim the support of a minority of their ethnic constituency—for example, the Irish Republic Army (IRA) and the Basque Homeland and Liberty (ETA)—can gain political resonance because of their deep roots in the national culture for which they claim to be the authentic voice. There is no sign that groups of this kind are disappearing from the terrorist scene.

Ideological Terrorists

These terrorists seek to change the entire political, social, and economic system either to an extreme left or extreme right model. In the 1970s and 1980s studies of ideological terrorism focused on the extreme left, because of the preoccupation with groups such as the Red Army Faction in Germany and the Red Brigades in Italy. Yet, as Walter Laqueur observes in his magisterial general history of terrorism,[7] the dominant ideological orientation of European terrorism between the world wars was fascist. And it is neo-Nazi and neo-fascist groups that are behind so much of the racist and anti-immigrant violence in present-day Germany and other European countries. The Red Army groups so active during the 1970s and 1980s have now largely faded away, victims of their own internal splits, determined law enforcement by their respective police and judicial authorities, and changing political attitudes among young people in the post-cold war era. However, in Latin America and parts of Asia and Africa, extreme left organizations using terrorism remain a significant challenge to governments.

Religio-Political Terrorists

The most frequently cited examples of this type of terrorism are groups such as Hezbollah and Hamas. Osama bin Laden's al Qaeda network is clearly religio-political. At its core his agenda is political, though it is dressed up in a language of Islamic holy war.[8] But it is important to bear in mind that militant fundamentalist factions of major religions other than Islam have also frequently spawned their own violent extremist groups. Striking examples can be found among Sikhs, Hindus, and Jews, and there is a well-documented link between certain Christian fundamentalist groups and extreme right-wing terrorism in North and Central America.[9]

Single Issue Terrorist Groups

These groups are obsessed with their desire to change a specific policy or practice within the target society, rather than with the aim of political revolution. Examples include the violent animal rights and anti-abortion groups.

State-Sponsored and State-Supported Terrorists

States use this type of terrorism both as a tool for domestic and foreign policy. For example, when the Iranian regime sent hit squads to murder leading dissidents and exiled political leaders, they did so for domestic reason, to intimidate and eradicate opposition to the regime. However, when North Korea sent its agents to mount a bomb attack on the South Korean government delegation on its visit to Rangoon, the communist regime was engaged in an act of covert warfare against its perceived "enemy" government in the South, designed at furthering their foreign policy aim of undermining the Republic of South Korea. State sponsors may use their own directly recruited and controlled terror squads or choose to act through client groups and proxies. They almost invariably go to some lengths to disguise their involvement, in order to sustain plausible deniability. The ending of the cold war and the overthrow of the East European communist one-party regimes and the former Soviet Union certainly removed the Warsaw Pact's substantial network of sponsorship and support for a whole variety of terrorist groups. But this does not mean that state sponsorship has ceased to be a factor in the international scene. Countries such as Iraq, Iran, and Syria are still heavily involved.[10] Others, such as Libya, appear to have been attempting to distance themselves from past major involvement in state-sponsored terrorism. The post-cold war environment has made such sponsorship potentially far more costly because of the likelihood of strong U.S. sanctions being imposed.

EFFECTIVENESS AND MOTIVATIONS

How effective has terrorism been as a weapon for attaining political objectives since 1945? History shows that terrorism has been more effective as an auxiliary weapon in revolutionary and national liberation struggles. Most of the key modern theorists and leaders of revolutionary insurgency, such as Mao Tse Tung and Che Guevara, have recognized the dangers of depending on terrorism and have come down against giving it a major role in the struggle for revolution. The few cases where terrorism played a major part in bringing about sweeping political change arose in a limited number of colonial independence struggles against foreign rule. Included in this group would be the circumstances surrounding the end of the Palestinian Mandate after the terrorist campaign of the Irgun (National Military Organization) and Stern (Fighters for the Freedom of Israel), and the British decision to withdraw from the Suez Canal zone base together with the campaigns that led the British to withdraw from Cyprus and Aden, and the French to withdraw from Algeria. In all these cases special conditions existed that made terrorism a more potent weapon: (1) due to humanitarian and judicial restraints, the occupying power was unwilling to carry through draconian measures to wipe out the terrorist organizations; (2) in each case there were intercommunal power struggles within the colony which rendered peaceful diplomatic settlement and withdrawal difficult if not impossible; (3) the terrorists who succeeded in these conditions (as in Aden up until 1968) enjoyed solid if not massive support from their own ethnic groups, and this created an almost impenetrable barrier for the intelligence branches on which the government security forces depended for success, and a vast reservoir of active and tacit collaboration and support for their terrorist operatives. Even taking into account the influence of terrorism as an auxiliary tactic in revolutionary and independence struggles and in the rise of fascism between the First and Second World Wars, the overall track record of terrorism in attaining major political objectives is abysmal.

But if this historical assessment is correct, we are left with the thorny problem of explaining why, at the beginning of a new millennium, political terrorism remains such a popular weapon among a wide range of groups around the world. There are at least four hypotheses that may help provide an answer to this question. They are by no means mutually exclusive: (1) some terrorists may be poor students of history and may continue to believe that they can repeat the success of the groups such as the National Organization of Cypriot Fighters (EOKA) in Cyprus and the National Liberation Front (FLN) in Algeria, not realizing that their own situations are not truly colonial in this sense and, therefore, not comparable; (2) some may fully recognize the severe limitation of terrorism as a means of attaining strategic goals, but may see sufficient tangible short-term rewards from terrorism—such as huge publicity, the gaining of ransoms, securing the release of fellow terrorists from jail—to make it worthwhile to use it as an auxiliary weapon; (3) some may be motivated by the *expressive* value of the activity rather than the *instrumental/ operational* value, and may wish to continue the campaign primarily because it is a relatively quick and easy way to express their hatred of their opponents and of the justice of their cause; and (4) some may be addicted to the business of terrorist operation and material gain from extortion and racketeering and may be unable to kick the habit. Politically motivated terrorism is generally justified to realize an alleged transcendental end (in Weber's terms,[11] "value rational" grounds) (5); closely linked to number (6) is the claim that extreme violence is intrinsically beneficial, regenerative, cathartic, and an enabling deed regardless of the other consequences; (7) terrorism can be shown to have "worked" in the past, and is held to be either the "sole remaining" or "best available" method to achieving success (in Weber's terms, "instrumental rational" grounds); (8) the morality of the just vengeance, "an eye for an eye, a tooth for a tooth"; and (9) the theory of the "lesser evil," which assumes that greater evils will befall us or our nation if we do not adopt terror against our enemies.

THE SIGNIFICANCE OF SEPTEMBER 11

Prior to September 11, 2001, the conventional wisdom was that the use of terrorism was endemic in low-intensity conflict around the world but that it rarely, if ever, posed a strategic threat to the security of a major power or the international community. Some specialists in the study of terrorism did point out the use of weapons of terror as having a strategic impact on international politics, for example in the hastening of the withdrawal of colonial powers from countries such as Cyprus and Algeria or derailing the peace process between the Israelis and the Palestinians.[12] Others warned of the dangers of terrorists obtaining and using a weapon of mass destruction, but these warnings were largely ignored.[13]

September 11, 2001, changed these conventional attitudes toward terrorism dramatically and irrevocably. These attacks had enormous strategic consequences for both the U.S.A. and the international community. At the time of writing, we are still too close to these tragic events to make a proper assessment of their wider impact and long-term implications. It is possible, however, to identify some of the most significant consequences:

- The scale of the loss of life caused in the World Trade Center attacks, unprecedented in the history of substate terrorism, led the U.S. president, government, and the vast majority of U.S. citizens to view them as an act of war rather than as crimes of terrorism.

- President Bush decided to respond by declaring a global war on terrorism, not only against the perpetrators of the September 11 attacks, but also against other terrorist groups described as having "global reach." This obviously had huge implications for U.S. foreign and security policy.

When President Bush took office, he and his advisors created the impression that the new administration would be placing its main emphasis on domestic issues, reducing foreign entanglements and avoiding new ones. This "Fortress America" approach has been completely reversed since September 11. The U.S. administration has embarked on a policy of global activism and military intervention unparallel since the early days of the cold war, and extending to a new doctrine of preemptive military attack that President Bush seems determined to implement in order to secure a "regime change" in Iraq.

President Bush, with the support of Prime Minister Blair of the United Kingdom and other close allies, has enthusiastically, and with a remarkable degree of success, sought to create an international coalition against terrorism. A remarkable feature of this coalition is that it includes two major powers traditionally deeply opposed to U.S. global activism, Russia and China. It is clear that the leaders of Moscow and Beijing view the activities of al Qaeda as a grave threat to their own national security. President Putin's demonstrated willingness to provide substantial assistance to the U.S.A. in the struggle against al Qaeda, including permission to overfly and use bases in Russia's sphere of influence, has led to much closer U.S./Russian relations.

Perhaps the most remarkable changes in the strategic environment caused by the September 11 attacks were the swift toppling of the Taliban regime in Afghanistan, which had provided al Qaeda with such a valuable safe haven and base, and the decision by General Musharraf, the leader of Pakistan, to reverse his country's policy of support of the Taliban, a policy that had helped the latter to seize control of most of Afghanistan. Moreover, against most predictions, the interim government in Afghanistan, set in place through the aegis of the UN, appears to have survived and is beginning the painful process of rebuilding Afghanistan's shattered economy.

WHAT IS "NEW" ABOUT THE AL QAEDA TERRORISM? WHY DOES IT STILL POSE A SERIOUS THREAT?

It would be foolish to try to assess the impact of the September 11 attacks without taking into account the responses of the U.S.A., other major states, and the wider world. Yet it would also be wanting to ignore the ways in which al Qaeda, the perpetrators, have changed the nature and severity of the terrorism threat.

Al Qaeda, "the Base," a global terrorist network largely created by bin Laden, can justifiably be characterized as the archetype of the "New Terrorism."[14] Unlike the more traditional types of terrorist groups, it is transnational in its fullest sense: it has a universalistic ideology aimed not only at forcing the U.S.A. to withdraw its forces from the Arabian Peninsula and to stop supporting Israel, but also at toppling the governments of Arab and other Muslim states it accuses of collaborating with the U.S.A. and its allies, and its ultimate aim is to establish a pan-Islamic Caliphate. It is not dependent on any single regime or government for its survival and financial resources. It has a presence in at least fifty countries. Its activists are drawn from a wide range of Muslim countries, and some originate from the Muslim Diaspora within Western societies.

Second, in addition to its central leadership and coordinating committees on military, legal, media, and other matters, al Qaeda has a worldwide network of operational and preparative cells and affiliated organizations capable of being activated at any time and carrying out terrorist attacks on their own initiative. It is because of this, despite the major setback of losing its safe haven in Afghanistan, that the global network is still capable of continuing its terrorist campaign. This has been clearly demonstrated by a series of terrorist attacks, including a number that have been thwarted by the authorities. The use of overseas support networks and international terrorist attacks is, of course, nothing new in the history of terrorism. What is new about the al Qaeda network is the scale of its diffusion around the world, and, as demonstrated in the September 11 attacks, the meticulous long-term planning and terrorist tradecraft the network had been able to deploy.[15]

Last, but not least, there are major differences between the more traditional terrorist groups and al Qaeda regarding *the nature and scale of the violence* the latter employs. Through its suicide airliner attacks on the World Trade Center and the Pentagon, al Qaeda has been responsible for the most lethal acts of terrorism by a substate group in history. It is no accident that bin Laden's network should have been the first substate group to have carried out mass destruction terrorism. An American scholar once stated, "terrorists want a lot of people watching, not a lot of people dead."[16] Sadly, for groups such as al Qaeda and its affiliates, this no longer holds. Therefore, while such deadly terrorist cells, aimed and equipped to cause carnage on a massive scale, are still at large, the threat to the U.S., the U.K., Israel, and other designated "enemies" of the bin Laden network remains an ever-present reality. Moreover, it is important to note that al Qaeda has carried out, planned, or attempted terrorist attacks in a wide range of countries, including Singapore, Pakistan, India, Tunisia, Morocco, Jordan, Italy, France, Kenya, Tanzania, Indonesia, Yemen, and Saudi Arabia. It is also very clear that a terrorist group like al Qaeda, which sets out to kill as many civilians as possible, would have no compunction about using chemical, biological, radiological, or nuclear (CBRN) weapons if they manage to weaponize the appropriate materials. Hence, the threat of CBRN terrorism has been brought a step closer by the September 11 attacks.

Is "Traditional" Terrorism in Decline? Does It Continue to Pose a Serious Threat?

It should be fairly obvious from the preceding discussion that al Qaeda and its affiliates constitute a particularly intractable and dangerous challenge to governments and the international community. Indeed, the author shares the widely held view of specialists in terrorism studies that bin Laden's network poses the most serious threat to innocent life in the history of terrorist groups. But what of the "traditional" groups? Are they being eclipsed by the new terrorism and forced to retire from the scene? Sadly, there is no real evidence of this. The roots of the ethnic, ideological, and religious conflicts that spawn such terrorism show no signs of withering away, and in the eyes of practitioners and sympathizers, terrorism appears an attractive low-cost, low-risk, and potentially high-yield weapon that they are unwilling to forgo.

One positive development is that, at least in a few of the cases, the terrorism appears potentially corrigible, because a combination of political initiatives, diplomacy, and peace processes can sometimes resolve even highly intractable conflicts. For example, against all predictions, the Northern Ireland peace process, though extremely fragile, is still surviving, and terrorist killings in the Province have been dramatically reduced.[17] Another remarkable example where a peace initiative has made a breakthrough is the Norwegian-inspired initiative in Sri Lanka, which has led to a cease-fire between the Tamil Tigers and the government security forces and to peace talks, following a conflict which has cost over 64,000 lives.

Unfortunately there are many deep-rooted conflicts that seem stubbornly incorrigible, like those between the Israelis and the Palestinians and the Indians and Pakistanis. In these situations terrorism only helps polarize the conflict. In both of these cases, terrorist attacks could all too swiftly escalate into full-scale wider interstate war, with a significant risk that weapons of mass destruction could be used by the belligerents.

Conclusions

Certain conclusions follow from this brief analysis: first, both "new" and "traditional" terrorism pose a significant strategic threat to nation-states and to international peace and security generally; second, because there are many different kinds of terrorism with a potentially international reach in the contemporary world, it is a dangerous illusion to believe that they can all be eradicated by "the war on terrorism" or by some simple military or political solution; and third, in view of the risks of terrorism triggering wider wars or escalating to the level where weapons of mass destruction are employed, it is vitally important to develop far more effective and widely supported conflict resolution and peace-building initiatives, as well as methods of more effectively preventing and combating terrorist violence.

Conflict resolution methods alone will not eradicate the terrorist violence of incorrigible groups fueled on hatred and revenge. But by significantly reducing the underlying causes of deep-seated conflicts, giving politics and diplomacy a chance to succeed, they can save thousands of lives.

12

Terrorism: Theory and Reality

Larry Hollingworth

THE SEMANTICS OF STUDIES on terrorism seem to strive more for political correctness than for presenting an accurate picture of the soil in which these terrible acts are usually born, gestate, and explode. Definitions divorced from reality offer, at best, a two dimensional view of a multifaceted problem. To focus solely on acts of desperate individuals and to not equally consider official or state terrorism is not only a simplistic approach but one that fails to make the obvious linkage of violence to violence.

I have served as a humanitarian worker for refugees and displaced persons, and as a negotiator, in areas of armed conflict in many parts of the world. I have personally witnessed the perverse impact of occupying governmental forces on innocent civilians in Srebrenica, Chechnya, Aceh, East Timor, Rwanda, and in Palestine.

Where there is an overt government policy to terrorize civilian populations into a dependent, even supplicant, state, the silence of the oppressed can be very deceptive. Hatred breeds where homes, fields, schools, hospitals, water and electricity supplies, and vital records are wantonly destroyed; when well-equipped armies use overwhelming force against entire townships, killing and maiming women and children; when targeted assassinations and torture instead of the rule of law are used by sovereign states.

In this chapter, I shall offer the reflections of a field worker on some commonly used definitions in the "war on terrorism," and then provide a view of terrorism as perceived and experienced on the ground by civilians under army occupation.

DEFINITION

Look up "terrorism" on the Web search engine "Google;" there are more than fifty pages of entries, many clamoring to define what it is. In the excellent book, *Political Terrorism*, the authors Alex Schmid and Albert Longman offer twenty-six choices.[1]

Noam Chomsky, in one of his numerous papers on the subject, offers two approaches to the study of terrorism: the literal and the propagandistic. "Pursuing the literal approach, we begin by determining what constitutes terrorism. We then seek instances of the phenomenon—concentrating on the major examples . . . and try to determine causes and remedies. The propagandistic approach dictates a different course. We begin with the thesis that terrorism is the responsibility of some officially designated enemy. We then designate terrorist acts as 'terrorist' just in the cases where they can be attributed (plausibly or not) to the required source; otherwise they are to be ignored, suppressed, or termed 'retaliation' or 'self defense.'" He adds, "It comes as no surprise that the propagandistic approach is adopted by governments generally, and by their instruments in totalitarian states."[2]

The U.S. Department of State definition is, "Terrorism is premeditated, politically motivated violence perpetrated against noncombatant groups by subnational groups or clandestine agents usually intended to influence an audience. International terrorism is terrorism involving citizens of the territories of more than one country."[3]

The U.S. Army *Operational Concept for Terrorism Counteraction* pamphlet 525–37 of 1984 defines terrorism with a commendable economy of words as "the calculated use of violence or threat of violence to attain goals that are political, religious, or ideological in nature. This is done through intimidation, coercion, or instilling fear."

Professor Igor Primoratz, a philosopher at Melbourne University, defines terrorism, "for the purpose of philosophical discussion . . . as the deliberate use of violence, or threat of its use, against innocent people, with the aim of intimidating some other people into a course of action they otherwise would not take." Thus, he states, "terrorism has two targets. One person or group is attacked directly, in order to get at another person or group to intimidate them into doing something they would not do. In terms of importance, the indirect target is primary and the direct target secondary. The secondary, but directly attacked target is innocent people."[4]

Professor Rakesh Gupta presents a simpler "philosophical" offering. "In any discussion on terrorism—whether it is criminal or political—denial of the right of life would be the basic philosophical category of analysis." This statement seems to suggest that political terrorist acts may be legal. But Professor Gupta continues and clears up the doubt: "Since a terrorist action today is a small group action against innocents and is against either national or international law, it is criminal."[5]

Back to Professor Primoratz to define who are the victims of terrorism: the "innocents . . . persons not guilty of any action or (omission) the terrorist could plausibly bring up as a justification of what he does to them. They are not attacking him; therefore he cannot justify his action in terms of self-defence. They are not waging war on him, nor on those on whose behalf he presumes to act; therefore he cannot say that he is merely waging war. They are not responsible, on any plausible understanding of responsibility, for the (real or alleged) injustice, suffering, or deprivation that is being inflicted on him or on those whose case he has adopted, and which is so grave that a violent response to it can be properly considered."[6]

Primoratz importantly further defines the "innocents": "In the context of war, according to the mainstream version of just war theory, this includes all except members of the armed forces and security services, those who supply them with arms and ammunition, and political officials directly involved in the conflict. In the context of a political conflict that falls short of war, the category of the innocent has similarly wide scope: it includes all except government officials, police and members of security services."

This seems to imply that, at least "philosophically," soldiers, politicians, and police are "legitimate" victims of acts of terrorism.

VIOLENCE

The key word in most definitions of terrorism is "violence," an action that has been around since Cain slew Abel. Is there good and bad violence; a violence that liberates and a violence that enslaves? St. Thomas Aquinas maintained that, "violence is good or bad depending on the use or purpose to which it is put." In his book, *Violence,* Jacques Ellul stresses the importance of who is responsible for an act of violence and introduces the concept of "force" by quoting the well-known example used by the theologian Suarez: "a man cannot lawfully kill his neighbor, nor can two men together, nor ten thousand, but a judge can lawfully pronounce a sentence of death. His indisputable legitimate power derives from the state. There is all the difference between violence and force."[7]

Does this "force" absolve a state from a crime of violence? Not all states and state decisions are necessarily just or right. The power that condemns to death may be tyrannical or oppressive or simply may make a mistake. How legitimate is the state? Did the state or the ruler of the state achieve power justly or unjustly? Does the state's use of force conform to law—national and international? Jacques Ellul again: "Force used by a state is just when its use conforms to the laws; when it does not conform to the laws, it is still force—not violence—but unjust force." Scant comfort for the victim but encouragement for retribution.

Ellul has five rules, which he cautions all who contemplate violence to remember:

1. Once begun there is continuity to violence
2. There is reciprocity: violence begets violence

3. Violence begets violence . . . and nothing else (I am not happy with this one)
4. There is sameness to violence—there are proportions and shades but essentially violence is violence
5. The perpetrators of violence always try to justify the violence and themselves

THE CYCLE OF VIOLENCE, . . . THE TANDEM OF RESPONSIBILITY

"Who started it?" Is there a parent or teacher who has not asked this question?

How often do we hear spokespersons, especially in parts of the Middle East, say, "In response to . . . we have carried out. . . ."? In any major crisis over the past decade, it would be very difficult to define when the crisis began and by whom: Sudan, Somalia, former Yugoslavia, Rwanda, Chechnya, Aceh, and Palestine, and I only choose some of those where I have served. But each and every side can point to the last incident as the one that they must revenge, and so the cycle continues. Once the violence begins it is difficult to effect reconciliation. A leader at any level who is prepared to attend talks with the other side risks the accusation of weakness or collaboration. But unless both sides can at least glimpse the view from the other side, there is no hope.

The French Franciscan Father Maillard, when Director of *Freres du Monde,* published in their magazine: "It is always the violence of the oppressor that unleashes the violence of the oppressed. The time comes when violence is the only possible way for the oppressed to state their case." Again, speaking only from personal experience, I cannot fault this.[8]

The black power leader, Pastor Albert Cleage Jr., said after the race riots in Detroit: "Now we are no longer afraid; now it is the white man who is afraid." The violence of the oppressed transfers fear to the oppressor previously secure in his dominance. This is particularly so today in Israel where the Palestinian retaliation includes a weapon that truly frightens the Israeli population: the suicide bomb. Rattle the bars of a caged lion and you must expect to be scratched or bitten.

THE PERPETRATOR

Who is a terrorist? It depends on who applies the label. One man's terrorist is another man's freedom fighter. Or, to quote Noam Chomsky: "actions undertaken against oppressive regimes and occupying armies (are) considered resistance by their perpetrators and terrorism by the rulers, even when they are nonviolent."[9]

Terrorists espouse a cause. The focus of the cause can be any shade of the rainbow. They may represent: the have nots—no land, no access to education, no money, no status, no resources; the religiously oppressed; the racially oppressed; the politically oppressed; or the culturally oppressed. More often they are to the left of the political spectrum but some of the most virulent are from the right wing. They can be from minority groups, fascists, racists. They come from all walks of life and all strata of society.

Jihad and Martyrs

A number of terrorist groups operate in and out of states where Islam is the major faith. Their campaigns are labeled "jihad" and their dead are honored as "martyrs."

Jihad is the verbal noun of the verb to strive, to struggle, to exert. While a number of other nouns can be linked to jihad to give it different connotations, it is now best known in its meaning "armed struggle" and, more specifically, "armed struggle against unbelievers." In effect, it has the same meaning as "crusade"! Jihad is often mentioned in the Koran as *is qitaal,* which means "fighting." The most relevant references are: K22:39, "Leave is given to those who fight because they were wronged"; K3:157–158, which encourages participation in the fighting; and K169–

172, which promises rewards in heaven to those martyrs *(shuhaada)* who die in battle. K2:190–194 has a chilling relevance in the Middle East today: "And fight in the way of God with those who fight you, but aggress not: God loves not the aggressors. And slay them wherever you come upon them, and expel them from where they expelled you."[10]

As scholars pore over holy books and interpret them in different ways, the Koran is no exception. There are at least two distinct schools, the Modernists and the Fundamentalists, and two different ways of approaching the interpretations; one is to take each verse in traditional order and to examine its content in depth, the other is to gather together all the verses on one topic and to examine their relationship. The latter produces the more moderate interpretation.

Rebels

Professor Gupta is keen to point out the difference between a terrorist and a rebel. He labels Bal Gangadhar Tilak, "who had no fetish for nonviolence," as "a mass leader and not an alchemist of revolution," and similarly labels Mahatma Gandhi "a rebel with his entire pacifist menace." I am happy so far but have reservations with his next statement that: "[a rebel's] commitment is to the cause of his people and not to himself or his group, which is the commitment of a terrorist." This may be true in the Indian examples he gives; I am not certain it is when applied more generally. I suspect that many, if not most, terrorists believe that they represent the true voice of the people. They may be deluded but their zeal is genuine.

Edward Herman and David Peterson, in *Z* magazine, introduce the concept of "retail" versus "wholesale" terror. "Bin Laden and his network . . . is a 'retail' terrorist network, like the IRA or Cuban refugee terrorist network: it has no helicopter gun ships, no offensive missiles, no 'daisy cutters,' no nuclear weapons. Really large scale killing and torture—'wholesale' terrorism—is implemented by states, not by no state terrorists."[11]

State Terrorism

> State terrorism is a taboo term. Politicians never utter it. Newspapers rarely describe it. Academic "experts" suppress it. It is by far the most menacing form of terrorism.
>
> John Pilger: www.mirror.co.uk

> We must recognize that by convention—and it must be emphasized only by convention—great power use, and the threat of the use, of force is normally described as coercive diplomacy, and not as a form of terrorism.
>
> Michael Stohl, "States, Terrorism and State Terrorism,"
> ed. Robert O'Slater and Michael Stohl
> (London: Macmillan, 1988)

There are states that support terrorism domestically, states that support terrorism externally overtly, states that support terrorism externally covertly, and states that do all three.

William Blum is the recorder *par excellence* of the activities of the United States of America as a purveyor of state terrorism. In his highly readable books he chronicles the participation of the U.S. interventions around the globe. In *Killing Hope,* there is a chapter for each intervention. And there are fifty-five chapters![12] The second book is entitled *Rogue State*. It has three sections: "Ours and Theirs: Washington's Love/Hate Relationship with Terrorists and Human Rights Violators"; "United States and the Use of Weapons of Mass Destruction"; and "A Rogue State versus the World."[13]

Mavis Cheek, who chose the book as one of the books of the year in the U.K. Sunday newspaper, *The Observer,* wrote, "William Blum, once of the U.S. State Department, gives a chilling reminder that while there may be no justification for September 11, there may be reasons."

William Blum is not the only U.S. citizen to criticize U.S. policy. "The guiding principle, it appears, is that the U.S. is a lawless terrorist state and this is right and just, whatever the world may think, whatever international institutions may declare" (Noam Chomsky).

John Pilger, who is much more catholic in his range of targets, writes in a Post Bali bombing report: "Today, largely unreported, the Indonesian military, with the tacit approval of the United States, Britain, and Australia, is terrorizing the populations of Aceh and West Papua. Most of the 'human rights violations' in these provinces—the euphemism for state terrorism—have been part and parcel of 'protecting' the American Exxon oil holdings in Aceh as well as the vast Freeport copper and gold mines and BP holdings in West Papua."[14] He refers to research by Edward Herman and Gerry O'Sullivan: "Covering the period since 1965, which points to the killing of several thousand people by nonstate terrorists such as al Qaeda, compared with 2.5 million civilians killed by state-sponsored terrorism. These include the violence of the South African apartheid regime, the Suharto regime in Indonesia, the 'Contras' in Nicaragua, and other American-backed terrorist states."

The U.S. State Department, which, if Mr. Blum is right, should know a thing or two about the subject, itself maintains an annual list of State Sponsors of Terrorism. It includes Cuba, Iran, Iraq, Libya, North Korea, Sudan, and Syria.

Is a state that pursues terrorism a terrorist state? Professor Primoratz: "I suggest we reserve this label for states that do not merely resort to terrorism on certain occasions, but employ it in a lasting and systematic way and, indeed, are defined in part by the sustained use of terrorism against their own population. These are totalitarian states."[15]

It is, however, important to note that a few non-totalitarian states have used terrorism against their own populations.

Is there ever a need for external interference? Irving Kristol believes so: "Insignificant nations, like insignificant people, can quickly experience delusions of significance . . . In truth, the days of 'gunboat diplomacy' are never over . . . Gunboats are as necessary for international order as police cars are for domestic order."[16]

A Case Study: Palestine

I choose Palestine for the simple reason that it is my most recent field appointment. I was United Nations Relief and Works Agency for Palestine Refugees (UNRWA) Emergency Coordinator in Jenin Camp on loan from the Center for International Health and Cooperation. I left there six weeks before writing this chapter. I begin with a caveat: it is difficult to serve in an occupied Palestinian community and be true to the tenets of our humanitarian faith—neutrality, impartiality, and independence.

"What is the difference between state terrorism and individual terrorist acts?" asks Lev Grinberg of the Humphrey Institute for Social Research at Ben Gurion University in an oft-quoted article from the May/June 2002 *Tikkun* magazine. "If we understand the difference," he continues, "we'll also understand the evilness of U.S. policies in the Middle East." He then answers the question he posed. "Israel's state terrorism is defined by the U.S. officials as 'self-defense,' while individual suicide bombers are called 'terrorists.'"[17]

Grinberg is not soft on Palestinian terrorists: "Suicide bombs killing innocent citizens must be unequivocally condemned; they are immoral acts, and their perpetrators should be sent to jail. . . . However, they cannot be compared to state terrorism carried out by the Israeli government. The former are acts of despair of a people that sees no future, vastly ignored by an unfair and distorted international public opinion. The latter are cold and 'rational' decisions of a state and a military apparatus of occupation, well equipped, financed, and backed by the only superpower in the world."

"Palestinian violence receives worldwide condemnation" (Chomsky[18]) with the silent rider booming in our ears that Israeli violence rarely does.

It is bitterly ironic that the modern state of Israel, conceived by a biblical promise, born out of a terrorist/freedom fighter struggle, growing up with a population of victims of generations of oppression and constantly led by leaders whose roots lie in the

Holocaust, is not able to understand the aspirations and desires of their neighbors with whom they share the land. "Do unto others what you would have them do unto you" is replaced with, "Do unto others what was done unto you."

It is sad that in the international arena "Palestinian" is associated closely with "terrorist," in some circles to the point of being synonymous. This image was beginning to change in the early days of the Second Intifada with frequent television coverage of the new "Davids" slinging stones at the new "Goliath" in his armored vehicle. Unfortunately, a faction of militant Palestinians—how easy it is to label all actions as Palestinian—returned to the suicide bomb as its most successful weapon. More unfortunate was the choice of target. If the suicide bombers had blown themselves up at checkpoints, in Israeli barracks, and in Israeli Defence Force Headquarters, and all their victims were military, I am sure they would have maintained the tide of sympathy and may even have earned admiration for their desperate courage. Better still would have been protest suicides outside embassies or other high-profile buildings where the suicide was the sole victim. Sadly, they chose civilian targets and killed and maimed innocent women and children. They have frightened the Israelis beyond expectation, but have brought upon themselves a ruthless military retaliation and the return of the dreadful epithet "terrorist."

I was in Jenin in late April 2002 after the Israeli incursion. The talk was of a massacre. A UN mission headed by Mary Robinson, UN High Commissioner on Human Rights, was refused entry into Israel. The United Nations assembled in Geneva a team of the most respected of international senior persons: Mr. Martti Ahtisaari, former Prime Minister of Finland; Madame Sadako Ogata from Japan, former UN High Commissioner for Refugees; and M. Cornelio Sommaruga, former President of the International Committee of the Red Cross from Switzerland, to go to Jenin to investigate what had happened. This fact-finding mission was agreed to between the UN Secretary General and the Israeli Foreign Minister and had the full support of the UN Security

Council. The mission was refused entry into Israel! As well as an insult, this was a grave strategic error. Human Rights Watch (HRW), with a speed and accuracy that should be a model for all agencies, produced in early May a comprehensive investigation report that stated that there was no massacre but many severe human rights violations. I will dwell no more on this incursion but recommend the reader to view the HRW report, which is available on the Internet and whose findings I fully support.[19]

I further recommend the more comprehensive and measured report, *Israel and the Occupied Territories, Shielded from Scrutiny: IDF Violations in Jenin and Nablus,* issued by Amnesty International on November 4, 2002. This covers the period of April–June 2002.

I left Jenin in early June and returned in mid-August to a Jenin under curfew. What did this mean? I soon discovered. The Israeli Defence Forces occupied the West Bank. It was not possible to get in and out without passing IDF checkpoints, which was time-consuming for internationals and almost impossible for the majority of Palestinians. The curfew was an added inconvenience. It was imposed either with warning or without. If with warning, the start time was given but rarely the end time.

If it was without warning, tanks and armored cars swept into the town, at least one with a loudspeaker. The population was told, "It is forbidden to move around. Go home and close your doors." From then on anyone who moved risked being shot.

The population of Jenin camp is 13,900. Together the town and camp number 41,000.

Forty-one thousand citizens were expected to clear the streets and get home rapidly. Not too easy; very difficult when you take into consideration that more than a third of the work force of Jenin live in outlying villages. Clear the streets, clear a checkpoint with no warning. Clear the schools, clear the hospital clinics. It would be easy with a considerate occupying force. It would be safe with an occupying force with tight rules of engagement: having clear rules of when they can shoot, at whom they can shoot, and with what warning. With aggressive and often nervous troops who were told that their own safety was of paramount importance, bursts of machine gun fire were common. Fatalities and injuries were frequent events. The terrorizing of the population, constant. It is hard to imagine the fear a tank generates as it growls along narrow streets sinisterly swiveling its main barrel from object to object. And if the barrel stops on you, there is a heart-stopping moment while you silently pray the tank commander has recognized that you present no threat. More than a dozen innocent civilians were shot dead during my time in Jenin. They included women and children. Some youths were shot dead throwing stones at tanks. In every exchange of weapon fire between Palestinian and Israeli, the Palestinian was the underdog, the odds-on favorite to lose. The Israeli response was so unequal, so disproportionate. There was no weapon in any hands in Jenin that was capable of penetrating tank armor. If there had been, they surely would have used it. The IDF could have fired paint ball or smoke or tear gas or rubber bullets and dispersed the Palestinians at no risk to themselves.

After weeks of on and off violence, more on than off, the IDF lifted the curfew and replaced it with a lesser imposition: closure. This was a reward for a lull in the attacks on Israelis.

Closure meant that the town and camp were completely blockaded. There were heavy armored checkpoints at every entrance and exit. Sounds easy. Stay within the camp and town and no problem. But what about the third of the work force who live outside the closed area? This includes doctors, dentists, nurses, teachers, tradesmen, humanitarian agency staff, the mayor of the town, the governor. And what about the staff of the schools and the clinics and the university who live within the closed area but whose workplace is in outlying villages? What about farm produce, grocery stocks, medicines, baby milk powder that comes into the town from outside?

Did everything stop? No. So what happened? Everyone from the mayor to the vegetable dealer used taxis to come into or out of the town using fields, tracks, culverts, whatever cover was available. Did the IDF turn a blind eye? It knew that this must happen, had to happen. No, taxi drivers and passengers were killed and wounded. Why?

Unfortunately, there were further suicide bombs, so closure was revoked and a military operation mounted. This was curfew and closure with a vengeance. Nothing moved. Houses with good views were commandeered, snipers were placed at vantage points, and armored vehicles were positioned at numerous static checkpoints or roamed the town at will. Anyone on the streets was shot at. It did not take many days before there was little food in the town, no baby milk, and, very importantly, no water. Because of two or three suicide bombers whose mission was not known by any more than a handful of controllers, 40,000 citizens suffered severe deprivation. After a while, some pipelines for essential personnel were opened. Passing through these checkpoints was time-consuming and humiliating. Hundreds were arrested; some interrogated and released, others disappeared into Israeli detention centers. Few were charged. Fewer released. Houses of known terrorists were demolished, their bewildered families left homeless.

When the town was on its knees and morale at its lowest, the operation ended, and, thanking the Lord for small mercies, we gratefully accepted the comparative liberty of closure.

I handed the office over to my successor, another international. Seven days later, he was shot dead by Israeli gunfire in the UN compound during an unannounced military operation. The IDF delayed the arrival of an ambulance, not that it would have been of any help.

It is hard to know where to begin categorizing the breaches of human rights. It will be fairest if I end this chapter with an extract from the list of recommendations of the Amnesty International report. Although written to cover April to June 2002 in Jenin, every observation is valid today.

It is not difficult to conclude that the population of Jenin is terrorized by the IDF.

It is also indisputable that suicide bombers came from Jenin. It is indisputable that there are terrorist cells operating within

Jenin. It is indisputable that there have been bomb-making factories in Jenin. It is indisputable that there are armed men shooting at Israeli troops in Jenin. Perhaps they number fifty or sixty. Because of them, 39,950 are collectively punished. IDF soldiers killed more Palestinians than suicide bombers killed Israelis. No one places curfews or closure in their towns. They are, however, now fencing themselves in, creating prisons for themselves mentally and physically.

Their tactics are increasing the numbers of hardliners in the camps and towns.

They fail to see that they escalate the cycle of violence. Suicide bombs are a reaction to violence, not an initiator of violence. Both sides have told me that there is no alternative to their tactics.

Sadly, the answer lies with the United States. As I write, an Israeli team consisting of the Defense Ministry director general, the Prime Minister's bureau chief, and the Finance Ministry director general are in Washington to present a request for $4 billion for special defense aid and $8 billion in loan guarantees. Few doubt that they will get it.

"It is absurd that we are still witnessing, in the twenty-first century, a case of occupation where the dominant side is seen as the victim" (Lev Grinberg).[20]

SUMMARY OF AMNESTY INTERNATIONAL RECOMMENDATIONS

Amnesty International calls on the government of Israel:

- To ensure the IDF operations are conducted in full respect of international human rights and humanitarian law
- To initiate a full, thorough, transparent, and impartial investigation into all allegations of violations of international human rights and humanitarian law, including those documented in this report, and to make the results public
- To cooperate with United Nations investigations
- To bring to justice those alleged to have committed serious vio-

lations of international human rights or humanitarian law in
proceedings that meet international standards for fair trial

- To ensure prompt and adequate reparation for victims of serious human rights or humanitarian law violations
- To respect and protect the human rights of all persons living in the Occupied Territories without discrimination
- To include the practices of Israeli authorities in the Occupied Territories in all reporting to UN human rights treaty bodies
- To take immediate action to prevent the IDF from compelling Palestinians to take part in military operations or to act as "human shields" and to take measures against any soldier or military commander who undertakes or sanctions such practices
- To fulfill its international legal obligations by ensuring that medical staff and ambulances are allowed to carry out duties without undue delays, and with safe passage
- To ensure safe access for humanitarian and medical supplies
- To immediately stop the use of lethal force to enforce curfews
- To end collective punishments, including house destruction, closures and curfews, and cutting off of water and electricity
- To end torture or other ill treatment of those in custody
- To end administrative detention and release all administrative detainees unless they are to be brought to trial for a recognizably criminal offence in a trial which is in accordance with UN fair trial standards
- To accept an international monitoring presence in Israel's Occupied Territories with a strong human rights component

Amnesty International calls on the Palestine Authority:

- To take all action to prevent anyone under its jurisdiction from attacking or otherwise endangering the safety of civilians

Amnesty International calls on the Palestinian armed groups:

- To respect fundamental principles of international law that prohibit the killing of civilians
- To end any use of children in armed operations[21]

13

Gender Exploitation

Ambassador Nancy Ely-Raphel

INTRODUCTION[1]

IN THIS INCREASINGLY globalized world where people and cultures are intersecting with ever-greater frequency, human trafficking for both labor and sexual exploitation has become an immediate concern for governments and individuals. Human trafficking is referred to as a form of modern-day slavery whose victims suffer sexual or labor exploitation involving indentured servitude, debt bondage, chattel slavery, and peonage, among other slavery-like practices.

This chapter examines gender exploitation as a consequence of human trafficking, and the economic and social crises that accelerate the exploitation of the disenfranchised, who are most often women and girls. I also focus on the denial of women's basic rights and protections that is borne out of gender discrimination, and its devastating consequences to the social fabric. In defining some important aspects of this problem, I will also highlight the U.S. government's responses and proactive efforts, both domestically and internationally.

Background

In October 2000, the U.S. government adopted into federal law the *Trafficking Victims Protection Act of 2000* ("TVPA"), Pub. L. No. 106–386, a multifaceted anti-trafficking law. The TVPA provides numerous forms of assistance to combat trafficking on both a macro and micro level. The harshest form of trafficking, for which maximum provision is made, is known as "severe forms of trafficking in persons" and includes two parts: "sex trafficking in which a commercial sex act is induced by force, fraud, or coercion, or in which the person induced to perform such act has not attained eighteen years of age," or, labor trafficking involving "the recruitment, harboring, transportation, provision, or obtaining of a person for labor or services, through the use of force, fraud, or coercion for the purpose of subjection to involuntary servitude, peonage, debt bondage, or slavery."

Globally, more and more societies are experiencing human trafficking. It knows no geographical, national, nor ideological boundaries: traffickers may transport their victims within one sovereign nation or across international borders; and may target victims of any age, race, ethnicity, and gender. Human trafficking may be caused by social or economic crisis in societies in which women are already the victims of age-old gender discrimination; by the destruction of social, cultural, and familial protections; or civil and military conflict that displaces people and populations. Large-scale social calamities have touched a good portion of the world during the last twenty years, including civil wars in Africa, the overwhelming epidemic of AIDS, the near-collapse of economies throughout Southeast Asia, and the increase in organized crime in the former Soviet Union. These crises have contributed to the tragic increase in human trafficking.

Traffickers target women, girls, men, and boys when exercising their criminal plots. Sometimes, the particular purpose for which they seek to traffick an individual is particular to one gender. For example, young boys are abducted and conscripted as child soldiers by rebel armies, or as camel jockeys, while adult men are recruited into forced labor for work in rubber and cocoa plantations. Women and girls, for example, are often sought out for work as domestic servants in the homes of diplomats and higher-income families, for work in clothing sweatshops, and for sexual exploitation and pornography.

While specific figures regarding the percentage of female versus male victims have not been gathered, trafficking for the purposes of sexual exploitation is a prevalent form of human trafficking, which indicates the destructive gender exploitation and discrimination occurring throughout the world. Women have struggled to gain equality and equity the world over, yet where this is still lacking, they remain vulnerable members of societies and easy prey for traffickers.

Trafficking in women and girls is a lucrative business for many reasons, some of which include social tolerance for the degradation of women as second-class citizens, women's changing roles in the family, and the fact that women's empowerment and decision-making authority has not increased proportionally to their responsibilities within a society. Women and girls in countless societies are subject to violence and abuse in the home and in public, a violence against women that is seldom confronted openly. Throughout the world, women have achieved greater equities in education and job skills, and more women are heading households, especially in emerging or otherwise struggling economies. Yet, demand for their labor often turns exploitive as they frequently bear the responsibility of providing for their families in very weak economies with few opportunities, especially for women. This plays into the hands of traffickers where women are unable to reach a sufficient level of employment in their home communities and they are forced to look elsewhere.

GENDER DISCRIMINATION'S CONTRIBUTION TO THE CAUSES AND CONSEQUENCES OF TRAFFICKING IN WOMEN AND GIRLS

It is important to put this theme into context through an actual trafficking story. The woman described below was victimized by traffickers and then subjected to continuing trauma throughout her experience with the criminal justice system. Her case illustrates the role gender discrimination plays in creating conditions for traffickers to target women and girls to a disproportionate degree, and subsequently how these women and girls are stigmatized by members of society who treat them as criminals, rather than victims of trafficking.

Case Study: Nina

Nina was born in a Southeastern European country with a faltering economy, political instability, high unemployment, and rampant organized crime. She was raised by her mother, who was mentally unstable. Nina could not find work that paid her enough to survive and, without the support of her extended family, she was determined to find work abroad. At the age of nineteen, Nina was recruited by an acquaintance who offered her a ride and assistance in getting a job in Italy. She went with him in his car, yet, before they even left their country, the journey ended at a brothel where she was sold and sexually exploited.

Nina was obstinate, and the traffickers beat her and drugged her into submission. She often became ill, but she courageously managed to escape once. Although fully aware of the dangers, she returned home to her village for lack of any other place to seek refuge. Soon after her return, the traffickers kidnapped her and took her back. Ultimately, the brothel where she was working was raided and the police took her into custody as a prostitute, a minor offense in that jurisdiction. She told her story of violence, rape, and forced prostitution to the police who, under much international pressure, decided to investigate. Despite concerns over retribution by the traffickers, she agreed to be a material witness at the trial.

The criminal code had no articles about human trafficking, so the defendants were charged with rape and other sexual offenses, as well as forced prostitution and pimping. Even with the defendants in pretrial custody, Nina needed a safe and secure location. None existed, so the police found her an apartment and assigned police protection. The very police officer assigned to protect her alerted the criminal gang of her whereabouts. She was threatened and security forces mobilized to find another, safer location.

When the trial finally took place, judges and defense counsel teased, mocked, and insulted her throughout the proceedings. The government's limited resources confined the trial to a courtroom so small that she shared a bench with the defendants. The rules of procedure mandated that she "accuse" the defendants in open court, the very men who beat, drugged, and raped her, and she did so from that shared bench, physically brushing arms with them. The criminal judicial proceedings only further victimized her as she was called derogatory names, her character and past sexual history were degraded, and the defendants threatened her life in front of the panel of judges. The judges did nothing to stop this.

When the trial was finished, the defendants were found guilty, but released from custody pending appeal. Again, they found her at the "safe location" where she was staying and threatened her life, even though she had twenty-four-hour protection. With the trial over, she had to find a long-term solution for herself. She could not return to her hometown and she could not remain where she was. Thanks to personal efforts by foreign diplomats familiar with her case, she was allowed to go to a third country as a student, where she has assumed a new name, and now tries to live a new life despite the horror of her victimization. She has no social, emotional, or physical assistance. Though safe, she is lonely and depressed, and desperate enough to consider returning home, despite the obvious dangers.

This graphic example is not unique, and illustrates the many ways in which various levels of gender discrimination and exploitation lead traffickers to target women.

Poverty, Migration, and Women   Nina's economic situation forced her to seek employment in a country with a stronger economy and more opportunities for work. Her case is not unusual. Numbers of women under the poverty line and who are migrating for economic reasons are increasing. These factors contribute to sexually exploitative trafficking. According to U.S. State Department figures, even though women are widely considered a growing majority of the workforce in export industries, women and children today represent 70 percent of the 1.3 billion people who live in absolute poverty. In many of these same societies, women have little prospect of advancement, are prohibited from owning or inheriting property, and are prevented from attending school with the same opportunities as their male counterparts. Societies that perpetuate this kind of gender discrimination in entitlements contribute to the vulnerabilities that encourage women to leave their homes in search of a profitable livelihood.

In keeping with today's economic realities, globalization trends bring competition for goods and services to even the remotest corner of the globe. As such, even where women are well represented in the domestic labor force, they often dominate informal economic and production sectors and produce goods that are sensitive to external competition. Moreover, women often work in clothing and textile industries, offering attractive skills to labor traffickers. When female laborers cannot provide for themselves or their families, and when their societies do not allow them to reap the fair profits of their work, they seek to migrate for better work opportunities. This situation is then ripe for traffickers to recruit these laborers for employment, and then subject them to deplorable conditions, or even into slavery-like conditions, such as Nina experienced.

Pervasive Violence Against Women While Nina's case illustrates how violence is a tool traffickers use to control victims, violence against women in other parts of society pushes women into the hands of traffickers. Where violence against women is pandemic, domestic violence—most often unspoken—forces women to escape abusive situations in search of new opportunities and new lives. State Department gender experts have looked closely at the phenomenon of gender-based violence—violence targeted at individuals because of their gender—and have noted that, while gender-based violence may affect both men and women, it principally affects women and girls. Gender-based violence exists across cultures, but is particularly prevalent in areas of conflict. State

Department refugee experts attribute this to specific, conflict-driven factors, including the frequent dissolution of the rule of law and basic legal protections, lack of physical security, male disempowerment, and the collapse of normal social roles and family units. Gender-based violence, like violence against women, operates as a factor pushing women out of their homes and societies and into the hands of traffickers who, at first glance, seem to offer a path out of the violence and into a new life.

Women in Civil and Military Conflicts   Civil conflicts have disproportionately negative effects on women and girls. In recent civil disorders around the world, men, quite naturally, account for the largest numbers of combatants while women and children comprise the largest section of civilians affected by conflict. In addition, U.S. figures indicate that up to 70 percent of the internally displaced persons and refugees around the world are women and children. International reports tell of traffickers preying upon these very vulnerable refugees and internally displaced persons, luring or kidnapping them from refugee camps.

While peacekeeping missions are vital elements for securing overall peace and stability, they may also bring with them an unfortunate byproduct when some police and soldiers deny their role as protector and become the abuser—reports of which are coming to light. In these same war-torn societies, local and regional criminal gangs often take advantage of the breakdown in law enforcement and security. During the reconstruction phase in many post-conflict societies, women have been marginalized or excluded entirely from the decision-making process while decision-makers relegate women's interests to a lower priority. Consequently, women seek a better life elsewhere. Hence, post-conflict societies are often both source and destination points for trafficking in women and girls.

Misunderstanding of Female Victims of Crime   Prevailing misconceptions of female victims of sexual crimes lead to an atmosphere that tolerates sex trafficking. Nina's example showed how a trafficking victim might experience re-traumatization through the judicial process if the people implementing the process lack appropriate sensitization and understanding of the crime and its effect on the victims. Sexual crimes are subjects people are often uncomfortable discussing in private, much less in public. Consequently, people remain ignorant of a woman's victimization, believing that she was "willing" when, in fact, she was a victim. Numerous case studies show that law enforcement investigators do not properly question victims but rather treat them as criminals, when they should be pursuing the perpetrators exploiting the victims. In the very few cases that advance to criminal judicial proceedings, many court monitoring reports indicate serious misperceptions about trafficking victims' involvement in acts of prostitution. Like Nina's experience, documented case studies tell of defense counsel taunting victims who testify, judges asking degrading questions in trial, and inappropriate character evidence being allowed into the record. This misunderstanding of victimization may make a woman fearful of reporting sex crimes and, consequently, less likely to testify, thus allowing traffickers to continue their criminal activities with little disincentive. Nina was unusually determined; most victims give up or disassociate themselves with prosecution efforts from the beginning.

Consequences

Gender exploitation as a consequence of human trafficking hinders governments' abilities to effectuate adequate protections. Many trafficking victims are afraid to return to their home countries for fear of being stigmatized as "unclean," and viewed solely as prostitutes. Many women also fear retribution and re-trafficking by the traffickers. Many victims are re-trafficked because police are unable or unwilling to protect against it. This unwillingness may be a result of corruption and complicity in trafficking, or perhaps a failure to prioritize such protection as important. Where there is an unwillingness to protect, options for victims to return home are compromised.

Reintegration is also complicated by misunderstandings of the needs of female victims of crime in general, and of sexual crimes in particular. Like any victim of a serious and traumatic crime, trafficking victims need rehabilitation, understanding, and the ability to reinsert themselves into a society where they can develop strength and independence. Female victims of sexual trafficking may also suffer serious and debilitating illnesses, including HIV/AIDS and other sexually transmitted illnesses. Many suffer in silence and in the shadows, afraid of telling anyone their story for fear of accusations that they are worthless and unclean. The continued social misperceptions about women and girls who are sexually exploited sometimes prevent them from seeking medical and psychological assistance.

The U.S. Response

The U.S. response to human trafficking is multifaceted. As the TVPA institutionalizes the mechanisms necessary to comprehensively address human trafficking, each federal agency charged with implementation is developing a wide-ranging plan to combat trafficking in its area. The section below offers details of just some of these responses.

Overview

The TVPA was adopted into federal law to fight sexual and labor exploitation both domestically and internationally. Combating human trafficking is a priority for the U.S. government both at home and abroad. According to the U.S. government's Department of Health and Human Services (HHS) Office of Refugee Resettlement (ORR), women and girls were the predominate victims of human trafficking into the United States who received a form of assistance from the federal government. According to HHS's fiscal year 2002 (FY02) annual report, 79.8 percent of trafficking victims who received ORR certification/eligibility letters were female. In HHS's assessment, this figure highlights the fact that women and girls tend to be the most vulnerable to these crimes. The circumstances these victims endured included aspects of sexual exploitation, involuntary domestic servitude, forced migrant agricultural labor, and sweatshop labor. The U.S. government is working toward eradication of gender exploitation and gender discrimination in many ways, and its focus on combating human trafficking is one part of that effort.

The U.S. government frames its response to trafficking within three key areas: protection, prosecution, and prevention. The following discussion provides a snapshot of some of the U.S. government's efforts, each of which falls under one or more of those key areas.

Coordinated Federal Response

The TVPA created mechanisms to assist and protect victims both at home and abroad, and to ensure that the U.S. government focuses on foreign governments' responses. The TVPA mandates the creation of an interagency task force chaired by the Secretary of State. This high-level commitment is coupled with working-level implementation through a senior policy advisory group, which coordinates policy and programs. The Departments of Labor (DOL) and Justice's (DOJ) Trafficking in Persons and Worker Exploitation Task Force coordinates the investigation and prosecution of domestic trafficking cases. It also supports a toll-free complaint line for trafficking victims and has produced brochures for law enforcement agents to give to victims. The Department of State (DOS), along with U.S. Agency for International Development (USAID), coordinates and monitors significant assistance programs the U.S. is sponsoring worldwide to address the prosecution of offenders, to offer protection to victims, and to prevent victimization.

A federal regulation implementing section 107(c) of the TVPA went into effect on August 23, 2001. It establishes overall implementation procedures and assigns responsibilities for the Departments of State and Justice to identify and protect victims of severe forms of trafficking in persons. Specifically it addresses: the identification and protection of victims of severe forms of trafficking in persons; access to information and translation services for these victims; legal mechanisms for allowing victims of severe forms of trafficking in persons who are potential witnesses continued presence in the United States, as well as the right to work; and development of appropriate training by the DOS and the DOJ.

The U.S. government seeks to help trafficking victims heal from the trauma they have experienced. Section 107(b)(2) of the TVPA authorizes the Attorney General to make grants to states, Indian tribes, units of local government, and nonprofit, nongovernmental victims' service organizations to develop, expand, or strengthen service programs for victims of trafficking through the Office for Victims of Crime in the Department of Justice. The HHS ORR is responsible for certifying victims and ensuring they receive their benefits. Trafficking victims who are certified as such receive benefits to the same extent as refugees.[2] The ORR also provides grant support to organizations assisting certified and/or eligible victims of severe forms of trafficking, and provides local and community outreach. In addition, the Department of Labor, Bureau of International Labor Affairs, provides grant funding through a cooperative agreement with the International Labor Organization's Program on the Elimination of Child Labor; these programs include awareness-raising campaigns, capacity building of governmental and nongovernmental partners, provision of rehabilitation services to child victims, and school or vocational training.

The State Department's Office to Monitor and Combat Trafficking in Persons

The TVPA created the Office to Monitor and Combat Trafficking in Persons in the U.S. Department of State. The office is responsible for collecting information about all countries in the world with significant trafficking problems and for drafting the annual Trafficking in Persons Report (TIP Report), which analyzes the efficacy of governments' response to their trafficking problems.

The TVPA ensures that elimination of human trafficking is, and will remain, a global priority by mandating sanctions, unless they are waived, beginning in 2003, including the termination of nonhumanitarian, nontrade-related foreign assistance,[3] against certain countries based on the State Department's TIP Report. The sanctions will be applicable to those countries of origin, transit, or destination for a significant number of victims of severe forms of trafficking whose governments do not fully comply with the minimum standards for the elimination of trafficking and are not making significant efforts to bring themselves into compliance.[4]

Protection

The drafters of the TVPA understood that once an individual falls into trafficking, she is at the mercy of ruthless traffickers. When the victim is rescued and cooperates with law enforcement, she knows that she may never be able to return safely to her previous life in her hometown or even country. The drafters of the TVPA understood the dangers posed by traffickers back at home both to the victims and their families, and provided victims with protective options.

In addition to the many immigration benefits generally available to qualifying individuals, victims of severe forms of trafficking, in particular, may be entitled to specific tools to prevent further victimization, including two new types of immigration statuses. Availability of relief will be determined by the individual circumstances surrounding the victimization and the specific eligibility requirements of the type of relief sought. While other immigration relief exists for qualifying aliens in the United States, the following options relate specifically to victims of severe forms of trafficking in persons.

- *Continued Presence.* In order to effectuate the prosecution of traffickers, eligible victims who lack legal immigration status, but who are potential trafficking witnesses, may receive temporary immigration relief under the continued presence provisions of section 107(c) of the TVPA. Only a federal law enforcement agency may petition the Immigration and Naturalization Service (INS) for continued presence. INS has the discretion to utilize one of several statutory and administrative mechanisms to authorize the continued presence of victims of severe forms of trafficking. Some of the mechanisms available to the INS for this purpose include parole, stay of removal, and deferred action.

- *T Status.* T status may be available to victims of severe forms of trafficking who have complied with any reasonable requests for assistance in the federal investigation or prosecution of acts of trafficking, and are physically present in the U.S. or a U.S. territory on account of such trafficking, and would suffer extreme hardship involving unusual and severe harm upon removal. While the TVPA requires an ongoing investigation for adult victims to qualify for a T status, minors under the age of fifteen are not required to comply with requests for investigative assistance in order to be eligible for a T status.
- *U Status.* U status will be available to aliens who have suffered substantial physical or mental abuse as a result of victimization of certain crimes designated by the *Violence Against Women Act of 2000* (VAWA)—including trafficking—that violate federal, state, or local laws or have occurred while in the United States (including in Indian country and military installations) or its territories or possessions. The conditions required for eligibility are defined in relevant law.

Recipients of both the T and U statuses are eligible for employment authorization and may be eligible after three years to adjust their status to that of lawful permanent resident in accordance with federal law and INS regulations, and perhaps eventually may be eligible for citizenship. In appropriate circumstances, these statuses may be available to family members of the victim. By statute, 5,000 T statuses and 10,000 U statuses may be issued to victims annually. These limits do not apply to family members.

Prosecution

Federal criminal offenses that are established by the TVPA and that may apply to trafficking in persons are related to slavery and peonage, sex and labor trafficking in children and adults, and the unlawful confiscation of a victim's documents.[5] In addition, there are many federal criminal statutes that may be applicable in trafficking cases. In brief, these include the crimes of: (1) forced labor; (2) visa and document fraud; (3) kidnapping; (4) transportation for prostitution or any criminal sexual activity (Mann Act); (5) importation of aliens for unlawful activities, including prostitution; (6) organized crime and racketeering, fraud and false statements, money laundering, and human smuggling.

Traffickers convicted of certain federal offenses under the TVPA and other statutes may receive prison sentences of up to twenty years for some offenses and up to life for others, they may be required to pay substantial fines, and must provide restitution to victims. They may also be subject to forfeiture of their property used in the commission of the crimes or obtained with proceeds from the criminal enterprise.

Prevention

The U.S. government seeks means to prevent trafficking before it happens, in addition to protecting victims and prosecuting traffickers. The U.S. has focused global programming on remedying the inequities of women's unequal access to education and decision-making, their greater subjection to poverty, and on assisting women in gaining access to essential social services, including health care and legal advocacy. U.S. foreign assistance programs address the gender discrimination and exploitation aspect of human trafficking via programs targeted at women's empowerment, ensuring they have the tools to be decision-makers in their societies and homes. Respect for women's rights is a non-negotiable demand of human dignity. Ensuring the basic human rights of women, and those of their families, strengthens democracy and is at the core of building a civil, law-abiding society.

Effective prevention strategies require cooperative efforts. This cooperation must occur bilaterally and multilaterally among various governments, but also between governments and civil society, including NGOs. Efforts must involve governmental coordination on national counter-trafficking strategies, as well as coordination at a local level. Destination countries must work with transit and source countries to stem the flow of trafficking. Source countries must work not only to prevent trafficking, but also to help with the reintegration of trafficking victims back into their home societies. The United States's international engagement, especially in the area of prevention, is focused on bolstering international political will to combat the issue, increasing a dialogue among countries, and strengthening nations' efforts to fight trafficking.

The State Department and the U.S. Agency for International Development support international programs assisting governments, as well as nongovernmental and international organizations, worldwide on projects to deter trafficking and to assist its victims. One avenue has been to build on existing resources such as women's shelters and legal advocacy programs for women. The U.S. also supports new initiatives, such as victim-centered anti-trafficking legal reform, job skills programs for at-risk populations, police and judicial sensitization training, police training manuals that include techniques to investigate trafficking, and migration information centers. Improving education, economic opportunities, and the position of women and girls in society are vital prevention efforts. Campaigns targeted to the at-risk are important, but must accompany efforts on the root causes and conditions that make victims vulnerable and the business lucrative for traffickers.

CONCLUSION

The phenomena of trafficking and exploitation may not be new, but the figures have grown and the faces have changed. The gender discrimination and exploitation aspects of trafficking highlight the destructive effects this evil has on affected societies. The U.S. government's approach recognizes that no one country can solve the trafficking problem alone. Governments can eliminate this transnational crime only by looking globally and understanding its complexities, including the aggravating role of gender exploitation. This pervasive criminality must be rooted out, but the task requires serious examination of social, educational, and economic factors making women and girls particularly vulnerable to traffickers. The global community cannot tolerate this violation of respect for women, human values, and humanitarian beliefs. Elimination of gender discrimination and trafficking are essential complementary goals for the twenty-first century.

Part 5

Some fault lines that can result in severely weakening or destroying the foundations of society are the result of intemperate reactions to new challenges. In the United States, the terrorist attacks of September 11 posed a very real threat to our way of life. But sometimes, as in medicine, one must make certain the cure is not worse than the disease. In this part, four chapters carefully consider some of the dangers in fashioning a secure society that continue to preserve the very reasons our country was founded.

Professor John D. Feerick, a distinguished constitutional lawyer, takes us back to the earliest days of our nation and demonstrates how our Founding Fathers carefully balanced the needs for security and for personal freedom. Michel Veuthey, an international humanitarian law professor, argues forcefully in his chapter that abandoning the rules established in the Geneva Conventions because of a new war on terrorism would be a tragic step backwards for the world community.

Edward Mortimer, the UN Secretary General's Director of Communications, reflects on a fault line in journalism, the difficulty in fully understanding the complexities of an alien culture. Such a failure can result in biased or even prejudiced analyses and reporting. Finally, I include another chapter on migration to complement the one in the Foundations section of this book. The rapidly growing number of migrants and asylum seekers poses political, economic, and even cultural challenges that go to the very heart of national pride and security. Kathleen Newland presents a comprehensive and insightful analysis of this current global crisis in the traditions and values of many societies that, until recently, prided themselves on welcoming and helping those in distress.

14

Balancing National Security and Civil Liberties

Professor John D. Feerick

ON SEPTEMBER 11, 2001, the United States experienced the worst terrorist attack in its history. It took the lives of almost 3,000 individuals of many different backgrounds and nationalities. It also inflicted untold harm on the loved ones of those who lost their lives, and on millions of others in every state and many nations of the world.

The response to this act has been swift, strong, and sustained, both militarily and legislatively. Freedoms heretofore enjoyed by citizens and noncitizens alike have given way to the imperatives of national security as seen through the eyes of officials in both the executive and legislative branches of government. As a result, substantial concerns have been raised regarding the reach of authority and the curtailment of liberty.

Some of these issues flow out of the *USA PATRIOT Act* (Uniting and Strengthening America by Providing Appropriate Tools Required to Intercept and Obstruct Terrorism) passed by Congress on October 26, 2001. The Act changed more than a dozen statutes designed to limit government surveillance of citizens and noncitizens, and gave broad powers to law enforcement and intelligence agencies.

Other actions by government have included closed immigration hearings; the arrest and detention of hundreds of individuals from Islamic countries on immigration and criminal charges and as "material witnesses"; the deportation of individuals; the limitation of access to government information; the denial of access to asylum seekers; the establishment of military tribunals for the trial of suspected terrorists; the designation of citizens and noncitizens as enemy combatants and therefore not covered by the ordinary criminal justice system; and the arrest of hundreds of citizens from other countries and the jailing of them at Guantanamo Bay, Cuba, without acknowledging their entitlement to the protection of any particular law. Lower federal courts have differed concerning the appropriateness of some of these actions, and debate on the issues presented has increased. The passage of the Homeland Security Act and the establishment of new programs in the defense department and elsewhere in the United States have added to the concerns expressed.

The legal framework from which to analyze many of these issues is murky and uncertain. In 1866, Justice Davis of the United States Supreme Court, writing for the five-member majority in *Ex Parte Milligan*, 4 Wallace (U.S.) 2, asked if there were one set of rules for wartime and another for times of peace, and answered that there was only one set for all times. Many years later, different sentiments were expressed by another Supreme Court Justice who supposedly said that, in times of danger, "constitutional rights only matter at the margins."[1]

Perhaps the time is ripe for another way of looking at these issues. In attempting to do so, I do not sift through the current issues specifically. Instead, I suggest a possible framework in which the issues might be considered—a framework that draws the Constitution of the United States more into the debate. Its language is often drowned out by the rhetoric and passions of the moment. For purposes of this chapter, my focus is on the Constitution as seen through the eyes of the writers of *The Federalist Papers*.

Why *The Federalist*? For many years, these eighty-five papers were the principal source upon which to draw to identify the thinking of the Framers of the Constitution. Frequent references to them can be found in the early decisions of the United States Supreme Court,[2] and in the great works on the Constitution, such as those by Story, Kent, and Rawle. Published in 1787 and

1788 over the pseudonym of "Publius," *The Federalist* were the handiwork of Alexander Hamilton, James Madison, and John Jay. Thomas Jefferson described *The Federalist* as the best commentaries on the principles of government "ever written."[3] George Washington said they "merit the Notice of Posterity," adding that the "principles of freedom and the topics of government" will always be "interesting to Mankind so long as they shall be connected in Civil Society."[4]

The revered Clinton Rossiter noted in his February 15, 1961, introduction to an edition of *The Federalist:* "[T]he message of *The Federalist* reads: no happiness without liberty, no liberty without self-government, no self-government without constitutionalism, no constitutionalism without morality—and none of these great goods without stability and order."[5] Abraham Lincoln put the dilemma underscored by *The Federalist* this way: "Must a government of necessity be too *strong* for the liberties of its people, or too *weak* to maintain its own existence?"[6]

Although I draw no specific conclusions from *The Federalist* as to the current clashes between national authority and civil liberty, I do suggest that in wrestling with such issues, the views of *The Federalist* writers are directly on point. Though expressed a long time ago, at a fragile time in the history of the United States, they are far from academic. Indeed, they deserve an informing and guiding role in any discussions of foundations and fault lines. They provide an important background for judging the degree of fidelity to the underlying principles of our constitutional system. In that regard, they make clear that national strength is an important object of the American Union, but always it must be expressed with "inviolable attention to" liberty and the republican form of government. *The Federalist* state over and over again that power under the Constitution is limited and that each branch of government must play its constitutional role in order to assure a free society, with a vigilant citizenry as the ultimate safeguard. When any of these forces are silent, the potential for erosion of the nation's foundations is greatest.

Before turning to a discussion of *The Federalist*,[7] some background is both instructive and necessary.

HISTORY

The Bill of Rights

The Constitution was the culmination of a long struggle by the American colonists against abuses of power and the deprivation of their liberties. Their surge toward independence led to continental congresses in 1774 and 1775, the Declaration of Independence in 1776, the American Revolution, and then the Articles of Confederation. In a few short years after that Revolution, rivalries, jealousies, and excesses of democracy so threatened the fabric of union that a Convention was called to render the Articles "adequate to the exigencies of government and the preservation of the Union." The danger to unity was substantial, with a possibility, very real, of the states separating into three or four confederacies. In the process, the Articles were scrapped and, in response to the claim that the Convention of 1787 had exceeded its authority, *Federalist* no. 40 stated: "Let them declare, whether it was of most importance to the happiness of the people of America, that the articles of confederation should be disregarded, and an adequate government be provided, and the Union preserved; or that an adequate government should be omitted, and the articles of confederation preserved."

The Constitution, in its original formulation, was rather quiet on the subject of individual rights. It contained no bill of rights for the reason that such a statement could be viewed as suggesting that government had more power than intended. The national government was considered limited, consisting only of delegated powers. Pointing to the Preamble and its reference to the blessings of liberty, *Federalist* no. 84 stated: "[H]ere is a better recognition of popular rights than volumes of those aphorisms which make the principal figure in several of our state bills of rights. . . ." However, because a number of the states ratifying the conventions demanded that specific limitations in favor of liberty be placed on the national government in the Constitution itself, the First Congress proposed the Bill of Rights.

An interesting backdrop to the Bill of Rights was reflected in a series of letters exchanged in the 1780s between Thomas Jefferson and James Madison. In one of these letters, Thomas Jefferson voiced strong support for a bill that would protect: "freedom of religion, freedom of the press, protection against standing armies, restriction against monopolies, the eternal and unremitting force of the *habeas corpus* laws, and trials by jury in all matters of the fact triable by the laws of the land and not by the laws of Nations." Madison responded that, "experience proves the inefficacy of a bill of rights on those occasions when its control is most needed. Repeated violations of these parchment barriers have been committed by over-bearing majorities in every State. . . ." In a follow-up letter, Jefferson expressed his confidence in the "legal check which [the Constitution] puts into the hands of the judiciary. This is a body, which if rendered independent, and kept strictly to their own department, merits great our confidence for their learning and integrity."[8]

Madison acted on Jefferson's observation when, in introducing the Bill of Rights in the First Congress, he stated: "If they are incorporated into the constitution, independent tribunals of justice will consider themselves in a peculiar manner the guardians of those rights; they will be an impenetrable bulwark against every assumption of power in the legislative or executive; they will be naturally led to resist every encroachment upon rights expressly stipulated for in the constitution by the declaration of rights." (*Annals of Cong.* 1 [ed. Joseph Gales, 1790]: 456–57.)

The liberties referenced in the Bill of Rights, of course, enjoy a long history. The Magna Carta of 1215 is the source of some of them, especially the right to trial by jury, which appears in Article 3 and the fifth and sixth amendments to the Constitution, and the imperative of due process of law, which appears in the fifth and fourteenth amendments. In its famous chapter 39, the Magna Carta declared: "No free man shall be taken or imprisoned or dispossessed, or outlawed, or banished, or in any way destroyed, nor will we go upon him, nor send upon him, except by the legal judgment of his peers or by the law of the land." The principle of due process of law was proffered by Daniel Webster as a law that "hears before it condemns; which proceeds upon inquiry, and renders judgment only after trial."[9]

Beyond the Magna Carta, there were other important constitutional milestones in English history. In 1628, the English Parliament adopted a Petition of Rights that spoke to the importance of the liberty of representation, strengthened the writ of *habeas corpus,* and condemned the quartering of soldiers in homes, imprisonment without cause shown, and trials of civilians under martial law in times of peace. Later in the century, the English Bill of Rights affirmed the importance of the freedoms of religion and press and the independence of the judiciary.

As these developments occurred, the American colonists staked out their own emphasis on liberty. They sought "unequivocal statements of the existence and extent of their liberties,"[10] and reacted strongly to their curtailment. In the Stamp Act Congress of 1765, they demanded that there be no taxation without representation and decried the removal of crimes from the ordinary courts to admiralty courts, thereby foregoing the requirement of a jury trial. They also expressed themselves forcibly on the subject of liberty in the Declaration and Resolves of the First Continental Congress, the Declaration of the Causes and Necessity of Taking up Arms of the Second Continental Congress, and, finally, in the Declaration of Independence, which concluded with the words, "we mutually pledge to each other our lives, our fortunes, and our sacred honour." Among the grievances cited in the Declaration of Independence, as justifying a complete break with England, were interference with the legislative process, taxation without representation, weakening of the judiciary, placing military authority ahead of civil, obstructing the laws of naturalization of foreigners, and eliminating the right to trial by jury.

Tensions Between Security and Liberty

Subsequent to the adoption of the Bill of Rights, moments appeared in American history when the demands of security and the blessings of liberty have collided with each other. In 1798, a war crisis with France led to the passage by Congress of four laws known as the Alien and Sedition Acts. Three of the four dealt with aliens, authorizing their deportation and detention and extending the period required for naturalization. The fourth prohibited false and malicious writings against the government. Although no alien was deported, a number of persons were convicted and imprisoned for violations of the Sedition Act. It was not long, however, before these laws, considered odious by many, passed away.

During the Civil War, martial law was put in place in various parts of the United States and the writ of *habeas corpus* was suspended by the President. On two different occasions, the Supreme Court took issue with the actions of the Executive. In *Ex Parte Merryman* (Fed. Cases no. 9487 (1861), Chief Justice Roger Taney admonished President Lincoln for suspending the writ of *habeas corpus* without the sanction of an act of Congress, and in *Ex Parte Milligan,* the Court set aside a conviction by a military commission of a citizen from a state not in rebellion where the civil courts had remained open. In finding the commission without jurisdiction, Justice Davis, speaking for the Court, said: "The Constitution is a law for . . . all times, and under the circumstances . . . No doctrine . . . was ever invented by the wit of man than that any of the provisions can be suspended during any of the great exigencies of government."

In the twentieth century, in the first of the world wars, the Supreme Court upheld a statute that criminalized the printing and distribution of leaflets urging resistance to the draft. Said Justice Holmes, for a unanimous Court, "when a nation is at war many things which might be said in time of peace are such a hindrance to its efforts that their utterance will not be endured so long as men fight. . . . No court could regard them as protected by any constitutional right."[11] Although the Court in this and another case was not receptive to the claims of civil liberty violations, it nonetheless spoke to the issues presented. In World War I, unlike during the Civil War, no trials before military tribunals took place, and the writ of *habeas corpus* remained available to individuals accused of violating the Espionage Act.

Less than a quarter-century later, during the Second World War, these issues returned to the Supreme Court, leading to six important decisions. In *Ex Parte Quirin*, 317 US 1 (1942), dealing with the arrest and prosecution by military commissions of German saboteurs, the Court upheld the constitutionality of the tribunals. In *In re Yamashita*, 327 US 1 (1942), it upheld the power of a military commission to try a Japanese general for offenses under the laws of war. Subsequently, actions taken by the government against American citizens of Japanese ancestry, as well as noncitizens of such descent living in the United States, led to decisions that remain controversial in the history of our jurisprudence. In *Hirabayashi v. United States*, 320 US 81 (1943), the Court upheld a curfew regulation directed against such individuals, and in *Korematsu v. United States*, 323 US 214 (1944), it upheld the constitutionality of their confinement and subjection to military authority. In doing so, in *Korematsu*, the Court expressed regret for the discrimination based on race but noted the difficulty of separating loyal from disloyal citizens, stating that "in time of war residents having ethnic affiliations may be a greater source of danger than those of a different ancestry."

But not every case went in favor of the government during World War II. In *Ex Parte Endo*, 323 US 283 (1944), an American citizen of Japanese nationality was released from confinement because he was able to establish his loyalty to the United States, and in *Duncan v. Kahanamoku*, 327 US 304 (1946), the Court found two German American citizens improperly detained, stating that a statute passed by Congress did not intend to supplant civil authority in favor of military authority for all purposes in Hawaii.

Most significant is that in each of the six cases, the Supreme Court reviewed the actions taken and expressed its view of the law. Indeed, in *Duncan,* the government cooperated in facilitating that review. History also records the disquiet some Justices of the Supreme Court who voted in the majority felt about the outcome in *Korematsu.*[12]

And now, in the present, some of the pending cases are likely to reach the Supreme Court, providing it with an opportunity to express a twenty-first-century view of the applicable framework of law to the battle against terrorism.[13] *The Federalist* offers illumination.

THE FEDERALIST

In *The Federalist,* the notion of a strong national government with "inviolable attention to liberty" and the republican form appear as dominant themes, with the rule of law as an animating force. Law, said *Federalist* no. 28, was the only "admissible principle" of the republican form of government.

No subject was more important to the Framers than that of the peace and safety of the American people. *Federalist* no. 3 stated: "Among the many objects to which a wise and free people find it necessary to direct their attention, that of providing for their safety seems to be the first, . . ." and *Federalist* no. 8: "Safety from external danger is the most powerful director of national conduct," with even liberty having to give way to its dictates. In *Federalist* no. 41, Madison declared that, "security against foreign danger . . . is an avowed and essential object of the American Union," and he added that, "a wise nation does not rashly preclude itself from any resource which may become essential to its safety. . . . [but it] will exert all its prudence in diminishing both the necessity and the danger of resorting to one which may be inauspicious to its liberties."

On the subject of liberties, the authors of *The Federalist* cautioned that abuses of liberty were a greater danger than those of abuses of power, pointing to the history of other countries, and within the colonies themselves. In *Federalist* no. 1, John Jay spoke of: "a dangerous mask for the zeal for the rights of the people [being] a much more certain road to the introduction of despotism than [power]." Madison, in *Federalist* no. 63, said, "that liberty may be endangered by the abuses of liberty, as well as by the abuses of power . . . and that the former rather than the latter is apparently most to be apprehended by the United States."[14]

Whenever speaking of the powers granted to the national government by the Constitution, *The Federalist* repeatedly noted their far-reaching nature. *Federalist* no. 45 said that the "operations of government will be most extensive and important in times of war and danger"; *Federalist* no. 31, that "a government ought to contain in itself every power requisite to the full accomplishment of the objects committed to its care"; and *Federalist* no. 59, that "every government ought to contain in itself the means of its own preservation." In *Federalist* no. 36, Alexander Hamilton noted his "aversion to every project that is calculated to disarm the government of a single weapon, which in any possible contingency might be usefully employed for the general defense and security." In the conduct of war, *Federalist* no. 70 said, "the energy of the executive is the bulwark of the national security." *Federalist* nos. 23 and 34 warned of the dangers involved in tying the hands of the government, but they emphasized that government must be "modeled in such a manner, as to admit of being safely visited with the requisite powers" (no. 41).

The Federalist acknowledged the necessary, occasionally awkward, balance between power and liberty, and envisioned a system of government that accommodated the two. In the words of *Federalist* no. 48: "It will not be denied, that power is of an encroaching nature, and that it ought to be effectively restrained from passing the limits assigned to it." "Mere demarkation on parchment of the constitutional limits of the several departments," said Madison, "is not a sufficient guard against those encroachments which lead to a tyrannical concentration of all the powers of government in the same hands" (no. 48). Hamilton said in *Federalist* no. 33: "If the Federal Government should overpass the just bounds of its authority, and make a tyrannical use of its powers, the people whose creature it is must appeal to the standard they have formed, and take such measures to redress the injury done to the constitution, as the exigency may suggest and prudence justify." As for the people, *Federalist* no. 84 declared: "the citizens who inhabit the country . . . will in all questions that affect the general liberty . . . stand ready to sound the alarm when necessary. . . ."

The Federalist viewed the design of the government as reflected in the Constitution as the model to provide the appropriate balance between authority and liberty. It placed powers with three separate branches of government, powers adequate to accomplish the purposes of each as well as to protect against the "encroachments" Madison and others feared. "[U]nless these departments be so far connected and blended, as to give to each a constitutional control over the others," said Madison in *Federalist* no. 48, the separation "essential to a free government, can never in practice be duly maintained." In *Federalist* no. 51, Madison gave classic expression to the idea of checks and balances when he said, "ambition must be able to counteract ambition. . . . It may be a reflection on human nature, that such devices should be necessary to control the abuses of government. . . . If men were angels, no government would be necessary. . . . A dependence on the people is no doubt the primary control on the government, but experience has taught mankind the necessity of auxiliary precautions."

Under the Constitution, all branches were to bear the imprimatur of the people (the House of Representatives by direct election, the Senate [originally] by appointment by the state legislatures, the President by selection by electors chosen in a manner directed by the state legislatures, and the Judiciary by the nomination of the President and confirmation by the Senate). Each branch of Congress would be a check on the other, with the House reflecting the passions and feelings of the people and the Senate bringing detachment and a broader outlook. The war powers were shared by Congress and the President. As to the Judiciary, *The Federalist* spoke of the "majesty of the national authority" being manifested through courts of justice (no. 16), described as the "bulwarks of a limited constitution" (no. 78). In the final analysis, however, the people would control the destiny of the country, and had it within their power to do so through elections and other expressions of their opinions and views.

What, therefore, might be drawn from this snapshot of the Constitution from the vantage point of *The Federalist* as it bears on the subjects of foundations and fault lines? I suggest the following:

First, a combination of strength, liberty, and republicanism was to be the centerpiece of American society. Its strength was expressed by the power and energy given to the national government, power intended to be at its height in times of national danger involving a serious threat to the safety of the people. Each branch of government at the same time was given the responsibility to check the others when necessary in order to assure fidelity to the purposes and objects of the nation. The country's republican form of government, and most important liberty, was considered crucial, grounded as it was on individuals who were chosen by the people, directly or indirectly, to exercise the powers of government. Said *Federalist* no. 28: "The whole power of the proposed government is to be in the hands of the representatives of the people. This is the essential, and, after all, the only efficacious security for the rights and privileges of the people which is attainable in a civil society."

The system designed by the Framers was premised on a close relationship between the governed and those who govern. The need for government to hear from people and for people to express themselves was assured and is paramount in times of serious conflict between the interests of public order and individual liberty. When governmental actions designed to promote public order collide with individual liberties, it is for the judiciary to step in and define whether constitutional limits have been surpassed. Although past history suggests that courts are reluctant to speak in times of war, the battle against terrorism may well become a permanent state of life, requiring a more active involvement by

American courts in dealing with these issues as a way of assuring an appropriate balance between order and liberty.[15]

To put it in different terms, I would note that safety itself is an important prerequisite for liberty. Without safety, the enjoyment of liberty is not possible, and without liberty, the happiness of people is not attainable. Both safety and liberty are values of the highest importance in the foundations of the United States. Safety alone, however, is not sufficient. It would be an irony of history if, after the colonists fought a revolution to secure liberty, important liberties were lost as the nation took upon itself the long-term challenge of meeting terrorism on a global basis. In facing this challenge, the words of Madison in *Federalist* no. 41 offer a useful signpost and bear repeating: "a wise nation does not rashly preclude itself from any resource which may become essential to its safety . . . [but it] will exert all its prudence in diminishing both the necessity and the danger of taking actions which may curb liberty." There is in these words an allowance for the derogation of liberty depending on the exigencies of the situation, but limited by a rule of necessity and principles of pro-portionality. Some liberties, of course, do not allow for deroga-tion such as when the Constitution speaks directly to where power lies, as, for instance, suspension of the writ of *habeas corpus.* Other liberties, such as the right of a free press, are key to the proper functioning of a republican government and restraint on such a press should have to meet a high burden of justification. The right to counsel, the oldest of the common law privileges, also has been an important ingredient in the success of the Amer-ican democracy, not only in terms of individual rights but also in enabling issues of constitutional limits to be presented to Ameri-can courts.

Beyond the question of constitutional limits is the question of what policies by government, even if constitutional, should be adopted as they impinge on important liberties enjoyed by citi-zens and noncitizens within the United States and its territorial jurisdiction. It is self-evident, I suggest and as *The Federalist* indi-cate, that the greater the danger to the safety of people, the greater the curtailment of liberty that should be permitted, and conversely, as the danger subsides, the lost liberties need to be restored. *The Federalist* make clear that it would be mischievous and wrong to disable government from anticipating and preparing for serious threats from abroad in ways, for example, that may need to be protected by considerations of secrecy in the interests of national security. Thus, in *Federalist* no. 34, Hamilton noted that in government "there ought to a capacity to provide for future contingencies," and suggested that it would be "the extreme of folly . . . to leave the government entrusted with the care of the national defense, in a state of absolute incapacity to provide for the protection of the community, against future invasions of the public peace, by foreign war or domestic convulsions."

The appropriate line between authority and liberty in most instances can only be defined, it seems to me, from an engagement of all parts of our system operating through its republican form. The line is incapable of being drawn appropriately without such engagement. A serious threat to the foundations of American society—its fault line, so to speak—is when there is a failure of such engagement either because one branch of government dominates another or is silent when it should be active or because the people fail to voice their views to their elected representatives or are unable to do so because of limited access to information from the press and other sources so essential to the functioning of a free society.

The approach that I take from my scrutiny of *The Federalist* is not unlike that found in the International Covenant on Civil and Political Rights. It allows states to derogate temporarily from obligations under the Covenant, but only in circumstances exceptional and temporary in nature, and only by means proportionate to the exigencies of the situation, with the objective of restoring as soon as possible the lost liberty. Under the Covenant, of course, some liberties may not be derogated from in the interests of security.

Foreign opinion also has a role to play under the Constitution.

The importance, in the eyes of other nations, of our actions is a theme that runs throughout *The Federalist*. Indeed, our relationships with other nations influenced the Framers, for example, to remove from the states a constitutional role in dealing with foreign nations lest the lack of respect for international undertakings repeat itself as had occurred when some of the thirteen original states violated the 1783 Treaty of Paris between Great Britain and the United States. The relevance of foreign opinion was captured in *Federalist* no. 63: "An attention to the judgment of other nations is important to every government for two reasons: The one is, that independently of the merits of any particular plan or measure, it is desirable on various accounts that it should appear to other nations as the offspring of a wise and honorable policy: The second is, that in doubtful cases, particularly where the national councils may be warped by some strong passion, or momentary interest, the presumed or known opinion of the impartial world, may be the best guide that can be followed." And, as *Federalist* no. 63 observed, errors could have been avoided by the states in the 1780s if account had been taken of the "[J]ustice and propriety of [measures] by the light in which they would probably appear to the unbiased part of mankind."

I conclude by calling attention to the Preamble of the United States Constitution, and the objects of the American Union:

> We the people of the United States, in order to form a more perfect Union, establish Justice, ensure domestic Tranquility, provide for the common defense, promote the general welfare, and secure the Blessings of Liberty to ourselves and our Posterity, Do ordain and establish this Constitution for the United States of America.

Of justice, Madison said in his famous *Federalist Paper* no. 51, that "it is the end of government [and] the end of civil society." In recommending the adoption of the Constitution, he and his colleagues stated: "Happy will it be for ourselves, and most honorable for Human Nature, if we have wisdom and virtue enough, to set so glorious an example to Mankind" (no. 37). This example is very much on the line in how the United States balances security and liberty in its war against terrorism.

15

Disregarding the Geneva Conventions on the Protection of War Victims

Michel Veuthey[1]

> The laws of war, that restrain the exercise of national rapine and murder, are founded on two principles of substantial interest: the knowledge of the permanent benefits which may be obtained by a moderate use of conquest, and a just apprehension lest the desolation we inflict on the enemy's country may be retaliated on our own.
>
> Edward Gibbon[2]

> We become the healers, not the killers of our species.
>
> Robert Lifton and Eric Markusen[3]

> Seek to understand the conditions, as far as possible without national prejudice, which led to past tragedies and should strive to determine the great fundamentals which must govern a peaceful progression toward a constantly higher level of civilization.
>
> General George C. Marshall[4]

> Since Auschwitz we know what man is capable of.
> And since Hiroshima we know what is at stake.
>
> Viktor E. Frankl[5]

> The object of war being the destruction of the enemy State, one has the right to kill its defenders only when

they have weapons in their hands; but immediately as they put them down and surrender, thus ceasing to be enemies or agents of the enemy, they at once become ordinary men and one no longer has any right to their life.

Jean-Jacques Rousseau[6]

THE GENEVA CONVENTIONS of August 12, 1949, on the protection of war victims are an impressive body of positive law in force, perhaps the most extensive and universal set of rules of international law, still not fully respected and implemented. The Geneva Conventions certainly have limitations, the most important being their possible application to weapons of mass destruction. The Geneva Conventions are not only positive law. They are the result of history, political experience and wisdom, military honor and interest, and universal ethical standards. The Geneva Conventions are today the core of international humanitarian law, or laws of war, which strikes a balance between military necessity and requirements of humanity.

Laws of war are not always rules of a game between gentlemen of the same club. Even if play and war are no longer synonymous,[7] restraints agreed upon in treaties should be respected.

The modern total war began with the Napoleonic Wars, where entire nations were pitted against each other. Sherman's march to the sea,[8] air bombings during World War II,[9] terror attacks against civilian populations in Africa, Asia, Latin America, and the Middle East were the precursors of today's protagonists of total war. The twentieth century—"the century of megadeath"[10]—invented both the terms genocide[11] and international humanitarian law. Will the twenty-first century consecrate genocide and discard international humanitarian law? Both the nineteenth and twentieth centuries have been a fertile ground for instruments of international law protecting human dignity even in time of war.[12] Will the twenty-first century start with lawlessness *(a-nomia)*, lack of restraints in the use of force, ignorance of standards and values for the protection of human dignity?[13]

After 9/11, some voices implied that the Geneva Conventions of August 12, 1949, on the protection of war victims were obsolete,[14] that they should they be disregarded in today's global war against terror,[15] that torturing prisoners[16] and attacking civilians should be necessary in order to conduct a successful war against terror.[17]

The "Law of Geneva" in Force

1. Geneva Convention for the Amelioration of the Condition of the Wounded and Sick in Armed Forces in the Field (First Convention of August 12, 1949)[18]
2. Geneva Convention for the Amelioration of the Condition of Wounded, Sick, and Shipwrecked Members of Armed Forces at Sea (Second Convention of August 12, 1949)[19]
3. Geneva Convention Relative to the Treatment of Prisoners of War (Third Convention of August 12, 1949)[20]
4. Geneva Convention Relative to the Protection of Civilian Persons in Time of War (Fourth Convention of August 12, 1949)[21]
5. Protocol Additional to the Geneva Conventions of August 12, 1949, and Relating to the Protection of Victims of International Armed Conflicts (First Protocol)[22]
6. Protocol Additional to the Geneva Conventions of August 12, 1949, and Relating to the Protection of Victims of Non-International Armed Conflicts (Second Protocol)[23]

The Geneva Conventions are the core instruments of international humanitarian law. International humanitarian law is usually defined as the set of principles and rules restricting the use of violence in armed conflicts, to spare the persons not (or no longer) directly engaged in hostilities (wounded, sick, and shipwrecked members of the armed forces, prisoners of war, and civilians). It also aims at limiting the use of methods and means of warfare causing superfluous injury (or excessive suffering, as in the case of "dumdum bullets," or gas warfare),[24] severe damage to the natural environment or betrayal of an adversary's confidence in agreed-upon obligations ("perfidy").

In contemporary written law, the principle of the limitation of armed violence is reflected in the Saint-Petersburg Declaration of 1868,[25] as well as in Article 22 of The Hague Regulations of 1907,[26] which stipulates that: "The right of belligerents to adopt means of injuring the enemy is not unlimited." This text is taken up again, slightly reworded, in paragraph 1 of Article 35 ("Basic Rules") of Protocol 1 of 1977: "In any armed conflict, the right of the Parties to the conflict to choose methods or means of warfare is not unlimited."

The terminology used to refer to international treaties may vary ("Humanitarian Law,"[27] "International Humanitarian Law Applicable in Armed Conflicts,"[28] "Laws of War,"[29] "Law of Geneva,"[30] "Red Cross Conventions,"[31] "Law of The Hague,"[32] "Human Rights in Armed Conflicts"[33]), but all seek the same objective—namely, to limit the use of violence in war.

Disregarding the Geneva Conventions is an important issue, larger than its purely legal dimension, which we shall examine along the following lines:

Is it legally admissible?
Is it politically advisable?
Is it militarily advantageous?
Is it ethically acceptable?

Is Disregarding the Geneva Conventions Legally Admissible?

The four 1949 Geneva Conventions and their two 1977 Additional Protocols are the main instruments in force of international humanitarian law. Their provisions embody the major development and reaffirmation of the legal restraints to violence in war of the twentieth century. Disregarding the Geneva Conventions would cause a great loss for a body of international law that has reached an exceptional level of universal respectability. The Geneva Conventions are universally ratified.[34]

Loss of Humanity

Disregarding the Geneva Conventions would entail, from a legal point of view, the weakening or even the disappearance of a land-mark of humanity[35] in international humanitarian law, fruit of the international community's efforts of the last two centu-ries[36]—if not longer,[37] if we consider early efforts to extend the benefit of international law to all human beings, regardless of their race, religion, civilization, or nation.

The Geneva Conventions have a long history in all civiliza-tions.[38]

Francisco de Vitoria (1480–1546), a member of the Dominican Order, is often mentioned as one of the founders of Western international law. He believed in *jus gentium,* a "law of nations"—considered universally valid—established on the basis of natural law. Living at the time of the conquest of the Americas, Vitoria developed his teaching partly in the context of the discussions of his contemporaries on the appropriate treatment of the native peoples of the Americas.[39]

Supported by Vitoria, Bartholomew de Las Casas (1474–1566) devoted himself to the defense of the indigenous peoples of the Americas against the ruthless exploitation and ferocious cruelty that they suffered from the Spanish conquerors.[40]

The four Geneva Conventions expanded from the original ten articles of the First Geneva Conventions in 1864—protecting only military personnel wounded in the field in land warfare—to nearly six hundred provisions protecting members of the armed forces as well as the entire civilian populations of countries at war.

Every step of the codification of international humanitarian law was marked by a pattern involving the following steps:

- Witnessing the needs for additional protection in the field, as did Henry Dunant on the battlefield of Solferino,[41] the International Committee of the Red Cross (ICRC), and other organizations of medical doctors amputating limbs of antipersonnel landmine victims in Afghanistan, Angola, Cambodia, and so many other places

- Consulting private military, political, and legal experts on a personal capacity[42]
- Convening experts from the Red Cross and Red Crescent National Societies[43]
- Convening a conference of government experts[44]
- Proposing draft instruments—based on the previous consultations—to a diplomatic conference convened by the Swiss government, as the state depositary of the Geneva Conventions[45]
- Campaigning for the ratification[46] and the adoption of national legislation for the implementation of the Geneva Conventions[47]
- Negotiating with belligerents on the applicability and implementation of the new instruments[48]

Contemporary international humanitarian law is the moving balance between two dynamic forces: *the requirements of humanity* and *military necessity*.[49] It is also a sum of tragic real-life experiences that need not be repeated: wounded and shipwrecked members of the armed forces—and the humanitarian personnel caring for them—must be rescued and respected; prisoners of war must be humanely treated and released at the end of active hostilities; and civilians should not be killed nor harmed.

Each stage of the codification of international humanitarian law was the result of a post-war shock wave among public opinion and governments, a collective painful learning process.

These humanitarian codifications occurred as follows:

- The Battle of Solferino (1859),[50] between Austrian and French armies in Lombardy, was the impetus for the First Convention, in 1864, protecting military wounded on land[51]
- The Naval Battle of Tsushima (1905),[52] between Japanese and Russian fleets, prompted the adjustment of the Convention on war at sea, in 1907,[53] extending protection to military shipwrecked[54]
- World War I brought about the two 1929 Conventions,[55] including a much broader protection for prisoners of war

- World War II led to the four 1949 Conventions,[56] an extensive regulation on the treatment of civilians in occupied territories and internment
- The Vietnam War and struggles for decolonization in Africa preceded the two 1977 Additional Protocols,[57] which brought written rules for the protection of civilian persons and objects against hostilities[58]
- A worldwide campaign promoted by governments, United Nations agencies, the Red Cross and Red Crescent Movement,[59] and a coalition of nongovernmental organizations (NGOs),[60] that stressed the human suffering and socio-economic costs caused by antipersonnel mines resulted on the total ban in antipersonnel landmines signed in Ottawa on December 4, 1997

Humanitarian law has evolved from rules protecting only certain categories of privileged individuals (from medieval knights to today's prisoners of war), to a set of provisions ensuring fundamental human rights guaranteeing the survival of civilian populations in wartime. This evolution was not only brought by the codification of new instruments and *ad hoc* negotiation, but also by the practice of states as well as by the decisions of International Tribunals.[61]

Among other significant developments, the International Tribunals on the former Yugoslavia[62] and on Rwanda[63] broke down the distinction between international and non-international armed conflicts regarding the prosecution of war crimes.[64]

Loss of Humanitarian Standards

Disregarding the Geneva Conventions would also entail the disappearance of the universality of humanitarian standards, ratified by practically all countries, that have acquired customary character, and whose fundamental provisions have even been recognized as nonderogable (*jus cogens*).[65]

The 1907 Hague Regulations, which establish laws for conducting war on land, are considered a part of international customary law since the International Military Tribunal of Nuremberg declared, on October 1, 1946, that these Regulations were declaratory of the laws and customs of war.[66]

The four 1949 Geneva Conventions are universally ratified. The two Additional Protocols are widely ratified, but still lack ratification by the U.S.A. and some other countries. Most of their provisions have customary character.[67]

As Dietrich Schindler wrote in 1999:[68]

> The International Criminal Tribunal, in its *Tadic* decision, came to the conclusion that many principles originally applicable in international armed conflicts had only in the course of time become customary rules applicable also in non-international conflicts; it enumerated a considerable number of such customary rules.[69] This finding constitutes one of the most important results of the post-cold war developments. It shows that non-international armed conflicts are regulated to a much greater extent by legal rules than had generally been assumed. The International Court of Justice, in its Advisory Opinion of 1996 on the legality of the use of nuclear weapons, also affirmed that a great majority of treaty rules on international humanitarian law had become customary. It did not, however, specifically refer to rules on internal armed conflicts.[70]

Antonio Cassese,[71] Christopher Greenwood,[72] and Theodor Meron[73] confirm the customary character of most provisions of the Geneva Conventions.

In particular, the customary nature of Common Article 3 of the Geneva Conventions has been affirmed by the International Court of Justice in the *Nicaragua* case[74] and, more recently, by the Appeals Chamber of the International Criminal Tribunal for the Former Yugoslavia in the *Tadic* case.[75] In its decision, the Appeals Chamber also held that many of the provisions of Protocol 2 can be regarded as customary law.[76]

As for *jus cogens*, according to Article 53 of the 1969 Vienna Convention on the Law of Treaties, "[a] treaty is void if, at the time of its conclusion, it conflicts with a peremptory norm of general international law. For the purposes of the present Convention, a peremptory norm of general international law is a norm accepted and recognized by the international community of States as a whole as a norm from which no derogation is permitted and which can be modified only by a subsequent of general international law having the same character."

In its Article 60, paragraph 5, the same Convention on the Law of Treaties exempted international humanitarian law from the rule of reciprocity.[77]

The International Court of Justice, in the *Nicaragua* case, considered Article 3 of the 1949 Geneva Conventions as "elementary considerations of humanity" binding all parties to conflicts:

> The Court considers that the rules stated in Article 3, which is common to the four Geneva Conventions, applying to armed conflicts of a non-international character, should be applied. The United States is under an obligation to "respect" the Conventions and even to "ensure respect" for them, and thus not to encourage persons or groups engaged in the conflict in Nicaragua to act in violation of the provisions of Article 3. This obligation derives from the general principles of humanitarian law to which the Conventions merely give specific expression.[78]

Loss of Responsibility

Disregarding the Geneva Conventions would be ignoring the collective responsibility of all states that consists in ensuring the respect for these instruments. According to Common Article 1 to the four 1949 Geneva Conventions and to Article 1 of Additional Protocol 1, all states parties to these instruments have the obligation "to respect and ensure respect" for them "in all circumstances." This wording has been widely understood as implying a double responsibility for every state party: for its own duties as well as a collective responsibility for the behavior of other states parties.[79]

The International Court of Justice holds that Common Article 1 to the 1949 Conventions had turned into customary law.[80]

Humanitarian rules and principles are to be respected in all circumstances. This is especially important today, in the case of "collapsed states,"[81] "postmodern wars,"[82] and anarchic conflicts.[83] According to the ICRC's Commentary to the 1949 Conventions:

> The words "in all circumstances" in Common Article 1 of the four 1949 Geneva Conventions refer to all situations in which the Convention has to be applied and these are defined in Article 2. It is clear, therefore, that the application of the Convention does not depend on whether the conflict is just or unjust. Whether or not it is a war of aggression, prisoners of war belonging to either party are entitled to the protection afforded by the Convention.[84]

This collective responsibility to ensure respect for the Geneva Conventions in all circumstances could take many forms.[85] It could be a very powerful tool for an effective implementation, and enforcement, of international humanitarian law. Even if this provision was only taken over in Protocol 1 in 1977,[86] Common Article 1 of 1949 could imply obligations both for internal[87] as well as international conflicts.[88]

Loss of Universal Jurisdiction

Disregarding the Geneva Conventions would mean abandoning the principle of universal jurisdiction for all states parties in terms of the prosecution of grave breaches of the Conventions and blurring the standards of the definition of war crimes.[89]

The four 1949 Geneva Conventions contain provisions defining "grave breaches" (which Additional Protocol 1 expanded and equated with war crimes) and asking the High Contracting Parties: "to enact any legislation necessary to provide effective penal sanctions for persons committing, or ordering to be committed, any of the grave breaches";[90] "to search for persons alleged to have committed, or to have ordered to be committed, such grave breaches, and shall bring such persons, regardless of their nationality, before its own court. It may also, if it prefers, and in accordance with the provisions of its own legislation, hand such persons over for trial to another High Contracting Party concerned, provided such High Contracting Party has made out a prima facie case."[91]

Loss of Special Agreements

Disregarding the Geneva Conventions would also entail losing a valuable tool for special agreements in non-international conflicts and with non-state actors.

Special agreements were concluded through ICRC delegates in the Spanish Civil War (for the application by both the Madrid Government and the Burgos Junta of the two 1929 Geneva Conventions),[92] in Palestine in 1948,[93] in the Yemen Civil War in 1963,[94] as well as in the Civil War in Nigeria[95] in 1969. Both sides accepted to abide by the four 1949 Geneva Conventions. In Afghanistan, the Soviet Union on one side and the Afghan mujahideens on the other side both signed the same agreement with the ICRC in order to ease the plight of prisoners: the Soviets let the ICRC visit prisoners in the Puli-Charki jail in Kabul and the mujahideens handed over their Soviet prisoners to the ICRC for a two-year internment in Switzerland before being repatriated to Mother Russia. In the former Yugoslavia, numerous special agreements were concluded in Geneva and elsewhere under the auspices of the ICRC.[96] The status of the conflicts—whether international or non-international—was left unclear on purpose so as not to jeopardize ICRC's activities in the field. In Somalia, ICRC was allowed to visit a U.S. prisoner of war (POW) in the hands of General Aidid, thanks to such a special agreement.[97]

In addition to the general applicability of the Geneva Conventions to a conflict and to the improvement of the treatment of prisoners on both sides, the establishment of protected areas was achieved by ICRC thanks to special agreements in Jerusalem in 1948, in Dacca/Dhakka in 1971, in Nicosia in 1974, in Jaffna in 1990, and in Dubrovnik and Osjek in 1991. The rejection by the UN Security Council of such a procedure for Srebenica—and the creation of the so-called "safe areas" instead—paved the way for the massacre of thousands of civilians.[98]

Loss of Antiterrorism Rules

Disregarding the Geneva Conventions would mean giving up a set of rules clearly prohibiting acts of terrorism[99] in times of armed conflict, such as attacks against civilian persons and objects, hostage taking, torture and ill-treatment, as well as collective punishments.

Article 33, paragraph 1, of the Fourth Geneva Convention reads as follows: "No protected person may be punished for an offence he or she has not personally committed. Collective penalties and likewise all measures of intimidation or of terrorism are prohibited."

Article 51, paragraph 2, of Additional Protocol 1 also specifically prohibits acts of terrorism: "The civilian population as such, as well as individual civilians, shall not be the object of attack. Acts or threats of violence the primary purpose of which is to spread terror among the civilian population are prohibited."

Disregarding the Geneva Conventions is certainly not legally admissible. But:

> Could the existing rules and implementation mechanisms be used more effectively?
> Could the limits of the existing rules and mechanisms be identified more clearly, both in regard to the use of mass destruction weapons and to low-intensity conflicts?

Existing rules and mechanisms could certainly be used more effectively on the domestic and international level. National implementation regulations as well as the criminal prosecution of violations by domestic courts could be improved. The role of regional organizations (African Unity, Arab League, Council of Europe, OSCE, Organization of American States) in ensuring respect for international humanitarian law "in all circumstances" could be enhanced.

The role of the UN, mentioned in Article 89 ("Cooperation") of Additional Protocol 1, could be clarified. This Article reads as follows: "In situations of serious violations of the Conventions or of this Protocol, the High Contracting Parties undertake to act, jointly or individually, in cooperation with the United Nations and in conformity with the United Nations Charter."

The use of weapons of mass destruction is not explicitly regulated in the 1949 Geneva Conventions or in the 1977 Additional Protocols.

Less than a month after Hiroshima and Nagasaki, the ICRC launched an appeal to all Red Cross and Red Crescent National Societies on September 5, 1945 ("The end of hostilities and the future task of the Red Cross") expressing its "anxiety for the future of the Red Cross work in face of the development of war techniques."[100] In an Appeal to the States Parties to the Geneva Conventions of April 5, 1950 ("Atomic Weapons and Non-Directed Missiles"), the ICRC stressed the incompatibility between the recently adopted 1949 Geneva Conventions and the use of the nuclear bomb. The ICRC then requested governments to make every possible effort in order to reach an agreement prohibiting this weapon and "non-directed weapons" in general, as a natural complement to the 1949 Geneva Conventions and the 1925 Geneva Protocol. The ICRC motivated this appeal by stressing the contradiction between weapons of mass destruction and the fundamental principles of international humanitarian law, the distinction between combatants and non-combatants, and the prohibition of unnecessary suffering:

> The use of this arm is less a development of the methods of warfare than the institution of an entirely new conception of war, first exemplified by mass bombardments and later by the employment of rocket bombs. However condemned—and rightly so—by successive treaties, war still presupposed certain restrictive rules, above all did it presuppose discrimination between combatants and non-combatants. With atomic bombs and non-directed missiles, discrimination becomes impossible. Such arms will not spare hospitals, prisoners of war camps, and civilians. Their inevitable consequence is extermination, pure and simple. Furthermore, the suffering caused by the atomic bomb is out of proportion to strategic necessity; many of its victims die as a result of burns after weeks of agony, or are stricken for life with painful infirmities. Finally,

its effects, immediate and lasting, prevent access to the wounded and their treatment.

In 1957, the ICRC presented "Draft Rules for the Limitation of the Dangers Incurred by the Civilian Population in Time of War." Article 14 ("Weapons with Uncontrollable Effects") prohibited the use of weapons "whose harmful effects—resulting in particular from the dissemination of incendiary, chemical, bacteriological, radioactive, or other agents—could spread to an unforeseen degree or escape, either in space or in time, from the control of those who employ them, thus endangering the civilian population." The Draft Rules were not adopted by the International Conference of the Red Cross at New Delhi in 1957. Western powers were against any regulation of the use of weapons of mass destruction within the framework of international humanitarian law, while the Soviet Union wanted a complete prohibition of nuclear weapons, not only a restriction of their use.

In 1965, the Twentieth International Conference of the Red Cross, in Vienna, in its Resolution No. 28, solemnly declared that:

All governments and other authorities responsible for action in armed conflicts should conform at least to the following principles:
  —That the right of the parties to a conflict to adopt means of injuring the enemy is not unlimited
  —That it is prohibited to launch attacks against the civilian population as such
  —That distinction must be made at all times between persons taking part in the hostilities and members of the civilian population to the effect that the latter be spared as much as possible
  —That the general principles of the Law of War apply to nuclear and similar weapons

On May 19, 1967, the ICRC sent a Memorandum ("Protection of Civilian Populations Against the Dangers of Indiscriminate Warfare") to the Governments Parties to the 1949 Geneva Conventions and to the Fourth Hague Convention of 1907 concerning the laws and customs of war on land reminding them of the Vienna Resolution and requesting governments to sanction these principles and "if need be, to develop them in an adequate instrument of international law." The ICRC also asked governments to reaffirm these principles in a resolution of the United Nations General Assembly and to include them in the instructions given to the armed forces.[101]

The United Nations General Assembly Resolution 2444 (XXIII) ("Respect for Human Rights in Armed Conflicts") reaffirmed the first three principles and left out the fourth principle.[102]

Before the ICRC could start the process of "Reaffirmation and Development of the Laws and Customs Applicable in Armed Conflicts" after the adoption of Resolution XX of the Twenty-first International Conference of the Red Cross, in Istanbul in 1969, it had to agree with the nuclear powers that its endeavor would only deal with conventional warfare, excluding from its scope weapons of mass destruction as well as chemical and bacteriological warfare.

As a result, the Additional Protocols of 1977 never make any specific mention of these arms.

The International Court of Justice dealt with the conformity of nuclear weapons with international humanitarian law in one Advisory Opinion following two requests.

The first request for an opinion was transmitted to the court under a World Health Assembly resolution of May 14, 1993, with the following question: "In view of the health and environmental effects, would the use of nuclear weapons by a state in war or other armed conflict be a breach of its obligation under international law including the WHO Constitution?"

The second was requested by the General Assembly of the United Nations in Resolution 49/75 K of December 15, 1994 ("Request for an Advisory Opinion from the International Court of Justice on the Legality of the Threat or Use of Nuclear Weapons"), pursuant to Article 96, paragraph 1 of the Charter of the United Nations, on the following question: "Is the threat or use of nuclear weapons in any circumstances permitted under international law?"

On July 8, 1996, the International Court of Justice gave its advisory opinion in response to the two inquiries. On one hand, the court did not find any international rule specifically prohibiting, in all circumstances, the threat or use of nuclear weapons during an armed conflict. On the other hand, the court decided unanimously that any use of nuclear weapons would be subject to the rules and requirements of international humanitarian law.

The issue is certainly not closed. As Judge Géza Herczegh said: "Given the importance of the Advisory Opinion and of the contrasting views expressed by the members of the court, it would seem most important that eminent experts in international humanitarian law thoroughly investigate the theoretical questions that may be raised in this connection."[103]

Is Disregarding the Geneva Conventions Politically Advisable?

Are the Geneva Conventions to be discarded by the new realists—in a time without mercy—as the remnant of idealists of the second half of the last century?

Loss of Time

Disregarding the Geneva Conventions would entail, from a political point of view, losing at least fifty years of campaigning for humanitarian standards in armed conflicts.

The 1949 Geneva Conventions, with the UN Charter in 1945 and the Universal Declaration on Human Rights in 1948, are the result of the tragic suffering of millions of civilians and prisoners, victims of total war and genocide in Europe and in Asia. The survivors pushed for the adoption of international instruments in order to avoid the repetition of such tragedies. Many governments, international and regional organizations, as well as the civil society, especially international humanitarian organizations and human rights NGOs, strived for decades to guarantee a better respect of these instruments.

Loss of Universality

Disregarding the Geneva Conventions would entail, from a political point of view, losing the universality of humanitarian standards, re-establishing different areas and levels of protection of human dignity in armed conflicts.

The Geneva Conventions, since the First Convention in 1864, did incorporate in a single body of international law—recently known as "international humanitarian law," and also as "laws of war," "laws of armed conflicts," or even "human rights in armed conflicts"—rules and customs originating from all civilizations. Before this progressive universalization of humanitarian customs, first limited to "civilized nations," humanitarian restraints in war were limited within the same tribe, nation, civilization; wars against adversaries outside of the group were usually not conducted according to the same restraints. The possible demise of the universal standards painstakingly attained through the Geneva Conventions could mean the return to various standards applicable within diverse groups. As the brief Kosovo campaign demonstrated, strikingly diverging interpretation of humanitarian restraints within a military alliance nearly provoked the breakdown of a coalition.[104]

Loss of Dialogue

Disregarding the Geneva Conventions would entail, from a political point of view, losing an important common ground for maintaining a minimal dialogue even in the midst of conflicts, as well as powerful tools for the re-establishment of peace and for the sustainability of peaceful settlements.

The exchange of names and messages between prisoners and their families, the passage of relief supplies, more importantly the release of prisoners or the repatriation of civilians, keep communication between warring parties open—directly or through intermediaries such as the ICRC. Such contacts give opportunity for belligerents to engage in truces, cease-fires, and even peace negotiations. The fact that prisoners are visited by ICRC delegates, identified, taken care of, their families reassured on their survival and well-being, and themselves certain of being released and repatriated contribute to the peaceful settlement and to its sustainability. On the contrary, attacks against civilians, mistreatment of prisoners, and denial of visits by the ICRC do nothing to create an atmosphere leading to dialogue. The re-establishment of normal, trustful relations between Germany and the USSR after 1945, on one hand, and between the U.S.A. and Vietnam after 1975, on the other hand, was considerably influenced by the treatment of POWs during the wars. The first American Ambassador in Hanoi was a former POW, who had to demonstrate that the noncompliance by the Democratic Republic of Viêt-Nam of the Third Geneva Convention was past history.

Loss of Restraint

Disregarding the Geneva Conventions would entail, from a political point of view, losing restraints in the use of violence that aim at avoiding degradation between adversaries and among one's own population.

Veterans coming back home often experience severe problems within their families and communities, partly because of lack of limitations while they were engaged in combat.[105]

Loss of Movement

Disregarding the Geneva Conventions would entail, from a political point of view, losing rules that could effectively prevent the movement of internally displaced persons (IDPs)[106] and of refugees.

Most internally displaced persons and refugees were compelled to move from their homes by violations of international humanitarian law. Implementing international humanitarian law would be the best way to prevent the creation of IDPs and refugees and avoid social and security problems in recipient countries and territories.

Loss of POWs and MIAs

Disregarding the Geneva Conventions would entail, from a political point of view, losing procedures allowing the repatriation of prisoners of war, civilian internees, and internally displaced persons as well as of refugees. Unsolved humanitarian issues become serious political issues (refugees, missing, disappeared,[107] MIAs,[108] etc.), necessarily leading to the renegotiation of issues that could have been solved easily through a faithful implementation of the Geneva Conventions.

The Third Geneva Convention explicitly provides for a clear and rapid identification of the prisoners, a location of their detention places, a monitoring of their health, and the exchange of messages between prisoners and their families. According to Article 118, the release of the prisoners shall happen "without delay after the cessation of active hostilities." The non-respect of this rule after the war between Iraq and Iran was unfortunately facilitated by a UN Security Resolution asking for—in this order—the cease-fire, the withdrawal of the troops on the border, and only then the release and repatriation of the POWs. As a result, thousands of POWs on both sides were not repatriated for many years after the end of hostilities. This leads to severe consequences on the individual, family, national, and regional level.

Loss of Private Property

Disregarding the Geneva Conventions would mean losing standards prohibiting the destruction of civilian objects indispensable for the survival of the civilian population. The violation of those standards generates the need for relief, medical, and food assistance during the conflict and reconstruction thereafter.

The 1949 Geneva Conventions and especially both 1977 Additional Protocols prohibit the destruction of objects indispensable for the survival of the civilian population.

Loss of Casualty Guidelines

Disregarding the Geneva Conventions would mean losing guidelines that aim at minimizing civilian casualties[109] and keeping a good image for one's cause, as well as standards of behavior that avoid alienating the civilian population of occupied territories and thus lessen the support for resistance movements.[110]

Loss of International Security

We would also lose a set of standards essential for international security referred to in many resolutions of the United Nations (Security Council, General Assembly, Commission on Human Rights, and other UN organs), of regional organizations, and international human rights NGOs in the last fifty years; and an important aspect of multilateral and international cooperation at a time when solidarity might be greatly needed on many levels.[111]

The four Geneva Conventions on the protection of war victims constitute an important part of international cooperation. They contribute to international security, facilitate dialogue between warring parties, aid in the re-establishment of peace and to the sustainability of peaceful settlements.

The first items to be discussed during negotiations are often humanitarian issues, such as visits by the ICRC to prisoners of war, their release,[112] or the plight of civilians.

Violations of the Geneva Conventions exacerbate conflicts, leading to escalations of hostilities and adding obstacles to the efforts for a peaceful settlement of conflicts.

Violations in one part of the world—if not met by an appropriate reaction by individual states and/or by the international community—are too often imitated on the spot in other parts of the world.

Violations of the Geneva Conventions often are the cause of movements of internally displaced persons and of refugees, and can facilitate criminal activities in the area of conflict and well beyond.

Violations of the Geneva Conventions represent a serious threat to international security, at the regional level and world-wide, because:

—They are a frequent cause of or pretext for foreign armed inter-vention. Violations of international humanitarian law thus served to justify armed intervention in Iraq, Somalia, Bosnia-Herzegovina, Kosovo, and East Timor.

—They lead to a geographical extension of conflicts, as shown by the wars in Algeria and Vietnam and the wars of liberation in Africa, or even the recent and current conflicts in the African Great Lakes region.

—They create a system of anarchic instability at national, regional, and international levels. The situations in Sierra Leone, Liberia, and Guinea are recent examples of this kind of anarchy, fomented and fueled by the warring parties, who lived by preying on the civilian population, or even on the humanitarian agencies. Af-ghanistan and Colombia are other current examples of anarchy leading to disturbances and giving rise to trafficking and various kinds of terrorism.

—They cause large-scale movements of displaced persons and refu-gees, which are sometimes recognized by the United Nations Se-curity Council as threats to security. Even during internal armed conflicts, population displacements are strictly prohibited. Article 3, common to the 1949 Geneva Conventions and their Additional Protocol 2 of 1977, contain rules that, if respected, would signifi-cantly reduce the number of refugees and internally displaced per-sons, and victims in general. Respect for international humanitarian law would also imply the separation of combatants from civilians, the disarming of camps, the careful placing of refu-gees, and preventing combatants from using refugees for cover or aid supplies.[113]

—They may contribute to or even cause terrorism. In the words of Madeleine Albright, former Secretary of State, quoted in the *Christian Science Monitor* of November 15, 2002: "We need to figure out what are the circumstances that cause unhappy people to strap bombs to themselves."[114]

IS DISREGARDING THE GENEVA CONVENTIONS MILITARILY ADVANTAGEOUS?

The Geneva Conventions and their Additional Protocols were discussed, adopted, and ratified by decision-makers, including military experts. Have they been overtaken by the new realities of war, both high-technology and low-intensity warfare?

Destruction of Humanitarian Values

Disregarding the Geneva Conventions would mean, from a military point of view, destroying humanitarian values largely based on universal military ethics, traditions, and honor;[115] and giving up decades—even centuries—of humanitarian customs embodied in the Geneva Conventions and incorporated in military manuals and instructions. Abiding by the Geneva Conventions is also an important part of military discipline[116] and legitimacy of an army[117] and of individual units.[118] In November 1847, one of the founders of the ICRC, Swiss General Dufour, issued the following proclamation to the Confederation troops under his command: "Confederates, I place in your keeping the children, the women, the aged and the ministers of religion. He who raises a hand against an inoffensive person dishonours himself and tarnishes his flag."[119]

Among the reasons for the military to abide by the Geneva Conventions, we could mention:

—International humanitarian law was developed in the real world of military practice, not in an ideal world imagined by academics or humanitarians, but out of expediency and mutual interest. The

input of military specialists was constant throughout the codification of the Geneva Conventions. International humanitarian law
is not divorced from the day-to-day military practices and professional military standards.

—Combatants do not get a free ride because they are fighting a liberation war or a war against terrorism. The forms of war change, but
the core of international humanitarian law does not.

As an important military document recently stated:

Military power must be wielded in an unimpeachable moral fashion, with respect for human rights and adherence to the Geneva
Conventions. This morality should not be a matter of legality, but
of conscience.

Moral behavior is essential for gaining and maintaining the positive worldwide reputation of American fighting men and women
as well as the confidence and support of the American people, a
basic source of American military strength.[120]

Jeopardizing Protection

Disregarding the Geneva Conventions would mean jeopardizing
clear and universally agreed-upon guarantees for the protection
of combatants in case of injury, sickness, shipwreck, and capture;
and undermining the probability that one's own soldiers would
be receiving POW status and treatment in case of capture.

Limiting Surrender

Disregarding the Geneva Conventions would mean limiting the
probability of the surrender of enemy combatants, in view of the
uncertainty they could have on their treatment and status; the
surrender of the enemy may be more easily obtained if the
enemy knows that it will be treated humanely.

The principle of humanity,[121] the cornerstone of humanitarian
law, has frequently been opposed to military necessities. Nevertheless, these two essential factors are not necessarily contradictory. On the contrary, humanity and military effectiveness are
often complementary; the best approach is, indeed, to highlight

the mutual military, political, and economic benefits of recognizing the enemy—civilian or combatant—as a human being with the same dignity as one would wish for oneself.

Besides, attacks against the civilian population, far from reducing it into submission, often incites it to resistance. One should use the dynamic role of humanitarian action to disarm the adversary or, in the words of the famous Chinese strategist Sun Tzu, to "build a golden bridge to the retreating enemy," meaning: "Treat the captives well, and care for them. Generally, in war, the best policy is to take a state intact; to ruin it is inferior to this. To capture the enemy's army is better than to destroy it; to take intact a battalion, a company, or a five-man squad is better than to destroy them."[122]

One of the fundaments of the four Geneva Conventions on the protection of war victims is military self-interest: the first three Conventions protect members of the armed forces when wounded or sick (First Convention), shipwrecked (Second Convention), captured (Third Convention). The Fourth Convention, relating to the treatment of civilians, could protect their own families in occupied territories, or if wounded or interned. Each of the four Conventions contributes to military discipline. Discipline of one's own troops must incorporate the respect of humanitarian restraints. History shows that when combatants are given free rein to kill and destroy indiscriminately, or to commit acts of savagery against the enemy, they will more likely turn against their own leaders and act ruthlessly against their own population. To assure that humanitarian principles are respected and implemented at this most basic level, credible instruction and rigorous training are essential. To this end, it is important that these rules be disseminated simply and clearly in military manuals or instructions[123] and that they be coupled with a system of disciplinary sanctions guaranteeing their observance.[124]

IS DISREGARDING THE GENEVA CONVENTIONS ETHICALLY ACCEPTABLE?

If one cornerstone of the Geneva Conventions is military self-interest, another is ethics—of religious or humanist origin, aim-

ing at the preservation of the survival of the group and at the
respect of fellow human beings, even in time of war. The most
universal formulation of this ethical basis for the Geneva Conventions is the Golden Rule, in its positive ("Do unto others . . .")
and negative ("Do not do . . .") forms.

Loss of Human Dignity

Disregarding the Geneva Conventions would mean, from an ethical point of view, undermining a cornerstone of our civilization
for the protection of human dignity in armed conflicts;[125] losing
the common denominator of humanitarian principles and rules
based on all civilizations, building a thin red line between all civilizations;[126] and recreating "islands of humanity" within the international community, with different levels of humanitarian
standards.

The Golden Rule can be found in several civilizations, not only
Judeo-Christian ones, and states: "So, whatever you wish that
men would do to you, do so to them."[127]

This rule was set to ensure the survival of a group, and forbade
behaviors that would have permanently endangered the group.[128]
Indigenous peoples of all continents have attempted to prevent
excesses that would turn conflicts into collective suicides. The
customs of Melanesians,[129] Inuit,[130] and Nilotic peoples;[131] Buddhism,[132] Hinduism,[133] Taoism,[134] Confucianism,[135] and Bushido[136] in Asia; Judaism,[137] Christianity,[138] and Islam[139] in the
Middle East; customary humanitarian law in Africa;[140] and mutual restrictions imposed by chivalry and military honor[141] in Europe contain examples of rules of "Life-Affirmative Societies," in
which the main emphasis of ideals, customs, and institutions is
the preservation and growth of life in all its forms.[142]

Loss of Legitimacy

Disregarding the Geneva Conventions would mean "destroying
one's cause by the very means used to defend it" (Camus):[143]

undermining the legitimacy of military actions. Civilian casualties, allegations of ill-treatment, torture, and execution of prisoners that stained various wars did bring these military operations to an end, due to the reaction of the "public conscience" against torture,[144] killing of civilians,[145] and mistreatment of prisoners.[146] This has also been true for peacekeeping operations.[147]

Loss of Civilian Population

Disregarding the Geneva Conventions could also be threatening the survival of the civilian population locally or on a broader scale. Over the course of time, we have seen in each civilization "islands of humanity" being formed, inside which certain rules limited violence in war-time, by imposing responsibilities toward victims.

The Geneva Conventions sum up these rules on a universal level. What is at stake today is not so much the survival of the tribe or the nation or a specific individual civilization, but humankind as a whole. We need to maintain those values of common humanity, cooperation, and equal respect.[148]

Breaking the Geneva Conventions (and underogable human rights such as the prohibition of torture) using the defense of democracy and freedom as a pretext would be fallacious.

Beyond the literal meaning of the Conventions, there is a need to stress the spirit of the Conventions, and the common interest in keeping up the standards for our survival.

CONCLUSION AND PROPOSALS

Can the Geneva Conventions survive such merciless wars, conflicts, where everything seems permissible, where every limitation is equaled to weakness?

As Georges Abi-Saab recently wrote, "There is no need to reinvent the law."[149]

What is really needed is a better application of existing rules, customs, and existing mechanisms, a stronger political will to abide by the fundamental principles and rules of humanity.

Here are three proposals to contribute to a reinforcement, a renewal, and a better implementation of the Geneva Conventions in today's conflicts:

—Reaffirm the fundaments
—Train, teach, educate, and research
—Implement and enforce essential existing rules

Reaffirm the Fundaments

Reaffirm the foundations of the Geneva Conventions through a declaration of the fundamental humanitarian rules, customs, and principles applicable in armed conflicts in a simple, easy-to-understand form.[150] The struggle for the respect of fundamental humanitarian rules in today's conflicts is not a lost cause; it is nevertheless an uphill battle to uphold the "principles of humanity and the dictates of public conscience."[151]

There is no need to redraft or to renegotiate the formulation of these fundamental rules. They already exist:

Common Article 1 to the four Geneva Conventions of 1949
Common Article 3 to the four Geneva Conventions of 1949
Article 12 ("Protection and Care") of the First Convention
Article 12 ("Protection and Care") of the Second Convention
Article 13 ("Humane Treatment of Prisoners") of the Third Convention
Article 27 ("Treatment. General Observations") of the Fourth Convention
Article 48 ("Civilian Population—General Protection against Effects of Hostilities—Basic Rule") of Additional Protocol 1 of 1977
Article 75 ("Fundamental Guarantees") of Additional Protocol 1 as well as:
—Article 10 ("Protection and Care")
—Article 11 ("Protection of Persons")
—Article 15 ("Protection of Civilian Medical and Religious Personnel")

—Article 16 ("General Protection of Medical Duties")
—Article 35 ("Methods and Means of Warfare—Basic Rules")
—Article 40 ("Quarter")
Articles 4 ("Fundamental Guarantees") and 5 ("Persons Whose Liberty has been Restricted") of Additional Protocol 2
—The Martens Clause

Train, Teach, Educate, and Research

Train, teach, and educate arm bearers,[152] troops, police, militias, armed groups, and trainers, including foreign trainers and foreign private security groups, in fundamental restraints of violence and essential humanitarian principles.[153]

This could include mobilizing public role models (such as artists[154] or athletes) in close contact with the local traditions[155] who can influence leaders or public opinion at large. Spiritual leaders should participate in those campaigns, especially when religious and spiritual values have been used to fuel conflicts.[156]

Implement and Enforce Essential Existing Rules

Strengthen the implementation of the existing rules through a better use of existing legal mechanisms and other remedies against violations.

The international community of States Party to the 1949 Geneva Conventions should reaffirm their collective responsibility according to Article 1, common to all four Conventions and to Protocol 1.[157] The role of the United Nations could also be clarified.[158]

Other remedies exist and could be used to improve the respect for the Geneva Conventions, by states and by non-state actors.[159]

The Geneva Conventions are not only the result of painful experiences of war victims, long negotiations, decisions by courts, practice of states, and writings of legal experts. The Geneva Conventions are based on the balance between military interest and universal humanitarian principles. What is needed today is a better application of the existing law and implementation mecha-

nisms, more creative interpretation and remedies to overcome
the limitations of the letter of the law and to support the spirit of
the Conventions and their Additional Protocols. Multidisciplinary research and training in history, anthropology, ethics, and
spiritualities would highlight the renewed necessity of humanitarian standards in conflicts. Such research would also give evidence
of the contribution of the Geneva Conventions to peace and security on the national, regional, and international level. It could
show as well that violations of the Geneva Conventions are short-
sighted, and do not meet the military and political interests of
any warring party. It might, indeed, be too easy for lawyers and
other experts without any battlefield experience to put aside the
Geneva Conventions. It might seem the easy way out for political
leaders to declare the Geneva Conventions inapplicable to a particular conflict, territory, category of prisoners or civilians. The
reality of conflicts could well bring back the mutual interest of
parties, even in asymmetrical conflicts, to abide by fundamental
principles. Even if one side is violating the Geneva Conventions,
there is a unilateral interest in respecting them. To grant humane treatment to an enemy who surrenders is less costly militarily than to corner him and face heroes and fanatics.
Respecting civilians is good for the image, and militarily sound,
because it avoids excessive resistance, even terrorism. The Geneva Conventions could prove very advantageous, both in today's
and tomorrow's conflicts, for everyone: for superpowers as well
as for smaller nations; for governments and non-state insurgents;
for regular armies as well as non-state actors. What is needed is
not the undermining of this vital set of rules, but rather the reinforcement of the Geneva Conventions on every possible level:
legal, political, military, ethical, and spiritual.

16

Media: Prism or Mirror

Edward Mortimer

MORE THAN TWENTY YEARS AGO, when I was just finishing my book, *Islam, Faith and Power*, I wrote a sort of spin-off article for the *Middle East Journal* called, "Islam and the Western Journalist." It was, in part, a review of, or a response to, Edward Said's book *Covering Islam*, which, in turn, was a kind of sequel to his more famous book, *Orientalism*.

It may seem tedious to recapitulate the arguments of that time today, but the fact is that they have lost nothing of their topicality. Or maybe they did, in between—but if so, they have regained it with a vengeance since September 11, 2001. In fact, one of the strongest sensations of the past year or so for me has been the feeling of déjà vu. And one of the most frightening things about it has been the realization that contemporary American society, at least as represented by its mass media, has an extraordinarily selective historical memory. One can read any number of articles comparing George W. Bush to John F. Kennedy, or 9/11 to Pearl Harbor, or discussing the nineteenth- and twentieth-century precedents for preemptive self-defense. But in all the discussion of the American reaction to 9/11, I have seen very few references to the Iranian revolution, and hardly any to the hostage crisis of 1979–81.

Yet the atmosphere at that time in the United States was quite similar to what it is now. Many of the same resentments were expressed, and many of the same questions asked. There was outrage and incomprehension at what seemed an unprovoked and gratuitous attack on American civilians who were only doing their jobs. There was exasperation at the inability of overwhelming military superiority to deliver a political solution. There was also a widespread desire to understand better "why they hate us," and a tremendous awakening of interest in Islam and almost everything to do with it. Indeed, it was largely to cater to that interest and, of course, to profit from it that I wrote my book.

I was a journalist, and my book had no pretensions to be other than journalistic. Edward Said, then as now, was a professor. His interest in Western images of Islam long predated the Iranian revolution, and *Orientalism* came out shortly before it. It was essentially a book written by a scholar about other scholars. One can hardly do justice to the argument by summarizing it in one or two sentences, but it had two main strands. First, Western scholarly investigation of Islamic societies had not, for the most part, been disinterested, but had been an instrument of imperial domination. Secondly, it had given a distorted image of those societies by exaggerating both what they had in common with each other and what made them different from the West.

Orientalism has little to say about the mass media because, at the time it was written, the mass media had little to say about Islam. In coverage of the Middle East, for example, from the 1950s to the 1970s, Western journalists tended either to ignore religion as a factor in politics or to assume that it was of diminishing importance. But with the advent of the Iranian revolution in 1978, that changed dramatically. Journalists like me found ourselves required to become instant experts on Islam, and expected to emphasize religion as a factor when we analyzed political events in the Muslim world. Inevitably, we turned to the very scholars whom Said had been criticizing, and we reproduced their approach with all the simplifications and exaggerations associated with our trade. Said therefore turned his attention to us, and *Covering Islam* was the result.

Said himself was not above a bit of simplification and exaggeration—or "reductionism," to use one of his favorite words. But his broad point was right. Much of the coverage did tend to emphasize the exotic and alien characteristics of Muslim societies, and to lump them all together. To a certain extent, this dehumanized ordinary Muslim people, assimilating them with the most violent and/or anti-Western political agitators among them. Such a portrayal did not make it easier for Western societies to envisage rational dialogue and negotiation as a productive way of dealing with Muslim societies. It encouraged them to think of the relationship as one inevitably, if regrettably, involving violence and confrontation.

Twenty years later, things do not appear to have changed much, or anyway not for the better. Islam is now seen almost entirely through the prism of terrorism, and anyone who questions this approach runs the risk of being vilified as at best naïve or at worst an appeaser. Lip-service is paid to the need for tolerance and respect for diversity, but in practice an understandable obsession with security leads to acceptance of racial profiling and a frantic effort to identify those aspects of Muslim belief or culture that might explain the willingness of young men (and, in some cases, women) to immolate themselves in the process of inflicting indiscriminate destruction on innocent civilians. And the search for such explanations is itself distorted by a bias toward subjective factors—those to do with Muslim perceptions—as opposed to objective reasons why some Muslims might feel anger toward the West or the United States. If a journalist shows too much interest in the latter, he or she can very quickly incur the accusation of justifying terrorism, which in the present atmosphere is almost equated with direct incitement.

In another respect, however, this interest in Muslim perceptions is an improvement. It leads to a somewhat more three-dimensional picture of Muslim societies, and, indeed, of Muslim people. If I were to rewrite my article now, I should have to say something about the Muslim journalist as well as the Western journalist.

Of course there have been Muslim journalists for the best part of 200 years. Yet it is really only since 9/11 that they have been deemed worthy of attention by their colleagues in the Western media, thanks almost entirely to the role of Al-Jazeerah. This Qatar-based Arab TV station has gained notoriety in the West as the preferred vehicle through which Osama bin Laden conveys his views to the world. It has also been blamed for its inflammatory coverage of the Palestinian Intifadha, and, more generally, for the strident anti-Western or anti-American tone of much of its commentary. The irony is that it is, in many respects, a follower of Western models. It does not have to toe a government line (except in the negative sense of avoiding direct criticism of, or embarrassing revelations about, the authorities in Qatar itself). It features attractive anchorwomen and advertisements clearly designed to stimulate consumer appetites through associations with sex, glamour, and status. The news coverage is technically slick but often superficial or one-sided. The discussion is lively but tends to remain within a received spectrum of Arab opinion; and the prevailing tone is sympathetic to conspiracy theories, particularly about foreign or Western influence within the Arab world. The core group of journalists that run it are graduates of the BBC Arabic service, but their product is close to being a mirror image of the stations owned by Rupert Murdoch.

We should not generalize too glibly from these examples. But a conclusion one might draw is that cultural similarities produced or encouraged by globalization will not necessarily reduce, and may even accentuate, political differences. And journalists reporting on one culture or society to another will continue to face a dilemma. Clearly they will not be doing their job if they fail to report what makes the two societies different from each other. Yet they also have a responsibility to see through those differences to the underlying common humanity, and enable their audience to achieve a degree of understanding, even empathy, for the words and actions of those they are reporting on.

An important step toward achieving this may be to stop thinking of "Western" and "Muslim" as mutually exclusive categories. We should remember that by now every "Western" society has a significant Muslim component, and every "Muslim" society has absorbed significant influences from the West.

17

International Migration: At the Boiling Point

Kathleen Newland

ALTHOUGH CONCERN about international migration is achieving a new intensity, migration itself is far from a new phenomenon. In fact, it considerably predates recorded history. The story of our species is the story of expansion, conquest, the transformation of vast landscapes by the arrival of man, and—the dark side—it is also the story of the suppression and disappearance of peoples—whether the Carib "Indians," Amazonian tribes, or the San people of Southern Africa. Is there anything new about migration and refugee flows in the late twentieth and early twenty-first centuries? Or are we simply witnessing the latest chapter in a saga that has continued for millennia? Why is migration now generating such extraordinary tensions?

One new ingredient is the sheer volume of migration. The absolute numbers of people on the move is greater than ever before—but this is a statement that can be made about almost every category of human activity. It reflects not only an increase in the tendency to migrate but also an increase in the number of people doing *anything*. The population of the world is about 6 billion people, and has risen very rapidly with the revolution in public health and basic medical care such as childhood immunization.

The conventional best estimate of the number of migrants in the world—defined as people residing in foreign countries for more than one year—is about 175 million. That is a very rough estimation, but it is a huge number—larger than the population of all but a handful of the biggest countries. And it has risen rapidly. The UN Population Division calculates that only 75 million people fit that definition in 1965; 105 million were migrants in 1985.

Apart from its absolute size, the other thing that is striking about that number is what a small *proportion* of the total human population it is. In the so-called "Age of Migration," less than 3 percent of people have left home. The proportions were, at least for some large parts of the world, greater 100 years ago. The U.S. Census of 1910 showed that nearly 15 percent of the people living in the United States had been born somewhere else. In the 2000 Census, it was just a little over 10 percent (10.4 percent).

In proportional terms, the period around the turn of the last century was more strikingly an age of migration. A great wave of people moved from Europe to the New World—not only to the United States, Canada, and Australia but also to Argentina, Chile, and Uruguay. There was a very substantial migration from Japan—then considered desperately overpopulated—to Peru and Brazil. A large exchange of populations also took place among the various elements of the British Empire—people moved from the Indian subcontinent to East Africa and the Caribbean, from Malaysia and India to South Africa. Another great global flow saw Chinese move to Southeast Asia, North America, and, in less concentrated streams, to Europe. So very large-scale migration is nothing new, although the absolute numbers of the late twentieth and early twenty-first centuries are unprecedented.[1]

Migration today also has developed a momentum that is unusual in historical terms. In the past, the great waves have been interrupted by catastrophes. Global depression and world war put a stop to the last great wave. People did not have the means or the ability to move. Without these catastrophic interruptions, migration acquires a tremendous momentum, in large part because of the phenomenon often called *chain migration,* which is driven by family reunification and community networks. One member of a family establishes himself—or, increasingly, her-

Figure 17.1

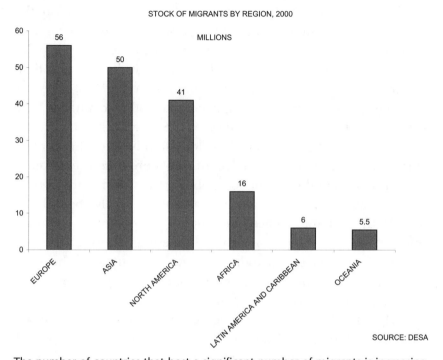

STOCK OF MIGRANTS BY REGION, 2000

The number of countries that host a significant number of migrants is increasing. In 2000, sixty-six countries hosted more than 500,000 migrants, an increase from twenty-six countries in 1965.

self—in a new country, and in time is able to bring a spouse or children or parents she left behind. Then the spouse brings his parents, and they bring their other adult children, who bring their spouses, siblings, in-laws, and so forth. The communities of origin often develop a culture and a political economy of migration, so that it becomes an expected part of life's pattern and develops a powerful momentum if it is not interrupted by some external factor.

The late twentieth century has not had a war or depression of such a scale as to disrupt global migration patterns since recovering from the after-effects of World War II. In fact, the cataclysmic events of the last twenty years have been such as to *promote* migration—the collapse of the Iron Curtain, removal of internal borders in Europe as part of the process of European integration, the technological revolution that put long-distance travel and communication within reach of people of modest means. The negative side can be seen in the protracted civil wars of the late twentieth century that, rather than disrupting migration patterns, have created new ones as refugees sought safety in other countries. The worldwide total of refugees peaked in the early 1990s and has remained high, as resolution to these long-standing conflicts proves elusive. Afghanistan is a case in point. For more than twenty years, Afghans have had the distinction of being the world's largest refugee population—7 million at the peak and currently about 4 million. With a fragile peace seeming to hold from late 2002, however, Afghan refugees are going home in great numbers.

Another new factor in today's migration context is the stark contrast between the demographic situation of countries of origin and receiving countries. Most of the receiving countries, particularly the Europeans, have entered demographic free-fall. Their birth rates have collapsed (in Italy and Spain it is about 1.1 child per woman, half the replacement level) and the average age of their populations is rising rapidly. As a result of somewhat higher levels of immigration and relentless fertility declines, immigration accounted for 84 percent of Western Europe's modest population growth in 1990–95. Its contribution to Germany's population growth was 130 percent—in other words, Germany would have shrunk substantially in the absence of immigration. These trends have continued in the late 1990s and early 2000s.

Two recent studies, from the Organization for Economic Cooperation and Development (OECD) and the UN Population Division, projected for several countries what levels of immigration would be required to maintain the size of the population, the labor force, and the dependency ratio (of workers to non-workers in the population). The projections were very sobering—huge multiples of present levels of immigration to Europe would be needed to maintain existing dependency ratios. (See Eliasson, in this volume.) The study galvanized a shift in some quarters in thinking about the need for immigration to prevent a collapse in productivity and in the financial underpinnings of European pension and medical insurance systems. Familiarity with the demographic facts of life have not, however, prevented—and may have encouraged—anti-immigration backlash in a number of countries where the prospect of greatly increased immigration gives rise to cultural and social insecurity.

The widespread perception that immigration is out of control and therefore dangerous exerts a strong influence on the current migration debate. Large-scale migration in the past was not frequently encouraged or sponsored by governments. Today, governments have much less control over who comes, and how. Generally, immigration flows through three major streams: the family stream, the employment stream, and the humanitarian stream.

In the advanced industrial countries, family reunification recounts for the great bulk of immigration: about 60 percent in the European Union and 75–80 percent in the United States. Governments set the rules for family migration but it is not easy for them to control the numbers. The right to integrity and unity of the family is widely recognized as a fundamental human right. Very few countries place legal restrictions on the right of citizens to sponsor a spouse or minor children for immigration. Some add parents under certain conditions. Legal permanent residents who are not citizens also normally have some rights to family reunification.

The second largest immigration stream to the United States is employment related. But it is small compared to the family—only about 107,000 for permanent residence, or 13 percent. (There is also a sizable temporary labor category, many of whom eventually gain permanent status.) The employment category is the most controllable, and most welcome in public policy terms. In Europe, however, it is only in third place among sources of immigrants, at about 7 percent.

The third stream of immigration—the humanitarian—is in some ways the most problematical today in the eyes of governments and public opinion in many countries. It is the one part of the immigration stream over which governments have deliberately relinquished a considerable degree of control. As of the end of 2002, 145 governments have signed the UN Convention Relating to the Status of Refugees, which obligates them not to return a refugee against his/her will to a place where his/her life or liberty would be in danger. Another clause of that treaty says that a refugee should not be penalized for entering a country illegally in order to seek asylum.

The asylum channel is one of the very few ways in which a person without previous ties in a country can legally remain there, and has become a major channel of migration—roughly one-third of all entries to European countries now are asylum seekers. Many of them are suspected of coming for economic motives rather than to escape persecution, although the greatest number come from some of the most violent and oppressive countries on earth—Afghanistan, Iraq, Iran, Somalia, and Sudan all being high on the list of countries of origin of asylum seekers in the industrialized countries. The United States, with more expansive family and employment programs, receives only 8 percent of its total legal immigration through humanitarian programs.

The sharp growth in the numbers of asylum seekers in the last quarter of the twentieth century played an important role in raising the anxiety level about uncontrolled and uncontrollable entry. In Western Europe, there were only about 13,000 asylum claims per year filed in the 1970s. The total had risen to 170,000 by 1985 and peaked at about 690,000 in 1992. The lifting of exit restrictions in the former Eastern Bloc was a major factor in this sudden rise in the early 1990s; one-third of the 1992 applicants in Western Europe were from Bulgaria and Romania.

Within this broad picture of international migration in the early twenty-first century, what accounts for the new and widening fault lines? There is a simple answer, and a whole series of extremely complex ones. The simple answer is, "more people want to come in than states are willing to accept." Like most simple answers, it isn't completely wrong, but it isn't very useful, either. The more complex answers include these factors:

- There are more countries in crisis, resulting in more violent conflicts and more human rights abuses affecting ever-larger numbers of people, some of whom are determined to escape by any available means;
- Growing income disparity between North and South and the powerful pull of job vacancies in wealthier countries makes migration an economically rational choice for many residents of developing countries;
- Proportionally fewer opportunities for legal migration invite people to try to use the asylum channel for labor or family migration, feeding an atmosphere of distrust toward migrants in many receiving countries;
- Easier and cheaper transportation and communication between source and destination countries make it easier for people to travel long distances, and to anticipate conditions at their destinations;
- The growth of a new industry of smugglers and traffickers of people is hardening both governmental and public attitudes toward clandestine entry;
- Cross-cutting political pressures on government authorities urge them to crack down on people who deliberately misuse the asylum system, but at the same time to respect human rights and show compassion for the unfortunate;
- There is a pervasive *fear* on the part of governments that their sovereignty and ability to control their borders is being eroded by the forces of globalization—which include migration—and a corresponding determination to reassert control. Along with this, of course, goes the fear of being punished at the polls if the government is perceived to have lost control or to be governing badly;
- Most importantly, perhaps, in the wake of the events of September 11, 2001, security concerns have focused in a very broad

way on immigrant populations and foreign visitors as potential sources of threat.

SECURITY AS A FAULT LINE

The last of these factors is genuinely new. It is ironic that economic reliance on immigration is growing at the same time that immigrants are increasingly seen as a security risk—particularly in the United States, where the security threats from foreigners that have been detected are not coming from immigrants but from temporary visitors. The September 11 hijackers, for example, entered as short-term tourists, businessmen, or students. The words of political leaders after the September 11 terrorist attacks were reassuring, but subsequent actions have indeed targeted immigrants along with foreign visitors. For example, long-resident legal immigrants from certain countries (mostly in the Middle East and Africa) are now required to submit to a special registration procedure with the Immigration Service that has landed many people in harsh detention conditions simply for minor technical violations or for lack of complete documentation. Citizenship applications have in some parts of the country been subject to a *de facto* freeze as the Service is overwhelmed with new requirements.

Refugee resettlement programs have taken a particularly severe hit, despite the fact that resettling refugees are among the most scrutinized of all people entering the United States or other countries. They have been through elaborate selection and processing procedures, and are the only group that arrive in the United States assigned to domestic agencies that assist in their integration into new communities. In the United States, a ceiling for resettlement is set each year in a consultation between the Congress and the Administration. In fiscal year 2002, the ceiling was 70,000, yet fewer than 27,000 refugees were admitted for resettlement. Security concerns were the main reason given for the dramatic shortfall. It is a sad fact that countries that, through violence and persecution, generate large numbers of refugees also generate terrorism or support for terrorists: Algeria, Afghanistan, Iraq, Somalia, and Sudan are among the top source countries for refugees and asylum seekers. The new security atmosphere has placed refugees from those countries in double jeopardy.

European countries have somewhat better reasons than the United States to be concerned about terrorist activities in immigrant communities. More and larger radical Islamist communities are found in European cities, and terrorists (including the September 11 hijackers) have been found to be living in Europe as immigrants, asylum seekers, and students. European systems are less effective in removing persons who may pose a threat; in particular, very long adjudication periods for asylum seekers in some countries and poor integration of existing immigrant communities create opportunities for those who intend harm to remain and find cover in communities disaffected from the mainstream of society. Nonetheless, the links that are being drawn between immigration in general and security threats are overdrawn, and often misrepresented.

There are, indeed, ways in which immigrants create security threats, and it is important to acknowledge them in order to separate reality from fiction. Some of the security threats to home or host countries that may arise from certain immigrant groups include the following:

- Immigrants may work against the regimes of their home countries, increasing the threats to those governments. The Tamil Diaspora, for example, has actively supported the Tamil separatist cause in Sri Lanka.
- Immigrants may directly or indirectly (through hospitality to visitor) attack the interests of their host country or another country. This has been evident from some of foiled plots hatched by al Qaeda cells in Hamburg, Rome, Paris, and other cities in Europe.

- The host country may use immigrant groups to threaten their country of origin (or at least tolerate the actions of such groups), or the home country may use or send immigrants to act against the host country. Both dynamics have been evident in U.S.-Cuba relations in the 1980s and 1990s.
- Mass influx of defeated fighters, who mix in among refugees in border areas, may pose a threat to their home or host countries, or both, as was the experience of Rwanda and neighboring Congo after the fighting that followed the 1994 genocide in Rwanda.
- In some settings, immigrants are perceived to pose a cultural threat to the host country. Bhutan asserted this fear in the face of immigration from Nepal, and subsequently dealt harshly not only with newly arriving would-be immigrants but with long-standing residents of Nepali descent.
- Obviously inefficient and ineffective border controls may create a crisis of confidence in government, undermining it from within.

How do these possibilities compare to the actual threats from immigration that have been the focus of policy attention in the West post-September 11?

The major security threats associated with migration in North America and Europe arise from four characteristics. First, particularly evident in Western Europe, is the lack of integration and the associated alienation of immigrant populations. Some minority groups, such as the Turks in Germany, have been there for years or even generations, but have very limited access to citizenship and are still regarded very much as "foreigners"—even those who were born in Germany. Being denied full membership in the host society keeps immigrants from developing feelings of loyalty and solidarity, and may even lead some among them to a destructive rage.

Second, the presence of large numbers of undocumented migrants, who do not have legal permission to reside in the country where they live, creates two levels of security concern. Those without regular status have no legal identity, and have an interest in remaining invisible to the authorities. Although their "invisibility" masks no ill intentions in the vast majority of cases, the mere presence of a large number of undocumented residents makes looking for the few who do intend harm a needle-in-the-haystack proposition. Security would be enhanced by getting as many people as possible out of the shadows of irregular migration by regularizing their status.

A third kind of security threat associated with current migration flows is the growing involvement of organized crime in the movement of people. Tighter controls on entry have made it more difficult for ordinary migrants to enter without authorization, and so have created a growth industry for smugglers. Annual turnover is estimated to be in the $12–$15 billion range. With this kind of revenue, smugglers can easily invest in corrupting border guards and immigration officials, creating genuine new security problems that go far beyond illegal immigration.

Each of these new security problems is a self-inflicted wound on the part of immigrant-receiving countries rather than a fault inherent in immigration itself. The immigrant-specific policy responses to September 11 and the kind of terrorist threat it represents have exacerbated rather than solved the problems. Investigation, registration, and detention based on ethnic and racial profiling have alienated immigrant populations that were reasonably well integrated previously. Not only might this bear bitter fruit in the long run, but also in the short run it makes disaffected immigrant communities less likely to cooperate with the authorities in intelligence-gathering and law enforcement. A closed and fearful community is more rather than less conducive to terrorism, even if unwittingly.

Movement toward greater opportunities for legal immigration and regularization of undocumented populations that were proceeding prior to September 11 have lost momentum or even been reversed. These include the progress toward a migration agreement between the United States and Mexico, and the broad, positive migration-harmonization agenda unveiled by the

European Union at the Tampere Summit in 1999. Moreover, the high costs of unauthorized entry means that many undocumented migrants who used to come and go between home and abroad now come and stay, as they can no longer afford frequent circular trips.

The opportunity for organized crime and criminalized political networks has expanded, both in scope and in profitability. Illegal immigration has not declined as governments have thrown more resources at their borders and ports of entry, but it has become professionalized, and much more dangerous (both for migrants and for those who try to keep them out) as criminal gangs come to dominate the traffic.

Immigration measures should have to pass some tests of value and effectiveness, as well as tests of humanity and consistency with the values of the society in whose name they are imposed. Philip B. Heyman, a Professor at Harvard Law School and a former U.S. Deputy Attorney-General, wrote: "For democratic nations, the primary concerns in dealing with terrorism are to maintain and protect life, the liberties necessary to a vibrant democracy, and the unity of society, the loss of which can turn a healthy and diverse society into a seriously divided and violent one." By his criteria, international migration policy in most countries is failing the test.

Figure 17.2

TOP 10 MIGRANT RECEIVING COUNTRIES, 2000

PERCENTAGE

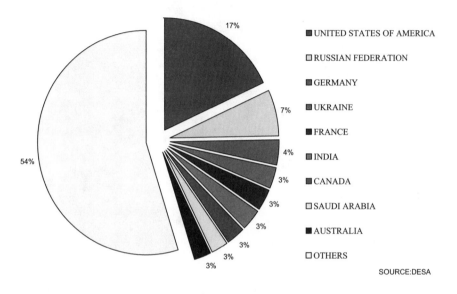

- ■ UNITED STATES OF AMERICA
- □ RUSSIAN FEDERATION
- ■ GERMANY
- ■ UKRAINE
- ■ FRANCE
- ■ INDIA
- ■ CANADA
- □ SAUDI ARABIA
- ■ AUSTRALIA
- □ OTHERS

SOURCE:DESA

CORRECTIONS

Part 6

In this final section, two very experienced diplomat-scholars consider what corrective actions are being—or could be—taken to address the fault lines that so threaten the foundations of our cultures and our political systems. Peter Tarnoff, an international consultant, has held leading positions in both the private and public sectors of foreign affairs. His practical considerations of possible corrective steps that might be taken by sovereign nations is grounded in a reality nurtured when he was President of the Council on Foreign Relations and then refined during his term as the U.S. Undersecretary of State for Political Affairs.

Professor Richard Falk contributes a fitting last chapter, one that notes the impressive upsurge in international humanitarian initiatives in the last decade of the twentieth century. Much of this was due to the efforts of civil society, human rights organizations, and even individuals participating in a normative revolution unknown in history. Falk then warns, however, of the detour in these global efforts and offers reasons why even the most powerful nation on earth must rely on our noble traditions, values, and moral position if we are to survive in a secure, humane world.

18

Government Responses to Fault Lines

Peter Tarnoff

MOST PEOPLE who serve in government want to be in office indefinitely. They also want to wield as much power as possible. In some cases, they are motivated principally by high ideals and commendable motives; in other instances, they are driven primarily by greed and ego. Over the course of time, however, their conduct and actions can change and evolve for better or for worse. At the same time, the way governments deal with the "fault lines" issues can be modified by internal and external forces and incentives.

Moreover, governments can gravitate closer to or away from belief systems or institutions ("foundations"). Religions, for example, can provide a framework of values for countries or regions, but governments generally decide opportunistically rather than spiritually how much influence to accept from an established faith and its clergy.

The "fault lines" are policy categories, not political objectives or moral ends. While there is general agreement that some of the "fault lines" are good (such as civil liberties) and some are bad (for example, torture, terrorism), most governments—even those widely regarded as "democratic"—tend to justify or condemn actions taken on "fault line" issues more on the basis of the motives of the perpetrator than on the nature of the action undertaken. Consider the adage: "one man's terrorist is another man's freedom fighter."

For the most part, value and theological systems provide governments with an rhetorical structure of belief rather than clear ethical prescriptions for the way to behave. The weakening of traditional authorities both secular and spiritual and the proliferation of sources of information have propelled governments into a state of perpetual motion, constantly in search of marginal advantage or popular favor. It is rare for governments to credibly align themselves consistently to an accepted value system. For the most part, political leaders decide what to do first and then wrap their actions in whatever inspirational or patriotic texts and beliefs they believe will impress the audiences they seek to persuade. Although some American politicians claim that they ask themselves "what Jesus would do?" when making hard decisions, it remains to be seen whether the answers they receive come from within or without.

But before lamenting the passing of the traditional structures of common values, we should remember that rigid belief systems sometimes have produced the most intolerant and fanatic of regimes. "True believers" may have once referred to men and women prepared to sacrifice themselves rather then denounce a caring and humanistic faith. Now, the term also applies to people so convinced of the exclusive rightness of their belief that they will brutalize those who refuse to convert or submit.

DIFFERENT PATHS TO COMMON GOALS

It is remarkable how much the preambles of constitutions have in common. Even when their authors come from different historical, religious, and cultural traditions, these documents extol the dignity of all citizens and defend the exercise of freedom and rights while proclaiming the unity of a people in a national politic. Founders of nations and their successors invariably appeal to universal sentiments common to all humankind. No doubt some of the constitution writers are sincere in evoking aspirations that elicit a general will to work for the common good. Other founders may be more cynical or manipulative, knowing full well that even a morally correct constitution does not always reflect the realities of governance.

In order to understand the true intentions of governments, we may want to distinguish between those that are value oriented and results oriented. Value-oriented regimes commit themselves to govern according to traditional—usually religious—texts or laws. The highest authorities in value-oriented states are clerics and the most venerated documents of state are scriptures. High religious authorities are empowered to interpret religious texts in ways that apply to everyday life including commerce, contracts, laws, and the definition and punishment of crime. In these societies, severe restrictions usually are imposed on the behavior of ordinary citizens and close ties with foreign powers are regarded with suspicion for fear of contamination or subversion.

Results-oriented governments aim to bring about tangible improvements in the well-being of society in areas such as health care, prosperity, education, public safety, national security, and infrastructure. When a government is results-oriented, its laws can be based on a body of traditional doctrine but its constitutional foundation is consistently being interpreted and reinterpreted by secular, often elected, judiciaries.

The United States government is, for the most part, results-oriented. Its constitution affirms the separation of church and state. A strong federal system and independent judiciary constrain the power of the central government. The two national political parties compete for public favor in terms of concrete deliverables. While public rhetoric, especially during electoral periods, embraces traditional values and moral principles, elections themselves usually are won or lost on the basis of policy prescriptions or records of achievement.

Can the same be said of American foreign policy? Is it also results-oriented or is the propagation of an American value system becoming more central to U.S. objectives around the world?

In the immediate post-World War II period, American foreign policy was driven principally by the need to establish a network of coalitions under U.S. leadership that were prepared to defend—militarily, if necessary—the Western world against encroachments from the Communist bloc, led by the Soviet Union. During the forty-five years of the cold war, there were superpower proxy wars in the developing world but no armed conflict between NATO and the Warsaw Pact. The two alliance adversaries made little effort to convert the other; both were principally concerned with controlling their own members and preserving their respective systems of governance and economic organization.

Suddenly, just over a decade ago, the USSR collapsed and the cold war ended.

An "end of history" was proclaimed by some and it looked to many Americans as if liberal democratic forms of government and free market economies had triumphed over the Communist and totalitarian alternatives and that there would be a universal recognition that something close to a U.S. model had become the system of choice for most societies. In the absence of overarching military and ideological threats and a diminished need for the "sole remaining superpower" to tend to minding its alliances, there was more talk in Washington than before about a moral foreign policy and greater confidence that American values (often portrayed as "universal values") would be a central component of Washington's worldwide reach.

A DOCTRINAIRE FOREIGN POLICY

Doctrines and values are not new to American foreign policy. In the early nineteenth century, the Monroe Doctrine alerted Europeans that the U.S. "should consider any attempt on their part to extend their system to any portion of this hemisphere as dangerous to our peace and safety."

Shortly after World War II, the Truman Doctrine made clear that the U.S. would act to oppose any Soviet attempt to extend its influence into Greece and Turkey. Under President Jimmy Carter, human rights were placed high on the U.S. foreign policy agenda and, although Carter was denounced by balance-of-power realists for sacrificing American interests on the altar of idealism, his successor, Ronald Reagan, strengthened democracy-building efforts primarily to weaken the hold of the Communist regimes. The first President Bush announced the coming of a "new world order" that was understood to rely heavily on the American experience and influence.

President Clinton came to stand for what some of his aides described as a doctrine of "humanitarian interventionism," where the international community—assisted and sometimes led by the U.S.—intervenes, with force if necessary, to prevent or stop human slaughter.

The second Bush Administration has been more ambitious than its recent predecessors in proclaiming the need for a new doctrinal structure and the obligation to spread American political, economic, and moral values far and wide. It justifies this redefinition of American interests and strategies on the basis of what is required to defend the U.S. against new enemies and new threats in the post-cold war world.

The new Bush Doctrine was published as the "National Security Strategy of the United States." Since it has been dissected and debated exhaustively in the press, academic circles, and in foreign ministries worldwide, I will not describe it in detail, but for this chapter there are features of this doctrine worth noting.

The document makes clear that the United States intends to preserve and use its position as the dominant military power in today's world. Washington will decide what threatens the American way of life and, while there are passing references to international partners, it is clear that the U.S. is prepared (even eager) to act alone. It is not hard to see in the text the strength of the Administration's unilateralist impulse that so concerns most of America's friends and allies and that the State Department gamely tries to minimize.

In the case of Iraq, the doctrinal and moral strains of Bush Administration thinking meet and fuse. President Bush repeatedly stated that the U.S. would act quickly, decisively, and alone (if necessary) to remove the threat that Saddam Hussein represented. He has been so clear and consistent that it is hard to imagine the President being satisfied by anything less than a convincing cleansing of all weapons of mass destruction in Iraq and the ouster of Saddam as well. Most world leaders, including those in the Arab nations, would like nothing better than to rid Iraq of such weapons, and there was little support around the world for the murderous regime of Saddam Hussein. Yet, why then was there so much suspicion regarding Washington's demands when America's objective (Iraqi disarmament) is so widely shared?

For two reasons: The first is that many governments believed that American policy in Iraq was not based on a legitimate fear of Iraqi intentions or capabilities, but that Washington was using Iraq as a convenient excuse to assert America's paramount political power and military superiority and its willingness to use them. In its first two years in office, the Bush Administration has given ample evidence of its preference for going it alone and its disdain for international treaties and commitments. International public and political opinion had already soured on the U.S. even before the President put regime change in Iraq at the top of his foreign policy priorities.

The second reason resonates especially in the Islamic world. Many Muslim leaders believe that the U.S. will endeavor to transform that country into a Western-style democracy. I do not argue that the Iraqi people were better off under Saddam Hussein than under a benevolent U.S. military occupation, but the prospect of an American democracy offensive starting in Iraq and spreading throughout the Middle East terrifies even some of America's best friends in the region. Lest any reader think that my description of Bush Administration intentions for a post-Saddam Iraq are fanciful, I invite them to read the many on-the-record comments made by high U.S. officials on how democracy will flourish first in Baghdad and spread rapidly throughout the Middle East. Some in the administration go so far as to predict that this rapid democratizing of the region will produce agreement between Israelis and Palestinians because two democratically elected leaders will find it easier to make peace.

But back again to doctrine and values. Now that there is an official Bush Doctrine, it becomes awkward for the administration to flexibly and creatively innovate new policies or react to new emergencies. The recent announcement by North Korea that it is pursuing a nuclear weapons program is a case in point. A threat from North Korea is a clear candidate for preemptive military attack by the U.S. It is tailor-made for the Bush Doctrine. However, the Bush Administration is reacting cautiously and cooperatively to the North Korean program—as it should—while defending itself against charges from the right wing that it is handling the challenge no differently from the way the much-maligned Clinton Administration would have reacted.

The U.S. forcibly installing democracy in Baghdad, and beyond, alarms many in the Middle East who will not soon forget the crusader spirit of those American officials eager to assert that the U.S. has the right to remake Muslim societies. Of course, those international norms of behavior contained in the Geneva Conventions and other international treaties should be part of American policy. But imposing Western ways by force of arms following a military victory on countries determined to preserve their distinctive cultures and religions would unleash a terrifying clash of civilizations.

Good Versus Evil: An Age of Absolutes

American presidents have called foreign adversaries "evil" before. Ronald Reagan labeled the Soviet Union an "evil empire," but he then went on to become a serious negotiating partner with Mikhail Gorbachev. Now, the second President Bush describes Iran, Iraq, and North Korea as constituting an "axis of evil" and he warns the rest of the world that countries have a choice: they can be either for or against the U.S. in the war on terror. "It's either us or them," the administration asserts and, in its view, neutrality is tantamount to appeasement.

What role there is now for American diplomacy is an open question, unless American leadership in the UN Security Council convinces hard-liners in Washington that multilateral diplomacy can be made to serve U.S. interests after all. Since World War II, the U.S. has worked harder at persuading and cultivating its political, military, and economic partners than at negotiating with its enemies. Presidents from Truman to Clinton understood how much American security depended on having close friends and allies, even when there were differences of views to bridge and difficult compromises to swallow.

It is also true that diplomatic conditions have changed: America's new enemies are both more and less threatening than the USSR at the height of the cold war. They are less threatening because, whatever their destructive power, they are unable to obliterate the planet (although some would do so if they could).

But they are more threatening because they do not seek to reach accommodations with us. They have no interest in summitry or state visits. In the Middle East, some have a political agenda: the destruction of the State of Israel and the overthrow of the Gulf monarchies, especially that of Saudi Arabia. They see the U.S. as the principal obstacle to their aims and have shown themselves ready to use terror to weaken and hurt us. In the case of the most fanatic extremists, no negotiation is possible and the U.S. has no choice but to work with others to destroy them.

Still, does their suicidal fanaticism make all of the terrorists' demands evil? What happens when countries in the Middle East that we need for security cooperation and oil express some sympathy for the political agenda of the terrorists? The problem with labeling governments and groups as either good or evil and demanding (rhetorically, at least) that they be for us or against us is that it may play well in American politics but it outrages many important non-Americans whose cooperation is essential to us in the war on terror and who insist on making a distinction between the aims and the methods of terrorist states and organizations.

The overuse of "evil" to describe countries and governments also places an implicit obligation on the U.S. to dispose of such regimes. Although the U.S. can fight and win wars in many places at once, few in America want Washington to be the world's enforcer. Indeed, less talk of good versus evil and us versus them might allow the U.S. to recapture the moral high ground in the war on terror. The more insidious the threat, the more important it will be for the U.S. to be less absolutist in its approach. During the cold war, the U.S. could have fought alone against the USSR. But there is no way that the U.S. can win the war on terror alone, even if America is statistically more powerful than ever before when compared to the rest of the world.

SHIFTING FAULT LINES

Living as I do in an earthquake zone in California, I am extremely sensitive to the dangers when fault lines start to shift, even to a small degree. I also know that it is hard to predict when and where these movements will occur and what will be the extent of the damage they are likely to cause. It is clear, however, that even the most democratic and well-intentioned governments behave uncharacteristically when they feel threatened or destabilized. For example, they can:

—relax their definition of what constitutes torture and permit a degree of corporal punishment and non-physical pressures (e.g., sleep deprivation, noise and light harassment, extreme and indefinite isolation, threats to family members, constant interrogation)

—resort to the extra-judicial and covert assassinations of suspected terrorists

—invoke a political form of "force majeure" as reason for selectively applying or ignoring the Geneva Conventions

—restrict immigration, especially from countries or cultures perceived to be strange or hostile. Anti-immigrant sentiment also leads to the formation of sometimes-powerful neo-fascist political movements even in developed countries

—pay less attention to issues of discrimination against women and children in countries that are important partners in confronting a common new enemy

—amend domestic judicial practices so that terms of indictment and confinement are radically tightened. Punishments then become much more severe for crimes stemming from the new threats

—impose restrictions on the media that result in less information being made available to the general public. Invoking national security considerations is a frequent excuse for withholding information that might prompt citizens to oppose the policies of their governments.

It is reasonable, even necessary, for societies under threat to resort to extraordinary measures to defend themselves. But it is also essential that in open societies there be a continuing public and political debate about how much security can be gained by limiting how much freedom. Such a debate can be acrimonious but it becomes unhealthy only if stifled. As frustrating as it is to policy makers, the struggle between security and liberty is endless. Should conditions change, practices can be loosened or tightened. The tectonic plates of policy are always shifting and the number of independent variables at play in a crisis can be huge. Nevertheless, as long as governments are committed to the proposition that it is ultimately desirable for there to be more freedoms not less and more information not less, citizens can expect that liberties and openness will someday be restored. But beware of those—even in democracies—who seek to make emergency restrictions permanent, because the threat is potentially infinite. Their aim is to transform, not simply defend, society because they live in a world of absolutes, including the illusion of absolute security.

Because the very nature of post-cold war threats is indefinite and universal, there are some who believe that it will be necessary to modify fundamentally the character of free societies in order to defeat them. We know wars that end with a V-E Day or V-J

Day, and where we can see the battle lines changing in our daily newspapers. But there will never be a V-Terrorism Day.

Like foreign policy itself, the campaigns against the new global threats will be an endless process where success will be measured incrementally, never conclusively. In the long haul, however, it will be the free and open societies that are best able to sustain the efforts and sacrifices necessary to stay the course in the interminable wars against the new challenges of the twenty-first century.

ALL ALONE OR ALL TOGETHER

When confronted with complex and ever-shifting fault lines, governments incline either toward the unilateral or the multilateral. Smaller and more vulnerable countries—especially those firmly embedded in regional political or economic alliances—are prone to turn to their neighbors for help in times of crisis. Most member states of the European Union act that way. Especially in matters of economic policy, the EU nations tend to stick together and face the rest of the world in a united fashion after setting common economic policies. However, EU solidarity is less firm in political and security matters. Since the U.K. and France are permanent members of the UN Security Council and most EU nations are also members of NATO, there are not yet common European diplomatic or security policies on most issues.

The unilateralist impulse is more prevalent in the case of major powers and those opaque and dangerous regimes sometimes identified as "rogue states." Major powers are the most inclined to act and stand alone. They have the wherewithal to operate with a high degree of autonomy and their domestic political climate favors policies of "national interest" over "international comity." China and the U.S. are prime examples of powerful countries that are readier than most to stand alone on matters of high policy and principle. In the case of what might be called "outcast regimes," their very isolation and opaqueness create a shield that makes it hard for outsiders to have a clear view of their intentions and capabilities. North Korea is such a case in point.

In principle, the world and the cause of peace would be better served if international organizations and agreements were effectively respected by all nations. In principle, most countries favor a rule of international law and order that prevents conflict and humanitarian chaos.

But problems occur when nations differ over whether a threat to international peace and stability exists and, if it does, how international players should react. The discussions in the UN Security Council over how to disarm Saddam tended to overshadow international concerns about the scope and nature of the threat itself. Since the U.S. and U.K. invaded Iraq, the multilateral approach to solving international problems have suffered a telling blow (irrespective of all the other ramifications—good and bad—resulting from this military action).

In principle, the new global threats of the twenty-first century are mostly multilateral in nature. They include environmental degradation, international crime, proliferation of weapons of mass destruction, ethnic and religious conflicts, disease, extreme poverty, and violations of human and civil rights. These threats know no borders and governments are not usually the sole entities with influence and resources. In fact, governments are coming to understand that nongovernmental organs (business, labor, the media, academia, religious groups, and private voluntary organizations) are active and important components of international affairs.

Today's multilateral diplomacy extends vertically to non-state entities and horizontally to like-minded governments and international organizations. Effective international coalitions are no longer limited to ministers and generals. Non-state players from business, academia, labor, private voluntary organizations, and the media are represented at the diplomatic negotiating table whether or not they are physically present. International diplomacy is now played like multidimensional chess.

SANCTIONS AND FENCE-MENDING

When countries clash over what they consider to be important issues of policy or principle, there is always a risk that they will resort to military force. However, most governments at least pay lip service to the proposition that they will use force only as a last resort and many leaders actually do their best to resolve disputes peacefully. Moreover, there has emerged in recent decades a long menu of ways that governments and international organizations can bring non-military pressure to bear on adversaries or outlaw states:

Economic Sanctions—Three Varieties

Multilateral Usually imposed by the UN Security Council. Generally regarded as the most effective because the most widely observed. Can be lifted once offending country meets certain conditions but requires a confirming vote by the UN Security Council to do so.

Unilateral Country-to-country. May have political/moral effect, but porous economically because most countries are not bound to restrict trade or investment with targeted regime. If sanctioning country has sufficient power in International Financial Institutions (IFIs), it can block IFI loans and grants as well.

Extraterritorial Sanctioning country applies economic penalties to third countries trading with targeted country. Hotly contested politically and legally by countries unwilling to accept jurisdiction of sanctioning country over their sovereign trading practices.

The imposition of economic sanctions can, however, be a

broad and blunt weapon. Unless they are targeted on the offending country's leadership, sanctions can cause serious suffering among the civilian population. If the pain from sanctions on innocents is prolonged and serious, states—especially in the region—will circumvent them. The U.S. has imposed sanctions more than any other country in recent years, but because most American sanctions are essentially bilateral, they have had only marginal economic effects.

Moral/Political Sanctions—Multilateral or Unilateral

This form of sanction is often applied in the area of human rights. The UN Human Rights Commission meets annually to pronounce itself on alleged human rights violators around the world. Charges and countercharges are debated in Geneva before the violations are put to a vote by the Commission. In addition, and uniquely, the U.S. publishes annually a series of human rights reports describing and condemning what it considers to be human rights violations around the world.

Shunning

A more discrete form of official displeasure occurs when a country decides to have no or limited diplomatic representation in another capital. Shunning can be augmented by ordering its diplomats to avoid all contact and dialogue with representatives of the foreign power.

Sanctions are non-military methods of pressure and punishment, but the diplomatic arsenal also contains devices to promote reconciliation and dispute resolution. They include:

Mediation/Arbitration

Ideally, such interventions occur before international disputes turn violent. Successful conflict prevention is better than settlement negotiations but resolving a conflict that has already erupted is sometimes the only way that peace can be restored. International organization negotiators (usually, but not always, with the UN) abound but there are skilled national mediators as well. For decades, the U.S. has played a unique role in the Middle East peace process and now, more recently, in the Balkans. Norway has become a powerful mediating force and the EU is reinforcing its dispute resolution capacities. Regional organizations should play greater roles in settling disputes, although the disputing parties must also be convinced that there are positive and negative economic consequences for them to settle. This means that the developed countries and the IFIs have to be prepared to provide substantial financial rewards for good political behavior.

Constructive Engagement

This is a diplomatic way to describe a "good cop, bad cop" routine for dealing with a recalcitrant state. It involves at least one outside government maintaining contact with the regime that is under pressure to change or to cease and desist. Constructive engagement works best when the "good cop" coordinates its initiatives with the international community pressing for change. Regional nations, even neighbors, are good in this role although it helps to have a major power perceived as supportive so that the country that is the object of all this attention believes that any eventual political and economic rewards it gains in return for compliance will have broad international support.

When governments are confronted with cataclysmic threats or emergencies, traditions, values, and humanitarian actions can be incinerated by the intense heat of the moment. Especially in democracies where public pressure on governments is greatest, political leaders often feel that they have to act first and ask (moral) questions afterwards. In the U.S. it is commonly accepted that the president's first responsibility is to come to the defense of the country. Voices calling for measured and appropriate responses consistent with a nation's traditions and values rarely penetrate into the command centers and cabinet rooms of governments under attack. There are, however, ways that a sense of morality and humanism can be inserted into the decision-making process.

The first is to have the public be as well informed as possible about exceptional measures that a government believes it must take to prosecute the war (or emergency) effort. Ultimately, it is the public and its elected representatives that should have the final say when it comes to deciding how drastic and how durable these measures must be. But without fairly full disclosure, the public will be kept in the dark.

The second is to improve the legislative oversight of foreign policy. For the first two hundred years of our nation, it was generally accepted that foreign policy was the purview of the executive branch. Only rarely were presidents and secretaries of state subjected to the degree of scrutiny that administrations received on domestic issues. Then came the Vietnam War and television news. Trust in government was further eroded by Watergate and serious oversight of foreign affairs by the Congress began. As a result, American foreign policy may be less coherent and well managed than before. But foreign policy is also more transparent than before and it turned out to be no harder than domestic policy for the American people to understand.

The third is to broaden the uniquely American practice of having high officials shuttle between private careers and public service. Government careerists find this system arbitrary and inefficient and they are probably right: it often is. But a government dominated by career politicians and civil servants runs the risk of isolation and excess. Moreover, having men and women who were successful in nongovernmental careers appointed to high public office increases the chances that decisions will better reflect the attitudes of society at large and that policies will be made by people who are used to being held accountable for their actions because they come from professions where rapid merit-based advancement and abrupt dismissals can occur.

Fourth, it is vital for citizens to understand that values are as essential to their security as military might and economic strength. A country true to a legacy of humanism is easier to defend and harder to attack. Its population will rally to the defense of the homeland. Its government will have standing in calling for international aid and support. Its enemies will know that world opinion will turn against them. Such a country is not guaranteed to be invulnerable in our turbulent world, but it will be much safer if it makes every effort to adhere to practices and conventions accepted by most of humanity as genuinely beneficial to all.

In modern societies, the pressures for demanding high levels of accountability, freedom, and openness come from the bottom up not the top down. Governments under threat will always seek greater control and autonomy and it is hard to strike a perfect balance between a government's ability to manage a crisis and a free people's need to know, judge, and change what a government is doing. Still, if the balance of power tilts too strongly and indefinitely in government's favor, the new global wars that it is trying to win will be lost.

19

Reviving Global Civil Society After September 11

Richard Falk

SEPTEMBER 11 has challenged the American way of life in a manner that is unprecedented, and evolving in ways the significance of which we are only beginning to grasp. To uphold the blessings of democracy, we must start with the understanding that as members of a constitutional republic, we are citizens and not subjects. Subjects discharge their political responsibilities to society by unconditionally obeying the government. Citizens face a more complex challenge. Their need, especially in periods of crisis, is to strike a balance between loyalty and patriotism on one side and conscience and independent judgment on the other. Blind submission by citizens, even in wartime, does not promote the national well-being, nor does it sustain and deepen our confidence in constitutional government. A passive citizenry forfeits the virtues of democracy as well as betrays a lack of confidence in public debate on controversial issues. Without the benefits of vigorous debate and a genuine political opposition, alternatives to war and militarism tend to be bypassed. The more extreme voices counseling political leaders tend to gain influence, a climate of chauvinistic nationalism is likely to dominate public discussion. This pattern of behavior represents both a general observation and is intended as a critical commentary on the drift of American domestic and foreign policy since September 11.[1]

This assertion of citizen responsibilities might have seemed too obvious in this country to comment upon only a few years ago. It has suddenly become a matter of some urgency in the aftermath of the mega-terrorist attacks in 2001. Because these attacks caused such great symbolic and substantive harm, and because the enemy was a concealed terrorist network operating by stealth in sixty or more countries in such a manner as to be everywhere and nowhere, there was a tendency on the part of the citizenry to close ranks behind our political leaders, relying on their capacity to fashion an effective response that would restore our sense of security in the face of this new enemy that demonstrated both its tactical ingenuity and its genocidal plan to kill as many Americans, Jews, "crusaders" as possible. This call for unity by the government was a natural response to such an unprecedented challenge, but it has had several serious unfortunate side-effects, including the disruption of some very positive global developments of a humanitarian character that had been moving forward in the decade after the end of the cold war. These developments owed a great deal to the activism of citizens from democratic societies around the world, as well as to their organizations, which often took the shape of voluntary transnational associations.[2] These initiatives arising out of civil society were both supplementing and challenging the policies of governments and international institutions in a number of key areas of international life.

What makes the present context particularly disturbing is a rediscovery of the fragility of societal reality, and for us here in America, that despite our power and wealth as a country, we are both vulnerable to hostile extremism and that our policies around the world are generating intense and widespread resentment. Despite the achievements of modernity, our political arrangements for governance seem unable to control either the passions that animate politics or the technologies that are relied upon to establish security. There may be a tragic predicament that is embedded in these realizations. Security for the citizenry is likely to remain elusive despite impressive technological innovations and the greatly intensified efforts of regulatory institutions.[3] We confront a serious possibility that the pursuit of security in our daily lives may prove to be both ineffectual and

repressive at the same time, thereby imperiling the quality of democracy without providing protection against these new forms of
extremism directed against our nation and people. What is more,
which is the relevant point in this essay, the pressures exerted
by the challenges of mega-terrorism have diverted energies and
resources away from some exceptionally promising developments in the humanitarian sector that were occurring in the
1990s. These developments were exciting in several distinct ways,
raising hopes for significant improvement in the human condition, as well as representing encouraging steps from the perspective of global justice. Such initiatives exhibited both the growth
of transnational social forces emerging out of civil society, often
acting internationally as nongovernmental organizations
(NGOs), and a new spirit of collaboration between governments
and NGOs that was giving rise to a new type of diplomacy that
could be described as "a new internationalism" motivated by ethical concerns, and distinct from the preoccupations with power
and wealth that formed the subject-matter of geopolitics as practiced by leading states. The historic Antipersonnel Landmines
Treaty (1998) was a notable illustration of this new and promising form of global reform.

It seems reasonable to maintain that prior to September 11
there was a multifaceted upsurge of humanitarian initiatives that
had already within the space of a decade established a rather
remarkable record of achievement, with prospects for continuing
progress. I have previously described this set of developments as
the first global normative revolution in human history, that is, a
definite trend of qualitative status suggesting the relevance of
ethical values and issues of justice that was beginning to challenge the dominant realist paradigm that reduced international
relations to calculations of power and self-interest, also called
"national interest."[4]

THE FIRST GLOBAL NORMATIVE REVOLUTION

The centerpiece of the emergent normative revolution was the
genuine rise of human rights from the outer margins of diplo-

macy and international concern to a position that seemed close to the center of foreign policy, bearing directly on issues of whether or not to seek economic gains in relation with countries whose governments were responsible for repressing their own populations. Michael Ignatieff, an influential commentator on global policy trends, argued that human rights had become the secular religion of our era.[5] Such a sweeping generalization undoubtedly reflected wishful thinking, but it was also a historic comment on some extraordinary reversals of expectations that had occurred in the 1990s. The collapse of the Soviet system of internal and regional domination was certainly hastened by strong grassroots resistance that claimed to be seeking and demanding the implementation of human rights. The amazing surprise transformation that took place in South Africa without bloodshed early in the decade was definitely hastened by the anti-apartheid movement that was inspired by the global consensus condemning the institutionalized racism of Pretoria as a crime against humanity. Such positive outcomes owed a great deal to pressures exerted by people acting on their own on behalf of human rights goals, organized at the level of civil society, and mounting moral outrage that led governments to override material and strategic interests by joining in the struggles to achieve change.

These encouraging initiatives reflected the interplay of many different influences, but in this discussion the focus will be on the distinctive contributions made by the NGO world, and civil society generally. This contribution is particularly evident in relation to the expanding role of human rights in world politics. The domain of human rights as a subject for NGO activism goes back to the period immediately after World War II.[6] It is doubtful that sovereign states in the late 1940s would have assented to an international framework imposing duties to respect human rights if their leaders had thought such standards were meant in any but an aspirational spirit. What made the Universal Declaration of Human Rights (UDHR, 1948) a feasible *political* project was the assurance that it was understood at the time to be unenforceable.

This expectation was signaled by shaping the framework in the form of a "declaration" endorsed by the membership of the UN General Assembly, but lacking the legal stature of a treaty that carries with it the implications that the standards set forth are obligatory. It was also evident after World War II that very few countries were governed in accordance with the UDHR, and that their governments would never have lent their approval to an international instrument that gave the UN or other states some sort of legal basis to push for implementation.

Human rights NGOs in the decades following 1948 were formed and immediately realized that a great opportunity existed to use this aspirational document to promote some desired modifications of behavior by repressive states, and at least to depict persuasively severe human rights abuses. Amnesty International took advantage of their realization that governments increasingly care about their reputation, and that allegations of human rights abuses are black marks when backed up by genuine information and given wide distribution by a world media. Such allegations could not be dismissed as the propaganda of ideological adversaries as was the case in the exchange of cold war charges and counter-charges being made by officials in Washington and Moscow. NGOs put human rights on the world policy map long before the 1990s, and paved the way for many governments to adjust their regulatory policies.[7] To begin with, the UDHR was converted in the mid-1960s into a pair of treaties called "covenants" that were widely ratified by states around the world. It became a matter of political legitimacy for states to commit themselves formally and existentially to the overall goal of conforming their political practices to human rights standards. This evolution, although welcome, was less attributable to changes of heart on the part of governments and more to a combination of the sustained pressure of human rights organizations and some parts of the media over the years and a closely related trend toward the democratization of political life. Thus, despite its modest beginnings, human rights NGOs and international institutions increasingly viewed the UDHR as a framework of rights to be seriously implemented, which included the push for treaty-making procedures and for the further elaboration of specific rights that deserved wider recognition (for instance, prohibition of racial discrimination, protection of women and children, prohibition of torture).[8]

This NGO role was then reinforced by historical circumstances that led opposition groups in authoritarian societies to rely on *international* human rights standards to back up their demands for political reform. This process of opposition was most dramatic in the settings of Eastern Europe and South Africa where the wider struggle for fundamental change showed that human rights could no longer be reduced to a set of pieties but were now a serious dimension of political conflict. The same dynamic was to a degree also visible in the Asian pro-democracy movements of the 1980s, which did not achieve success in all instances, but exhibited the degree to which people everywhere were inspired by the conviction of an entitlement to fundamental human rights.[9]

What happened in the 1990s that was so encouraging was that human rights seemed to become an active ingredient of international public policy, generally exhibiting a sincere concern of the general public about the suffering endured by vulnerable populations, groups, and individuals victimized by governmental wrongdoing and subject to media exposure.[10] This upgrading of human rights was also institutionally expressed within the United Nations, principally by establishing a High Commissioner for Human Rights, which in turn led to more prominence being accorded to the work of the Geneva-based UN Human Rights Commission. Thanks to the combined pressures of an increasingly democratized world and a heightened global public opinion strengthened by media attention, human rights were becoming an essential facet of international political life in the 1990s.

The second development in the previous decade that formed part of the normative revolution getting underway, even though it remained controversial in some settings, was the willingness of the organized international community, or portions of it, to undertake humanitarian intervention designed to rescue or protect vulnerable populations or minorities from oppressive practices of their government.[11] The idea behind humanitarian intervention is the claim by an *external* political actor that it refuses to respect the supremacy of territorial sovereignty in those circumstances of extreme abuse of human rights. The occasion giving rise to humanitarian intervention in the 1990s was the accusation of ethnic cleansing of a disfavored ethnic or religious component of the territorial population with the goal of expulsion, an abusive policy that was also often coupled with genocidal practices involving massive rape and massacres directed against the targets of abuse. Humanitarian intervention generated the sort of debate that was also in the background of discussion about the implementation of human rights generally.[12] There were several issues: Should the obligation to uphold human rights be implemented by force? Were the motives underlying humanitarian intervention truly humanitarian or were these claims masking geopolitical goals? Must humanitarian intervention in all instances be authorized by the UN Security Council? Did the results of such interventions bring real benefit to the vulnerable peoples?

To be sure, there were disappointments and ambiguities associated with purported humanitarian interventions in this period. The Kosovo intervention of 1999 seemed to reward the violence of the KLA; it relied on tactics that caused extensive death among Serbian civilians; it proceeded without formal mandate from the United Nations; and during its aftermath, insufficient effort was made by occupying forces under NATO authority to protect the Serbian minority against "reverse ethnic cleansing." At the same time, the intervention provided the only available means to ensure that the great majority of the Kosovars would be rescued from a catastrophic prospect, to have some confidence in the avoidance of a repetition of the ethnic cleansing that had in the early 1990s caused so much death and destruction in Bosnia, and to repudiate decisively the criminal policies associated with the Milosevic government in Belgrade.

Of potentially even greater significance for the future of world order, a consensus seemed to be slowly taking shape among leading states insisting that sovereignty was no longer an absolute grant of authority, and that the moral, political, and legal prerogatives of rulership were conditioned upon adhering to the most basic human rights standards. If a government henceforth severely abused its people, or a portion thereof, beyond a certain threshold, then respect for its sovereign rights would be diminished, if not ignored, and such tarnished sovereign rights need no longer to be respected by the international community. And in some instances, that loss of sovereignty becomes permanent, taking the form of affirming the right of the abused minority to exercise a right of self-determination that could lead to *de facto,* and even to *de jure,* independence. Human rights NGOs cannot take the major credit for instances of humanitarian intervention, but it has often been their presence on the ground in the society experiencing, and their credibility in validating, oppressive circumstance that leads to media emphasis, which in turn tips the balance toward intervention within governmental circles and at the United Nations.

Before concluding against humanitarian intervention, it would be appropriate to consider the massacre of upwards of 800,000 in Rwanda in 1994, where the UN refused to respond to urgent calls for humanitarian protection, and in Bosnia during the first half of the 1990s when tepid engagement by the UN led to the spectacle of a particularly brutal enactment of ethnic cleansing, culminating in the 1995 massacre of some 7,000 Muslim males at Srebrenica.[13] What I think it is possible to say is that this subject-matter of humanitarian intervention remained problematic whether the decision was to take positive action or to refrain from doing so. There is no doubt that powerful states used the cover of humanitarian intervention to advance strategic goals, and refused to allow such responses in comparable situations if their interests were linked to the status quo. It is reasonable for smaller states and for ex-colonial states, and the non-Western world generally, to be deeply suspicious of humanitarian intervention as it invariably has involved the Euro-American complex of states imposing its political will with mixed motives on one or another non-Western state. Such suspicions are deepened if, as in Kosovo, the UN is bypassed to avoid a veto of a resolution in the Security Council authorizing force, and if supporters argue that in the future, not even the imprimatur of a regional grouping such as NATO is necessary, but that it is sufficient to enlist "coalitions of the willing."

Let it be understood that not all of the opposition to instances of humanitarian intervention comes from leftist skepticism in the North and anti-interventionism in the South. The political right is also generally opposed to humanitarian intervention on principled reasons, believing that foreign policy should be guided by strategic, and possibly ideological, goals, but not by any ethos of human solidarity. Such conservative views in the United States opposed the whole idea of humanitarian intervention as a basis for foreign policy, especially to the extent that it was regarded as sincere! The shift in American leadership that occurred at the end of the 1990s represented a move from liberalism to conservatism on this issue, with the new president, George W. Bush, emphasizing throughout his campaign his unwillingness to engage in "nation-building," by which he meant the policies guided by humanitarian motivations pursued by the Clinton Administration in sub-Saharan Africa, and especially in the Balkans. In effect, the left criticized humanitarian intervention because it was hiding geopolitical motives and was hypocritical while the right attacked the same policies because they were not convincingly geopolitical.

The third dimension of this new focus on the ethical side of international relations that assumed great significance in the 1990s and reflected the growing potency of civil society was the surge of efforts by individuals and their associations to obtain redress in various forms for historic grievances.[14] This surge of concern disclosed an increased willingness to treat the crimes of the past as unresolved: the activism of Holocaust survivors; of comfort women in the Japanese setting; of a variety of slave labor initiatives seeking compensation after the clouds of the cold war; of claims for reparations associated with the institutions of slavery and colonialism; of an array of commissions devoted to "truth and reconciliation"; and of grievances advanced by indigenous peoples who had been dispossessed from their historic lands and endured humiliation and deprivations.[15] This sense of the obligations of present society for past abuses of state power, most of which were treated as legal and valid at the time of their occurrence, represented an extraordinary recognition that these historic wounds continued to cause suffering to victims and their descendants, and would never be healed without some active curative response. Many of these grievances had persisted without serious notice for decades, if not centuries. Why had these past injustices abruptly generated formal responses and increased activism in the 1990s when they had been ignored for so long? There is no simple response, no one explanation. Certainly, the end of the cold war removed some of the obstacles that had shielded governments from accountability. Also relevant was the previously mentioned trends toward upholding human rights and democratization. But perhaps most important was the spreading awareness of civic empowerment. Holocaust survivors and their descendants led the way, but also led others with grievances to push for acknowledgement, compensation, apology, and other types of redress.

In this climate of opinion, the credibility of claimants was greatly enhanced. To be sure, there was also practical and principled resistance. Those accused tended to be defensive, contending that there was no current responsibility for what had been done previously in an atmosphere where values and legalities were different. There was no consistent response from issue to issue, and from country to country. There were some impressive symbolic and substantive steps taken toward reconciliation, and in the direction of reversing past injustice. Swiss banks were induced to return deposits and settle many claims of Holocaust victims valued in the billions. Corporations using slave labor in Germany offered fairly large amounts of compensation. Apologies were expressed by leaders such as President Bill Clinton for the institution of slavery, and by the British queen for the imposition of colonial rule. Several governments, including the Canadian and the Australian, established education and compensation funds that are trying at least to rescue the traditional remnants of indigenous civilizations from complete extinction, and to provide at least symbolic recompense for past wrongs.

These evidences that the international community and civil society were coming to some sort of acknowledgment of these historic injustices was again, I think, an important element in this unexpected normative revolution that was beginning to take shape in the 1990s. Its essential character was to exhibit the interaction of governments and civil society with respect to a series of issues bearing on the responsibility of the state. The state, as well as other international actors, was being humanized by this process by which injustices, even if in the distant past, were being heeded, and to some extent addressed. Such a process reflected the capacity of NGOs to help generate an ethical climate of accountability that exerted influence on all global actors, including the United Nations.

There was a still further fourth major element of this normative revolution that again exhibited the growing strength of civil society to reshape the role of the state and its institutions with regard to issues of global justice. This element concerned dramatic efforts to make leaders individually accountable for crimes of state committed against their own peoples.[16] The objective was to make leaders accountable for severe abuses carried out against their own people. The Pinochet litigation, arising out of action taken in Spanish courts leading to an extradition request directed at the British government, came about as a result of tireless efforts by those individuals and their relatives who had been victimized in Chile during the period of dictatorship not giving up on the pursuit of justice when living in exile in Spain. The dramatic fact of Pinochet's 1998 detention in Britain and the series of legal challenges associated with the detention produced some notable achievement. The practice of torture was confirmed by the House of Lords, the highest British judicial tribunal, as an international crime that can be apprehended and punished anywhere in the world, not just in the country where it occurred.[17] Of even greater importance was the renewal of the Nuremberg idea that even leaders of sovereign states are not exempt from individual criminal accountability for their official deeds, that the shield of sovereign immunity is not available. What happened unexpectedly in the 1990s after a lapse of more than forty-five years—first in relation to the Balkans and Rwanda—was this revival of the radical idea applied to defeated countries after World War II that political and military leaders of sovereign states are not above the law. Of course, the pursuit of Pinochet, which in the end failed because he was found medically unfit to stand trial and returned to Chile, suggested the analogous criminality of a host of other leaders still at large around the world. Some of those accused were linked to powerful states. The most widely discussed instances were Henry Kissinger, especially for his role in the wrongdoing of the Pinochet government, and Ariel Sharon for his alleged responsibility for the massacres that took place in the Palestinian refugee camps of Sabra and Shatila back in 1982. Questions were raised as to whether the world is ready for such criminal accountability, which, given the realities, would lead to very uneven and selective enforcement of such standards of accountability.

The moves to detain and prosecute Pinochet stimulated civil society by suggesting that the rule of law might reach those responsible for the worse excesses of governmental and military authority. The Pinochet controversy, together with the experience of the ad hoc tribunal in The Hague dealing with crimes attributed to individuals associated with managing the breakup of former Yugoslavia, led civil society activists to embark upon an ambitious project to institutionalize the process in some enduring way through the establishment of a permanent international criminal court entrusted with the prosecution of the most serious international crimes. What ensued was a notably effective collaboration between a large coalition of NGOs and a series of moderate governments that generated a political process that led in 1998 to the Treaty of Rome and then to the establishment of the International Criminal Court (ICC) in 2002. Such a major institutional innovation was brought into being with surprising speed, securing more than the required sixty ratifications in a period of a few years.

This experiment in institutionalization is still in its infancy. It is opposed vigorously at present by the United States, and ignored by several other powerful countries, including China and Russia. If it could come later to obtain universal participation (as is the case with the UN), it would likely be viewed as the greatest institutional innovation since the United Nations itself. Its significance, symbolically and substantively, is that it expresses a determination to extend accountability and the rule of law to those who represent the state at the highest level. The creation of procedures by which to impose such accountability is a step forward in the efforts to overcome the impunity, at least on the international level, previously enjoyed by those who control sovereign states. Also, even compared to Nuremberg, the ICC is ambitious. The earlier criminal prosecutions of leaders were linked to a war, and embodied "victors' justice," the winners judging the loser.[18] Here, any leader at any point is, theoretically at least, subject to indictment, whether of a powerful or a weak country. The establishment of the ICC in an interdependent globalizing world could yet become an extraordinary step forward in the struggle to create global democracy as a complement to national democracy, yet to reach this goal there are major obstacles that must be overcome. At present, strong resistance to such an expansion of accountability and the consequent strengthening of the global rule of law has mainly come from such leading countries as the United States and China. Both countries are definitely unwilling at this point to join in the effort to qualify sovereignty as the last word on legality.

The fifth and final component of the normative revolution that I am depicting is the rise of global civil society, which has become a source of lawmaking and global policy formation. Literally thousands of NGOs are now associated with the representation of transnational social forces in a variety of regional and global arenas. Their presence was a robust and influential feature in the first half of the 1990s of such UN conferences as those on population, environment, human rights, and women's rights that advanced a people-oriented agenda on these matters of global concern. This agenda clashed with the priorities of leading governments and global corporations and banks.[19] Increasingly, the focus of efforts emanating from global civil society was placed upon the supposed excesses of neo-liberal globalization. The emphasis on globalization led to demonstrations around the world that gained major attention from the media, particularly in the aftermath of "the battle of Seattle" in late 1999. The demonstrators and their discussion forums highlighted the antidemocratic practices of the International Monetary Fund (IMF) and the World Trade Organization (WTO), as well as the lending practices of the World Bank.

This antiglobalization movement, although diverse and inchoate, is properly considered as part of the normative revolution that is being described. Its main thrust was to resist some of the capital-driven impacts of globalization that seemed to be producing increasing inequality within and among states, as well as leaving some states that lacked investment trade opportunities out in the cold. These global civil society criticisms were mainly not opposed to globalization as such, but were insisting on reforms that would lead to what might be described as "humane globalization." These criticisms were increasingly engendering a response from some of those most closely associated with the world economy in its recent globalizing phase. Such figures as George Soros and Joseph Stiglitz echoed many of the complaints that were being shouted by the demonstrators about the way the global economy policy was proceeding.[20] As a result, the language associated with globalization began to exhibit more concern with such issues as the reduction of world poverty, the promotion of greater economic equality, the protection of human rights, particularly labor rights, and matters of environmental protection.

In the background was an acknowledgement by policymakers and leaders that just as early industrial capitalism had to come to terms with the labor movement there was a need for global capitalism to reach a compromise with its critics. Even business circles were beginning to recognize that continued economic growth depended on striking a win/win bargain with this deepening grassroots struggle for equity of result and for some kind of democratic participation in the policy-forming process. What had been evident earlier in the strident street demonstrations was also reflected in the changed mood of the business and finance elites that gathered each year in Davos at the World Economic Forum. To continue this dialogue, civil society forces have organized their own annual event in recent years, pointedly called the World Social Forum and deliberately held in Porto Allegre in Brazil. The conclusion here is that these transnational social forces, and their NGOs, were overwhelmingly dedicated to the promotion of global justice and the range of humanitarian concerns that constituted the normative revolution of the 1990s.

September 11: Detour or Derailment?

Against this background of positive initiatives, I want to raise the question as to whether the September 11 attacks have resulted in a detour from this normative revolution, or merely caused its temporary derailment. There is little doubt that the energies and attention given to the initiatives discussed above have been superseded during the last year or so, especially in the United States, by the renewed foreign policy preoccupation with security and the dynamics of the war against global terror. In light of this shift how should we interpret the overall impact of September 11? Its negative aspects are quite obvious. Instead of seeking to build the structures of global governance, and strengthen further a global rule of law as a means of exerting constraints on sovereign states,

the new emphasis is on claiming the authority to engage in whatever actions contribute to antiterrorist goals. This kind of claim
to carry on violent conflict has two particularly disturbing aspects.

The first concern is that there has resulted the first borderless
war in which the both principal adversaries disavow respect for
the territorial sovereignty of states. The al Qaeda network has
declared *jihad* against America, its allies, and its people, and is
prepared to launch attacks wherever such targets can be found,
that is, anywhere in the world. The United States, in turn, claims
the right to attack anywhere that it can find an al Qaeda presence
or threat. This pattern of conflict is quite subversive from the
perspective of international law, which evolved to deal with conflicts among territorial sovereigns. Of course, international law
never enjoyed great success in relation to wartime situations, but
it did have some role in moderating the scope of conflict by con-
fining the zone of violent operations to the territorial domains
of the combatants. Now, as President Bush has pointed out, other
countries are denied the option of neutrality and war-avoidance;
either they join with the United States or they will be treated as
siding with the terrorists.

The United States is the most powerful country in human history. Since September 11 its leadership portrays itself as the vehicle of good against this evil of anti-state terrorism. To destroy this
evil, it is determined, as is the case with its al Qaeda adversary, to
suspend limits on the way force is used to achieve goals. Already
prisoners suspected of al Qaeda connections are denied rights
under the Geneva Conventions governing the standards of international humanitarian law. Already the White House has issued
orders permitting assassination of suspects in foreign countries
as a permissible tactic, reversing an earlier ban on assassinations.
There are authoritative indications that American investigative
procedures are directly and indirectly relying on torture.[21] When
the leading state treats its national security in such absolute and
unconditional terms, there are grounds for concern as to

whether the claims being made do not *unnecessarily* infringe on individual and sovereign rights.

But there are additional reasons to be troubled. The antiterrorist banner is being waved, but the goals of American foreign policy were extravagant before September 11, and now seem to be pretending that the struggle against terrorism validates the project to exert control over virtually the entire planet. Such contentions can best be understood by reference to such other American strategic undertakings as the militarization of space, the realization that U.S. defense spending exceeds that of the next fifteen countries combined, and there have been Pentagon leaks disclosing an increased willingness to rely on nuclear weaponry in battlefield situations. Our president has been saying very clearly that the U.S. possesses and will take whatever steps it needs to maintain a degree of military dominance that makes it futile for any country or group of countries to mount a challenge. In effect, President Bush has instructed foreign governments not to waste their resources on trying to compete with the United States. This stricture applies to both friend and foe. For neither is it worth trying to challenge the military dominance that the U.S. now exercises over other states. Foreign governments are explicitly advised, as in the president's West Point Commencement Address of 2002, to concentrate on trade and peaceful pursuits, leaving the business of global security to the United States.

In effect, American security planners are proposing post-realist arrangements that follow from the facts of unipolarity. Such ideas as the balance of power, containment, and deterrence are essentially outmoded. Whatever stability achieved during the several centuries of modernity, which was organized with reference to the interaction of a few leading sovereign states, was premised upon ideas of countervailing power. International law played a modest role, reinforcing the intended results of countervailing power by counseling peaceful settlement of international disputes, seeking to be useful by finding the humanitarian niches in the framework of war that would not undercut actions of warring states based on considerations of military necessity. These niches related to the protection of prisoners of war, of sick and wounded soldiers caught on the battlefield, and, to some extent, the prohibition on direct attacks on civilians and non-military targets. What made these legally imposed limits generally effective was that they were based on a logic of reciprocity and embodied mutual interests of the conflicting parties.

But this new framework of American power, so far unchallenged by other states, but vulnerable to attack by concealed transnational terrorist networks, makes us think of the relevance of one of the basic maxims of political theory. Its formulation is usually associated with Lord Acton's statement that power corrupts and absolute power corrupts absolutely.

Under these circumstances can we, should we, search for new limits on the discretion to use force in world politics? This is a vital question, especially for Americans, that needs to be addressed in this new post-September 11 setting. I want to answer such a question rather subjectively, by offering some tentative thoughts about the reconstruction of limits, and how this might bear upon the wider agenda of humanitarian action. As a starting point, the only acceptable way to rediscover a framework of limits is to recognize that our own values and traditions as a free society based on constitutionalism depend upon nurturing a respect for law and for the opinions of others, including those situated beyond our borders, and a reluctance to embark upon warfare outside of the Western Hemisphere. This ethical outlook is part of the federalist idea and the republican vision that has guided our sense of ourselves as a country, despite notable departures from time to time, since the national point of origin in the American Revolution. To protect this heritage at this point, given the pressures of the mega-terrorist challenge and the ambitions of the geopoliticians in the White House and Pentagon, will require massive citizen vigilance. Unfortunately, this vigilance will obviously not come from governmental institutions centered in Washington. If it comes at all it will be from the American people, from interior states such as Kansas and Minnesota, from activism on college campuses, and from a new energy in the religious community and the labor movement. Even to contemplate such prospects may seem utopian at this point, given the patriotic mood that still grips the country, as well as the disturbing passivity of the Congress, the opportunistic virtual silence of the Democratic Party, and the bellicose cheerleading of the mainstream media.

At stake here also is the matter of fundamental national identity. Aside from this acceptance of the self-limiting character of the state is the traditional American claim to be a republic and not an empire. However, if you assess the plans put forth by the Pentagon or peruse recent issues of *Foreign Affairs,* it is assumed that America has become, whether intentionally or not, an empire. The issue that remains more uncertain in these interpretations is whether the United States is likely to be a benevolent empire or whether it will be its fate to be an irresponsible, and probably, self-destructive empire.[22] The question that has so far not been raised, at least in these discussions within the American establishment, is whether being an empire is itself subversive of the self-proclaimed constitutional identity of this country as a republic. To be a republic is to be sensitive to the fragility of power, including the acute dangers of its abuse. The main purpose of the constitutional structure, based on checks and balances, is to protect the society against the destructive effects and multiple dangers of unchecked power. This prospect threatens our liberties as citizens, but internationally, the menace of unchecked power involves ignoring the well-being and viewpoints of others who lack the means of resisting.

The second problematic aspect of the response to September 11 should have been part of our foreign policy and political consciousness for years, that is, diagnosing and responding to the legitimate grievances that exist throughout the world, and if ignored, give rise to severe resentment. This resentment is especially directed against those political actors that are perceived to be responsible for unacceptable conditions and possess the capabilities to fashion just solutions to outstanding conflicts. The

United States, as the predominant actor throughout the world, is seen as having contributed to the suffering of peoples due to its relationship to some of these legitimate grievances. From the moment of the attacks, the American leadership has failed to connect anti-American sentiments, including those that give rise to political and religious extremism, and terrorist tactics with their real causes. Instead, avoiding the slightest willingness to allow self-criticism, the explanation of "why they hate us" is reduced to envy directed at our values and achievements. Supposedly, in such self-serving explanations, those who most resent America's role in the world do not have our institutions or wealth, and hate us as a result. Given the actualities surrounding America's presence in many parts of the world, especially the Middle East, such an explanation does not convince beyond our borders.

These spiraling patterns of resentment pertain to the relations between the United States and the Islamic world, and especially the Arab Middle East. Of course, commentary is speculative. But it certainly seems much more likely that September 11 would not have happened if the Palestinian problems of self-determination had been solved years ago in a manner that was fair to both peoples. This conflict should have been dealt with long ago in a balanced way, not only for prudential reasons associated with regional stability, but as part of a more intrinsic commitment to a realization of the right of self-determination for the Palestinian people, who had been denied independence and statehood despite the dynamics of decolonization having swept across the world in recent decades. The United States possessed the leverage to push toward such a solution, but instead allowed the issue to be shaped by domestic politics. The contours of a fair solution have been widely supported at an international level for more than a decade. To stand aside or to lend support to the Israeli refusal to allow a solution that would give both peoples their own states is to flaunt global public opinion and to overlook the reasonable expectations of the Palestinian people. This failure, so long sustained, inflames Arab and Islamic sensibilities, creating a resonance for conspiratorial accounts of Islamic frustrations and a ready constituency for political militancy.

Not all the legitimate grievances arising from American policies are associated with Islam. And yet September 11 has had a negative impact on efforts to address substantively unrelated issues, as well. For instance, a promising initiative by the Mexican government to humanize the circumstances of 20 million Mexican immigrants living in the United States had met with a positive response in the early period of the Bush presidency. But since September 11 it has been cast aside, apparently indefinitely. So much so that the Mexican foreign minister, Jorge Castañeda, who had made immigration reform the centerpiece of his efforts to improve the character of the U.S.-Mexican relationship, resigned his post in disillusionment.[23] If anti-American extremism were to emerge in Mexico sometime in the future, we could look back and ask ourselves why we failed to address the arbitrary hardships endured by so-called undocumented Mexican immigrants that live in this country while remaining vulnerable to exploitation and hardship because of their unresolved immigration status.

REVIVING THE NORMATIVE REVOLUTION: TEMPTATIONS AND COMMITMENTS

In effect, the construction of a humane framework for global governance, which was proceeding in a generally encouraging way in the 1990s, has been abandoned in this period after September 11. Can it be revived? Can global civil society renew its pressures that proved effective in the prior decade? What sorts of issues should take priority? Despite adverse trends, wherever integrity and courage are found, there remains the possibility of positive action with respect to the agenda of the normative revolution. The security obsessions generated by September 11 are not a valid excuse for a denial of human rights under most circumstances. Nothing has illustrated this potentiality better than the decision by a conservative Republican governor of Illinois, George Ryan, to commute all 167 death row sentences in his state just prior to leaving office. Such an act challenges the United States to question the overall moral viability of capital punishment at the very moment when the federal government has made the death penalty increasingly easy to apply in any case touching on the terrorist menace. After all, from a human rights perspective, America lags far behind our traditional European allies on this issue, and finds itself aligned with some of the worst human rights offenders in the world, including China, Iraq, and Iran.

One direction of response is to argue that war policies favored by Washington in relation to "axis of evil" countries are really "humanitarian interventions" under a different name. In the background is the claim that the Afghanistan War emancipated the people of Afghanistan from the oppressive cruelties of the Taliban regime. Although the evidence is conflicting in several respects, the Taliban collapse seems to be providing the Afghan people with enhanced possibilities for the achievement of minimal human rights, especially with respect to the treatment of women. The same position may result from the change of Saddam Hussein's regime in Iraq. True, the Bush Administration does not rely on a humanitarian rationale to validate its thrust toward war, but rather the threat associated with Iraq's undisclosed weapons of mass destruction and the possible linkage to the al Qaeda network. Outside of America, this justification for war had few adherents. But why not support the war as an instance of humanitarian intervention, taking comfort from the effects of the Kosovo intervention and the outcome of the Afghanistan War?

It is true that the removal of the Saddam Hussein Baathist regime will have an emancipatory impact on Iraq, possibly even allowing its return to normalcy in relation to the outside world and enabling economic recovery to occur, as well as installing in power a more moderate leadership. Such prospects are clouded by serious uncertainties about the ease and repercussions of an

American-led intervention. The complexities of the situation are such that such an intervention, followed by an augmented American military presence in the region, will fan the flames of anti-Americanism, likely worsening the problems arising from terrorism. Beyond this, some informed observers believe that the control of a post-Saddam Iraq will be exceedingly difficult, with the dangers of the fragmentation of the Iraqi state and/or a civil war lurking close to the surface. If these negative scenarios occur, then it is quite possible that anti-American moves in countries such as Jordan, Egypt, Saudi Arabia, and even Pakistan could occur, widening the arena of violent conflict.

There are other problems with the suggestion that those who favor humanitarianism and human rights at the global level should advocate support for the Iraq war. American hypocrisy on the issue is awkward. The worst crimes of Baghdad were committed in the 1980s, quite long ago, when Iraq was a virtual regional ally of the United States, and criticism deliberately muted. This includes criminal Iraqi uses of chemical weaponry against Iranian soldiers in the Iraq-Iran War and against Kurdish villages, especially Halabja. It also overlooks the degree to which the American insistence on sustaining a harsh sanctions policy following the Gulf War has contributed to the deaths of more than a half million Iraqi civilians, according to impartial UN and NGO documentation. And finally, in relation to the al Qaeda threat, there exists a strong argument that Saddam's Iraq had nothing to do with this terrorist network, and that the U.S. government needs to concentrate its political and military efforts on this danger. There are great dangers in a costly and risky campaign for regime change in Iraq, despite the well-documented case depicting the brutalities and oppressiveness of the Saddam regime. It is not, accordingly, a good enough case for humanitarian intervention to overcome the objections, and thus opposition to the Iraq war policies was justified.

In conclusion, returning to the spirit of the normative revolution in the 1990s is not immediately feasible. There is a sufficient active and continuing security threat to validate the current diversion of energies and resources. But if this direct security threat can be minimized by the American response, then the deeper security argument strongly supports the revival of the normative revolution, starting with fashioning equitable responses to legitimate grievances around the world. Without resuming the struggle to achieve humane global governance, the likelihood is that forces of resistance will occur in forms that will jeopardize security in additional ways. We need the moral and political imagination to realize that the security of the rich and powerful in a globalizing world depends over time on improving the circumstances and raising the hopes of the poor and weak. If September 11 has taught us anything, it should be that the weapons and tactics of the weak are capable of inflicting severe harm with significant adverse material and psychological consequences. To learn from such a traumatic experience means nurturing our ethical impulses as well as sharpening our swords!

APPENDIX

ESSENTIAL PROVISIONS OF THE 1949 GENEVA CONVENTIONS
AND 1977 ADDITIONAL PROTOCOLS

—Common Article 1 to the four Geneva Conventions of 1949:

The High Contracting Parties undertake to respect and to ensure respect for the present Convention in all circumstances.

—Common Article 3 to the four Geneva Conventions of 1949:

In the case of armed conflict not of an international character occurring in the territory of one of the High Contracting Parties, each Party to the conflict shall be bound to apply, as a minimum, the following provisions:

1. Persons taking no active part in the hostilities, including members of armed forces who have laid down their arms and those placed "hors de combat" by sickness, wounds, detention, or any other cause, shall in all circumstances be treated humanely, without any adverse distinction founded on race, color, religion or faith, sex, birth or wealth, or any other similar criteria.

   To this end, the following acts are and shall remain prohibited at any time and in any place whatsoever with respect to the above-mentioned persons:

   a) violence to life and person, in particular murder of all kinds, mutilation, cruel treatment, and torture;

   b) taking of hostages;

   c) outrages upon personal dignity, in particular humiliating and degrading treatment;

   d) the passing of sentences and the carrying out of executions without previous judgment pronounced by a regularly constituted court, affording all the judicial guarantees which are recognized as indispensable by civilized peoples.

2. The wounded and sick shall be collected and cared for.

An impartial humanitarian body, such as the International Committee of the Red Cross, may offer its services to the Parties to the conflict.

The Parties to the conflict should further endeavor to bring into force, by means of special agreements, all or part of the other provisions of the present Convention.

The application of the preceding provisions shall not affect the legal status of the Parties to the conflict.

—Article 12 ("Protection and Care") of the First Convention:

Members of the armed forces and other persons mentioned in the following Article, who are wounded or sick, shall be respected and protected in all circumstances.

They shall be treated humanely and cared for by the Party to the conflict in whose power they may be, without any adverse distinction founded on sex, race, nationality, religion, political opinions, or any other similar criteria. Any attempts upon their lives, or violence to their persons, shall be strictly prohibited; in particular, they shall not be murdered or exterminated, subjected to torture or to biological experiments; they shall not willfully be left without medical assistance and care, nor shall conditions exposing them to contagion or infection be created.

Only urgent medical reasons will authorize priority in the order of treatment to be administered.

Women shall be treated with all consideration due to their sex.

The Party to the conflict which is compelled to abandon wounded or sick to the enemy shall, as far as military considerations permit, leave with them a part of its medical personnel and material to assist in their care.

—Article 12 ("Protection and Care") of the Second Convention:

Members of the armed forces and other persons mentioned in the following Article, who are at sea and who are wounded, sick, or shipwrecked, shall be respected and protected in all circumstances, it being understood that the term "shipwreck" means shipwreck from any cause and includes forced landings at sea by or from aircraft.

Such persons shall be treated humanely and cared for by the Parties to the conflict in whose power they may be, without any adverse distinction founded on sex, race, nationality, religion, political opinions, or any other similar criteria. Any attempts upon their lives, or violence to their persons, shall be strictly prohibited; in particular, they shall not be murdered or exterminated, subjected to torture or to biological experiments; they shall not willfully be left without medical assistance and care, nor shall conditions exposing them to contagion or infection be created.

Only urgent medical reasons will authorize priority in the order of treatment to be administered.

Women shall be treated with all consideration due to their sex.

—Article 13 ("Humane Treatment of Prisoners") of the Third Convention:

Prisoners of war must at all times be humanely treated. Any unlawful act or omission by the Detaining Power causing death or seriously endangering the health of a prisoner of war in its custody is prohibited, and will be regarded as a serious breach of the present Convention. In particular, no prisoner of war may be subjected to physical mutilation or to medical or scientific experiments of any kind which are not justified by the medical, dental, or hospital treatment of the prisoner concerned and carried out in his interest.

Likewise, prisoners of war must at all times be protected, particularly against acts of violence or intimidation and against insults and public curiosity.

Measures of reprisal against prisoners of war are prohibited.

—Article 27 ("Treatment. General Observations") of the Fourth Convention:

Protected persons are entitled, in all circumstances, to respect for their persons, their honor, their family rights, their religious convictions and practices, and their manners and customs. They shall at all times be humanely treated, and shall be protected especially against all acts of violence or threats thereof and against insults and public curiosity.

Women shall be especially protected against any attack on their honor, in particular against rape, enforced prostitution, or any form of indecent assault.

Without prejudice to the provisions relating to their state of health, age, and sex, all protected persons shall be treated with the same consideration by the Party to the conflict in whose power they are, without any adverse distinction based, in particular, on race, religion, or political opinion.

However, the Parties to the conflict may take such measures of control and security in regard to protected persons as may be necessary as a result of the war.

—Article 48 ("Civilian Population—General Protection against Effects of Hostilities—Basic Rule") of Additional Protocol 1 of 1977:

In order to ensure respect for and protection of the civilian population and civilian objects, the Parties to the conflict shall at all times distinguish between the civilian population and combatants and between civilian objects and military objectives and accordingly shall direct their operations only against military objectives.

—Article 75 ("Fundamental Guarantees") of Additional Protocol 1 as well as:

1. In so far as they are affected by a situation referred to in Article 1 of this Protocol, persons who are in the power of a Party to the conflict and who do not benefit from more favorable treatment under the Conventions or under this Protocol shall be treated humanely in all circumstances and shall enjoy, as a minimum, the protection provided by this Article without any adverse distinction based upon race, color, sex, language, religion or belief, political or other opinion, national or social origin, wealth, birth or other status, or on any other similar criteria. Each Party shall respect the person, honor, convictions and religious practices of all such persons.

2. The following acts are and shall remain prohibited at any time and in any place whatsoever, whether committed by civilian or by military agents:

   a) violence to the life, health, or physical or mental well-being of persons, in particular:

   (1) murder;

   (2) torture of all kinds, whether physical or mental;

   (3) corporal punishment; and

   (4) mutilation;

   b) outrages upon personal dignity, in particular humiliating and degrading treatment, enforced prostitution, and any form of indecent assault;

   c) the taking of hostages;

   d) collective punishments; and

   e) threats to commit any of the foregoing acts.

3. Any person arrested, detained, or interned for actions related to the armed conflict shall be informed promptly, in a language he understands, of the reasons why these measures have been taken. Except in cases of arrest or detention for penal offences, such persons shall be released with the minimum delay possible and, in any event, as soon as the circumstances justifying the arrest, detention, or internment have ceased to exist.

4. No sentence may be passed and no penalty may be executed on a person found guilty of a penal offence related to the armed conflict except pursuant to a conviction pronounced by an impartial and regularly constituted court respecting the generally recognized principles of regular judicial procedure, which include the following:

   a) the procedure shall provide for an accused to be informed without delay of the particulars of the offence alleged against him and shall afford the accused before and during his trial all necessary rights and means of defense;

   b) no one shall be convicted of an offence except on the basis of individual penal responsibility;

   c) no one shall be accused or convicted of a criminal offence on account of any act or omission which did not constitute a criminal offence under the national or international law to which he was subject at the time when it was committed; nor shall a heavier penalty be imposed than that which was applicable at the time when the criminal offence was committed; if, after the commission of the offence, provision is made by law for the imposition of a lighter penalty, the offender shall benefit thereby;

d) anyone charged with an offence is presumed innocent until proved guilty according to law;

e) anyone charged with an offence shall have the right to be tried in his presence;

f) no one shall be compelled to testify against himself or to confess guilt;

g) anyone charged with an offence shall have the right to examine, or have examined, the witnesses against him and to obtain the attendance and examination of witnesses on his behalf under the same conditions as witnesses against him;

h) no one shall be prosecuted or punished by the same Party for an offence in respect of which a final judgement acquitting or convicting that person has been previously pronounced under the same law and judicial procedure;

i) anyone prosecuted for an offence shall have the right to have the judgement pronounced publicly; and

j) a convicted person shall be advised on conviction of his judicial and other remedies and of the time-limits within which they may be exercised.

5. Women whose liberty has been restricted for reasons related to the armed conflict shall be held in quarters separated from men's quarters. They shall be under the immediate supervision of women. Nevertheless, in cases where families are detained or interned, they shall, whenever possible, be held in the same place and accommodated as family units.

6. Persons who are arrested, detained or interned for reasons related to the armed conflict shall enjoy the protection pro-

vided by this Article until their final release, repatriation or re-establishment, even after the end of the armed conflict.

7. In order to avoid any doubt concerning the prosecution and trial of persons accused of war crimes or crimes against humanity, the following principles shall apply:

   a) persons who are accused of such crimes should be submitted for the purpose of prosecution and trial in accordance with the applicable rules of international law; and

   b) any such persons who do not benefit from more favorable treatment under the Conventions or this Protocol shall be accorded the treatment provided by this Article, whether or not the crimes of which they are accused constitute grave breaches of the Conventions or of this Protocol.

8. No provision of this Article may be construed as limiting or infringing any other more favorable provision granting greater protection, under any applicable rules of international law, to persons covered by paragraph 1.

—Article 10 ("Protection and Care"):

1. All the wounded, sick, and shipwrecked, to whichever Party they belong, shall be respected and protected.

2. In all circumstances they shall be treated humanely and shall receive, to the fullest extent practicable and with the least possible delay, the medical care and attention required by their condition. There shall be no distinction among them founded on any grounds other than medical ones.

—Article 11 ("Protection of Persons"):

1. The physical or mental health and integrity of persons who are in the power of the adverse Party or who are interned, detained, or otherwise deprived of liberty as a result of a situation referred to in Article 1 shall not be endangered by any unjustified act or omission. Accordingly, it is prohibited to subject the persons described in this Article to any medical procedure which is not indicated by the state of health of the person concerned and which is not consistent with generally accepted medical standards which would be ap-

plied under similar medical circumstances to persons who are nationals of the Party conducting the procedure and who are in no way deprived of liberty.

2. It is, in particular, prohibited to carry out on such persons, even with their consent:

   a) physical mutilations;

   b) medical or scientific experiments;

   c) removal of tissue or organs for transplantation, except where these acts are justified in conformity with the conditions provided for in paragraph 1.

3. Exceptions to the prohibition in paragraph 2*(c)* may be made only in the case of donations of blood for transfusion or of skin for grafting, provided that they are given voluntarily and without any coercion or inducement, and then only for therapeutic purposes, under conditions consistent with generally accepted medical standards and controls designed for the benefit of both the donor and the recipient.

4. Any willful act or omission which seriously endangers the physical or mental health or integrity of any person who is in the power of a Party other than the one on which he depends and which either violates any of the prohibitions in paragraphs 1 and 2 or fails to comply with the requirements of paragraph 3 shall be a grave breach of this Protocol.

5. The persons described in paragraph 1 have the right to refuse any surgical operation. In case of refusal, medical personnel shall endeavor to obtain a written statement to that effect, signed or acknowledged by the patient.

6. Each Party to the conflict shall keep a medical record for every donation of blood for transfusion or skin for grafting by persons referred to in paragraph 1, if that donation is made under the responsibility of that Party. In addition, each Party to the conflict shall endeavor to keep a record of all medical procedures undertaken with respect to any person who is interned, detained, or otherwise deprived of liberty as a result of a situation referred to in Article 1. These

records shall be available at all times for inspection by the Protecting Power.

—Article 15 ("Protection of Civilian Medical and Religious Personnel"):

1. Civilian medical personnel shall be respected and protected.
2. If needed, all available help shall be afforded to civilian medical personnel in an area where civilian medical services are disrupted by reason of combat activity.
3. The Occupying Power shall afford civilian medical personnel in occupied territories every assistance to enable them to perform, to the best of their ability, their humanitarian functions. The Occupying Power may not require that, in the performance of those functions, such personnel shall give priority to the treatment of any person except on medical grounds. They shall not be compelled to carry out tasks which are not compatible with their humanitarian mission.
4. Civilian medical personnel shall have access to any place where their services are essential, subject to such supervisory and safety measures as the relevant Party to the conflict may deem necessary.
5. Civilian religious personnel shall be respected and protected. The provisions of the Conventions and of this Protocol concerning the protection and identification of medical personnel shall apply equally to such persons.

—Article 16 ("General Protection of Medical Duties"):

1. Under no circumstances shall any person be punished for carrying out medical activities compatible with medical ethics, regardless of the person benefiting therefrom.
2. Persons engaged in medical activities shall not be compelled to perform acts or to carry out work contrary to the rules of medical ethics or to other medical rules designed for the benefit of the wounded and sick or to the provisions of the Conventions or of this Protocol, or to refrain from performing acts or from carrying out work required by those rules and provisions.

3. No person engaged in medical activities shall be compelled to give to anyone belonging either to an adverse Party, or to his own Party except as required by the law of the latter Party, any information concerning the wounded and sick who are, or who have been, under his care, if such information would, in his opinion, prove harmful to the patients concerned or to their families. Regulations for the compulsory notification of communicable diseases shall, however, be respected.

—Article 35 ("Methods and Means of Warfare—Basic Rules"):

1. In any armed conflict, the right of the Parties to the conflict to choose methods or means of warfare is not unlimited.
2. It is prohibited to employ weapons, projectiles, and material and methods of warfare of a nature to cause superfluous injury or unnecessary suffering.
3. It is prohibited to employ methods or means of warfare which are intended, or may be expected, to cause widespread, long-term and severe damage to the natural environment.

—Article 40 ("Quarter"):

It is prohibited to order that there shall be no survivors, to threaten an adversary therewith or to conduct hostilities on this basis.

—Article 4 ("Fundamental Guarantees") of Additional Protocol 2:

1. All persons who do not take a direct part or who have ceased to take part in hostilities, whether or not their liberty has been restricted, are entitled to respect for their person, honor, and convictions and religious practices. They shall in all circumstances be treated humanely, without any adverse distinction. It is prohibited to order that there shall be no survivors.
2. Without prejudice to the generality of the foregoing, the following acts against the persons referred to in paragraph 1 are and shall remain prohibited at any time and in any place whatsoever:

a) violence to the life, health, and physical or mental well-being of persons, in particular murder as well as cruel treatment such as torture, mutilation, or any form of corporal punishment;

b) collective punishments;

c) taking of hostages;

d) acts of terrorism;

e) outrages upon personal dignity, in particular humiliating and degrading treatment, rape, enforced prostitution and any form of indecent assault;

f) slavery and the slave trade in all their forms;

g) pillage;

h) threats to commit any of the foregoing acts.

3. Children shall be provided with the care and aid they require, and in particular:

a) they shall receive an education, including religious and moral education, in keeping with the wishes of their parents, or in the absence of parents, of those responsible for their care;

b) all appropriate steps shall be taken to facilitate the reunion of families temporarily separated;

c) children who have not attained the age of fifteen years shall neither be recruited in the armed forces or groups nor allowed to take part in hostilities;

d) the special protection provided by this Article to children who have not attained the age of fifteen years shall remain applicable to them if they take a direct part in hostilities despite the provisions of sub-paragraph *(c)* and are captured;

e) measures shall be taken, if necessary, and whenever possible with the consent of their parents or persons who by law or custom are primarily responsible for their care, to remove children temporarily from the area in which hostilities are taking place to a safer area within the country and ensure that they are accompanied by persons responsible for their safety and well-being.

—Article 5 ("Persons Whose Liberty Has Been Restricted") of Additional Protocol 2:

1. In addition to the provisions of Article 4, the following provisions shall be respected as a minimum with regard to persons deprived of their liberty for reasons related to the armed conflict, whether they are interned or detained:

    a) the wounded and the sick shall be treated in accordance with Article 7;

    b) the persons referred to in this paragraph shall, to the same extent as the local civilian population, be provided with food and drinking water and be afforded safeguards as regards health and hygiene and protection against the rigors of the climate and the dangers of the armed conflict;

    c) they shall be allowed to receive individual or collective relief;

    d) they shall be allowed to practice their religion and, if requested and appropriate, to receive spiritual assistance from persons, such as chaplains, performing religious functions;

    e) they shall, if made to work, have the benefit of working conditions and safeguards similar to those enjoyed by the local civilian population.

2. Those who are responsible for the internment or detention of the persons referred to in paragraph 1 shall also, within the limits of their capabilities, respect the following provisions relating to such persons:

    a) except when men and women of a family are accommodated together, women shall be held in quarters separated from those of men and shall be under the immediate supervision of women;

    b) they shall be allowed to send and receive letters and cards, the number of which may be limited by competent authority if it deems necessary;

    c) places of internment and detention shall not be located close to the combat zone. The persons referred to in paragraph 1 shall be evacuated when the places where they are interned or detained become particularly exposed to danger arising out of the armed conflict, if their evacuation can be carried out under adequate conditions of safety;

d) they shall have the benefit of medical examinations;

e) their physical or mental health and integrity shall not be endangered by any unjustified act or omission. Accordingly, it is prohibited to subject the persons described in this Article to any medical procedure which is not indicated by the state of health of the person concerned, and which is not consistent with the generally accepted medical standards applied to free persons under similar medical circumstances.

3. Persons who are not covered by paragraph 1 but whose liberty has been restricted in any way whatsoever for reasons related to the armed conflict shall be treated humanely in accordance with Article 4 and with paragraphs 1*(a)*, *(c)*, and *(d)*, and 2*(b)* of this Article.

4. If it is decided to release persons deprived of their liberty, necessary measures to ensure their safety shall be taken by those so deciding.

—Martens Clause (Article 1, para. 2 of Protocol 1):

In cases not covered by this Protocol or by other international agreements, civilians and combatants remain under the protection and authority of the principles of international law derived from established custom, from the principles of humanity, and from the dictates of public conscience.

CHAPTER NOTES AND REFERENCES

NOTES TO CHAPTER ONE
CHRISTIANITY AND HUMANITARIAN ACTION
Avery Cardinal Dulles, S.J.

1. Rodney Stark, *The Rise of Christianity* (Princeton, NJ: Princeton University Press, 1996), 161.

2. Vatican II, Pastoral Constitution *Gaudium et spes,* 24.

3. Karol Wojtyla (John Paul II), *Love and Responsibility* (New York: Farrar, Straus, Giroux, 1981), 26, and 290–91, note 6.

4. Vatican II, *Gaudium et spes,* 24.

5. Vatican II, Decree on the Apostolate of the Laity *Apostolicam actuositatem,* 8.

6. Vatican II, Decree on Ecumenism *Unitatis redintegratio,* 23.

7. Peter T. Kilborn, "Nuns Bring Hope to a Destitute Town in Mississippi," *New York Times,* 20 November 2002, A20.

8. Joseph Cardinal Bernardin, "Catholic Identity: Resolving Conflicting Expectations," in *The Future of Catholic Institutional Ministries,* eds. Charles J. Fahey et al. (New York: Fordham University Third Age Center, 1992), 75–84, at 77.

9. Quoted from Fred Kammer, "Ten Ways Catholic Charities are Catholic," Catholic Charities Web site: *catholiccharitiesusa.org/beliefs/10ways.*

10. "The Pope's Address to Catholic Charities," *Origins* 17 (October 8, 1987): 286–88, at 288.

11. *Gaudium et spes,* 42, 45.

12. Vatican II, Decree *Unitatis redintegratio,* 12.

13. Text in *Origins* 32 (June 20, 2002): 81–84.

14. Francis Arinze, *Meeting Other Believers* (Huntington, Ind.: Our Sunday Visitor Publishing Co., 1997), 29.

15. "John Paul II Angelus Address of September 23, 2001," *Origins* 31 (October 4, 2001): 287, 289, at 289.

NOTES TO CHAPTER TWO
FOR THE SAKE OF MY KIN AND FRIENDS:
TRADITIONS, VALUES, AND HUMANITARIAN ACTION IN JUDAISM
Rabbi Harlan J. Wechsler

1. Compare this, as well, to Plato's idea in the *Timaeus* that creation is so lowly a task that it needs to be done by the *demiurgos* and not by God Himself.

2. Abraham Joshua Heschel, *The Prophets* (New York: Harper and Row, 1962), 234–59.

3. Cf. Yohanan Muffs, *Love & Joy: Law, Language and Religion in Ancient Israel* (New York: The Jewish Theological Seminary of America, 1992), 9–48.

4. Harlan J. Wechsler, "The Artisan's Touch: Jewish Ethics and the Doctrine of Creation," *Conservative Judaism* (Summer 1974): 54–60.

5. Gen. 1:27.

6. Maimonides *The Guide for the Perplexed* 1.1.

7. Commentary to Gen. 1:27.

8. Abraham Joshua Heschel, *The Insecurity of Freedom* (New York: Schocken, 1972), 153.

9. Babylonian Talmud (BT) Sanhedrin 38a.

10. Gen. 2:7.

11. Nahmanides to Gen. 1:26.

12. Gen. 2:18.

13. Gen. 2:23. See Joseph B. Soloveitchik, "The Lonely Man of Faith," *Tradition* (Summer 1965): 5–67.

14. BT Taanit 23a.

15. Cf. the writings of the modern Jewish philosopher Emanuel Levinas. See, for example, Ira F. Stone, *Reading Levinas/Reading Talmud* (Philadelphia: The Jewish Publication Society, 1998), 3–22.

16. BT Sanhedrin 38a.

17. Ibid., 37b.

18. Ibid., 38a.

19. Ibid., 37b.

20. Gen. 2:16–17.

21. Gen. 6:6.

22. Martin Buber, *I and Thou*, trans. Walter Kaufman (New York: Charles Scribner's Sons, 1970), 53–85.

23. Deut. 6:5. This is part of the first paragraph of the Shema, the Scriptural recitation that is the center of both morning and evening prayers.

24. Ibid., 11:13–21. This is the second paragraph of the Shema. See BT Berakhot 13a.

25. As the paragraph recited before the Shema in the daily prayers puts it: "A great love you have loved us." It then goes on to speak of the Law, its teachings, and commandments.

26. BT Sanhedrin 56a; Maimonides, Mishneh Torah (Code of Jewish Law), Laws of Kings, chaps. 9 and 10.

27. Maimonides, Mishneh Torah, Laws of Repentance, 3:5. Also Laws of Kings, 8:11. This is based on the Talmud, BT Sanhedrin 105a. In that chapter, Balaam is noted as a king (obviously a gentile king) who will not be rewarded with life in the world to come. His lack of righteousness is emphasized. It follows, therefore, that those who *are* righteous will have a place in that eternal abode.

28. Coming from a different place, I echo the view expressed by Pope John Paul II in the 1991 encyclical *Centesimus Annus*.

29. See M. A. Casey, "How to Think About Globalization," *First Things* (October 2002): 47–56.

30. Exod. 20:12. This is complemented by Lev. 19:3 ("You shall each revere his mother and his father . . .") in the development of the law.

31. The laws of honoring and revering parents are discussed in BT Kiddushin 30b–32b. The laws of standing up and revering the old are discussed in the same tractate, 32b–33a.

32. BT Kiddushin 33a.

33. These discussions are in BT Shabbat 151b–152a, Midrash Vayikra Rabbah, Parashah 18:1, and Midrash Koheleth Rabbah, chap. 12.

34. See Harlan J. Wechsler, "The View of Rabbinic Literature," in *Justice Across Generations: What Does It Mean?* (Washington: AARP, 1993), 19–34.

35. The classic work on the subject is *Hafetz Hayyim* by Rabbi Israel Meir HaCohen.

36. Rabbi Joseph Caro, *Shulhan Arukh* (Code of Jewish Law), Orah Hayyim 329:1.

37. BT Sanhedrin 74a.

38. For a review of the laws of warfare, see Elliot Dorf, *To Do the Right and the Good* (Philadelphia: Jewish Publication Society, 2002).

39. Lev. 19:3–18.
40. Gen. 3:21.
41. Deut. 34:6.
42. BT Sotah 14a.
43. Deut. 13:5.
44. Ibid., 4:24.
45. Gen. 3:21.
46. Ibid., 18:1. The previous verses speak of Abraham's circumcision. The visit of God thus follows immediately after.
47. Ibid., 25:11.
48. Deut. 34:6.
49. BT Sotah 14a.
50. Jer. 9:22–23.
51. The words of the "Aleynu" prayer recited three times daily. In modern Jewish thought, social action is often termed, *tikkun olam,* perfection of the world. This use of this terminology is derived from these words.
52. Midrash Tanhuma (Buber), Tazria 7.
53. Quoted in Norman Lamm, *The Good Society: Jewish Ethics in Action* (New York: Viking, 1974), 219.
54. Mishnah Avot 2:16.
55. Lev. 19:34; also Deut. 10:19.
56. Deut. 5:15.
57. Ibid., 15:14–15.
58. Ibid., 24:17–18.
59. Ibid., verse 22.
60. Zech. 14:9, 16–17.
61. Num. 6:26.
62. Ps. 37:11.
63. See Midrash Leviticus Rabbah 9:9, and Midrash Numbers Rabbah 11:7.
64. Jer. 31:15–16.

NOTES TO CHAPTER THREE
STRATEGIES FOR DISAGREEMENT
His Royal Highness Prince El Hassan bin Talal

1. This paper was delivered at the "Traditions, Values, and Humanitarian Action" symposium by Professor Mustapha Tlili, Founder

and Director of Dialogues-Islamic World-U.S.-the West and Senior Fellow at the World Policy Institute.

2. H. Küng and H. Schmidt, eds., *A Global Ethic and Global Responsibilities: Two Declarations* (London: SCM Press, 1998), 8–42 (texts in parallel).

3. A. Toynbee, *An Historian's Approach to Religion,* 2nd ed. (London: Oxford University Press, 1979), 313–14.

4. In this regard, it is my hope that the Parliament of Cultures in Istanbul, devoted to cross-cultural dialogue on values with a focus on media and education, and the project "Partners in Humanity," which I have undertaken with John Marks of the *Search for Common Ground,* devoted to the promotion of responsible and representative media, will have some positive effect.

5. M. Khatami, "Dialogue among Civilizations and the World of Islam," in his *Islam, Dialogue and Civil Society* (Karachi: Foundation for the Revival of Islamic Heritage, 2000), 1–5, at 3.

6. See especially pages 1–2 in El Hassan bin Talal, "A Personal Vision," in *Continuity, Innovation and Change: Selected Essays* (Amman, 2001), 1–6; and see pages 1–13 in "The Ethics of Human Solidarity," in *Winning The Human Race? The Report of the Independent Commission on International Humanitarian Issues,* foreword by Sadruddin Aga Khan and Hassan bin Talal (London and New Jersey: Zed Books, 1988).

7. Issues touched upon in the context of humanitarian benefit in the professional sphere by Reinhard Mohn in *Humanity Wins: A Strategy for Progress and Leadership in Times of Change* (New York: Crown Business, 2000), 74–75.

8. Tarif Khalidi, ed. and trans., *The Muslim Jesus: Sayings and Stories in Islamic Literature* (Cambridge, MA, and London: Harvard University Press, 2001), 57:84. Another tradition reports that a man asked Jesus to teach him how a servant could be truly pious before God. Jesus replied that [to be pious] would be to truly love God, work in His service, and be merciful to all the people of the questioner's race. Further questioned as to who constituted this race, Jesus replied, "All the children of Adam. And that which you do not wish done to you, do not do to others." (Ibid., 48:79.) Cf. Matt. 22:34–40.

9. B. A. Dar, "Ethical Teachings of the Qur'an," in *A History of Muslim Philosophy,* vol. 1, ed. M. M. Sharif (Delhi: Pakistan Philosophical Congress, 1961; reprint 1995), 155–78, at 158.

10. Ibid., 168.

11. For example, readings of Article 26, items 2 and 3, on freedom of education and the parents' right to determine education for their child in the context of the current debates in the U.K. and Europe on whether or not government should lend financial support to single-faith schools; Article 16, item 3, on the protection of the family unit and its relation to recent objections by Christian groups to U.S. contributions to UN family-planning programs; Article 14, item 1, on the right to asylum, and the difficulties of negotiating the huge influx of Palestinian refugees into Jordan over the past fifty years.

12. See, for example, the outline of the Saudi representative's misgivings concerning the UNDHR document and the Pakistani representatives differing comments, described in D. Little, J. Kelsay, and A. Sachedina, *Human Rights and the Conflicts of Culture: Western and Islamic Perspectives on Religious Liberty* (Columbia: University of South Carolina Press, 1988), 35–37.

13. Cf. J. L. Esposito on Islamic modernizers: "On the one hand, they identified with premodern revivalist movements and called for the purification of internal deficiencies and deviations. On the other, they borrowed and assimilated new ideas and values from the West. For some, like Sayyid Ahmad Khan, this was accomplished by maintaining that Islam was the religion of reason and nature par excellence. For others, like Afghani and Iqbal, the rubric was the reclaiming of progressive, creative past whose political and cultural florescence demonstrated that the very qualities associated with the power of the West were already present in Islam and accounted for its past triumphs and accomplishments," *Islam: The Straight Path* (New York: Oxford University Press, 1991), 140–41.

14. Qur'an 24:35.

Notes to Chapter Four
The World of the Dinka: A Portrait of a Threatened Culture
Ambassador Francis Mading Deng

1. The author's writings on the Dinka include: *Tradition and Modernization* (New Haven and London: Yale University Press, 1971); *The Dinka of the Sudan* (New York: Holt, Rinehart and Winston, 1972); *The*

Dinka and Their Songs (Oxford: The Clarendon Press, 1973); *Dinka Folktales* (New York and London: Africana Publishing Company, 1974); *Dynamics of Identification: A Basis of National Integration in the Sudan* (Khartoum: Khartoum University Press, 1974); *Africans of Two Worlds* (New Haven and London: Yale University Press, 1978); *Dinka Cosmology* (London: Ithaca Press, 1980); *Recollections of Babo Nimir* (London: Ithaca Press, 1982); and *The Man Called Deng Majok: A Biography of Power, Polygyny, and Change* (New Haven and London: Yale University Press, 1986).

2. Major Court Treatt, who traveled throughout Africa during the first quarter of the twentieth century, reaching the land of the Ngok Dinka of Abyei in 1928, wrote: "As we drew nearer and obtained a clearer view of the village standing on rising ground, it seemed that we had stumbled on the master-builders of the tribes; instead of the usual undersized, vermin-infested native huts we beheld large, clean-looking dwellings about twenty-five feet in diameter, decorated with twisted grass-work and magnificently thatched." *Out of the Beaten Track* (New York: E. P. Hutton & Co., 1931), 60. In another context, Major Treatt described the inside of a Dinka dwelling:

> My first impression of roominess and excellent workmanship was pleasantly buttressed by the realization that the floor was dry and the hut itself warm, and I subsequently found that this temporary home of mine measured twenty-five feet in diameter beneath a domed roof twenty feet high. Excluding the center pole, at a height of seven feet was a wooden platform covered with clean grassmats, and beneath this platform was a small open fire, the smoke from whose hearth of lumps of based ant-hill earth protected the sleepers from mosquitoes (79).

Major Treatt concludes his account of Dinka dwellings: "Their huts, whose thatching is beyond all praise, are the most efficiently built native dwellings I have ever seen. And even the remnants of former huts . . . bear testimony to the excellence of their architecture" (124).

In a private letter dated February 24, 1932, one of the letters to relatives and friends which he kindly passed on to me, K. D. D. Henderson sketches pictures of a dwelling hut and a cattle-byre and observes that the latter holds about fifty head of cattle a night. Since every animal is tied to a peg with sufficient space left between the animals to avoid entanglement, this evidently means that the byre is very spacious.

3. Among the varieties that Henderson mentioned in a letter

dated March 3, 1932, were: "Teal, whistlers, pintail duck, comb duck, Egyptian geese, sacred ibis, wood ibis, maribou storks, saddle storks, greater and lesser egrets, golden crested crane, cormorants, herons, pelicans, fish eagles," all of which he describes as "almost as common hereabouts as sparrows." Major Treatt also observed "small water-holes speckled with myriads of water birds. . . . Duck and geese grubbed in the lush water grass of these pools while numerous species of storks would swoop down in shining curves, and once or twice we saw the rare pygmy goose sliding with its deceptive apparent slowness above the surface of the pools" (59–60).

4. Yet, as Godfrey Lienhardt noted, "The agnatic genealogical structure of his whole clan . . . is not known to a Dinka; he knows that there are likely to be many sub-clans of his clan, all descended from wives or sons of the clan founder, whose name and existence have been forgotten long ago by members of his own sub-clan." "The Western Dinka," in *Tribes Without Rulers,* eds. Middleton and Tait (Oxford: Oxford University Press, 1958), 105–6; see also Paul Howell, "Notes on the Ngok Dinka," *Sudan Notes and Records* 32 (1951): 256.

5. According to Paul Howell, "The initiative does not have to come from the junior age-set but usually does, and in the form of rude songs which cast reflection on the waning popularity among the girls of the age-set senior to them" ("Notes on the Ngok Dinka," 252). To my knowledge, the initiative is always taken by the older age-set in the form of scandalous songs in which they imply a challenge to the qualification of the younger generation to rise to the level of warriors and eligible partners of the corresponding female age-set. The theme of their songs is to identify the members of the younger age-set with their mothers as children still and to insult their mothers by association, even if they had sibling brothers in the senior age-set. For the younger age-set to insult their seniors, even in retaliation, would be totally inappropriate and unacceptable.

6. Godfrey Lienhardt, *Divinity and Experience: The Religion of the Dinka* (Oxford: The Clarendon Press, 1961), 26.

7. Charles Seligman and Brenda Seligman, *The Pagan Tribes of the Nilotic Sudan* (London: G. Routledge and Sons, 1932), 173. David Cole and Richard Huntington observed, in their *African Rural Development,* "If it is possible to rank peoples according to their religiosity, then the Dinka must be counted among some of the most religious peoples of

the world. They are intensely respectful of Divinity in all of its many manifestations."

8. Major Titherington, "The Raik of Bahr el Ghazar Province," *Sudan Notes and Records* 10 (1927): 159, 169.

9. *Divinity and Experience*, 46–47. Dinka religion can be described as monotheistic in that they believe there is only one God, *Nhialic*, a word with the connotation of "above" or "in the Sky." As Lienhardt observed, the Dinka "assert with a uniformity that makes the assertion almost a dogma that 'Divinity (God) is one.' They cannot conceive of Divinity as a plurality and, did they know what it meant, would deeply resent being described as polytheistic" (156). But they also believe in a complex set of spirits, some of whom have godly attributes and are sometimes described as gods.

10. The manner in which the clans divide into segments, resulting in a parochialism of loyalties at the expense of the wider unity of the clan, is sometimes attributed to the effect of women and maternal kin. For the story of how women allegedly caused the original break into clans, see Father Nebel, *Dinka Grammar* (1948), 129. For another story that demonstrates the tensions and conflicts between paternal and maternal loyalties, see *Dinka Grammar*, 134.

11. Francis Mading Deng, *The Dinka and Their Songs* (Oxford University Press, 1974), 241.

12. Lienhardt, "Western Dinka," 106–7.

13. Father Nebel, *Dinka Dictionary* (1954), 315.

14. Francis Mading Deng, *Dinka Cosmology* (London: Ithaca Press, 1980), 58. Quoted in Francis M. Deng, *War of Visions: Conflict of Identities in the Sudan* (Washington, D.C.: The Brookings Institution, 1995), 196.

15. Deng, *Dinka Cosmology*, 42; and Deng, *War of Visions*, 197.

16. Major Court Treatt, *Out of the Beaten Track* (1931), 115–16.

17. Major Titherington, "The Raik Dinka," *Sudan Notes and Records* 10 (1927): 159.

18. Quoted in Deng, *War of Visions*, 282.

19. Godfrey Lienhardt, "Man in Society," in *The Listener* (London: BBC, 1963), 828. See also Lienhardt, *Divinity and Experience*, 248.

20. Howell, "The Ngok Dinka," 262–63. See also Deng, *Tradition and Modernization*, 149–50.

21. Titherington, "The Raik Dinka," 168.

22. Deng, *The Dinka and Their Songs*, 142. These and other extracts

from songs are reproduced from original translations, occasionally with minor revisions for greater clarity.

23. Deng, *The Dinka and Their Songs,* 236.

24. Francis Mading Deng, *Tradition and Modernization* (New Haven and London: Yale University Press, 1971), 219–24.

25. For examples of divorce and breach of engagement, see Deng, *The Dinka and Their Songs,* 219–224.

26. Deng, *Dinka Cosmology,* 46.

27. Ibid., 99.

28. Francis Mading Deng, *The Man Called Deng Majok* (New Haven and London: Yale University Press, 1986), 227.

29. John S. Trimingham, *The Christian Church in Post-War Sudan* (London and New York: World Domination Press, 1949), 34.

30. Audrey Butt, *The Nilotics of the Anglo-Egyptian Sudan and Uganda* (London: International African Institute, 1952), 41.

31. Francis Mading Deng, *The Dinka of the Sudan* (New York: Holt, Rinehart and Winston, 1972), 172.

32. Deng, *The Dinka of the Sudan,* 162.

33. Deng, *The Dinka of the Sudan,* 139; and Deng, *The Dinka and Their Songs,* 157–58.

34. Deng, *The Dinka of the Sudan,* 228.

35. Ibid., 229.

36. Deng, *The War of Visions,* 214.

37. See Deng, *Dinka Cosmology,* 269.

38. Godfrey Lienhardt, "The Dinka and Catholicism," in *Religious Organization and Religious Experience,* ed. J. Davis (London and New York: Academic Press, 1982), 89–90.

39. The accounts quoted here are reproduced, sometimes with minor revisions in the original translation.

40. Francis Mading Deng, *Africans of Two Worlds: The Dinka in Afro-Arab Sudan* (New Haven and London: Yale University Press, 1978), 50.

41. Ibid., 64.

42. Deng, *Dinka Cosmology,* 61.

43. Ibid., 196.

44. Ibid., 197.

45. Ibid., 201.

46. Ibid., 203.

47. For arguments in favor of a culturally oriented approach to development, see Francis M. Deng, "Crisis in African Development: A

Social and Cultural Perspective," *Annual Report* (New York: The Rockefeller Brothers Fund, 1984); Francis M. Deng, "Cultural Dimensions of Conflict Management and Developments: Some Lessons from the Sudan," in *Culture and Development in Africa,* eds. Ismail Serageldin and June Tabaroff (Washington, D.C.: The World Bank, 1994), Technical Paper 225, 466; Afterword in David Cole and Richard Huntington, *Between a Swamp and a Hard Place* (Cambridge: Harvard University Press, 1997); and Francis M. Deng and Terrence Lyons, eds., *African Reckoning* (The Brookings Institution, forthcoming).

NOTES TO CHAPTER FIVE
MILITARY VALUES AND TRADITIONS
Major General Timothy Cross, CBE, FCIT, FILT

1. The booklets, issued to every officer and soldier in the British Army, include statements on the ethos and values of the British Army. It defines the ethos as: "That spirit which inspires soldiers to fight. It derives from, and depends upon, the high degrees of commitment, self-sacrifice, and mutual trust which together are so essential to the maintenance of morale." It lists the values of the British Army as:

- Selfless Commitment—to put others before yourself
- Courage—to face up to danger and what is right
- Discipline—to maintain the highest standards, so that others can rely on you
- Integrity—to earn the respect and trust of your comrades
- Loyalty—to be faithful to your comrades and your duty
- Respect for others—to treat others with decency at all times

2. All members of the British military are subject to all aspects of civil as well as military law.

3. Leadership and discipline are, in my view, the primary "traditions." There are others. For example, during research on "The Right to Be Different" paper conducted for the British Armies Adjutant General Department in 1995–96, numerous senior officers were interviewed and a series of discussion groups held to discover what the ethos of the British Army was thought to be and what made it unique, compared to public institutions and private organizations. By re-analyzing

the list of values made at the time, a list of military virtues was drawn up as follows:

Personal integrity. To be willing to accept hazard, danger, and self-sacrifice; courageous—morally, physically, and intellectually; honorable and self-controlled; humane, conscienced, and restrained in operations and war.

Trustworthy, with regard to: intelligent conformity and obedience; loyalty and powers of self-discipline; confidence, based appropriately on openness and confidentiality; the sublimation of self-interest in the legitimating interests of the group and no curtailment or suspension of labor.

Competence. To have acquired necessary functional competence based on best practice in military doctrine, planning, training, and use of resources; tolerance to sustained hardship and stress in adverse conditions; judgement in military matters (and the ability to lead others); personal standards to withstand any detrimental pressures from outside the military profession or from within.

4. Sun Tzu, *The Art of War* (500–300 B.C.).

5. General Franks, Commander, 7 U.S. Corps (A.D. 1997).

6. A slightly more modern example: "It is singular how a man loses or gains caste with his comrades from his behaviour, and how closely he is observed in the field. The officers, too, are commented upon and closely observed. The men are very proud of those who are brave in the field, and kind and considerate to the soldiers under them. An act of kindness done by an officer has often during the battle been the cause of his life being saved. . . . I know from experience that in our army the men like best to be officered by gentlemen, men whose education has rendered them more kind in manners than your course officer, sprung from obscure origin, and whose style is brutal and overbearing." *Recollections of Rifleman Harris,* Peninsula, 1808.

7. "A good example of this is the story of the wreck of the *Warren Hastings,* which was carrying four companies of the King's Royal Rifle Corps and as many of the York and Lancaster Regiment, on the island of Reunion in 1897. When the ship struck, sentries of the Rifles were at once posted at various points on the lower deck, to guard the access to the spirit room and such like; and there they remained while boats were lowered to take the battalion ashore. The water rose steadily upon them inch by inch, and had reached their chests, when at last an officer came to summon them also, last of all, to take their place in the boats. He

collected them all, as he thought, but in the noise and darkness he missed one man and left him behind. The man saw his comrades disappear up the ladder, and the officer about to follow them, and not till then did he ask, *without quitting his post,* 'Beg pardon, sir, may I come, too?' If ever you hear any man speak lightly of military discipline, tell him that story, for that Rifleman is worthy to be placed alongside the Roman sentry at Pompeii." Sir John Fortescue, *Military History Lectures delivered at Trinity College, Cambridge.*

    8. Field Marshall The Viscount Slim, coverage and other broadcasts.

    9. Sir Arthur Bryant, *Years of Victory.*

    10. From Colonel Henderson, *The Science of War.*

    11. Josh. 1:5–7.

    12. A good example is this extract from an N.C.O.'s Report from the Ruthven Redoubt, August 30, 1745:

> HON. GENERAL—This goes to acquaint you that yesterday there appeared in the little town of Ruthven about three hundred of the enemy, and sent proposals to me to surrender the Redoubt upon condition that I should have liberty to carry off bags and baggage. My answer was, "I am too old a soldier to surrender a garrison of such strength without bloody noses!" They threatened to hang me and my men for refusal. I told them I would take my chance. This morning they attacked me about twelve o'clock with about one hundred and fifty men; they attacked the foregate and sally-port. They drew off about half an hour after three. I expect another visit this night, but I shall give them the warmest reception my weak party can afford. I shall hold out as long as possible.

> I conclude, Honourable General, with great respects,
> Your most humble servant,
> J. Molley, Sergt. 6th[Foot] *(Quoted in Britain at Arms)*

    13. When deployed on operations, soldiers are subject to the Laws of Armed Conflict and to the local law wherever they are serving—together they form the baseline for the standards of personal conduct of the soldier as a citizen. The constraints of Just War *(jus ad bellum)* impose severe limitations on soldiers—as well as politicians. Imperatives of military effectiveness increasingly conflict with other needs, particularly on complex emergencies/operations short of declared war. This poses great difficulties in defining the appropriate rules of engagement. Overall every serviceman and woman faces real practical difficulties with regard to the Laws of War *(jus in bello).*

14. Captain Farrar-Hockley, *The Edge of the Sword.*

15. "I do not believe that today a commander can inspire great armies, or single units, or even individual men, unless he has a proper sense of religious truth. All Leadership is based on the spiritual quality, the power to inspire others to follow." Field Marshall Montgomery.

16. Bill Slim tells a story of one of his experiences early on after taking command in Burma:

> In the camps on the line of communications, all reinforcements to the various fronts were held often for weeks until required. . . . Almost without exception I found these places depressing beyond words. Decaying tents, or dilapidated *bashas,* with earth floors, mosquito ridden, and lacking all amenities, were the usual accommodation; training and recreation were alike unorganised; men were crowded together from all units. No wonder spirits sank, discipline sagged, and defeatist rumours spread.

REFERENCES TO CHAPTER FIVE
MILITARY VALUES AND TRADITIONS
Major General Timothy Cross, CBE, FCIT, FILT

Bryant, Sir Arthur. *Years of Victory 1802–1812.* London: Collins, 1944.

Churchill, Sir Winston. *Marlborough, His Life and Times.* London: Harrap, 1933–38.

Farrar-Hockley, Capt. *The Edge of the Sword.* London: Muller, 1954.

Fergusson, Brig. Bernard. *The Wild Green Earth.* London: Collins, 1946.

Fortescue, Sir John. *A Gallant Company.* London: Williams and Norgate, 1927.

———. *A History of the British Army.* London: Macmillan, 1910.

———. *Following the Drum.* London: W. Blackwood, 1931.

———. *Military History: Lectures Delivered at Trinity College.* Cambridge: Cambridge University Press, 1914.

Fraser, Edward. *The Soldiers Whom Wellington Led.* London: Methuen, 1913.

Gilby, Thomas. *(Collected) Britain at Arms.* London: Eyre & Spottiswood, 1953.

Gurwood, Lt. Col. J. *The Dispatches of Field-Marshal The Duke of Wellington.* London: John Murray, 1837.

Hamilton, Gen. Sir Ian. *The Commander.* London: Hollis and Carter, 1957.

Harris, Henry Curling, ed. *Recollections of Rifleman Harris*. Peter Davies, 1848. New edition, Windrush Press, 1998.

Henderson, Col. *The Science of War*. London: Longmans, Green, 1993.

Majdalany, Fred. *The Monastery*. London: Bodley Head, 1946.

Moran, Lord. *The Anatomy of Courage*. London: Constable, 1945.

Munson, Col. *Leadership for American Army Leaders*. Washington, D.C.: Infantry Journal, 1942.

Purdom, C. B., ed. *Everyman at War*. London: Dent, 1930.

The Royal Military Academy. *Serve to Lead—An Anthology*. Sandhurst, 1994.

Slim, Field-Marshal The Viscount. *Courage and Other Broadcasts*. London: Cassell, 1957.

———. *Defeat into Victory*. London: Cassell, 1956.

Turner, E. S. *Gallant Gentlemen*. London: Michael Joseph, 1956.

Walker Trust. *Lectures on Leadership*. London: Oxford University Press, 1930–49.

Wavell, Field-Marshal Earl. *The Good Soldier*. London: Macmillan, 1948.

Selected Further Reading

Adair, J. E., M.A., Ph.D. *Leadership*. London: Macmillan.

Baynes, Major John. *Morale: A Study of Men and Courage*. London: Cassell, 1967.

Brett-James, Antony. *Wellington at War, 1794–1815*. London: Macmillan, 1961.

British Army Review 124 (spring 2000).

Bush, Captain Eric, RN (Retd). *Salute the Soldier*. London: George Allen and Unwin, 1966.

Costello, Edward. *The Peninsular and Waterloo Campaigns*. Edited by Antony Brett-James. London: Longmans, 1967.

Hackett, Lt. General Sir John Wintrop, KCB, CBE, DSO, MC. *The Profession of Arms* (Lees Knowles Lectures). London: Times Publishing Co., Ltd., 1962.

"The Royal United Services Institute for Defence Studies." *International Security Review* (2000).

Worsley, Commander F. A., DSO, OBE, RD, RNR. *Shackleton Boat Journey*. New York: W. W. Norton, 1998.

NOTES TO CHAPTER EIGHT
HUMAN RIGHTS AND THE MAKING OF A GOOD DOCTOR
Eoin O'Brien, M.D.

1. K. Cahill, *A Bridge to Peace* (New York: Haymarket Doyma Inc, 1988), 18.

2. K. M. Cahill, "Medicine and Diplomacy: An Introduction," in *The Untapped Resource: Medicine and Diplomacy,* ed. Kevin Cahill (New York: Orbis Books, 1971), 2.

3. H. L. Carey, "A War We *Can* Win: Health as a Vector of Foreign Policy," in *The Untapped Resource: Medicine and Diplomacy,* ed. Kevin Cahill (New York: Orbis Books, 1971), 96, 103.

4. G. B. Shaw, "Preface," in *The Doctor's Dilemma* (London: Penguin, 2002).

5. *http://mchip00.med.nyu.edu/lit-med/syllabi.for.web/syllabi.menu.page.html*

6. "What's a Good Doctor and How Do You Make One?" *BMJ* 325 (2002).

7. M. A. Elgizouli, "Medical Profession Needs Input from Belief in Humanity and Ethics," *BMJ* 325 (2002): 713.

8. P. Toynbee, "Between Aspiration and Reality," *BMJ* 325 (2002): 718–19.

9. C. Douglas, "Doing Better; Looking Worse: The Portrayal of Doctors in Art, Literature and Television," *BMJ* 325 (2002): 720.

10. *http://mchip00.med.nyu.edu/lit-med/syllabi.for.web/syllabi.by.topic.html*

11. *http://www.mhrd.ucl.ac.uk/*

12. E. O'Brien, *The Beckett Country: Samuel Beckett's Ireland* (Dublin: The Black Cat Press & Faber and Faber, 1986), 315–44.

13. E. O'Brien, "Samuel Beckett and the Weight of Compassion," *The Recorder* 10 (1997): 154–65.

14. L. Bernstein, "A View of the Author: The Medicine Man," in *A Bridge to Peace,* ed. K. Cahill (New York: Haymarket Doyma Inc., 1988), 98.

15. British Medical Association, *Medicine Betrayed* (London: Zed Books, 1992), Recommendation 19.

16. *Tomorrow's Doctors: Recommendations on Undergraduate Medical Education.* (London: The General Medical Council, 1993), 14–15.

17. British Medical Association, "Teaching and Human Ethics," in

The Medical Profession and Human Rights: Handbook for a Changing Agenda (London and New York: Zed Books, 2001), 483. Web site address: *www.-wma.net/e/policy/20-4-99_e.html*

18. *Guidelines for National Plans of Action for Human Rights Education.* Human Rights Questions, including alternative approaches for improving the effective enjoyment of human rights and fundamental freedoms. United Nations Decade for Human Rights Education (1995–2004) and public information activities in the field of human rights. Report of the Secretary-General.

19. Amnesty International, *Ethical Codes and Declarations Relevant to the Health Professions* (London, 1994).

20. S. Fluss, *International Guidelines on Bioethics* (Geneva: Council for International Organizations of Medical Sciences [CROMS], 1999).

21. Physicians for Human Rights–U.K. Response to the U.K. Government's Fourth Report under the International Covenant on Economic, Social, and Cultural rights, Article 12—The Right to Health. 2002.

22. K. Boyd, R. Higgs, A. Pinching, eds., *The New Dictionary of Medical Ethics* (London: BMJ Publishing, 1997), 126.

23. Shaw, "Preface" in *The Doctor's Dilemma.*

24. American Association for the Advancement of Science, Physicians for Human Rights, American Nurses Association, Committee for Health in South Africa. *The Legacy of Apartheid* (Washington, D.C., 1998).

25. Physicians for Human Rights–U.K. Response to the U.K. Government's Fourth Report, Article 12—The Right to Health.

26. Mary Robinson, *Physicians for Human Rights Newsletter* 13, no. 2 (2002): 6.

27. Brian D. Smedley, Adrienne Y. Stith, and Alan R. Nelson, eds., *Unequal Treatment: Confronting Racial and Ethnic Disparities in Health Care* (Washington, D.C.: National Academy Press, 2002).

28. S. Bharet, P. Aggleton, P. Tyrer, *India: HIV and AIDS-Related Discrimination, Stigmatization, and Denial* (Geneva: UNAIDS, 2001), 16–24.

29. P. Hall, "Human Rights in the Hippocratic Oath," presented at the International Federation of Health and Human Rights Organizations Conference, Amersfoort, 2002.

30. Article 12. International Covenant on Economic, Social, and Cultural Rights (CESCR).

31. P. Hunt, "The Right to Health: From the Margins to the Mainstream," *Lancet* 360 (2002): 1878.

32. *http://193.194.138.190/html/menu6/2/index.htm*

33. P. Hall, "Doctors Urgently Need Education in Human Rights," *Lancet* 360 (2002): 1879.

34. British Medical Association, "Teaching and Human Ethics," in *The Medical Profession and Human Rights: Handbook for a Changing Agenda,* 478–502.

35. Ibid., 492.

36. Ibid., 480.

37. Ibid., 492–94.

38. HURUMA, Makerere Medical School, P.O. Box 16749, Kampala, Uganda. E-mail: *huruma@uga.healthnet.org*

39. Commonwealth Medical Association, *Training Manual on Ethical and Human Rights Standards for Health Care Professionals* (London: BMA, May 1999).

40. "Teaching and Human Ethics," in *The Medical Profession and Human Rights: Handbook for a Changing Agenda,* 494.

41. Ibid., 497–98.

42. R. P. Claude, "Human Rights Education: The Case of the Philippines," *Human Rights Quarterly* 13 (1991): 453–524.

43. "Teaching and Human Ethics," in *The Medical Profession and Human Rights: Handbook for a Changing Agenda,* 494.

44. Johannes Wier Stichting, Postbus 1551, 3800 BN Amersfoort, Netherlands. Web site: *www.johannes-weir.nl*

45. "Teaching and Human Ethics," in *The Medical Profession and Human Rights: Handbook for a Changing Agenda,* 481–83.

46. Ibid., 485.

47. Ibid., 483.

48. Physicians for Human Rights (U.K.), The University Department of Forensic Medicine, The Royal Infirmary, Barrack Road, Dundee, Scotland. *phruk@dux.dundee.ac.uk*

49. *Physicians for Human Rights Newsletter* 13, no. 1 (2002): 4.

50. *www.dundee.ac.uk/med&humanrights/SSM/home.html*

51. "Teaching and Human Ethics," in *The Medical Profession and Human Rights: Handbook for a Changing Agenda,* 496.

52. *Physicians for Human Rights Newsletter* 13, no. 1 (2002): 4.

53. CIHC Headquarters, 850 Fifth Avenue, New York, NY 10021. E-mail: *cihcnyc@aol.com*

54. "Teaching and Human Ethics," in *The Medical Profession and Human Rights: Handbook for a Changing Agenda,* 497.

55. "Teaching and Human Ethics," in *The Medical Profession and Human Rights: Handbook for a Changing Agenda,* 485–92.

Notes to Chapter Nine
Immigration in Europe: Promise or Peril?
Ambassador Jan Eliasson

1. Olov Liljeborg contributed substantially to this chapter.

2. Swedish State Secretary Gun-Britt Andersson, Ministry of Foreign Affairs, statement at Lanzarote, April 5, 2002.

3. Better World Campaign, UN Current Events, Financing the Millennium Development Goals; *http://www.betterworldfund.org/about/current_index.shtml*

4. Number includes all fifteen current member states.

5. *Number of Asylum Applications Submitted in 30 Industrialized Countries, 1992–2001,* UNHCR (Population Data Unit); *www.unhcr.ch* (Statistics).

6. "The Key to Europe," *Migration News* 2, no. 1 (January 1995); *migration.ucdavis.edu*

7. *Racism and Xenophobia in Europe,* Eurobarometer Opinion Poll no. 47.1, 1997; *europa.eu.int/comm/public_opinion/archives/eb/ebs_113_en.pdf*

8. As quoted in "Cautious Welcome for Berlusconi Victory," *BBC News,* May 15, 2001; *www.bbc.co.uk*

9. *Country Report: Italy, 2002,* U.S. Committee for Refugees (USCR); *www.refugees.org*

10. "Presidency Conclusions," Seville European Council, June 21 and 22, 2002; *www.arena.uio.no/PDF/sevilleconclusions.pdf*

11. "The Welcome-Mat Has Gone," *The Economist,* June 4, 2002; *Economist.com*

12. "Northern Europe," *Migration News* 9, no. 9 (September 2002); *migration.ucdavis.edu*

13. "Germany: Law, Labor," *Migration News* 9, no. 5 (2002); *migration.ucdavis.edu*

14. "Huddled Masses, Please Stay Away," *The Economist,* June 13, 2002; *Economist.com*

15. "EU War on 'Illegal Immigration' Puts Human Rights at Risk," p. 3, *Amnesty International Appeal to the Sevilla Summit,* Amnesty International, June 12, 2002; *www.amnesty-eu.org/1/Sevilla_Summit_Appeal_12June2002.doc*

16. Ibid., 9.

17. Jessika ter Wal, ed., *Racism and Cultural Diversity in the Mass*

Media: An Overview of Research and Examples of Good Practice in the EU Member States, 1995–2000 (Vienna: ERCOMER, February 2002), 42.

18. *Number of Asylum Applications Submitted in 30 Industrialized Countries, 1992–2001* (UNHCR: Population Data Unit, 2002); *www.unhcr.ch* (Statistics).

19. Steve Schifferes, "Who Gains from Immigration?" *BBC News Online,* June 17, 2002; *news.bbc.uk.co*

20. Ibid.

21. "U.K.: Asylum, Economics," *Migration News* 9, no. 9 (September 2002); *migration.ucdavis.edu*

22. *Sweden in 2000—A Country of Migration,* Ministry for Foreign Affairs, Sweden, 2001; *http://www.utrikes.regeringen.se/*

23. *Asylum Applications Submitted in the European Union: Top 10 Origins, 1992–2001* (UNHCR: Population Data Unit, 2002); *www.unhcr.ch* (Statistics).

24. Herbert Brücker, Gil S. Epstein, Barry McCormick, Gilles St-Paul, Alessandra Venturini, and Klaus Zimmermann, *Managing Migration in the EU Welfare State,* Report to the Third European Conference of the fondazione (Migration Policy and the Welfare State), fondazione Rodolfo DeBenedetti, June 23, 2001; *www.frdb.org*

25. Carnegie Endowment for International Peace, "Research Perspectives on Migration," *International Migration Policy Project* 1, no. 1.

26. "Commission Autumn Economic Forecasts 2002–2004 for the Euro Area and the European Union," *The European Union Online,* Press release, November 13, 2002; *europa.eu.int*

27. *Statistik 2001,* p. 10, Swedish Migration Board, May 2002; *www.migrationsverket.se*

28. *Number of Asylum Applications Submitted in 30 Industrialized Countries, 1992–2001* (UNHCR: Population Data Unit, 2002); *www.unhcr.ch* (Statistics).

29. "Knocking on Europe's Door," *Time Europe* 155, no. 25 (June 3, 2000).

30. Ibid.

31. "U.K.: Asylum, Economics," *Migration News* 9, no. 9 (September 2002); *migration.ucdavis.edu*

32. "Invandringen lönsam affär," Anna Danielsson, *Svenska Dagbladet,* August 23, 2002.

33. "'Wanted' Immigrants," CNN Specials—Immigration, 2001; *www.cnn.com*

34. *Migration News* 9, no. 9 (September 2002); *migration.ucdavis.edu*

35. "'Wanted' Immigrants," CNN Specials—Immigration, 2001; *www.cnn.com*

36. *Moder Sveas rynkor,* Tankesmedjan, May 29, 2002; *www.tankes medjan.se*

37. Daniel T. Griswold, *Willing Workers: Fixing the Problem of Illegal Mexican Migration to the United States,* Trade Policy Analysis, no. 19 (Cato Institute, 2002), 8.

38. "Immigrants in the U.S.," *Migration News* 9, no. 9 (September 2002); *migration.ucdavis.edu*

39. Griswold, *Willing Workers: Fixing the Problem of Illegal Mexican Migration to the United States,* Trade Policy Analysis, no. 19.

40. Steve Schifferes, "Who Gains from Immigration?" *BBC News Online,* June 17, 2002; *news.bbc.uk.co*

41. Ibid.

42. Sheila Barter, "Europe Gripped by Migrant Myths," *BBC News Online,* June 19, 2002; *new.bbc.co.uk*

43. As quoted in Peter Ford, "Across Europe, the Far Right Rises," *The Christian Science Monitor,* May 15, 2002.

44. German Marshall Fund and the Chicago Council on Foreign Relations, *Worldviews 2002,* 2002; *www.worldviews.org*

45. Imperial powers England and France have a somewhat different immigration history, as they have received many immigrants from their former colonies.

46. "France: Le Pen," *Migration News* 9, no. 5 (2002); *migration.ucdavis.edu*

47. As quoted in Peter Ford, "Immigration Issue Grips Europe," *The Christian Science Monitor,* June 21, 2002.

48. United Nations Secretariat, *Replacement Migration: Is It a Solution to Declining and Aging Populations?* (Population Division: Department of Economic and Social Affairs, March 21, 2000).

49. Ibid.

50. *Demography and the West: Half a Billion Americans?* August 22, 2002; *Economist.com*

51. Schifferes, "Who Gains from Immigration?" *BBC News Online,* June 17, 2002.

52. John L. Helgerson, *The National Security Implications of Global Demographic Change,* National Intelligence Council, April 30, 2002.

53. Andrew Geddes, "Europe's Aging Workforce," *BBC News Online,* June 20, 2002; *news.bbc.uk.co*

54. Robin Oakley, "Europe's Tangle Over Immigration," *CNN Online,* 2001; *www.cnn.com*

55. *Observations by the European Council on Refugees and Exiles on the Presidency Conclusions of the European Council Meeting in Laeken, December14 and 15, 2001,* ECRE, January 2002; *www.ecre.org/statements/laeken con.shtml*

56. "How Do Asylum Seekers Arrive in the Countries Where They Make Applications?" *ECRE Quick Facts; www.ecre.org* (Fact File/Quick Facts).

57. "What is a Safe Third Country?" *ECRE Quick Facts; www.ecre.org* (Fact File/Quick Facts).

58. "EU War on 'Illegal Immigration' Puts Human Rights at Risk," *Amnesty International Appeal to the Sevilla Summit,* Amnesty International, June 12, 2002; *www.amnesty-eu.org/1/Sevilla_Summit_Appeal_12June2002 .doc*

59. "In Rotterdam It Is Another Vanishing, Another Consignment Gone Wrong," *Guardian Unlimited,* June 24, 2000; *www.guardian.co.uk/ Refugees_in_Britain/Story/0,2763,335897,00.html*

60. *Migration News* 9, no. 9 (September 2002); migration.ucdavis.edu

61. "Huddled Masses, Please Stay Away," *The Economist,* June 13, 2002; *Economist.com*

62. "Opening the Door: Whom to Let in to the Richer Countries and Why," *The Economist,* October 31, 2002; *Economist.com*

NOTES TO CHAPTER TEN
TORTURE
Timothy W. Harding, M.D.

1. J. Swain, *A History of Torture* (London: Tandem Books, 1986).

2. E. Peters, *Torture* (Oxford: Blackwell, 1985).

3. D. Forrest, ed., *A Glimpse of Hell* (London: Amnesty International/Cassel, 1996).

4. S. Milgram, "Behavioural Study of Obedience," *Journal of Abnormal Social Psychology* 67 (1963): 277–85.

5. Y. Tanaka, *Hidden Horrors: Japanese War Crimes in World War II* (Boulder, CO: Westview, 1996).

6. K. Farrington, *History of Punishment and Torture* (London: Hamlyn, 2000). See also M. Kerrigan, *The Instruments of Torture* (Guilford, CT: Lyons Press, 2001).

7. For the relationship between the terms "torture" and "cruel, inhuman, or degrading treatment," see chapter 3 of N. Rodley, *The Treatment of Prisoners Under International Law* (Oxford: Oxford University Press, 1987).

8. P. Tavernier, "Article 15" in L-E. Petititi, E. Decaux, and P-H. Imbert, *La Convention européenne des droits de l'homme: commentaire article par article* (Paris: Economica, 1995).

9. The full judgement can be found at *www.hudoc.echr.coe.int*

10. See report under Turkey at *www.cpt.coe.int*

11. Editorial, "Doctors and Torture," *British Medical Journal* 319 (1999): 397–98.

12. British Medical Association, *Torture Report* (London: Tavistock, 1986).

13. British Medical Association, *Medicine Betrayed: The Participation of Doctors in Human Rights Abuses* (London: Zed books, 1992).

14. R. J. Lifton, *The Nazi Doctors: The Psychology of Medical Killing* (London: Papermac, 1986). (New edition available from Basic Books [2000] with modified title: *The Nazi Doctors: Medical Killing and the Psychology of Genocide.*)

15. E. Staub, "The Psychology and Culture of Torture and Torturers," in *Psychology and Torture Hemisphere,* ed. P. Suedfeld (New York, 1990).

16. *British Medical Journal:* contributions by T. Marshall, 324 (2002): 235; J. Leaning, 319 (1999): 393–94; J. Immanuel, 310 (1995): 339.

17. World Health Organization, *The ICD-10 Classification of Mental and Behavioral Disorders: Diagnostic Criteria for Research* (Geneva: WHO, 1993).

NOTES TO CHAPTER ELEVEN
TERRORISM: THE CONCEPT
Professor Paul Wilkinson

1. Alex P. Schmid and Albert J. Jongman et al., eds., *Political Terrorism: A New Guide to Actors, Authors, Concepts, Data Bases, Theories and Literature,* 2nd ed. (Amsterdam: North Holland Publishing Co., 1988), 1–32.

2. Robert Friedlander, *Terrorism: Documents of International and Local Control,* vols. 1–4 (Dobbs Ferry: Oceana Publications, Inc., 1970–84), for a valuable collection of these measures.

3. Raymond Aron, *Peace and War* (London: Weidenfeld and Nicholson, 1966), 170.

4. Hannah Arendt, "On Violence," in *Crises of the Republic* (Harmondsworth: Penguin, 1973), 141 ff.

5. Alison Jamieson, *The Modern Mafia,* Conflict Studies no. 224, London Research Institute for the Study of Conflict and Terrorism, 1989.

6. Richard Clutterbuck, *Terrorism and Guerrilla Warfare* (London: Routledge, 1990), 89–114.

7. Walter Laqueur, *Terrorism* (London: Weidenfeld and Nicholson, 1977).

8. See Rohan Gunaratna, *Inside Al Qaeda* (London: CSTPV-Hurst Series on Political Violence, 2002).

9. See Jeffrey Kaplan, "Right Wing Violence in North America," in *Terror from the Extreme Right,* ed. Tore Bjørgo (London: Frank Cass, 1995), 182–220.

10. Department of State, *Patterns of Global Terrorism, 2001* (Washington, D.C.: Government Printing Office, 2002).

11. Max Weber, *Essays in Sociology,* ed. and trans. H. H. Gerth and C. W. Mills (London: Routledge and Kegan Paul, 1947).

12. See, for example, Paul Wilkinson, "Politics, Diplomacy and Peace Processes," *Terrorism and Political Violence* 11, no. 4 (1999): 66–82.

13. For example, Walter Laqueur, *The New Terrorism* (New York: Oxford University Press, 1999).

14. Ibid.

15. See Gunaratna, *Inside Al Qaeda.*

16. Brian Michael Jenkins, *Future Trends in International Terrorism* (Santa Monica, CA: Rand, 1985), 12.

17. Wilkinson, "Politics, Diplomacy and Peace Processes," *Terrorism and Political Violence.*

NOTES TO CHAPTER TWELVE
TERRORISM: THEORY AND REALITY
Larry Hollingworth

1. Alex P. Schmid and Albert J. Longman, et al., *Political Terrorism: A New Guide to Actors, Authors, Concepts, Data Bases, Theories and*

Literature (Amsterdam, Oxford, New York: North Holland Publishing Co., 1988).

2. Noam Chomsky, "International Terrorism: Image and Reality," in *Western State Terrorism,* ed. Alexander George (New York: Routledge, 1991).

3. U.S. State Department, *Annual Review of Global Terrorism 2002.*

4. Associate Professor Igor Primoratz, "State Terrorism and Counterterrorism," Centre for Applied Philosophy and Public Ethics, University of Melbourne.

5. Professor Rakesh Gupta, "Changing Conceptions of Terrorism," *JNU: www.idsa-India.org*

6. Primoratz, "State Terrorism and Counterterrorism."

7. Jacques Ellul, *Violence* (London and Oxford: Mowbrays, 1978).

8. *Frere du Monde* magazine, edition unknown. Source: Jacques Ellul, *Violence,* 56.

9. Chomsky, "International Terrorism: Image and Reality."

10. Extracts from Rudolph Peters, "Jihad," Princeton Series on the Middle East.

11. Edward S. Herman and David Peterson, "The Threat of Global State Terrorism: Retail versus Wholesale Terror," *Z* Magazine (January 2002).

12. William Blum, *Killing Hope* (Monroe, ME: Common Courage Press, 1999).

13. William Blum, *Rogue State* (Monroe, ME: Common Courage Press, 2000).

14. "Lethal Hypocrisy—John Pilger on State Terrorism," John Pilger Pacific Media Watch, 2002.

15. Primoratz, "State Terrorism and Counterterrorism."

16. Irving Kristol, "Where Have All the Gunboats Gone?" *Wall Street Journal,* 13 December 1973.

17. Lev Grinberg, "State Terrorism in Israel?" *Tikkun* (May/June 2002).

18. Chomsky, "International Terrorism: Image and Reality."

19. "Israel, the Occupied West Bank and Gaza Strip, and the Palestinian Authority Territories. Jenin: IDF Military Operations," *Human Rights Watch* 20, no. 10 (May 2002): 10.

20. Grinberg, "State Terrorism in Israel?"

21. "Israel and the Occupied Territories," *Amnesty International* (November 2002).

NOTES TO CHAPTER THIRTEEN
GENDER EXPLOITATION
Ambassador Nancy Ely-Raphel

1. This chapter, "Gender Exploitation as a Cause and Consequence of Human Trafficking and the U.S. Response," is based on the practical work of the State Department's Office to Monitor and Combat Trafficking in Persons and represents observations made by State Department experts regarding discrimination and exploitation of women in the context of human trafficking. Because of the breadth of this topic, the chapter will focus on specific aspects deemed to be illustrative of the issue.

2. Adult victims must be certified, whereas victims under the age of eighteen do not require certification to receive benefits.

3. Nonhumanitarian, nontrade-related assistance is defined in the TVPA as any assistance under the Foreign Assistance Act (FAA) (with stated exceptions) and sales or financing under the Arms Export Control Act (AECA) (with stated exceptions). The TVPA also instructs the president of the United States to instruct the U.S. Executive Directors to international financial institutions to vote against, and to use the Executive Directors' best efforts to deny, any loans or other utilization of the funds of the respective institution (other than for humanitarian, trade-related, or certain types of development assistance) with respect to countries on Tier 3 of the 2003 and later TIP Reports.

4. The act defines "minimum standards for the elimination of trafficking," which are summarized as follows:

1. The government should prohibit trafficking and punish acts of trafficking.
2. The government should prescribe punishment commensurate with that for grave crimes, such as forcible sexual assault, for the knowing commission of trafficking in some of its most reprehensible forms (trafficking for sexual purposes, trafficking involving rape or kidnapping, or trafficking that causes a death).
3. For knowing commission of any act of trafficking, the government should prescribe punishment that is sufficiently stringent to deter, and that adequately reflects the offense's heinous nature.
4. The government should make serious and sustained efforts to eliminate trafficking.

The act also sets out seven criteria that "should be considered" as indicia of the fourth point above, "serious and sustained efforts to eliminate trafficking." Summarized, they are:

1. Whether the government vigorously investigates and prosecutes acts of trafficking within its territory.
2. Whether the government protects victims of trafficking, encourages victims' assistance in investigation and prosecution, provides victims with legal alternatives to their removal to countries where they would face retribution or hardship, and ensures that victims are not inappropriately penalized solely for unlawful acts as a direct result of being trafficked.
3. Whether the government has adopted measures, such as public education, to prevent trafficking.
4. Whether the government cooperates with other governments in investigating and prosecuting trafficking.
5. Whether the government extradites persons charged with trafficking as it does with other serious crimes.
6. Whether the government monitors immigration and emigration patterns for evidence of trafficking, and whether law enforcement agencies respond appropriately to such evidence.
7. Whether the government vigorously investigates and prosecutes public officials who participate in or facilitate trafficking, and takes all appropriate measures against officials who condone trafficking.

The act also states three factors that the department is to consider in determining whether a country is making significant efforts to bring itself into compliance with these minimum standards. Summarized, these considerations are: (1) the extent of trafficking in the country; (2) the extent of governmental noncompliance with the minimum standards, particularly the extent to which government officials have participated in, facilitated, condoned, or are otherwise complicit in trafficking; and (3) what measures are reasonable to bring the government into compliance with the minimum standards in light of the government's resources and capabilities.

5. The Thirteenth Amendment to the U.S. Constitution outlaws slavery, including involuntary servitude (holding another in service through force or threats of force), and provides a basis for criminal statutes penalizing those activities.

NOTES TO CHAPTER FOURTEEN
BALANCING NATIONAL SECURITY AND CIVIL LIBERTIES
Professor John D. Feerick

1. Quoted by Evan Chesler at a talk given to the Scarsdale League of Women Voters, Friday, November 15, 2002.
2. See *Fletcher v. Peck*, 10 US 87 (1810); *McCulloch v. Maryland*, 17

US 316 (1819); *Marbury v. Madison*, 5 US 137 (1803); *Cohens v. Virginia*, 19 US 264 (1821).

3. John Adams, *The Works of John Adams, Second President of the United States* (Little, Brown, and Company, 1865), 23.

4. George Washington, *The Writings of George Washington from the Original Manuscript Sources, 1745–1799* (Washington, D.C.: U.S. Government, 1931).

5. Alexander Hamilton, John Jay, and James Madison, *The Federalist Papers* (A Mentor Book, 1961), xvi.

6. *Minersville Sch. Dist. v. Gobitis*, 310 US 586, 596 (1940).

7. My source for purposes of this chapter is *The Federalist: American State Papers* (Washington, D.C.: The Franklin Library, 1980).

8. These Letters are summarized as notes 5 and 8 in *The Constitution of the United States of America: Analysis and Interpretation*, eds. Johnny H. Killian and George A. Costello (Washington, D.C.: U.S. Gov't. Printing Office, 1996), 955–56.

9. Richard L. Perry, *Sources of Our Liberties* (American Bar Foundation, 1978), xi.

10. *Dartmouth College v. Woodward*, 17 US 518, 581 (1819) (argument of Daniel Webster).

11. *Schenk v. U.S.*, 249 US 47, 52 (1919).

12. See also Chief Justice Rehnquist's book, *All the Laws But One* (New York: Knopf, 1998), 203.

13. See, for example, *Padilla v. Bush*, no. 02 Civ. 4445, 2002 US Dist. Lexis 23086, at *132 (S.D.N.Y. Dec. 4, 2002) (Holding that the president has the authority to direct the military to detain enemy combatants); *Hamdi v. Rumsfeld*, no. 02–7338, 2003 US App. Lexis 198, at *55 (4th Cir Jan. 8, 2003) (Denying *habeas* relief to American citizen captured in a zone of active combat operations abroad and designated an enemy combatant).

14. Madison witnessed several historical abuses of liberty prior to penning *Federalist* no. 63, including the Boston Massacre of 1770, the Boston Tea Party of 1773, and Britain's passage of the Intolerable or Coercive Acts between 1765 and 1774. H. Richard Uviller and William G. Merkel, *The Second Amendment in Context: The Case of the Vanishing Predicate* 76 Chi.-Kent L. Rev. (2000), 403, 463–66.

15. Chief Justice Rehnquist noted in his thoughtful book, "it is both desirable and likely that more careful attention will be paid by the courts to the bases for the government's claims on necessity as a basis

for curtailing civil liberty. The laws will thus not be silent in times of war, but they will speak with a somewhat different voice." Rehnquist, *All the Laws But One, supra* n. 12, at 224–25.

NOTES TO CHAPTER FIFTEEN
DISREGARDING THE GENEVA CONVENTIONS ON THE PROTECTION OF WAR VICTIMS
Michel Veuthey

1. Personal Web sites: *veuthey@fordham.edu; www.idha.ch; www.cihc .org.* All Web sites mentioned in this chapter have been accessed in January 2003.

2. Edward Gibbon, *History of the Decline and Fall of the Roman Empire,* chap. 34, quoted by Geoffrey Best, *Humanity in Warfare: The Modern History of the International Law of Armed Conflicts* (London: Weidenfeld and Nicolson, 1980), 31.

3. Robert Jay Lifton and Eric Markusen, *The Genocidal Mentality: Nazi Holocaust and Nuclear Threat* (New York: Basic Books, 1990), 279.

The full final paragraph of this book reads as follows: "No one can claim knowledge of a single, correct path. Rather, there must be endless combinations of reflection and action and, above all, the kind of larger collective adaptation we have been discussing. At the same time, we must remain aware of persisting genocidal arrangements and expressions of genocidal mentality. We cannot afford to 'stop thinking.' Nor can we wait for a new Gandhi or Saint Joan to deliver us. Rather, each of us must join in a vast project—political, ethical, psychological—on behalf of perpetuating and nurturing our humanity. We are then 'people getting up from their knees' to resist nuclear oppression. We clear away the 'thick glass' that has blurred our moral and political vision. We become healers, not killers, of our species."

4. General George C. Marshall, speaking to students at Harvard. Quote from the brochure of the George C. Marshall European Center for Security Studies, Garmisch-Partenkirchen, Bayern, Germany, available at: *http://www.marshallcenter.org/table_of_contents.htm.*

5. Viktor E. Frankl, *Man's Search for Meaning* (New York: Washington Square Press, 1985), 179. (Conclusion of the *Postscript 1984: The Case for a Tragic Optimism.*)

6. Jean-Jacques Rousseau, *Le Contrat Social,* translated and quoted in G. I. A. D. Draper, *The Red Cross Conventions* (London: Stevens & Sons Ltd., 1958), 1–2.

7. See Johan Huizinga, *Homo Ludens: A Study of the Play Element in Culture* (Boston: Beacon Press, 1955), esp. chap. 5, "Play and War," 89–104.

8. See J. F. C. Fuller, *The Conduct of War, 1789–1961: A Study of the Impact of the French, Industrial, and Russian Revolutionary War and Its Conduct* (London: Eyre & Spottiswoode, 1961), 108. "When Sherman set out on his famous march through Georgia, he made this new concept of war his guiding principle, and waged war against the people of the South as fully as against its armed forces."

9. See *The United States Strategic Bombing Survey: Overall Report (European War)* and *The United States Strategic Bombing Survey: Summary Report (Pacific War),* quoted by Fuller, *The Conduct of War, 1789–1961,* 282–303.

10. Zbigniew Brzezinski, "The Century of Megadeath," chap. 1 in *Out of Control: Global Turmoil on the Eve of the Twenty-First Century* (New York: Charles Scribner's Sons, 1996).

11. The most recent definition of "Genocide" can be found in Article 6 of the Rome Statute of the International Criminal Court: "For the purpose of this Statute, 'genocide' means any of the following acts committed with intent to destroy, in whole or in part, a national, ethnical, racial, or religious group, as such:

(a) Killing members of the group
(b) Causing serious bodily or mental harm to members of the group
(c) Deliberately inflicting on the group conditions of life calculated to bring about its physical destruction in whole or in part
(d) Imposing measures intended to prevent births within the group
(e) Forcibly transferring children of the group to another group."

12. See Antonio Cassese, *International Law* (Oxford: Oxford University Press, 2001), especially Part 3: "Contemporary Issues in International Law," with chap. 15 ("Legal Restraints on Violence in Armed Conflict"), chap. 16 ("Protection of Human Rights"), and chap. 17 ("Protection of the Environment"). See also Dieter Fleck, ed., *The Handbook of Humanitarian Law in Armed Conflicts* (Oxford: Oxford University Press, 1995), especially pages xix–xxi, the list of international instruments, from the Declaration respecting Maritime Law (Paris, April 16, 1856) and the Convention for the Amelioration of the Condition of the Wounded in Armies in the Field (Geneva, August 22, 1864) to the International Convention

Against the Recruitment, Use, Financing, and Training of Mercenaries (December 4, 1989). From 1989 onwards, see Liesbeth Zegveld, *The Accountability of Armed Opposition Groups in International Law* (Cambridge: Cambridge University Press, 2002), xi–xii; with, among others: the 1989 UN Convention on the Rights of the Child; the 1993 Statute of the International Tribunal for the Prosecution of Persons Responsible for Serious Violations of International Humanitarian Law Committed in the Territory of the Former Yugoslavia Since 1991; the 1994 Statute of the International Tribunal for the Prosecution of Persons Responsible for Genocide and Other Serious Violations of International Humanitarian Law Committed in the Territory of Rwanda and Rwandans Citizens Responsible for Genocide and Other Such Violations Committed in the Territory of Neighboring States Between January 1, 1994, and December 32, 1994; the 1997 Ottawa Convention on the Prohibition of the Use, Stockpiling, Production, and Transfer of Antipersonnel Mines and on their Destruction; the 1998 Rome Statute of the International Criminal Court; and the 1999 Second Protocol to The Hague Convention of 1954 for the Protection of Cultural Property in the Event of Armed Conflict.

13. See Xavier Emmanuelli, Co-founder of *Médecins sans frontières* (MSF—Doctors Without Borders), at a conference in Saint-Maurice, Switzerland, November 23, 2002, speaking of a time of anomia, without marks (*époque d'anomie, sans repères . . .*).

14. Marco Sassoli, "Nebenopfer der Angriffe vom 11. September? Die Gefangenen in Guatanamo und die Genfer Abkommen," *Neue Zürcher Zeitung,* Zurich, January 23, 2002. Hans-Peter Gasser, "Total War Against Terrorism? The Geneva Conventions Also Apply to the Anti-Terror Effort," *NZZ Online English Window,* August 22, 2002 (first published in German on August19). Pierre Hazan, "La guerre contre le terrorisme nécessite-t-elle de modifier les Conventions de Genève?" *Le Temps,* Geneva, Octobre 2, 2002.

15. White House Counsel Alberto R. Gonzales, quoted by Stuart Taylor Jr., "We Don't Need to Be Scofflaws to Attack Terror. Disregarding the Geneva Conventions Will Undermine the Ability of the United States to Wage War, *The Atlantic Monthly* (February 2, 2002), available online: *http://www.theatlantic.com/politics/nj/taylor2002–02–05.htm* (accessed on January 7, 2003).

16. See the cover page story, "Is Torture Ever Justified? Even Faced with Monstrous Terrorism, Democracies Break the Taboo at their Peril," *The Economist* (London) (January 11–17, 2003): 11; also "Ends, Means, and Barbarity. Torture Has Been Outlawed in All Circumstances Everywhere. But Global Terrorism May Be Leading America to Bend the Rules," 20–22. See also Holly Burkhalter, "No to Torture," *The Washington Post,* January 5,

2003, B7. The author quotes reports that U.S. intelligence operatives and military police are torturing al Qaeda and Taliban suspects, and that U.S. Special Forces in Afghanistan turned over surrendered combatants to their local allies, who reportedly murdered hundreds of the prisoners in captivity.

17. See Ralph Peters, "Civilian Casualties: No Apology Needed," *Wall Street Journal,* July 24, 2002, available online at: *http://www.likud.nl/press 232.html;* Nicole Gaouete, "Attention Builds Over a Slain Civilian," *The Christian Science Monitor,* 11 January 2003, especially this paragraph, entitled "The Fog of War:"

> "Palestinian civilian deaths are a problem for Israel. This is war, many Israelis say. It's often hard for soldiers to tell if someone is civilian or terrorist. Palestinian militants show little regard for their own civilians when they attack Israeli troops from residential areas, exposing innocents to return fire. Some say this may even be part of the militants' goal, since it draws international condemnation for every Palestinian woman or child it kills. But Israel has an ethical obligation to take civilian deaths seriously," says Col. Daniel Reisner, head of the IDF's international law department. "A country's moral fiber is revealed in how it handles itself in times of adversity."

18. Geneva Convention 1, 75 U.N.T.S. 31.

19. Geneva Convention 2, 75 U.N.T.S. 85.

20. Geneva Convention 3, 75 U.N.T.S. 135.

21. Geneva Convention 4, 75 U.N.T.S. 2.

22. Additional Protocol 1, 1125 U.N.T.S. 3.

23. Additional Protocol 2, 1125 U.N.T.S. 609.

24. Protocol for the Prohibition of the Use of Asphyxiating, Poisonous or Other Gases, and of Bacteriological Methods of Warfare, Geneva, June 17, 1925.

25. Declaration Renouncing the Use, in Time of War, of Certain Projectiles, Saint Petersburg, November 29–December 11, 1868.

26. Convention (4) Respecting the Laws and Customs of War on Land and Its Annex: Regulations Concerning the Laws and Customs of War on Land, The Hague, October 18, 1907.

27. See Jean Pictet, *The Principles of Humanitarian Law* (Geneva: ICRC, 1966).

28. This was the term used by the Diplomatic Conference on the Reaffirmation and Development of International Humanitarian Law Applicable in Armed Conflicts (CDDH), which met in Geneva from

1974 to 1977 to adopt the two Additional Protocols to the 1949 Conventions.

29. "Laws of War" is the expression most widely used today in military circles. Cf. Frederic de Mulinen, *Handbook on the Law of War for Armed Forces* (Geneva: ICRC, 1987); or Thomas B. Baines, "The Laws of War and the Rules of Peacekeeping," presented to the Joint Services Conference on Professional Ethics at the National Defense University, Washington, D.C., January 30–31, 1997, available at: *http://www.usafa.af.mil/jscope/JSCOPE97/Baines97.htm* (accessed on January 7, 2003).

30. "Law of Geneva" is sometimes used with the intention of stressing aspects relating to the protection of victims of war, as opposed to the regulation of conduct with regard to methods and means of destruction between combatants, designated by the expression "Law of The Hague."

31. G. I. A. D. Draper, *The Red Cross Conventions* (London: Stevens & Sons Ltd., 1958).

32. The 1977 Protocols have, to some extent, merged the "Law of Geneva" and the "Law of The Hague"; this was merely the culmination of a trend that began when the rules of The Hague relating to the treatment of prisoners of war were incorporated and expanded upon in the Second Geneva Convention of 1929, and later in the Third Convention of 1949. Similarly, the Fourth Convention of 1949 incorporated most of The Hague Regulations of 1907 on military occupation. All this is of considerable significance: apart from the historical memory, it is the customary nature of the rules of The Hague (and hence of the provisions incorporated in 1949 and 1977) that should be emphasized.

33. This was the term used by the United Nations for almost ten years following the International Conference on Human Rights in Teheran (April 22–May 13, 1968). Numerous resolutions of the United Nations General Assembly, advocating further codification and describing how this was to be done, were adopted under the heading of "Respect for Human Rights in Armed Conflicts," as well as reports by the Secretary-General of the United Nations (A/7720 in 1969, A/8052 in 1970, A/8370 in 1971, A/8781 in 1972, A/9123 in 1973, A/9669 in 1974, A/10195 in 1975).

34. One hundred ninety states have ratified the four 1949 Geneva Conventions. One hundred sixty states have ratified Additional Protocol 1; 153, Protocol 2.

35. See Dietrich Schindler, "Significance of the Geneva Conven-

tions for the Contemporary World," Twenty-fourth Round Table on Current Problems of International Humanitarian Law, International Institute of Humanitarian Law, San Remo, September 1999. Nagard, ed., *Current Problems of International Humanitarian Law* (Milano: Dragan European Foundation, 2001), 133–41. This text was published in the *International Review of the Red Cross* 836: 715–29, and is available online at: *http://www.icrc.org/Web/eng/siteeng0.nsf/iwpList99/AE4906265A2A7 F0AC1256B66005 DCA3D.*

36. On the development of modern humanitarian law, see:

Geoffrey Best, *Humanity in Warfare: The Modern History of the International Law of Armed Conflicts* (London: Weidenfeld and Nicolson, 1980).

Eric David, *Principes de droit des conflits armés. Troisième édition* (Bruxelles: Bruylant, 2002), 38–51.

Leslie C. Green, *Essays on the Modern Law of War,* 2nd ed. (Ardsley: Transnational Publishers, 1999), 6–40; 41–74.

Frits Kalshoven and Liesbeth Zegveld, *Constraints on the Waging of War: An Introduction to International Humanitarian Law* (Geneva: ICRC, 2001).

Marco Sassoli and Antoine Bouvier, *How Does Law Protect in War? Cases, Documents and Teaching Materials on Contemporary Practice in International Humanitarian Law* (Geneva: ICRC, 1999), 99–104.

37. See among others:

Geoffrey Best, *War and Law Since 1945* (Oxford: Oxford University Press, 1994).

P. Bordwell, *The Law of War Between Belligerents: A History and Commentary* (Chicago: Callaghan, 1908).

Richard A. Falk, *Law, Morality and War in the Contemporary World* (New York: Praeger, 1963).

Wilhem G. Grewe, *The Epochs of International Law,* trans. and rev. Michael Byers (Berlin/New York: Walter de Gruyter, 2000), especially chap. 7 ("Law Enforcement") of Part 1 ("The Structure of the Law of the Nations during the Middle Ages"), Part 2 (*"Ius inter gentes*—The Law of Nations in the Spanish Age"), Part 3 (*"Droit Public de l'Europe*—The International Legal Order during the French Age, 1648–1815"), Part 4 ("International Law—The International Legal Order of the British Age, 1815–1919"), Part 5 ("International Law and the League of Nations—The International Legal Order of the Inter-War Period, 1919–1944"), Part 6 ("United Nations—International Law in the Age of American-Soviet Rivalry and the Rise of the Third World, 1945–1989"). See also chap. 5 ("The Formation of Legal Rules: The Role of the United Nations in the Creation of Law"), III (*"Bellum iustum* or *bellum legale?"*), IV

("American Conceptions of the 'Just and Limited War'"), V ("'Wars of Liberation' and Other Interpretations of the Just War Conflicting with the United Nations Charter"), and Part 7 ("Epilogue"), IX ("Adjudication: International Tribunals for War Crimes"), X ("Law Enforcement: War, Civil War, Internal Anarchy").

38. Christopher Greenwood, *The Handbook of Humanitarian Law in Armed Conflicts,* ed. Dieter Fleck (Oxford: Oxford University Press, 1995), 12–23.

39. On Francisco de Vitoria, see:

Prof. Alexander Broadie, *The Oxford Companion to Philosophy,* available online: *http://www.xrefer.com/entry/553829* (accessed January 7, 2003).

The bilingual Latin-German edition of: Francisco de Vitoria, "Relectiones," in U. Horst, H. G. Justenhoven, and J. Stüben eds., *Vorlesungen,* 2 vols. (Stuttgart, Berlin, Köln: W. Kohlhammer, 1995–1997).

"Vitoria, Francisco de," *Encyclopædia Britannica: http://www.britannica.com/eb/article?eu= 77565* (accessed January 7, 2003).

40. On Bartholomew (or Bartolomé) de Las Casas, see *A Short Account of the Destruction of the Indies,* ed. and trans. Nigel Griffin, with an introduction by Anthony Pagden (London: Penguin, 1992).

41. See Henry Dunant, *A Memory of Solferino* (Geneva: ICRC, 1986).

42. See the report by the ICRC on the consultations of private experts that led to the adoption of the 1977 Additional Protocols to the 1949 Geneva Conventions: ICRC, *Reaffirmation and Development of the Laws and Customs Applicable in Armed Conflicts,* Report submitted by the International Committee of the Red Cross to the Twenty-first International Conference of the Red Cross (Istanbul, September 1969), Geneva, May 1969.

43. Conference of Red Cross Experts on the Reaffirmation and Development of International Humanitarian Law Applicable in Armed Conflicts, The Hague, March 1–6, 1971. Report on the Works of the Conference, Geneva, April 1971.

44. On the 1971 and 1972 sessions of the Conference, in the following reports:

—Conference of Government Experts on the Reaffirmation and Development of International Humanitarian Law Applicable in Armed Conflicts, Geneva, May 24–June 12, 1971. Report on the Work of the Conference, ICRC, Geneva, August 1971.

—Conference of Government Experts on the Reaffirmation and Development of International Humanitarian Law Applicable in Armed Conflicts, Second Session, Geneva, May 3–June 3, 1972. Report on the Work of the Conference, vols. 1 and 2 (Annexes), ICRC, Geneva, July 1972.

45. The last Diplomatic Conference adopted both Additional Protocols. It met in four sessions in Geneva from 1974 to 1977. See the Official Records of the Diplomatic Conference on the Reaffirmation and Development of International Humanitarian Law Applicable in Armed Conflicts, Bern, Geneva, 1974–1977.

46. See Hans-Peter Gasser, "Steps Taken to Encourage States to Accept the 1977 Protocols," *IRRC* 258 (May 1987).

47. See the ICRC Advisory Service Web site: *http://www.icrc.org/web/eng/ siteeng0.nsf/iwpList2/Humanitarian_law:National_implementation* (accessed January 7, 2003); and its database on IHL National Implementation: Laws, Regulations and Case Law; and the Online National Implementation Law Biennal Report (2000–2001). See also Anna Segall, *Punishing Violations of International Humanitarian Law at the National Level: A Guide for Common Law States* (Geneva: ICRC Advisory Service on International Humanitarian Law, 2001).

48. See Pierre Boissier, *History of the International Committee of the Red Cross: From Solferino to Tsushima* (Geneva: ICRC, 1985); and André Durand, *History of the International Committee of the Red Cross: From Sarajevo to Hiroshima* (Geneva: ICRC, 1984). Jean-Daniel Tauxe, "Faire mieux accepter le Comité international de la Croix-Rouge sur le terrain," *Revue internationale de la Croix-Rouge* 833 (31 mars 1999): 55–61; English Summary ("Founding and Early Years of the International Committee of the Red Cross"), as well as the ICRC Web site at: *http://www.icrc.org/Web/Eng/siteeng0.nsf/htmlall/57 JNVM?OpenDocument* (accessed January 7, 2003).

49. See Georges Abi-Saab, "The Specificities of Humanitarian Law," in *Studies and Essays on International Humanitarian Law and Red Cross Principles in Honour of Jean Pictet,* ed. Christophe Swinarski (Geneva: ICRC, 1984), 265–80.

50. Dunant, *A Memory of Solferino.*

51. Convention for the Amelioration of the Condition of the Wounded in Armies in the Field, Geneva, August 22, 1864 (now replaced by the First Geneva Convention of 1949).

52. See a brief account of this battle by Captain Vladimir Semenoff ("The Battle of Tsushima") on the *War Times Journal* Web site: *http://www .wtj.com/archives/semenoff1.htm* (accessed January 7, 2003); as well as the description of casualties on both sides on this Russian Web site: *http://www .neva.ru/EXPO96/book/chap10-4.html* (Regional University and Science Network—accessed January 7, 2003).

53. Hague Convention (X) for the Adaptation to Naval War of the Principles of the Geneva Convention (now replaced by the Second Geneva Convention of 1949).

54. Geneva Convention for the Amelioration of the Condition of

Wounded, Sick, and Shipwrecked Members of Armed Forces at Sea, 75 U.N.T.S. 85, entered into force October 21, 1950. Available online at: *http://www1.umn.edu/humanrts/instree/y2gcacws.htm*. See Waldemar A. Solf, "Development of the Protection of the Wounded, Sick and Shipwrecked under the Protocols Additional to the 1949 Geneva Conventions," in *Studies and Essays in International Humanitarian Law and Red Cross Principles in Honour of Jean Pictet,* ed. Christophe Swinarski (Geneva, The Hague: ICRC, Nijhoff, 1984), 237–48.

55. Convention for the Amelioration of the Condition of the Wounded and Sick in Armies in the Field, Geneva, July 27, 1929 (now replaced by the First Geneva Convention of 1949); and the Convention Concerning the Treatment of Prisoners of War, Geneva, July 27, 1929 (now replaced by the Third Geneva Convention of 1949).

56. Geneva Convention for the Amelioration of the Condition of the Wounded and Sick in Armed Forces in the Field, August 12, 1949; Geneva Convention for the Amelioration of the Condition of the Wounded, Sick and Shipwrecked Members of the Armed Forces at Sea, August 12, 1949; Geneva Convention Relative to the Treatment of Prisoners of War, August 12, 1949; Geneva Convention Relative to the Protection of Civilian Persons in Time of War, August 12, 1949.

57. Protocol Additional to the Geneva Conventions of August 12, 1949, and relating to the Protection of Victims of International Armed Conflicts (Protocol 1); Protocol Additional to the Geneva Conventions of August 12, 1949, and relating to the Protection of Victims of Non-International Armed Conflicts (Protocol 2).

58. See Michael Bothe, Karl Josef Partsch, Waldemar A. Solf, *New Rules for Victims of Armed Conflicts: Commentary on the Two 1977 Protocols Additional to the Geneva Conventions of 1949* (The Hague/Boston/London: Martinus Nijhoff Publishers, 1982).

59. On the ICRC's role in the origin and drafting of the Ottawa Convention, see Louis Maresca and Stuart Maslen, eds., *The Banning of Antipersonnel Landmines: The Legal Contribution of the International Committee of the Red Cross, 1955–1999* (Cambridge: Cambridge University Press, 2001).

60. On the role of NGOs and civil society on behalf of the Ottawa Convention, see Mary A. Ferrer, "Affirming our Common Humanity: Regulating Landmines to Protect Civilians and Children in the Developing World," *Hastings International Law and Comparative Law Review* 20, no. 1 (fall 1996): 135–82. See also Kenneth Anderson, "The Ottawa Convention Banning Landmines: The Role of International Nongovernmental Organizations and the Idea of International Civil Society," *EJIL* 11, no. 1 (2000). The full text of the article is available online: *http://www.ejil.org/journal/Vol11/No1/art8.html* (accessed January 7, 2003).

61. See William J. Fenrick, "The Development of the Law of Armed Conflict through the Jurisprudence of the International Criminal Tribunal for the Former Yugoslavia," *JACL* 3 (1998): 202–4.

62. The International Tribunal for the Prosecution of Persons Responsible for Serious Violations of International Humanitarian Law Committed in the Territory of the Former Yugoslavia since 1991 was established by the Security Council on May 25, 1993.

63. The International Criminal Tribunal for the Prosecution of Persons Responsible for Genocide and Other Serious Violations of International Humanitarian Law Committed in the Territory of Rwanda and Rwandan Citizens Responsible for Genocide and Other Such Violations Committed in the Territory of Neighboring States between January 1 and December 31, 1994, was established by the Security Council on November 8, 1994.

64. See the Tadic Case: International Criminal Tribunal for the former Yugoslavia, *Prosecutor v. Dusko Tadic a/k/a "Dule"*: Decision on the defense motion for interlocutory appeal on jurisdiction. Decision of October 2, 1995, case no. IT-94–1-AR72. On this case, two articles in the *International Review of the Red Cross:* John Dugard, "Bridging the Gap Between Human Rights and Humanitarian Law: The Punishment of Offenders," no. 324 (September 1998): 445–53; and Thomas Graditzky, "International Criminal Responsibility for Violations of International Humanitarian Law Committed in Non-International Armed Conflicts," no. 322 (March 1998): 29–56.

65. On international humanitarian law and *jus cogens,* see:

Antonio Cassese, "The Introduction of *Jus Cogens* in the 1960s," in *International Law* (Oxford: Oxford University Press, 2001), 138–48, esp. p. 141.

Georges Perrin, "La nécessité et les dangers du jus cogens" in *Etudes et essais sur le droit international humanitaire et sur les principes de la Croix-Rouge en l'honneur de Jean Pictet,* ed. Christophe Swinarski (Geneva: ICRC, 1984), 751–59.

Steven R. Ratner and Jason S. Abrams, *Accountability for Human Rights Atrocities in International Law: Beyond the Nuremberg Legacy* (Oxford: Oxford University Press, 2001), 20, 24, 41 (Genocide), 112 (Slavery), 117, and 296 (Torture).

66. See ICRC, *Commentary on the Additional Protocols of 8 June 1977 to the Geneva Conventions of August 12, 1949* (Geneva, 1987), 381, para. 1364.

67. See Fausto Pocar, "Protocol 1 Additional to the 1949 Geneva Conventions and Customary International Law," *Israeli Yearbook on Human Rights* 31 (2001): 146–59. See also Theodor Meron, *Human Rights and Humanitarian Norms as Customary Law* (Oxford: Clarendon Press/Oxford University Press, 1989); and Marco Sassoli and Antoine Bouvier, *How Does Law*

Protect in War? Cases, Documents and Teaching Materials on Contemporary Practice in International Humanitarian Law (Geneva: ICRC, 1999), 108–9 ("Customary Law").

68. Schindler, "Significance of the Geneva Conventions for the Contemporary World."

69. United Nations, International Tribunal for the Prosecution of Persons Responsible for Serious Violations of International Humanitarian Law Committed in the Territory of the Former Yugoslavia since 1991, case no. IT-94-1-AR72, October 2, 1995, *Prosecutor v. Dusko Tadic a/k/a "Dule,"* para. 96–127. Quoted by Sassoli and Bouvier, *How Does Law Protect in War?* 1180–91 ("Customary Rules of International Humanitarian Law Governing Internal Armed Conflicts").

70. International Court of Justice (ICJ) Reports 1996, 256–59, para. 75–84.

71. Cassese, *International Law,* 330, 344–46.

72. Christopher Greenwood, *The Handbook of Humanitarian Law in Armed Conflicts,* ed. Dieter Fleck (Oxford: Oxford University Press, 1995), 24, para. 125: "It seems likely that most, if not all, of the provisions of the Conventions would now be regarded as declaratory of customary international law."

73. Theodor Meron, *Human Rights and Humanitarian Norms as Customary International Law* (Oxford: Oxford University Press, 1989).

74. ICJ Reports 1986, at 218.

75. Ibid., para. 98 ff.

76. Ibid., para. 117 ff. See Paola Gaeta, "The Armed Conflict in Chechnya Before the Russian Constitutional Court, *EIJL* 7, no. 4, available online at: *http://www.ejil.org/journal/Vol7/No4/art7.html*

77. Article 60 ("Termination or suspension of the operation of a treaty as a consequence of a breach"):

"1. A material breach of a bilateral treaty by one of the parties entitles the other to invoke the breach as a ground for terminating the treaty or suspending its operation in whole or in part. . . ."

"5. Paragraphs 1 to 3 do not apply to provisions relating to the protection of the human person contained in treaties of a humanitarian character, in particular to provisions prohibiting any form of reprisals against persons protected by such treaties."

78. International Court of Justice, *Case Concerning the Military and Paramilitary Activities in and against Nicaragua (Nicaragua v. United States of America),* Judgement of June 27, 1986 (Merits), vol. 114, para. 218. On this case, see Rosemary Abi-Saab, "The 'General Principles' of Humanitarian

Law According to the International Court of Justice," *International Review of the Red Cross* (July/August 1987): 367–75.

79. Jean S. Pictet, ed., *The Geneva Conventions of 12 August 1949. Commentary. IV. Geneva Convention Relative to the Protection of Civilian Persons in Time of War* (Geneva: International Committee of the Red Cross, 1958), 15–17.

80. International Court of Justice, *Case Concerning the Military and Paramilitary Activities in and against Nicaragua (Nicaragua v. United States of America)*, Judgement of June 27, 1986 (Merits), vol. 114, para. 220. See Antonio Cassese, "Collective Responsibility," *International Law*, 6–8, 182 ss.; Antonio Cassese, "State Responsibility," *International Law*, especially pp. 207–10 and 419.

81. See I. William Zartman, ed., *Collapsed States: The Disintegration and Restoration of Legitimate Authority* (Boulder: Lynne Rienner, 1995), 301; and "Armed Conflicts Linked to the Disintegration of State Structures," the preparatory document drafted by the ICRC for the first periodical meeting on international humanitarian law, Geneva, January 19–23, 1998, mentioning Resolution 814, para. 13 (Somalia), Res. 788, para. 5 (Liberia).

82. See Robert Fox, "On the Age of Postmodern War. Beyond Clausewitz: The Long and Ragged Conflicts of the Coming Millennium," *The Times Literary Supplement* (London), 15 May 1998.

83. As Martin Van Crefeld puts it in *The Transformation of War* (New York: Free Press, 1991): "Once the legal monopoly of armed force, long claimed by the State, is wrestled out of its hands, existing distinctions between war and crime will break down."

84. ICRC Commentary 3, Art. 1, available online at: *http://www.icrc.org/ihl.nsf/b466ed681ddfcfd241256739003e6368/49cfe5505d5912d1c 12563cd004 24cdd?OpenDocument* (accessed January 7, 2003).

85. See Umesh Palwankar, "Measures Available to States for Fulfilling Their Obligation to Ensure Respect for International Humanitarian Law," *IRRC*, no. 298 (1994): 9–25. See also Marco Sassoli, "State Responsibility for Violations of International Humanitarian Law," *IRRC*, no. 846 (2002): 401–34. Available online: *http://www.icrc.org/Web/eng/siteeng0.nsf/iwpList 113/35289C31F0187A41C1256B6600591427*

86. On Art. 1, para. 1 of Additional Protocol 1, see Yves Sandoz, Christophe Swinarski, and Bruno Zimmermann, eds., *Commentary on the Additional Protocols of 8 June 1977 to the Geneva Conventions of 12 August 1949* (Geneva: International Committee of the Red Cross, 1987), 34–38.

87. See Birgit Kessler, "The Duty to 'Ensure Respect' Under Common Article 1 of the Geneva Conventions: Its Implications on International and Non-International Armed Conflicts," *German Yearbook of International Law* 44 (2001): 498–516.

88. Laurence Boisson de Chazournes and Luigi Condorelli, "Common Article 1 of the Geneva Conventions Revisited: Protecting Collective Interests," *IRRC* 82, no. 837 (March 2000): 67–87.

89. See Steven R. Ratner and Jason S. Abrams, *Accountability for Human Rights Atrocities in International Law: Beyond the Nuremberg Legacy* (Oxford: OUP, 2001); especially the Conclusions, 331 ss., 333 (criminality of offenses during internal conflicts); 335 ("[. . .] violations of widely ratified treaties or of customary international law are more likely than other offenses to form the subject-matter jurisdiction of any future *ad hoc* international criminal tribunals"). See also Antonio Cassese, *International Law*, 207 (special regime for the prosecution of grave breaches of the Geneva Conventions); 246–48 ("War Crimes"); 261 (principle of *aut prosequi et judicare, aut dedere*); 262–64 ("Are States Internationally Empowered or Even Obliged to Prosecute International Crimes?"), with the judgement of November 6, 1995, in *Reporters sans frontières v. Mille Collines,* where the Paris Court of Appeal held that it lacked jurisdiction over genocide, grave breaches of the four 1949 Geneva Conventions, crimes against humanity, and torture allegedly committed abroad by foreigners against foreigners. Cassese ends with this comment: "It must be added that, strikingly, for about forty years the repressive system instituted by the 1949 Geneva Conventions with regard to grave breaches has not been put into practice. Only after the establishment of the ICTY and the ICTR have States commenced to resort to it." (265)

90. Art. 49, para. 1, of the First Convention; Art. 50, para. 1, of the Second Convention; Art. 129, para. 1, of the Third Convention; Art. 146, para. 1, of the Fourth Convention.

91. Art. 49, para. 2, of the First Convention; Art. 50, para. 2, of the Second Convention; Art. 129, para. 2, of the Third Convention; Art. 146, para. 2, of the Fourth Convention.

92. See Dr. Marcel Junod, *Warrior Without Weapons,* trans. Edward Fitzgerald from the French *Le Troisième Combattant* (London: Jonathan Cape and New York: Macmillan, 1951).

93. See Jacques de Reynier, *1948 à Jérusalem* (Geneva: Georg, 2002). First and second editions published by Neuchâtel: Editions de la Baconnière, 1950 and 1969. On this conflict and other special agreements, see also Michel Veuthey, *Guérilla et droit humanitaire,* 2nd ed. (Geneva: ICRC, 1983), 50–51.

94. See K. Boals, "The Internal War in Yemen," in *The International Law of Civil War,* ed. Richard A. Falk (Baltimore: Johns Hopkins Press, 1971).

95. ICRC, *Rapport d'activité 1967,* 37; and John Stremlau, *The International Politics of the Nigerian Civil War* (Princeton, NJ: Princeton University Press, 1977).

96. See Jean-François Berger, *The Humanitarian Diplomacy of the ICRC and the Conflict in Croatia (1991–1992)* (Geneva: ICRC, 1995).

97. See Physicians for Human Rights, *No Mercy in Mogadishu: The Human Cost of the Conflict and the Struggle for Relief* (Boston, 1992); and the University of Pennsylvania African Studies Center: *http://www.sas.upenn .edu/African_Studies/Newsletters/HAB395_SOM.html.*

98. See the UN and the Dutch official reports on Srebrenica:

"The Fall of Srebrenica," A/54/549, November 15, 1999, available: *http:// www.hri.ca/fortherecord1999/documentation/genassembly/a-54–549.htm* (accessed January 7, 2003).

Netherlands Institute for War Documentation (NIOD), "Srebenica, Een 'veilig' gebied. Reconstructie, achtergronden en analyses van de val van een Safe Area." ("Srebrenica, A 'Safe' Area. Reconstruction, Background, Consequences and Analyses of the Fall of a Safe Area.") Summary and order form of the Dutch original and English translation available at: *http://www.srebrenica.nl/* (accessed January 7, 2003).

99. See Hans-Peter Gasser, "Prohibition of Terrorist Acts in International Humanitarian Law," *International Review of the Red Cross,* no. 253 (July/August 1986): 1986; and from the same author, "Acts of Terror, 'Terrorism,' and International Humanitarian Law," *International Review of the Red Cross* 84, no. 847 (September 2002): 547–58.

100. See the *International Review of the Red Cross,* no. 313 (August 31, 1996): 500–502.

101. ICRC, *Reaffirmation and Development of the Laws and Customs Applicable in Armed Conflicts,* report submitted by the International Committee of the Red Cross to the Twenty-first International Conference of the Red Cross, Geneva, May 1969 (Istanbul, September 1969), 51.

102. Dietrich Schindler and Jiri Toman, *The Laws of Armed Conflicts* (The Hague: Nijhoff, 1988), 263–64.

103. *International Review of the Red Cross,* no. 316 (February 28, 1997): 4–5. See also Henri Meyrowitz, "La stratégie nucléaire et le Protocole 1 additionnel aux Conventions de Genève de 1949," *Revue générale de droit international public,* no. 4 (1979): 905–61.

104. Such were the divergences between NATO members toward the end of the air bombings during the Kosovo campaign.

105. See Lt. Col. Dave Grossman, *On Killing: The Psychological Cost of Learning to Kill in War and Society* (Boston: Little, Brown, 1995); Chris Hedge, "Ex-Soldier, Now a Bishop, Deals With Blood on His Hands," *The New York Times,* 20 December 2002.

106. On the protection of refugees and internally displaced persons in international humanitarian law, see:

Roberta Cohen and Francis M. Deng, *Masses in Flight: The Global Crisis in International Displacement* (Washington, D.C.: Brookings Institution Press, 1998); especially the third chapter, "Legal Framework."
Special issue: "Fiftieth Anniversary of the 1951 Refugee Convention: The Protection of Refugees in Armed Conflict," *International Review of the Red Cross*, no. 843 (2001).

107. See the Special ICRC Report, *Unknown Fate, Untold Grief: ICRC Activities on Behalf of Missing Persons and Their Families from the Conflicts in Croatia, Bosnia-Herzegovina and Federal Republic of Yugoslavia/Kosovo*, Geneva, August 2002, available in PDF format on the ICRC Web site: *www.icrc.org*

108. On MIAs, see among others: *http://www.aiipowmia.com* (Advocacy and Intelligence Index for POWs-MIAs Archives); *http://www.mia.org.il/* (The International Coalition for Missing Israeli Soldiers).

109. See Benjamin S. Lambeth, *NATO's Air War for Kosovo: A Strategic and Operational Assessment* (Santa Monica, CA: Rand, 2001); and especially page 136 ("Stray Weapons and the Loss of Innocents"): "Pressures to avoid civilian casualties and unintended damage to nonmilitary structures were greater in Allied Force than in any previous campaign involving U.S. forces."

110. See Uri Avnery, "A Queue of Bombers," available online on Media Monitors Network: *http://www.mediamonitors.net/uri63.html.* Here are a few lines of it:

When a whole people is seething with rage, it becomes a dangerous enemy, because the rage does not obey orders. When it exists in the hearts of millions of people, it cannot be cut off by pushing a button.

When this rage overflows, it creates suicide bombers—human bombs fueled by the power of anger, against whom there is no defense. A person who has given up on life, who does not look for escape routes, is free to do whatever his disturbed mind dictates [. . .] Pronouncements like, "We have intercepted attacks," "We have taught them a lesson," "We have destroyed the infrastructure of terrorism," show an infantile lack of understanding of what they are doing. Far from "destroying the infrastructure of terrorism," they have built a hothouse for rearing suicide-bombers. A person whose beloved brother has been killed, whose house has been destroyed in an orgy of vandalism, who has been mortally humiliated before the eyes of his children, goes to the market, buys a rifle for forty thousand shekels (some sell their cars for this), and sets out to seek revenge. "Give me a hatred gray like a sack," wrote our poet, Nathan Alterman, seething with rage against the Germans. Hatred gray like a sack is now everywhere. Bands of armed men now roam all the towns and villages of the West Bank and the Gaza Strip, with or without black masks (available for ten shekels in the markets). These bands do not belong to any organization. Members of Fatah, Hamas, and the Jihad team up to plan attacks, not giving a damn for the established institutions. [. . .] American politicians, like Israeli officers, do not understand what they are doing. When an overbearing vice-president dictates humiliating terms for a meeting with Arafat, he pours oil on the flames. A person who lacks empathy for the suffering of the occupied people, who does not understand its condition, would be well advised to shut up. Because every such humiliation kills dozens of Israelis. After all, the suicide-bombers are standing in line.

111. See Joseph S. Nye, *The Paradox of American Power: Why the World's Only Superpower Can't Go It Alone* (Oxford University Press, 2002).

112. See General H. Norman Schwarzkopf, *The Autobiography: It Doesn't Take a Hero* (New York: Bantam Books, 1992), 485: "The first thing that we would like to discuss is prisoners of war."

113. Ben Barber, "Feeding Refugees, or War? The Dilemma of Humanitarian Aid," *Foreign Affairs* 76, no. 4 (July/August 1997).

114. Faye Bowers, "A Lesson in Defeating a Terrorist," *The Christian Science Monitor,* 15 November 2002.

115. See the following Web sites (accessed January 7, 2003):

http://www.tandf.co.uk/journals/tfs/15027570.html (Journal of Military Ethics): Journal of Military Ethics (JME) is an international, peer-reviewed journal devoted to normative aspects of military force. The journal publishes articles discussing justifications for the resort to military force *(jus ad bellum)* and/or what may justifiably be done in the use of such force *(jus in bello).* The scope of JME also includes research/discussion on ethical issues in military training, as well as the post-conflict role of military forces.

http://d4.dir.dcx.yahoo.com/government/military/ethics/ with the following site listings:

—Center for the Study of Professional Military Ethics: works to promote and enhance the ethical development of current and future military leaders through education, research, and reflection

—Defense Industry Initiative on Business Ethics and Conduct: a consortium of U.S. defense industry contractors that subscribes to a set of principles for achieving high standards of business ethics and conduct

—Joint Services Conference on Professional Ethics (JSCOPE): JSCOPE is an academic conference of military officers and academics with the objective of exploring and discussing issues in military ethics

—Military Ethics (Selected Topics)—a course examining the ethical dilemmas encountered in military life and service

—Stanford Encyclopedia of Philosophy: War: discusses the ethics of war and peace, just war theory, realism, and pacifism related to war. *http://plato .stanford.edu/entries/war/*

—U.S. Department of Defense—Standards of Conduct Office: oversees the ethics and standards of conduct programs throughout the Department of Defense

http://www.usna.edu/Ethics/ (Center for the Study of Professional Military Ethics).

116. G. I. A. D. Draper, "The Implementation and Enforcement of the Geneva Conventions of 1949 and the Additional Protocols of 1977," *Recueil des Cours* 3, The Hague (1979): 31: "There is a point at which indiscriminate atrocities dissipate discipline on the battlefield and thereby impair or impede the operations."

117. See Richard R. Baxter, "The First Modern Codification of the Law of War: Francis Lieber and General Order No. 100," *International Review of the Red Cross* (Geneva) (April 1963): 171–89; (May 1963): 234–50.

118. See the case of the Canadian Airborne Regiment that was disbanded on January 24, 1995 by Canada's Defence Minister after violations of international humanitarian law were committed by some of its members. See the following web sites (accessed January 7, 2003):

—*http://www.commando.org/* Unofficial Canadian Airborne Regiment Home page.

—*http://www.cnn.com/WORLD/9704/17/belgium.somalia/* "Brussels, Belgium (CNN): Belgian military officials Thursday promised a thorough review of training exercises, following the publication of photos of alleged atrocities by elite paratroopers during the 1993 UN Somalia peace mission. Defense Minister Jean-Pol Poncelet said he was considering disbanding the elite Belgian paratrooper unit at the center of the scandal."

119. Translated from the original French and quoted by G. I. A. D. Draper, *The Red Cross Conventions* (London: Stevens & Sons, 1958), 3.

120. Joint Warfare of the Armed Forces of the United States, Joint Publication 1, 3:6, November 14, 2000: *http://www.dtic.mil/doctrine/jel/new_pubs/ jp1.pdf*

121. See the following writings by Jean Pictet:

—*The Principles of International Humanitarian Law* (Geneva: ICRC, 1966).

—*Development and Principles of International Humanitarian Law* (Dordrecht: Martinus Nijhoff, 1985).

122. Sun Tzu, *The Art of War,* trans. Samuel B. Griffith, introduction by Samuel B. Griffith and foreword by B. H. Liddell Hart (Oxford: Oxford University Press, 1963), 2:19, 76.

123. On military training courses on international humanitarian law, see:

—the military courses organized by the Institute of International Humanitarian Law in San Remo (Italy): *www.iihl.org*
—the reference curriculum of the Partnership for Peace Consortium: *www.isn.ethz.ch/wgcd/5-currdev/rc_IHL_2002–06–06.pdf*

and the following publications:

—Cees de Rover, "Police and Security Forces: A New Interest for Human Rights and Humanitarian Law," *International Review of the Red Cross*, no. 835 (September 1999): 637–47.
—Cees de Rover, *To Serve and to Protect: Human Rights and Humanitarian Law for Police and Security Forces* (Geneva: ICRC, 1998).

124. See Dieter Fleck, ed., *The Handbook of Humanitarian Law in Armed Conflicts* (Oxford: Oxford University Press 1995).

125. See Paul Grossrieder, "Humanitarian Action in the Twenty-First Century: The Danger of a Setback," in *Basics of International Humanitarian Missions*, ed. Kevin M. Cahill, M.D. (New York: Fordham University Press and The Center for International Health and Cooperation, 2003), 3–17.

126. Roberto Toscano, "The Ethics of Modern Diplomacy," in *Ethics in International Affairs*, eds. Jean-Marc Coicaud and Daniel Warner (Tokyo: United Nations University Press, 2001).

127. New Testament, Matt. 7:7–12; but also: Muhammad; thirteenth Hadiths of Nawawi; Mahavira: Yogashastra 2,20; Bouddha; Sutta Pitaka, Udanavagga 5, 18; Confucius; Analecta 15, 23; Mahabaharata 5; 15, 17; Talmud bab, Shabbat 31a; Baha'u'llah: Kitab-i-aqdas 148; Isocrate: Nicoclès 61. *Calendrier inter religieux 2001–2002* (Genève: Enbiro Lausanne & Plate-Forme inter religieuse, 2000).

128. Platon, *La République, introduction, traduction et notes de R. Baccon* (Paris: Garnier-Flammarion, 1966), 224–27. See also André Bernand, *Guerre et violence dans la Grèce antique* (Paris: Hachette, 1999); Pierre Ducrey, *Le traitement des prisonniers de guerre dans la Grèce antique des origines à la conquête romaine* (Paris: Ecole française d'Athènes, 1999); and Jacqueline de Romilly, *La Grèce antique contre la violence* (Paris: Ed. de Fallois, 2000).

129. F. Keitsch, *Formen der Kriegführung in Melanesien* (Doctoral diss., University Press of Bamberg, Germany, 1967), 380.

130. M. R. Davie, *The Evolution of War: A Study of Its Role in Early Societies* (New Haven: Yale University Press, 1929).

131. E. E. Evans-Pritchard, *The Nuer: A Description of the Modes of Livelihood and Political Institutions of a Nilotic People* (Oxford University Press, 1940).

132. Buddhism contains two fundamental principles, *maitri* (friendli-

ness, benevolence) and *karuna* (mercy, compassion), closely related to the principle of humanity.

133. For Hinduism, numerous rules on the kind treatment to be granted to the vanquished are found in the Mahabharata (XII;3487, 3488, 3489, 3782, 8235), which also prescribes loyalty in combat (XII:3541–42, 3544–51, 57–60, 64, 3580, 3659, 3675, 3677). See also the famous Laws of Manu, VII, 90 to 93 (*The Laws of Manu,* Oxford, 1886).

134. On Taoism, see Lao Tse, *Tao Te Ching,* a new translation by Gia-Fu and Jane English (New York, 1972), in particular no. 68 ("a good winner is not vengeful") and no. 38.

135. See Barbara Aria and Russell Eng Gon, *The Spirit of the Chinese Character* (San Francisco: Chronicle Books, 1992), 51. "Compassion: *Tz'u*"—"It is natural for us to want to help those in need, especially the young and helpless. This is why many Confucians believed in the essential goodness of human nature. If we see a child fall into a well, for instance, we automatically try to save the child." And also page 47: "Benevolence: *Jên*"—"This ideogram combines the radical for 'human being' (also pronounced jên), showing the legs and trunk of a person, with the pair of horizontal strokes that denotes 'two.' Benevolence: the essential kindness that one person shows to another."

136. On Bushido, see Sumio Adachi, "Traditional Asian Approaches: A Japanese View," in *Australian Yearbook of International Law* 9 (1985): 158–67; and, by the same author, "The Asian Concept," in *International Dimensions of Humanitarian Law* (Paris: UNESCO, 1986), 13–19, which also considers Buddhism.

137. On Judaism, see Erich Fromm's *You Shall Be as Gods* (New York: Holt, Rinehart and Winston, 1966).

138. On Christianity, Max Huber, *The Good Samaritan: Reflections on the Gospel and Work of the Red Cross* (London: Gollancz, 1945). See also Joseph Joblin, *L'Eglise et la Guerre. Conscience, violence, pouvoir* (Paris, Desclée de Brouwer, 1988); and in particular, for *jus in bello,* page 193 ff.; Alfred Vanderpol, *La doctrine scolastique du droit de la guerre* (Paris: A. Pedone, 1919).

139. On Islam, see among others, Hamed Sultan, "The Islamic Concept," in *International Dimensions of Humanitarian Law* (Geneva/Paris: UNESCO/Nijhoff, 1988), 29–39; Marcel Boisard, *L'Humanisme de l'Islam* (Paris: Albin Michel, 1979); Jean-Paul Charnay, *L'Islam et la guerre. De la guerre juste à la révolution sainte* (Paris: Fayard, 1986). See also the article published in the *International Review of the Red Cross* by M. K. Ereksoussi, "The Koran and the Humanitarian Conventions" (May 1962); Ameur Zemmali, *Combattants et prisonniers de guerre en droit islamique et en droit international humanitaire* (Paris: Pedone, 1997).

140. On African customs, see Emmanuel Bello, *African Customary Hu-*

manitarian Law (Geneva: ICRC, 1980); the articles by Yolande Diallo published in February and August 1976 in the *International Review of the Red Cross* under the title "Humanitarian Law and African Traditional Law."

141. See Geoffrey Best, *Humanity in Warfare: The Modern History of International Law of Armed Conflicts* (London: Weidenfels and Nicolson, 1980). Michael Ignatieff, *The Warrior's Honour: Ethnic War and the Modern Conscience* (New York: Viking, 1998) compares this warrior's honor with today's ethnic conflicts.

142. Eric Fromm, *The Anatomy of Human Destructiveness* (New York: Holt, Rinehart and Winston, 1973), 168. See also: *http://nativenet.uthscsa.edu/archive/nl/91c/0022.html*

143. Albert Camus, *Actuelles III. Chroniques algériennes (1939–1958)* (Paris: Gallimard, 1958), 24. Original French: "Se battre pour une vérité en veillant à ne pas la tuer des armes mêmes dont on la défend."

144. The French war in Algeria was not lost militarily but because of reactions from the Algerian and French population, as well as from international public opinion, mostly against torture. See, among others, Henri Alleg, *La question* (Paris: Pauvert, 1965); P. Vidal-Naquet, *La torture dans la République. Essai d'histoire et de politique contemporaines (1954–1962)* (Paris: Editions de Minuit, 1972); and John Talbott, *The War Without a Name: France in Algeria, 1954–1962* (New York: Knopf, 1980).

145. Such as in Vietnam, by the air bombings in the North and killings like the My Lai massacre in the South.

146. Such as in Somalia, where Belgian, Canadian, and Italian troops were prosecuted for mistreatment of prisoners and civilians.

147. On peacekeeping operations and international humanitarian law, see:

—Robert Kolb, *Droit humanitaire et opérations de paix internationales* (Genève/Bâle/Munich/Bruxelles: Helbing & Lichtenhahn/Bruylant, 2002).
—Daphna Shraga, "UN Peacekeeping Operations: Applicability of International Humanitarian Law and Responsibility for Operations-Related Damage," *AJIL* 94, no. 2 (April 2000): 406–12.
—Claude Emanuelli, *Les actions militaires de l'ONU et le droit international humanitaire* (Montréal: Wilson & Lafleur Itée, 1995).

148. See Zbigniew Brzezinski, *Out of Control* (New York: Charles Scribner's Sons, 1992), xv: "This is the critical historical challenge that America now faces in the postutopian age. The point of departure for an effective response is the recognition that only by creating a society that is guided by some shared criteria of self restraint can it help to shape a world more truly in control of its destiny. Only with such recognition can we ensure that we

will be the masters, and not the victims, of history as we enter the twenty-first century."

149. Georges Abi-Saab, "There is No Need to Reinvent the Law," *Crimes of War: A Defining Moment—International Law Since September 11*. Available at: *www.crimesofwar.org/sept-mag/sept-abi-printer.html*

150. There have been many proposals to draft simple humanitarian rules, applicable in all situations of conflict:

—in the early 1970s, Prof. J. Patrnogic, President of the International Institute of Humanitarian Law (San Remo, Italy): *www.iihl.org*

—in 1976, Michel Veuthey, "Propositions," the conclusion of *Guérilla et droit humanitaire* (Geneva: ICRC), 373–78, as well as in the second (1983) edition.

—in 1983, Theodor Meron, "On the Inadequate Reach of Humanitarian and Human Rights Law and the Need for a New Instrument," *AJIL* 77: 589; Theodor Meron and Allan Rosas, "A Declaration of Minimum Humanitarian Standards," *AJIL* 85 (1991): 375; Asbjoern Eide, Allan Rosas and Theodor Meron, "Combating Lawlessness in Gray Zone Conflicts Through Minimum Humanitarian Standards," *AJIL* 89 (1995): 215.

—David Petrasek, "Moving Forward on the Development of Minimum Humanitarian Standards," *AJIL* 92: 557–63.

—Jean-Daniel Vigny and Cecilia Thompson, "Fundamental Standards of Humanity: What Future?" *Netherlands Quarterly of Human Rights* 20, no. 2 (2002): 185–99.

151. On the Martens Clause, see:

—A. Cassese, "The Martens Clause: Half a Loaf or Simply Pie in the Sky?" *EJIL* 11, no. 1.

—A. Cassese, *International Law*, 121–23.

—Robert Kolb, "The Relationship Between International Humanitarian Law and Human Rights Law: A Brief History of the 1948 Universal Declaration of Human Rights and the 1949 Geneva Conventions," *International Review of the Red Cross*, no. 324: 409–19.

—Theodor Meron, "The Martens Clause, Principles of Humanity, and Dictates of Public Conscience," *AJIL* 94, no. 1 (January 2000): 78–89.

—UN Commission on Human Rights, Report of the Secretary-General on Minimum Humanitarian Standards (E/CN.4/1998/87 and Add. 1).

152. See ICRC Annual Report 1999, pages 135, 162, 171, 275, 385.

153. See the excellent "Respect for International Humanitarian Law," *Handbook for Parliamentarians* (Geneva: ICRC and the IPU, 1999), 56–57, with many practical recommendations ("What can you do?"). Available online: *http://www.ipu.org/english/handbks.htm* and in PDF at: *www.icrc.org*

154. See the "Woza Africa" Project by the ICRC in 1997. See the following document online: *http://www.icrc.org/Web/eng/siteeng0.nsf/iwpList75/644CDEA605D33696C1256B66005AD038*

155. See also this recommendation by the Brahimi Report (A/55/305-S/2000/809):

> 272. United Nations personnel in the field, perhaps more than any others, are obliged to respect local norms, culture, and practices. They must go out of their way to demonstrate that respect, as a start, by getting to know their host environment and trying to learn as much of the local culture and language as they can. They must behave with the understanding that they are guests in someone else's home, however destroyed that home might be, particularly when the United Nations takes on a transitional administration role. And they must also treat one another with respect and dignity, with particular sensitivity towards gender and cultural differences. *http://www.un.org/peace/reports/peace_operations/docs/part6.htm*

156. On the role of spiritual leaders for the promotion of common human values, see:

—Daniel L. Smith-Christopher, ed., *Subverting Hatred: The Challenge of Nonviolence in Religious Traditions* (Maryknoll, New York: Orbis Books, 2000).
—The message of His Holiness Pope John Paul II for the World Day of Peace 2003 ("*Pacem in Terris*—A Permanent Commitment") with the following headings: "A new awareness of human dignity and inalienable human rights," "The universal common good," "A new international moral order," "A culture of peace": *http://www.vatican.va/holy_father/john_paul_ii/messages/peace/documents/hf_jp-ii_mes_20021217_xxxvi-world-day-for-peace_en.html*

157. Including on the monitoring of violations and prosecution of war criminals. See, for example, the resolution adopted by the NATO Parliamentary Assembly on November 15, 1999, concerning the armed intervention in Kosovo ("Respecting and Ensuring Respect for International Humanitarian Law") reproduced in the *International Review of the Red Cross*, no. 837 (Geneva) (March 31, 2000): 263–64.

158. On the United Nations and the implementation and enforcement of humanitarian law, see:

—The Presidential Statement of the President of the UN Security Council with the *Aide Mémoire*
—The meetings the Security Council on the protection of civilians in armed conflict in 2001 (April 23, 2001, 4312th meeting, and November 21, 2001, 4424th meeting), in 2002 (March 15, 2002, 4492nd meeting, and December 10, 2002), as well as the meetings of the Security Council on Children and Armed Conflicts (November 20, 2001, and May 7, 2002)

—The statement by Angelo Gnaedinger, Director-General of the ICRC, before the Security Council on December 10, 2002 ("The protection of civilians in armed conflicts") with the promotion of a "culture of compliance"

—Human Rights Watch reports and appeals on Indonesia, Somalia, Sierra Leone

—Adam Roberts, "The Exceptional Role of Humanitarian Issues in International Politics since 1989," Third International Security Forum, Zürich, October 19–21, 1998, available online at: *http://www.isn.ethz.ch/security forum/Online_Publications/WS5/WS_5C/Roberts.htm*

—The Final Report of the Carnegie Commission on Preventing Deadly Conflict, available online at: *http://wwics.si.edu/subsites/ccpdc/pubs/rept97/ toc.htm*

159. On remedies, see:

—C. F. Amerasinghe, *Local Remedies in International Law* (Cambridge: Grotius Publications, 1990).

—Dinah Shelton, *Remedies in International Human Rights Law* (Oxford: Oxford University Press, 1999).

—Michel Veuthey, "Remedies to Promote the Respect of Fundamental Human Values in Non-International Armed Conflicts," *The Israeli Yearbook on Human Rights* 30 (2001): 37–77.

Notes to Chapter Seventeen
International Migration: At the Boiling Point
Kathleen Newland

1. Although some simplistic explanations see the growth of world population as all the explanation that is needed for resurgent migration, the demographic data show very little, if any, correlation between population growth and migration or population density and migration. Some of the most densely populated countries, such as Indonesia, are not major sources of migrants, and the least densely populated, such as Russia, are.

Notes to Chapter Nineteen
Reviving Global Civil Society After September 11
Richard Falk

1. For amplification, see R. Falk, "Testing Patriotism and Citizenship in the Global Terror War," in *Worlds in Collision: Terror and the*

Future of Global Order, eds. Ken Booth and Tim Dunne (New York: Palgrave Macmillan, 2002), 325–35.

2. For useful depiction of these dynamics, see Margaret E. Keck and Kathryn Sikkink, *Activists Beyond Borders: Advocacy Networks in International Politics* (Ithaca, NY: Cornell University Press, 1998).

3. This combination of chaos and complexity has reminded analysts of the contemporary world of the medieval period that preceded the emergence of a framework for world order that was based on the primacy of the sovereign state.

4. See R. Falk, "The First Normative Global Revolution: The Uncertain Future of Globalization," in *Globalization and Civilizations,* ed. Mehdi Mazaffari (London: Routledge, 2002), 51–76.

5. See Michael Ignatieff, *Human Rights as Politics and Idolatry* (Princeton, NJ: Princeton University Press, 2001).

6. See George J. Andreopoulos, ed., *Concepts and Strategies in International Human Rights* (New York: Peter Lang, 2002), esp. 1–20, 213–20; see also Paul Gordon Lauren, *The Evolution of International Human Rights* (Philadelphia, PA: University of Pennsylvania Press, 1999).

7. For overall assessments, see Thomas Risse, Stephen C. Ropp, and Kathryn Sikkink, eds., *The Power of Human Right: International Norms and Domestic Change* (Cambridge, UK: Cambridge University Press, 1999).

8. For a convenient collection of the major human rights instruments, see Burns H. Weston, Richard A. Falk, and Hilary Charlesworth, eds., *Supplement of Basic Documents to International Law and World Order,* 3rd ed. (St. Paul, MN: West Group, 1997), 368–670.

9. See Thomas Franck, "The Emerging Right of Democratic Governance," *American Journal of International Law* 86, no. 1 (1992): 46; for a more skeptical and sophisticated view of democracy and human rights, see Susan Marks, *The Riddle of All Constitutions: International Law, Democracy, and the Critique of Ideology* (Oxford: Oxford University Press, 2000).

10. There was a growing public appreciation that it was not only governments that were responsible for repressive practices. In the Indian context, cultural practices in defiance of the law, such as brideburning or *suti,* were responsible for cruelty to individuals that departed from international human rights norms. The same pattern is associated with "honor-killings" in the Middle East and "female circumcision" in Africa. Even in the United States, it is the citizenry that

has exerted pressure on governmental institutions to reestablish capital punishment.

11. For a discussion of cases and principles pertaining to humanitarian intervention, see Nicholas J. Wheeler, *Saving Strangers: Humanitarian Intervention in International Society* (Oxford: Oxford University Press, 2000); for a focus on the debate occasioned by the NATO intervention in Kosovo, see Independent International Commission on Kosovo, *Kosovo Report: Conflict, Response, Lessons Learned* (Oxford: Oxford University Press, 2001).

12. For a useful overview of the debate, see Ken Booth, ed., *The Kosovo Tragedy: The Human Rights Dimensions* (London: Frank Cass, 2001); see also sources cited in note 11 above.

13. On Rwanda, see particularly Linda Melvern, *A People Betrayed: The Role of the West in Rwanda's Genocide* (New York: Zed, 2000); on Bosnia, see David Rieff, *Slaughterhouse* (New York: Simon & Schuster, 1995).

14. A perceptive overview of these developments can be found in Elazar Barkan, *The Guilt of Nations: Restitution and Negotiating Historical Injustices* (New York: Norton, 2000); for a philosophical inquiry into these issues, see Janna Thompson, *Taking Responsibility for the Past: Reparation and Historical Injustice* (Cambridge, UK: Polity, 2002).

15. For an approach to justice and reconciliation for indigenous peoples, see Maivan Clêch Lam, *At the Edge of the State: Indigenous Peoples and Self-Determination* (Ardsley, NY: Transnational Publishers, 2000).

16. Two excellent books examine this development. See Martha Minow, *Between Vengeance and Forgiveness: Facing History after Genocide and Mass Violence* (Boston: Beacon Press, 1998); Gary Jonathan Bass, *Stay the Hand of Vengeance: The Politics of War Crimes Tribunals* (Princeton, NJ: Princeton University Press, 2000).

17. For an attempt to provide national courts with a standardized framework with which to deal with these issues, see *The Princeton Principles on Universal Jurisdiction*, published by the Program in Law and Public Affairs, Princeton University, 2001.

18. Victors' justice is well depicted in Richard H. Minear, *Victors' Justice: The Tokyo War Crimes Tribunal* (Princeton, NJ: Princeton University Press, 1971).

19. For a sense of the range and depth of concerns arising from this transnational peoples perspectives, see Robin Broad, ed., *Global Backlash: Citizen Initiatives for a Just World Economy* (Lanham, MD: Rowman & Littlefield, 2002); *Alternatives to Economic Globalization: Another*

World Is Possible, Report of The International Forum on Globalization (San Francisco: Barrett-Koehler Publisher, 2002).

20. See George Soros, *George Soros on Globalization* (New York: Public Affairs, 2002); Joseph E. Stiglitz, *Globalization and Its Discontents* (New York: Norton, 2002).

21. See cover story of *The Economist* bearing the caption, "Is Torture Ever Justified?" *The Economist* (Jan. 11–17, 2003): 18–20.

22. Such an issue is posed vividly by Michael Ignatieff, "The Burden," *NY Times Magazine* (Jan. 5, 2003): 22–27, 50–54; for a far more skeptical rendering see Alain Joxe, *Empire of Disorder* (Los Angeles: Semiotext[e], 2002).

23. See Denise Dresser, "Setback for Fox and U.S.-Mexico Relations," *Los Angeles Times,* January 12, 2003, M5.

THE CENTER FOR INTERNATIONAL HEALTH AND COOPERATION AND THE INSTITUTE OF INTERNATIONAL HUMANITARIAN AFFAIRS

The Center for International Health and Cooperation (CIHC) was founded by a small group of physicians and diplomats who believed that health and other humanitarian endeavors sometimes provide the only common ground for initiating dialogue, understanding, and cooperation among people and nations shattered by war, civil conflicts, and ethnic violence. The Center has sponsored symposia and published books that reflect this philosophy, including: *Silent Witnesses; A Framework for Survival: Health, Human Rights, and Humanitarian Assistance in Conflicts and Disasters; A Directory of Somali Professionals; Clearing the Fields: Solutions to the Land Mine Crisis; Preventive Diplomacy: Stopping Wars Before They Start;* and *Tropical Medicine: A Clinical Text.* It is co-publisher with Fordham University Press of an International Humanitarian Affairs series. The series includes *Basics of International Humanitarian Missions, Emergency Relief Operations,* as well as this book.

The Center and its Directors have been deeply involved in trying to alleviate the wounds of war in Somalia and the former Yugoslavia. A CIHC amputee center in northern Somalia was developed as a model for a simple, rapid, inexpensive program that could be replicated in other war zones. In the former Yugoslavia, the CIHC was active in prisoner and hostage release, in legal assistance for human and political rights violations, and facilitated discussions between combatants. The Center directs the International Diploma in Humanitarian Assistance (IDHA) in partnership with Fordham University in New York, the University of Geneva in Switzerland, and the Royal College of Surgeons in Ireland. The CIHC cooperates with other centers in offering specialized training courses for humanitarian negotiators and international human rights lawyers. The Center has offered staff support in recent years in crisis management in East Timor, Aceh, Kosovo, Palestine, Albania, and other trouble spots.

The Center has been afforded full Consultative Status at the United Nations. In the United States, it is a fully approved public charity.

The CIHC is closely linked with Fordham University's Institute of International Humanitarian Affairs (IIHA). The Directors of the CIHC serve as the Advisory Board of the Institute. The President of the CIHC is the University Professor and Director of the Institute, and two of the CIHC officers, Larry Hollingworth and Michel Veuthey, are adjunct professors of Fordham. The Institute offers courses in various aspects of international humanitarian affairs and sponsors symposia on cutting edge topics in this field.

Directors

Kevin M. Cahill, M.D.
(President)
Lord David Owen
Boutros Boutros-Ghali
Peter Tarnoff
Jan Eliasson

Peter Hansen
Francis Deng
Joseph A. O'Hare, S.J.
Abdulrahim Abby Farah
Lady Helen Hamlyn
Eoin O'Brien, M.D.

ABOUT THE AUTHORS

H. E. Kofi Annan is the Secretary-General of the United Nations.

Tom Brokaw is News Anchor at NBC Television and author of several books, including *The Greatest Generation*.

Kevin M. Cahill, M.D., is University Professor and Director of The Institute of International Humanitarian Affairs at Fordham University; President and Director of the Center for International Health and Cooperation; Professor and Chairman, Department of Tropical Medicine, Royal College of Surgeons in Ireland; Clinical Professor Medicine, New York University; Director, The Tropical Disease Center, Lenox Hill Hospital; and Chief Medical Advisor, Counterterrorism, New York Police Department.

Major General Timothy Cross, CBE, FCIT, FILT, has served with the British Army for over thirty years. His operational experience ranges from working as a bomb disposal officer in Northern Ireland in the 1970s to serving with the UN in Cyprus in the 1980s, the Coalition in the Gulf War in 1990–91, and three times with NATO in the Balkans in the 1990s. He commanded the 101 Logistic Brigade in Macedonia, Albania, and Kosovo, leading the NATO response to the 1999 Easter Refugee Crisis in Northern Macedonia, and assisting the UNHCR and other relief agencies in Southern Albania and Kosovo. He was appointed CBE in the subsequent operational awards and is currently Director General of the United Kingdom's Defense Supply Chain.

Ambassador Francis Mading Deng is a Director of the Center for International Health and Cooperation. He is also the UN Secretary-General's Special Representative for Internally Displaced

Persons; Ralph Bunche Professor of International Affairs at the City University of New York; and, Senior Fellow, the Brookings Institution. He was Secretary of State for Foreign Affairs, Sudan.

Avery Cardinal Dulles, S.J., is the Laurence J. McGinley Professor of Religion and Society, Fordham University, New York.

Ambassador Jan Eliasson is a Director of the Center for International Health and Cooperation; Swedish Ambassador to the United States; former UN Under-Secretary for Humanitarian Affairs; and Swedish Minister of State for Foreign Affairs.

Ambassador Nancy Ely-Raphel is Head of the Office to Combat Trafficking in Persons, U.S. State Department; former U.S. Ambassador to Slovenia.

Richard Falk is Albert G. Milbank Emeritus Professor of International Law and Practice, Princeton University; Visiting Distinguished Professor, University of California, Santa Barbara.

Professor John D. Feerick is Leonard J. Manning Professor and former Dean, Fordham University School of Law, New York.

Timothy W. Harding, M.D., is Professor, Forensic Medicine Institute, University of Geneva, Switzerland.

Larry Hollingworth is Humanitarian Programs Director for the Center for International Health and Cooperation. He is also Adjunct Professor in the Graduate School of Social Service of Fordham University in New York. He served with UN High Commission for Refugees in Bosnia and Chechnya. Prior to that he was a British Army officer for thirty years. He is a frequent lecturer on relief and refugee topics in universities and is a commentator on humanitarian issues for the BBC.

Edward Mortimer is Director of Communications, UN Secretary-General; former Chief Foreign Correspondent, *The Financial Times.*

Kathleen Newland is Director, Migration Policy Institute; former Co-Director, Carnegie International Migration Policy Program.

Eoin O'Brien, M.D., is a Director of the Center for International Health and Cooperation; Professor of Cardiovascular Medicine, the Royal College of Surgeons in Ireland; author of some 500 scientific papers on hypertension research, as well as *Blood Pressure Measurement, ABC of Hypertension, Conscience and Conflict: A Biography of Sir Dominic Corrigan,* and a literary work on Samuel Beckett—*The Beckett Country: Samuel Beckett's Ireland.*

Joseph A. O'Hare, S.J., is a Director of The Center for International Health and Cooperation. He is also President, Fordham University, New York, and former Editor in Chief, *America* magazine.

H.R.H. Prince El Hassan bin Talal of Jordan is moderator of the World Conference for Religion and Peace. He is the President of the Club of Rome and also serves as President of the Arab Thought Forum.

Peter Tarnoff is a Director of The Center for International Health and Cooperation, former U.S. Undersecretary of State for Political Affairs, and President of the Council on Foreign Relations.

Michel Veuthey, Doctor of Laws (Geneva University), is the Geneva Representative and Academic Director of the Center for International Health and Cooperation's International Diploma in Humanitarian Assistance (IDHA). He also directs the Summer Course with the International Institute of Humanitarian Law. He is an Adjunct Professor at the Fordham University School of Law and Board Member of MSF—Switzerland and the Geneva Fund. Prior to joining the CIHC he had served for thirty years with the ICRC in many positions including Assistant to the President.

Dr. Harlan J. Wechsler is Professor of Jewish Philosophy, Jewish Theological Seminary of America and Rabbi of Congregation Or Zarna.

Professor Paul Wilkinson is Director of the Centre for the Study of Terrorism and Political Violence, University of St. Andrews, Scotland.

INDEX